WELLINGTON'S HERITAGE

plants, gardens, and landscape

To the memory of my grandfather, J. C. Blackmore,
an early New Zealand horticulturist

WELLINGTON'S HERITAGE

plants, gardens, and landscape

WINSOME SHEPHERD

TE PAPA PRESS
Wellington

Te Papa Press
Museum of New Zealand Te Papa Tongarewa

First published 2000, reprinted with corrections 2001

Te Papa Press is an imprint of the Museum of New Zealand Te Papa Tongarewa

ISBN 0-909010-73-0

Title page image: 'Wellington in 1843', William Fox, Hocken Library
Image on p 1: A view from Bolton St, overlooking Bolton St Cemetery.
Large *Pinus radiata* planted c 1880 frame the office blocks of 1990.
John Johns, 1990

Edited by Anne French
with Michael Keith and David Cauchi
Index by David Cauchi
Original design by Nikolas Andrew, A Design
Designed by Walter Moala, with layout assistance from Tasman Image
Digital imaging by Jeremy Glyde
Printed in New Zealand by Brebner Print

Published by Te Papa Press
Museum of New Zealand Te Papa Tongarewa
PO Box 467
Wellington

CONTENTS

Foreword vi

Introduction vii

Acknowledgements viii

1 Emigration and survival 3

2 Country Acres in the Hutt Valley 17

3 Country Acres around Lambton Harbour 55

4 The Town Acres: settlers' gardens 95

5 Gardens of special significance 125

6 The Horticultural and A&P Societies 151

7 Wellington's pioneer nurserymen and seedsmen 165

8 Tea Gardens 185

9 The city landscape 197

10 Wellington's parks 217

11 Nursery catalogues and early plant introductions 242

Appendix 245

Index 254

FOREWORD

Like most people, I'm no expert on the trees and plants in and around Wellington. I think they make our city look great but that's about the sum total of my knowledge. That's what is so remarkable about *Wellington's Heritage – plants, gardens, and landscape*. This beautifully illustrated history of plants and gardens in Wellington shows that our plants are as much a part of our history as they are of our scenery, and is possibly the first of its kind to do so.

Any armchair historian or passionate gardener will find *Wellington's Heritage* fascinating. We can literally see the topography of Wellington change and develop through the years. We are treated to rare glimpses of nineteenth-century frontier Wellington with its rough wilderness of bush, fern, flax, and swamp. And out of that harsh landscape we can see our capital city emerging – larger homes, substantial buildings, and the beginnings of a second colonial landscape that arose from the successful conifer plants in our Botanic Garden. This vibrant landscape dominates our Town Belt today. And what a gorgeous sight it is! Although a modern cosmopolitan city, Wellington is anything but a concrete jungle. I know of few cities in the world where their office buildings enjoy the kind of lush green scenery we do.

As someone committed to the 'greening' of Wellington, I was also interested to read about the development of our city's parks, the introduction of trees to our streets, and a description of the city's major gardens.

This colourful book has made me appreciate our city's beauty. And it preserves our horticultural heritage even as it takes us into the new millennium. I congratulate the efforts of the author, the photographers, and the skills of the publishing team at Te Papa for producing such a significant work.

Mark Blumsky
Mayor of Wellington

INTRODUCTION

> *There are many who still think there is no need to remember, for whom the only reality is the present, for whom colonial beginnings, 'the 1840s time warp', are irrelevant to contemporary New Zealand. Without the sense of nature that comes from regular encounter, what does identity with country mean?*
>
> Geoff Park, *Ngā Uruora*

Wellington, when viewed from the harbour, at the beginning of the twenty-first century, shows the central high-rise buildings characteristic of any modern city; but houses and buildings on the slopes nestle and in some cases are almost submerged under and among a canopy of greenery. Closer examination of the city itself shows that trees invade the streets and small parks soften by their tracery the sometimes harsh lines of the man-made structures.

It augurs well for the future, but it was not always so. By 1865 the early settlers had destroyed the forest-clad tranquility of the land surrounding Port Nicholson, creating a harsh, desolate, windswept backdrop to the small struggling settlement that they were trying so hard to establish. Little has been documented about this destruction of existing vegetation which strangely enough went hand-in-hand with efforts to bring in an alien flora. Today it is this flora, together with the endemic one, that gives us that special environment now so characteristic of Wellington. It is a green city.

To date the introduction of plants to New Zealand by the early settlers has received little attention, particularly in regard to Wellington. It is easy to forget that our present gardens and landscape result from considerable toil and expenditure of money over a period of more than 150 years. Information on restoration or creation of New Zealand period gardens is scanty and where it does occur much of it has been based on information from overseas sources as for instance the fashion for cottage and herb gardens. Only by the study of archival information can we really understand recreate, if desired, the authentic early New Zealand garden. The following chapters, concentrating on Wellington and its landscape are the result of such a study. In this last half of the decade before the turn of the century and the year 2000, the city is evolving rapidly so it is appropriate and timely to place on record its past.

The introduction of plants to Wellington also impinges on social issues and conclusions deduced by historians in other fields. On arrival at Petone labourers worked alongside the gentry and it was not long before the class divisions strong in Britain had only limited carry-over in Wellington and in New Zealand. Initially all settlers had to rely on the own muscles – hand labour with pick, axe, and saw. Colonial landed interests on the Country Acre blocks divide into five main groups – firstly, the 'gentry'; then the family farmer or 'yeoman farmer'; then the cottager; followed as settlement problems were overcome by those who serviced the community: the carriers, millers, inn-keepers, blacksmiths and such like, and finally the farm labourers.

In the town the urban gentry included wealthy landowners, professionals, politicans, clergymen, army officers, and merchants; domestic servants and general labourers were at the lower end of the scale.

Whether urban or rural, the gentry were to the forefront in politics at regional, local, and national levels. As well as leading the way in founding townships, churches, schools, racecourses, and cricket clubs they played a major role in the Horticultural Society and the Agricultural and Pastoral Association. They led the way in both plant and livestock introductions, adapting machinery for different purposes. Examples can be read in every chapter of the book. Molesworth and Ludlam were landed gentry in the Hutt; further up the valley Thomas Mason was an excellent wealthy yeoman farmer. Unfortunately, after a promising start Molesworth died young, but Ludlam and Mason went on to serve in both the local and national political arenas. Trotter, a small yeoman farmer, a judge at the horticultural shows, worked outside his property augmenting his income by using his professional skills in working for Ludlam.

On the old Porirua Road Susan and Anthony Walls were cottage farmers – all members of the family, including the children shared in the work – milking the cows, making the butter and candles and making most of their clothes. At an early age, some children went out to work for wages, for instance splitting shingles.

After Molesworth's death his gardener James Bryant obtained some land at the Hutt, then worked as a publican in Johnsonville until acquiring land in Ohariu. Ultimately he became known as a wool king – something which could never have happened in England. The following chapters give a number of similar cases illustrating the breakdown of the English class system. Firstly, however, some of the conditions in England which decided settlers to emigrate are examined.

Acknowledgements

The book's origins go back to 1979 when I was asked by the New Zealand Historic Places Trust to research plant introductions to New Zealand after the missionary period. The subject was vast and each area of New Zealand needed to be examined before an overview for the whole country could be determined. After two years John Wilson, the Trust's Editor, believed a book was possible in the Botanic Garden material uncovered by the research. In 1988 the history of The Botanic Garden co-authored by myself and Walter Cook was published. In this the major introduction and dissemination of conifers in New Zealand for the years 1870–1885 was documented for the first time. Research material for plant introductions continued to accumulate, however, and now the information is presented in this eco-history of Wellington, thus fulfilling the original brief given me all those years ago.

Many people have helped me both directly and indirectly and I thank all for their help and encouragement. From Historic Places Trust I thank the late Pat Adams, John Daniels, John Wilson, Gavin McLean (now Historical Branch, Internal Affairs) and Peter Richardson; from the Wellington City Council the Mayor Mark Blumsky, Derek Thompson, Mike Oates and Photographer Neil Price; from the Historical Societies, Karori – Don Silver, Kitty Woods, Jan Heynes, Margaret Alington; Onslow – Judy Siers, Lawson Robertson; Lower Hutt – Neil Coup (City Librarian); Wellington Early Settlers and Historical Association; Vonne Nunns and Cecily Worsefield; the British High Commisioner, H.E. Mr Martin Williams, and Mrs Williams; Sutherland Trust, Graham Sutherland; Katherine Mansfield Birthplace Trust, Oroya Day and Wendy Tolley; Royal New Zealand Institute of Horticulture, Ron Flook, (Institute of Landscape Architects), Denis Hicks, Jack Hobbs, Alan Mason, Richard Nanson and Dr Eric Godley; Property Manager Government House, Dianne Johnson; the Institute of Landscape Architects, Frank Boffa, Boyden Evans and

Shona McCahon; Architect, Martin Hill; Museum of Wellington – City & Sea, Wendy Adlam; Alexander Turnbull Library, Walter Cook and Marian Minson; Canterbury Museum; The Hocken Library; Nelson Provincial Museum; the Lower Hutt City Library; Wellington Public Library; the State Library of New South Wales Mitchell Library, Sydney; the Royal Tasmanian and Museum Library; Kathleen Coleridge, Beaglehole Library, Victoria University of Wellington; David Mealing, Petone Settlers Museum; Pat Marpin, Petone Public Library; Bill Main; John Hall Jones, Ann Moffat, Murray Henderson, Helen Waugh, June and Richard Orr; Golders Cottage, Janice Browne; Rodney Reid, Professor Rodney Graves, L. Homer, Hilda Walker, Clive Lind, Evening Post. A special thank you to Walter Cook and Nancy Adams for reading, advising on the text, and encouragement.

Without the staff and services of Te Papa this book would not have been possible: Manuela Angelo and staff from the Hector Library; Jan Nauta for his splendid photographs; Libby Palmer and Eymard Bradley for searching out photographs in the Museum's Photographic Archives; the Archivist Eamonn Bolger; Desiree Wilkinson for the onerous job typing the manuscript; Anne French and the publishing team – Diana Minchall, Jeremy Glyde, Michael Keith, Walter Moala and Alma Van den Assem; Kevin Tso and others.

Finally, financial contributions from the Denton Trust, R.F. Blackmore and the Deepwater Trust; The Wellington Branch of the Royal New Zealand Institute of Horticulture, and a generous contribution from W. Bennett, a long-term Hutt Valley resident, have enabled this book to retail at an affordable price.

I thank you all.

Winsome Shepherd
12 October 2000

Chapter 1

EMIGRATION AND SURVIVAL

In the early part of the nineteenth century, England was changing from a rural economy to an industrial one. Many previously pleasant small towns had become monstrous coal-fired factory areas, their air polluted by heavy clouds of poisonous smoke. Workers' housing was inadequate and often squalid. Coal-mining activities had disfigured vast areas of the countryside and miners' homes were crowded hovels. The term 'Black Country' was certainly appropriate to describe the English Midlands. Children were forced to work at an early age and were lucky if they could stay at school until they were twelve years old. Punishment for petty crimes, often caused by hunger, were harsh in the extreme. Rural areas were depressed.

Like the industrial cities of the Midlands, London was overcrowded. In the early years of the century it expanded over its surrounding farmlands, from Kensington through to Hammersmith, Chiswick, Brentford, Isleworth, and Twickenham. The fertile fields were swallowed up by the city, and produce came from market gardens and orchards further away, some as far as Cornwall. Grain-growing in Britain, where climate and soil conditions had never been ideal, was similarly affected by the population explosion. Britain had to import grain, as its total grain production could no longer feed its population.

With conditions as they were in the 1830s, the prospect of new lands over the seas and the chance of a fresh start brought a glimmer of hope to people whose lives had been blighted by industrialisation, or whose land had been taken over to meet the needs of a rapidly expanding population. Emigration fever fired their imagination. Organised emigration to Australia and New Zealand was seen as a way of giving opportunity to England's surplus population. Emigration companies such as the New Zealand Company offered the hope of escape from poverty, harsh penal laws, restricted liberty, and oppressive living conditions, and the chance to establish farms and orchards in a new land. Visions of clear skies and lands of opportunity overcame any doubts, and even the prospect of many months at sea before the settlers reached the promised land did not deter them.

The majority of immigrants to New Zealand between 1840 and 1870 were rural labourers. Many came from rural Ireland, where millions were starving during the potato famine, from Cornwall, after the closure of the tin and copper mines, from northern Ireland, after the collapse of the linen industry around Belfast, and from Glasgow, after the failure of its cottage-based textile industry.

The founder of the New Zealand Company, Edward Gibbon Wakefield, believed that the new colony would become 'the granary of the Pacific'; capable of growing not only grain, together with some mixed farming, but also grapevines and perhaps olive trees as well.

But where Wakefield and the New Zealand Company failed both itself and the settlers was by failing to describe with any accuracy the climate and the inadequate amount of land available for cultivation. No thousands of acres of pasture for grazing awaited the new settlers, and the dense vegetation that covered the land was not going to be cleared easily or cheaply. It had taken hundreds of years for the English landscape to be cleared of forest. The historian James Belich says:

> Settlers were enticed by a crass and transparent advertising campaign which promoted New Zealand as a paradise where Anglo-Saxon could flourish, where the undulating plains at Port Nicholson were perfect for wheat, grapevines and olives, where the Hutt River was as broad as the Thames and navigable for several miles or so.[1]

Hundreds of articles published in British newspapers and periodicals promoted the myth. The first issue of the *Gardener's Chronicle* carried a New Zealand Company advertisement for land allotments in the new colony in Wellington. The 'Emigrants' Song', written by the well-known poet Thomas Campbell and published in the *New Zealand Gazette* in 1839, evokes the emigrants' feelings of hopefulness.[2] England is mentioned with pride, with no hint of the harsh conditions that the colonists were leaving behind.

SONG OF THE EMIGRANTS TO NEW ZEALAND

Steer helmsman, till you steer our way
By stars beyond the line -
We go to found a realm – one day -
Like England's Self to shine

Chorus

Cheer up! Cheer up! Our course we'll keep
With dauntless heart and hand,
And when we've ploughed the stormy deep
We'll plough a smiling land

A land whose beauties importune
The Briton to its bowers,
To sow but plenty's seeds and prune
Luxuriant fruits and flowers

A sunny land with varying sweets
Of healthy plains and hills
ith giant woods to build our fleets,
And floods to drive our mills

These tracts uncheered by human words
Seclusion's widest holds
Shall hear the lowing of our herds
The tumbling of our folds

Like rubies set in gold shall blush
Our vineyards, girt with corn
And wine, and oil, and gladness gush
From Amalthaea's horn

Britannia's pride is in our hearts
Her blood is in our veins
We'll girdle earth with British arts
Like Arnel's magic chains

Thomas Campbell

---

1 Belich, James, *Making Peoples*, Penguin Books, 1996.
2 *New Zealand Gazette*, Wednesday 21 August 1839. Thomas Campbell, 'Bard of Hope', lies entombed among England's illustrious dead, in Westminster Abbey.

When the ship *Tory* sailed into Port Nicholson on 20 September 1839, the young artist and draughtsman Charles Heaphy was on board. Forty years later, he recalled his first impressions of the land, and provided the first reliable account of the extent and density of the plant cover before European settlement. Heavy bush did not clothe the land uniformly.

> Along the eastern shore from the mouth of the Hutt river to outside of Ward Island the forest was uninterrupted and the trees overhung the water giving shelter to a great number of wild fowl. About Kaiwhara, Ngahauranga, and the Korokoro, the earthquakes had not then raised the coast, and caused the beach, now occupied by the railway, to appear, and there, also, the trees overhung the water, leaving only at the ebb tide a space sufficient for a pathway .... As seen from the ship, or the hills, a lofty pinewood appeared to occupy the whole breadth and length of the Hutt Valley, broken only by the stream and its stony margin. This wood commenced about a mile from the sea, the intervening space being a sandy flat and a flax marsh. The cultivations of the Natives were nearly all on the hillsides, and chiefly about what is now the Petone railroad station .... The site of the City of Wellington was, in 1839, covered at the Te Aro end with high fern and tupakihi tutu, rush, flax, and a great deal of impassable swamp. The Basin Reserve was a deep morass with an outlet to the sea at Clyde Quay, and to get to Newtown one had to keep to the high land to either side of the wide valley. About the upper part of Willis Street and Polhill's Gully, there were high pine trees, partly felled for native cultivations. Wellington Terrace was timbered with high manuka, some of the trees forty feet high. Thorndon Flat, about Mulgrave and Pipitea Street, was fern covered, but with high trees towards Tinakori Road. The native cultivations were along what is now Hawkstone Street, Tinakori Road, and the base of Tinakori Hill, sides and summit were densely timbered, the rata with its crimson flowers being conspicuous.

EMIGRATION

TO

NEW ZEALAND.

The Directors of the New Zealand Company, do hereby give notice that they are ready to receive Applications for a FREE PASSAGE to the

TOWN OF WELLINGTON,

AT LAMBTON HARBOUR,

PORT NICHOLSON, COOK'S STRAITS,

NEW ZEALAND,

From Agricultural Laborers, Shepherds, Miners, Gardeners, Brickmakers, Mechanics, Handicraftsmen, and Domestic Servants, BEING MARRIED, and not exceeding Forty years of age; also from SINGLE FEMALES, under the care of near relatives, and SINGLE MEN, accompanied by one or more ADULT SISTERS, not exceeding, in either case, the age of Thirty years. Strict inquiry will be made as to qualifications and character.

Apply on Mondays, Thursdays, and Saturdays, to Mr. JOSEPH PHIPSON, 11, Union Passage, Birmingham,

AGENT TO THE COMPANY.

TOWN and COUNTRY SECTIONS of LAND on sale, full particulars of which may be had on application as above.

Public Records Office, London.

Thorndon Flat and part of the city of Wellington, *April 1841. The view from Clay Point, above the present junction of Lambton Quay with Willis Street. This early watercolour by Charles Heaphy looks north and shows the forest on Tinakori Hill and beyond. Colonel Wakefield's house is visible on the green rise above Barrett's Hotel, the two-storeyed building on the foreshore. Two potato gardens are clearly visible on the slopes of Tinakori Hill. Heaphy's key to this painting indicates numerous potato gardens on the Wadestown hills.*

Alexander Turnbull Library, National Library of New Zealand, Te Puna Mātauranga, C-025-010

Lithograph by Thomas Allom, early 1840s, from drawings made during Colonel Wakefield's survey in 1839. This view of Port Nicholson was very misleading – the Hutt Valley seems endless. Burnham Water can be seen on the Miramar peninsula.

Alexander Turnbull Library, National Library of New Zealand, Te Puna Mātauranga

> At the beach, the head of Evan's Bay, were to be found waterfowl with flocks of Paradise ducks, and growing behind the beach was a quantity of wild turnip [horuhoru], alleged to have been grown from degenerated seed left on the New Zealand coast by Captain Cook. In the low fern and sandy shores of Lyall and Island Bays the indigenous quail was very common, and would rise in hundreds at one's foot with their shrill startling whistle. Along the rocks would be found slate coloured cranes, two and two, making erratic darts after shrimps, or patiently waiting for a passing fish.
>
> At this time the Native population of Port Nicholson, extending from the Hutt to Te Aro, was perhaps, not more than 500.[3]

The *Tory* carried out a survey of Port Nicholson. Thomas Allom prepared a lithograph from the *Tory's* charts and a drawing by Heaphy that circulated widely in England. Although excellent as an imaginary bird's-eye view of Port Nicholson, it was misleading, portraying the Hutt Valley as an extensive coastal plain that would be able to support pastoralists and the park lands of gentlemen's estates. The valley appears endless. Compare Allom's lithograph with the aerial photograph that shows the rugged topography to see the extent of the deception.

---

[3] Heaphy, Charles Henry V.C., 'Notes on Port Nicholson and the Natives in 1839', *Transactions of the New Zealand Institute*, Vol 12, 1879.

The intended layout for the new town was based on the universally accepted grid system, a system that could not cope with steep contours. Company instructions were that there were to be 1,100 Town Acres, with space for a cemetery, market place, public buildings, wharfage, a park, botanical garden, and extensive boulevards. Town Acres were to be separated from the Country Acres by a broad zone of open space.

The idea of having open spaces in a town had started in Britain in the 1830s, when it became clear open space benefited the health of those living in the over-crowded conditions of expanding industrial towns. The 'public park movement', as it came to be known, was a concept promoted strongly by John Claudius Loudon, a well-known English horticulturist. The idea was first introduced in the southern hemisphere when the survey of Adelaide, an early Wakefield settlement, provided for an extensive belt of park land around its urban centre. But that land was flat.

Before Wakefield sailed with the *Tory* for the Hokianga, in order to select, as instructed, the second place for a Company settlement, he had decided that the Company's first settlement, to be called Britannia, should be located across the harbour from where they were anchored at Petone. Instructions to this effect were left for the surveyor William Mein-Smith, who was following in the *Cuba*.

The *Cuba* anchored off Petone on 4 January 1840. Mein-Smith, required to use the grid system and provide 1,100 Town Acres, preferred the Hutt Valley to Wakefield's choice of site across the harbour, where there seemed not to be enough flat land. Mein-Smith may have been influenced by

This aerial view of Port Nicholson demonstrates just how misleading the Allom lithograph was to intending settlers. There is no wide valley capable of supporting the growing of large areas of wheat. The land surrounding the valley is also very hilly.

New Zealand Aerial Mapping Ltd

Looking north across the floor of the Hutt Valley in 1939. Market gardens are about to give way to industry and urban sprawl, a far cry from the pastoralists' dream for the area suggested by the Allom lithograph. The Hutt Motorway follows the line of the Wellington Fault.

Hutt City Library

A proposed plan of the city of Wellington in the first settlement in New Zealand founded 1839–40. Containing 1361 acres, exclusive of streets & terrace round the town: thus allowing 261 acres for government purposes, squares, public buildings, hospitals, schools, markets, wharfage, &c., &c.; and 1100 acres for the colonists for building purposes, &c., &c. *Designed by Samuel Cobham, this plan may have influenced Mein-Smith in his decision to lay out the town at Petone.*

Alexander Turnbull Library, National Library of New Zealand, Te Puna Mātauranga, F-51659-1/2, MapColl 832.4796a/[1839]/Acc. 1269

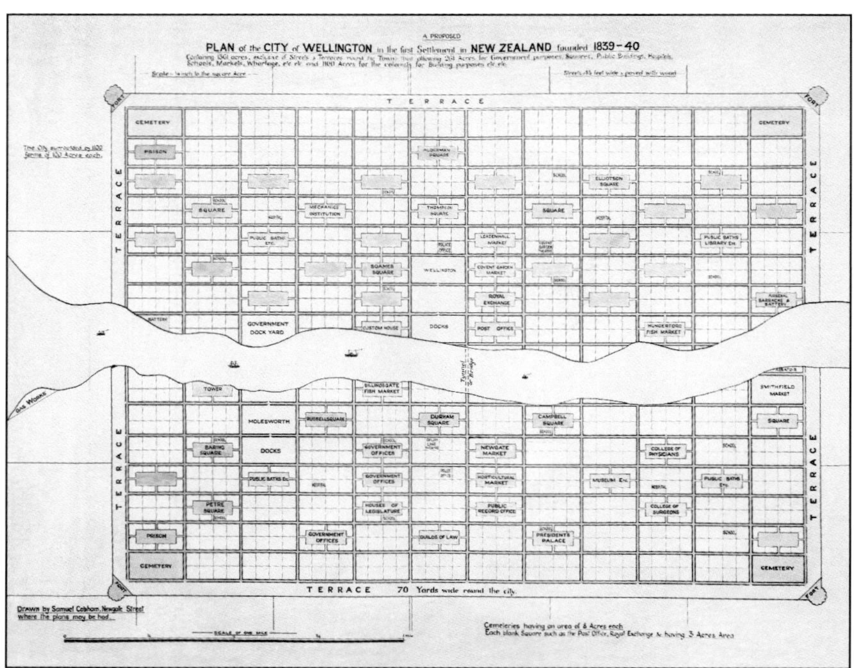

Samuel Cobham's plan, which he had with him, and which seemed suitable for the Hutt Valley.

The *Cuba* also brought an important change in instructions. Instead of two settlements in different parts of New Zealand, there was to be only one, combining both agricultural and mercantile aspects. Wakefield returned to Port Nicholson on 18 January and the survey continued at the Hutt.

Meanwhile, the ships full of settlers began to arrive. The *Aurora* came on 22 January, the *Oriental* on 31 January, the *Duke of Roxburgh* on 7 February, and the *Bengal Merchant* on 21 February.

As the ships sailed into the harbour, some settlers admired the untouched beauty of the land. One of them, Thomas Mason, was impressed by what he saw: 'mountain rising above mountain, the beauty of the scenery I never saw equalled – was grand and sublime'.[4] But others were dismayed by the primitive scene before them, without any welcoming shelter, and with no land available for immediate settlement. The discharging of settlers and goods was slow, as everything had to be rowed ashore.

The difficulties were many. Behind the sandy beach the land was swampy, the river frequently flooded, and further up the valley there was dense forest. The survey of the Town Acres was still progressing, and many watched with incredulity as the surveyors' lines were laid through the gardens of the Te Atiawa people. Mein-Smith advised that the problem of flooding could be overcome at a cost, but not within the sum allowed by the directors. On 5 April, Wakefield decided to establish the town across the harbour at what is now called Thorndon. The land at the Hutt would now become Country Acres, not Town Acres.

The difficulties with the survey and the decision to change the site of Britannia made life extremely hard for settlers that first winter. Some plants

---

[4] Mason, T., *Diary on Voyage to New Zealand*, Alexander Turnbull Library.

Britannia (Pito-one) in 1840, from the sketch drawn by Charles Heaphy, as from the Korokoro hill. Tents and houses are on the beach, emigrants' ships are anchored near Somes Island, and animals are grazing on the open land in the foreground where people are working. This was probably a Māori garden.

Alexander Turnbull Library, National Library of New Zealand, Te Puna Mātauranga

and seeds were sown at Petone while the settlers waited for land to become available, but a limited sowing of crops was only possible towards the end of that first year.

Gradually, as land was surveyed and allocated, the settlers moved on to their Town Acres in Wellington, as Britannia soon became known, or outwards to Country Acres at Wadestown, Karori, the Hutt, and Porirua. The physical difficulties of surveying and settling the hilly areas of the region are described in Chapters 3 and 4. But in hilly areas or on flat ones, such as the Hutt Valley, surveyors and settlers alike had to contend with swamp, fern and scrub, and dense forest.

Preparing the land

Clearing the forest that covered so much of the land was a huge task. Axemen found that it sometimes took an entire day to clear a patch that was large enough to pitch a tent, and this certainly compounded the frustratingly slow progress of the survey.

When clearing, it was necessary to first slash and clear the undergrowth, throw the trees using either a cross saw or an American axe, and leave all to dry out over the summer before firing it in the autumn. The remaining unburnt material, tree trunks and large branches, were then collected into heaps and burnt again.

Stumps often remained in the ground for several years before they could be torn up using a pair or two of bullocks and a strong stump chain. The use of a timberjack was slow and expensive. Even after burning, the soil was still full of roots, and a mattock or hoe had to be used to break it up. Sometimes seed was sown by hand shortly after the initial burning directly among the branches and stumps still in the ground. Settlers' letters and diaries tell of these difficulties and of the huge cost of bringing the land in.

Pencil sketch by William Swainson, c 1845. Settlers are felling the forest with American axes. Mantell Scrapbook, E.295, p 45.

Alexander Turnbull Library, National Library of New Zealand, Te Puna Mātauranga, E-295-q-045

'The settler came with axe and fire sticks and in a few hours unsightly ashes and black funeral stumps had replaced the noble woods which nature took centuries to grow.' Settlers sowing seed amidst the ashes of recently burnt-off bush.

C.E. Wildbore, Palmerston North Library

Seeds and plants

Food, housing, and then land was the order of priority for the first settlers. Fresh pork and potatoes were available locally, but with no bread, milk, or butter being produced, and only a few eggs available, thrift was necessary for several years.

Colonel Wakefield had anticipated that after a long voyage at sea settlers would require fresh vegetables. Before the *Tory* set sail for Kaipara in October 1839, he gave Mr Smith, a Te Awaiti whaler and trader known to the local Mäori, a stock of garden seeds and tools. Smith was asked to oversee the building of temporary shelters, to prepare the ground, and get crops sown, all in preparation for the arrival of the settlers.[5] These seeds, the first to be used in the colony, were mainly grown at Kaiwharawhara, near Smith's toetoe cottage. Henry Petre wrote:

> When we arrived we found turnips, cabbages and other stuff in great perfection. They had been raised from seed taken out by the Tory. They were grown between the present site of Wellington and the Hutt and as some of them were left to seed anyone who chose to do so helped himself in passing by which means excellent sorts of every species have been spread over the colony.[6]

Emigrants were asked to take seeds with them, but were seeds readily available in the new colony? The first edition of *The New Zealand Gazette*, printed in England on 21 August 1839, carried two advertisements:

> T. and C. Lochart, Seedsman and Florists, 156 Cheapside, London, beg most respectfully to call the attention of the Company and emigrants to New Zealand to their stock of agricultural, Garden and Flower Seeds, catalogues of which may be had gratis and post-paid applications.
>
> Agricultural and Kitchen Garden Seeds in large or small Assortments for Settlers in New Zealand, and all other Colonials, carefully packed by Gordon, Thomson and Co. Seedsman, 25 Fenchurch Street, London.

---

5 Wakefield, E.J., *Adventure in New Zealand, 1839–44*, London, 1845.

6 Petre, H.W., *Account of the Settlement of the New Zealand Company*, London, 1842.

These advertisements were repeated in the second issue of the *Gazette*, published at Port Nicholson on 18 April 1840, and again in August of that year.

The settlers were quick to sow the seeds they had brought with them or had had sent to them. Nonetheless, conditions in those first few years were harsh. Local Māori supplied potatoes and pork, but butter, beef, and mutton were almost unknown luxuries. John Kilmister, who arrived on the *Lady Nugent* in March 1841, asked:

> What would the settlers have done for food if it had not been for the Maori. They drove pigs in from Otaki. 40–50 in a mob and sold them at 10/- per head. Potatoes, hauled around the homes by Maori women sold for 1/- per cwt.
>
> Pigeons and tuis were shot, taken into town where the pigeons sold for 6d per pair and tuis 3d per pair.[7]

Seventy years after arriving on the *Birman* in 1842, an elderly woman recalled those early days:

> Food was a great problem in those days – such hungry days they were too. Cockles in plenty we found on the beach, fish we bought from the Maories, and pork, as well as potatoes and a kit would sometimes weigh up to 60 to 70 lbs. We also bought weed from the same source, the women carrying it on their backs. At first we did not dream of cutting down the bush.
>
> I think the spirit of the land fell upon us that first summer. It was so fine and hot, the waters were blue, and the skies arching high and clear. We had not passed by the joy of the morning. The sorrow of life came later of course but you will meet with that at every clime.
>
> Our staple vegetable was puha, commonly called sow thistle. It grew on the bank from Pipitea to Kaiwara. Boiled it was delicious – at least we thought so then. We cooked many queer things in those days. The seed of potatoes made capital pies, and we cooked the brown fern frond with tartarie and essence of lemon and sugar. We used stalks of dock leaves; we belied that rhubarb pie, and we carried home bunches of sorrel which like four and twenty blackbirds we baked in a pie and when the pie was opened like so much cabbage. Yes it was the herb for the use of man and the simple life. We were like children playing houses. When did we have mutton? Not for years and years. Every family had goats on Tinakori hills – big ones for milk and kids for meat. Roast kid is delicious. Yes it was a Robinson Cruso life – but we were spinning our wool. A native fruit that we ate was called puru puru [poroporo]. It was a yellow berry not unlike a gooseberry, but it has long since disappeared.
>
> There was joy over the first watercress. It was found growing at the little waterfall near Grant Road. I believe the spring is there now. The first cress was carried in triumph to my mother and she shed tears at the sight of it. Afterwards we used to boil watercress. Roasted 'kids' flesh and watercress. They were bygone and happy feasts.
>
> All the children of Wellington gathered to see the milking of the first cow. The cow which was owned by Mrs Miller, was accommodated on a verandah, and was quite conscious of its own importance. How we enjoyed the first taste of her milk.[8]

Within a few months, agents, auctioneers, and even the *Gazette* Office became distributors of seeds and fruit trees. Newspapers that first year show that imported crop seeds such as wheat, seed corn, seed peas, etc. were

---

[7] Kilmister, Albert, *Some Early History of the Kilmister Family and Early Wellington as they Remembered it*, MS, Alexander Turnbull Library.

[8] 'Pioneers of Seventy Years Since', *Evening Post*, 7 May 1912.

Painted by Charles Heaphy in September 1841, this early view of Wellington looks south-east across Te Aro Flat, with the bare slopes of Mount Victoria on the left and the swamp of the Basin Reserve area beneath them. Willis Street is on the right, and Wakefield Street skirts the shore. Forest covers the Brooklyn Hills.

Alexander Turnbull Library, National Library of New Zealand, Te Puna Mātauranga, C-025-009

obtainable from agents such as Luke Natrass, William Lyon, and G.H. Coglund, while T. Roskell had garden seeds for sale in May. The first locally-grown wheat and garden seed grown by Alzdorf were available in July 1841.[9] Two months later, Catchpool advertised Hutt-grown blue pea and radish seed, grown by 'the late Mr Eaton'. Fruit trees were first mentioned in February 1841, when John and George Wade offered to take orders for plants to be obtained from Van Diemen's Land.[10] The first record of fruit trees for sale in Wellington appears to have been in September 1841, when Johnson Moore advertised fruit trees from Sydney.[11] Fruit trees came from London in February 1843.

Advertisements in 1842 show a considerable increase in locally grown seed. The *Gazette* newspaper office distributed some of these as well as some of the imported seeds. As the young settlement grew and nurserymen became established, agents acted for nurserymen by taking orders for plants. Mr Spinks took orders for F.W. Hurst of Karori, John McBeth for Stockbridge of Brooklyn, and James McBeth for Lumsden of Tinakori Road. The Appendix gives a chronological listing of plant material advertised for sale for those first two years, indicating that crop and garden seeds as well as fruit trees were available fairly quickly.

In the 1840s, it was not unusual to see such a large number of vegetables and their varieties advertised at the *Gazette* Office. It is noteworthy that so

---

[9] *New Zealand Gazette and Wellington Spectator*, 18 September 1841.

[10] *New Zealand Gazette and Wellington Spectator*, 13 February 1841.

[11] *New Zealand Gazette and Wellington Spectator*, 11 September 1841.

many were available as early as this in Wellington. There is no indication whether they were Australian or British grown.

The anticipation and illusion that colonial fortunes were to be made through the cultivation of grain soon disappeared. By 1855, fifteen years after settlement, only 10,530 of the 27,500 acres sold were intensively farmed and only 13 per cent of these were in grain, as settlers realised that the climate was not suitable for ripening this crop.[12] Swainson estimated that it cost 8/- per bushel to put on the wharf; yet grain from New South Wales and Van Diemen's Land could be obtained for as little as 3/- and 4/- per bushel.[13] Raising sheep and cattle was easier and more profitable. John Kilmister said:

> **The first cattle came to Wellington from Sydney although some cows came from Scotland. They used to dump them into the sea and let them swim with a boat to guide them ashore near Cambridge Street where there was a stockyard also used as a saleyard. Best Bullocks sold at £3 per head.**[14]

Many of the cattle were turned out to fend for themselves. Most survived, but because cleared land was limited there was little export of livestock to Sydney in the 1840s. Some scrub cattle became wild and caused problems later.[15]

As the end of the first decade approached, the heady optimism of the first days of settlement was tempered by realism and a measure of despondency. Gradually, though, the settlers became more comfortable, as the native vegetation was succeeded by pasture and familiar plants from home. The range of plants available expanded surprisingly quickly, thanks to suppliers in Australia, which had been settled much earlier. J.W. Saxton noted in his diary on 4 May 1842 that he had:

> **reached Colonel Wakefield's home delightfully situated on what will by and by form a beautiful lawn. We walked over the garden where I saw growing strawberries, oaks, filberts, apples, cherries, vines, cape gooseberries, rhubarb, Indian corn, tomatoes, gilliflowers, stocks and most common vegetables. Geese, duck, and turkeys were pecking about. In a dairy we saw pans of milk. Received a box of cuttings from Colonel Wakefield including sage.**[16]

By the end of 1842, Robert Stokes, the Horticultural Society Treasurer, could boast:

> **I have cherries, filberts, mulberries, quinces, the magnolia, camellia, daphne, oleander, passion flowers, honeysuckle, jasmine, ranunculus, tulip and picottee. These were mostly obtained from Sydney and I have every reason to believe they will do well.**[17]

Francis Bradey, together with his wife and five children, arrived on the *Adelaide* in March 1840. When after a short time he returned briefly to England, he wrote:

---

[12] Patterson, B., 'The Grain Mirage', *Stout Centre Review*, May 1992.

[13] Ibid.

[14] Kilmister, Albert, *Some Early History of the Kilmister Family and Early Wellington as they Remembered it*, MS, Alexander Turnbull Library.

[15] Ibid.

[16] *New Zealand Journal*, 1842.

[17] Ward, Louis E., *Early Wellington*, Whitcombe & Tombs Limited, 1928.

> I advise all persons to take garden seeds with them, the sweetbriar, the hawthorn berry in particular; though the country abounds with the most beautiful shrubs and myrtles there is nothing so suitable for hedges.
>
> All persons interested cannot do better than read The Hon. H. Petre's work on New Zealand. The country will grow anything and when we saw our first crops of wheat and barley, and all kinds of vegetables we were quickly delighted ... . I intend to return myself in the spring. I may add that I was carrying on the business of a master bootmaker for 20 years in Old Kent Road and a rate payer of the parish of St George's, Southwark and a freeholder of the country of Surrey and I transferred the whole of my property to New Zealand. It was the most fortunate speculation I have ever made.[18]

Conditions for growth

Settlers were delighted with the realisation that soil conditions favoured plant growth. In 1840, George Duppa wrote in the *New Zealand Journal*:

> The soil is perfectly wonderful: the rapid growth of anything planted in it is something extraordinary. Every one appears to agree that it is capable of producing from five to seven quarters of wheat per acre as any of the most highly manured soils in England. A dense forest which has enriched the soil for ages, covers the country in this district .... The native potato-grounds show what the land is; they grow enormous crops by merely scratching the surface with a sharpened stick ....

Some plants, such as gorse, broom, sweet briar, watercress, blackberry, and Scotch thistles, proved to be too successful in the new country. On St Andrew's Day, 30 November 1840, Scottish settlers planted seeds of the Scotch thistle, celebrating the occasion with a picnic at William Lyon's farm, Petone.[19] This was but one of several introductions of Scotch thistle to New Zealand (some arrived in the first stocks of grass seed), and the plant soon became a nuisance. Scotch thistles became prolific after a burn. There was a time when the edges of the Rangitikei Line in the Manawatu were so covered with them that a rider would arrive in town with his clothes covered in prickles. Some years after their first introduction, Parliament had cause to enact the Thistle Act.

Gorse and broom became a serious problem in Wellington. The sweet briar obtained by early settlers such as Bradey established itself in the Botanic Garden Reserve. When formal development of the garden began in 1870, it was taken up and planted as a hedge, but it doesn't seem to have become a nuisance in Wellington as it did in Canterbury, where both sweet briar and watercress proved troublesome.

At first, early settlers were understandably nostalgic for the familiar plants and landscapes of their homeland, but after a time of adjustment to their new environment they were keen to acquire newly discovered plants.

It is surprising how quickly plants new to cultivation did reach New Zealand. By the 1870s, New Zealand nursery catalogues listed most plants available in the northern hemisphere as well as many plants from Australia and the Pacific. Walter Cook describes the founders of the Wellington

---

[18] Ward, Louis E., *Early Wellington*, Whitcombe & Tombs Limited, 1928.

[19] Shepherd, W. and Cook, W., *The Botanic Garden, Wellington*, 1840-1987, Wellington, 1988.

The stark reality of a small habitation set amongst burnt-off bush slopes. There are no picturesque herb or cottage gardens in this backyard. Angela Jacob at Apiti, near Feilding, 1890s.

Museum of New Zealand Te Papa Tongarewa

Botanic Garden as 'adventurous, curious, intelligent, educated, mid Victorians who brought together materials for a new landscape arising from what they saw as the present needs of a developing colony'.[20]

The Gardener's Magazine, the first English periodical devoted to horticulture, was edited by John Claudius Loudon from 1826 until his death in 1843. Loudon had a significant influence on garden design during the nineteenth century. He published extensively, aiming particularly at the professional gardener, and many of the women settlers brought a knowledge of the works of J.C. Loudon with them to the new country. Even more of them owned a copy of his wife Jane's book, *Gardening for Ladies*.[21] But it is doubtful if any early immigrant to Wellington, whatever his or her background, would have been aware of trends in landscaping and the use of terms such as 'gardenesque' and 'picturesque'.[22] Even if there were one or two with some understanding, the nature of the terrain, the dense plant cover, and the lashing of the winds that Cook Strait vented on the region made any artistry impossible in those first difficult years. All these factors are to be borne in mind in later chapters, where plant introductions and the development of homes and gardens are examined.

---

20 Ibid

21 Loudon, J., *Gardening for Ladies*, John Murray, 1840.

22 Howard, Leathlean, *Garden History*, Vol. 23 No 2.

Chapter 2

COUNTRY ACRES IN THE HUTT VALLEY

> Once we have tamed land like we believe we have this floodplain, are we immune from the life forces that shaped the land and the plants and animals that inhabit it? For the history of the European in the Pacific, the grey beach at Petone and the broad flat behind it is one of most telling places. Nothing quite like what happened here when the buyers of utility arrived in the first few weeks of 1840 had ever happened before.
>
> Geoff Park, *Ngā Uruora*

In 1840, there was chaos on that grey beach at Petone. It was a very muddled beginning for the new settlement. The wooden houses carried on each ship were hastily erected to provide shelter for the new arrivals and their baggage, and thatched whares were also built by local Māori, but no one anticipated that it would take four or five months before land for homes and businesses would become available.

The Petone foreshore was composed of sand dunes pierced by a large estuary fed by three rivers. The Hutt river was navigable by large boats for about six miles before snags and large fallen trees prevented further progress upstream. The map of the Lower Hutt Valley opposite shows the river systems and vegetation, sand dunes, swamps, and the southern limits of the forest. But although after the first few weeks most new arrivals went south across the harbour, those without land orders were directed to the original beach settlement at Petone, which continued to grow throughout the winter of 1840, reaching about 1500 settlers and 400 Māori by the end of the year.

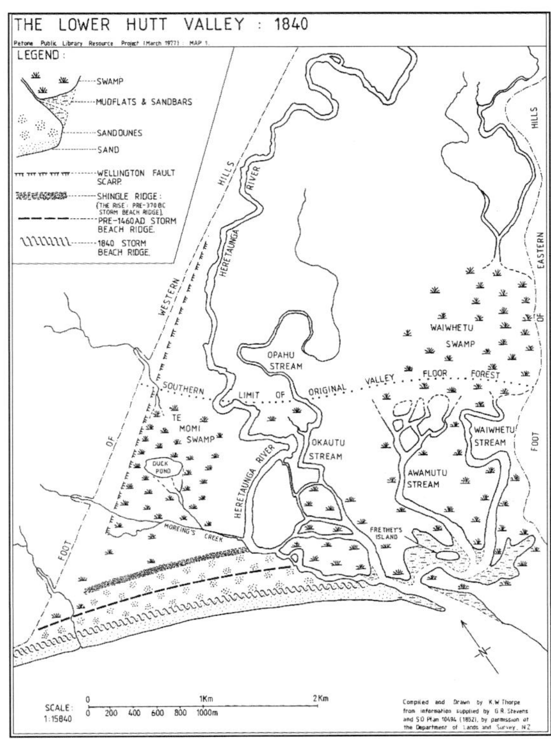

Map of the Lower Hutt Valley, 1840, a patchwork of swamps, rivers, and streams.

Petone Public Library

Near the mouth of the Hutt River in 1843. Watercolour by William Swainson, F.R.S.

Hutt City Library

Petone Road, with Wellington in the distance. S.C. Brees, 1847.

Alexander Turnbull Library, National Library of New Zealand, Te Puna Mātauranga

It was September 1840 before Thorndon was gazetted as the site for Britannia and the Bank was moved by boat from Petone to its new location on the other side of the harbour. Settlers followed, moving to Town Acres around Lambton Harbour or to Country Acre blocks elsewhere. But the extensive area of flat land at the Hutt commanded attention even after the New Zealand Company had endorsed Thorndon as the site for its settlement.

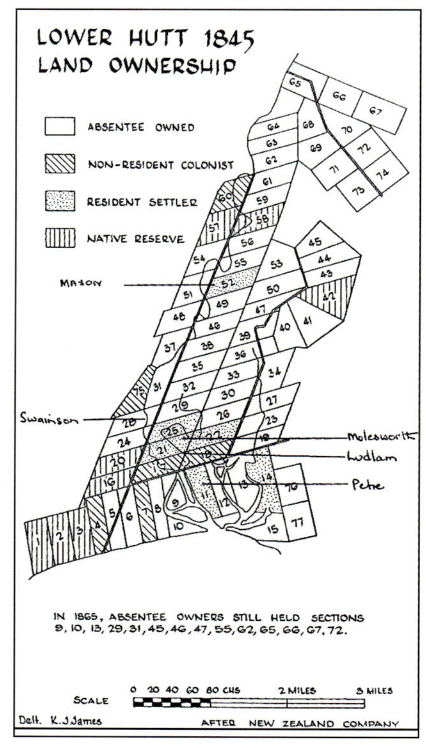

The location of some prominent settlers.

W. Shepherd

Some early Hutt Valley settlers

There were 80 100-acre blocks laid out in the valley by the survey. In this chapter, we look at the stories of some of the people who settled on Country Acres in the Hutt Valley.

Herrongate Farm, the residence of Henry Moreing, was leased by Henry Petre from the end of May 1843. The house stood on a ridge of shingly soil less than half a mile from the mouth of the Hutt River.

Further up the valley, Francis Molesworth's property, promoted by the Company as a model farm, spanned two branches of the river. The land was a mixture of swamp, open area, and heavy forest. Adjoining Molesworth's property on the east at Waiwhetu was a block owned by Alfred Ludlam. Some of this was low-lying but forested. Baron Charles Von Alzdorf's property was to the west of Molesworth's and south of William Swainson's. It fronted the Heretaunga River and was open and swampy, with some forest.

William Swainson had three 100-acre blocks more or less heavily forested, some fronting the river. Further up the valley, and with some river frontage, was Thomas Mason's land with its dense podocarp forest.

All settlers had difficulty in clearing their land, according to the position and lie of the land – near the river or heavily clothed in forest – but these difficulties were mostly glossed over. The *New Zealand Gazette* and *Spectator* reported on 29 January 1842 that:

> Johnson, Baron Alzdorf etc. etc. are clearing and cultivating acres by the fifties and hundreds. These gentlemen are not dismayed at the

The Hutt River with the Aglionby Arms Hotel on the right; to the left, buildings on the the Riddiford property. Molesworth's property is across the river. Dense native forest surrounds all. Reproduced from a painting by S.C. Brees, c 1846.
Alexander Turnbull Library, National Library of New Zealand, Te Puna Mātauranga, B-031-021

> cost of clearing, for they keep a steady eye in their sure market and large returns. There are few who possess the capital to cope with them but combined or rather contemporaneous efforts of persons with smaller means are producing unlooked for results.

The optimism and the acreage being cleared were both exaggerated. William Swainson's sketch of the Hutt Valley Road looking north from the entrance to his home illustrates just how thick the remaining bush was more than six years after settlement. By 1845, no more than six of the 80 blocks were occupied as estates. A further four had been briefly occupied between 1841 and 1845.[1] Some absentee owners leased small areas and thereby managed to get some of their land cleared for them.

William Swainson's sketch of the entrance to his property Hawkshead in 1848 shows dense forest along the new Hutt Valley road.
Hutt City Library

No provision had been made for a town or village, but in time a small cluster of buildings formed at the bend of the Hutt River where it turned east, on part of Daniel Riddiford's Section No 17. By 1848, it had become known as the village of Aglionby. It boasted an excellent tavern with good stabling and accommodation run by Mr Burcham, a small building used as a church and a school, a blacksmith's forge, several shops, one or two good farm houses, and numerous labourers' cottages. The European population of the Hutt Valley in 1845 totalled 644.

The Petres at Herrongate

Henry Petre was one of several young capitalists who arrived on board the *Oriental* in January 1840. He stayed for only a short time, mainly on the beach at Petone. He made a trip to Sydney in May 1840, buying barley seed, mulberry, peach and plum trees, and filberts. Petre returned

[1] Patterson, B., 'The Grain Mirage', *Stout Centre Review*, May 1992.

to England in 1841 and in 1842 his notes on Wellington formed the background for an essay published as *An Account of the Settlements of the New Zealand Company*. The essay is thought to have been ghost-written by H.S. Chapman (who later emigrated to New Zealand and whose story we take up in Chapter 4), and it gave an overly optimistic view of the possibilities for the settlement:

> Olives, and vines obtained from Sydney gave promise, mulberry trees yielded fruit, filberts were flourishing but walnuts, unobtainable in New South Wales, could not be tried. Apples, peaches and plums had been planted. One drawback upon the cultivation of the vine, the olive and the mulberry is that the English really know nothing about it. To cultivate them to any extent we shall require French and German cultivators to whom the most liberal encouragement should be given. The few French at Akaroa, on Bank's Peninsular have begun to make a success of cultivating the vine. …
>
> … The cattle landed lean from on board ship were fat in a short time when turned loose to shift for themselves.[2]

In February 1843, Petre returned to New Zealand with Eleanor, his seventeen-year-old bride, twenty brood mares from the Cape, and two thoroughbred horses from England. Three months later, the Petres took a two-year lease on about 80 acres of Henry Moreing's Herrongate Farm. Mary Swainson, the daughter of William Swainson and the same age as Eleanor Petre, described the place as bare, with no trees, only flax. Mary, although surprised at his choice, understood Henry Petre's need to have grazing land for his horses. The property was partly cultivated and sown with grass and clover. The Petres were to move in as soon as the stables were built.[3]

The land, as can be seen from Geoffrey Swainson's illustration, was very swampy and, being near the river, subject to flooding. In June,

Crayon sketch by William Swainson's son Geoffrey of Henry Moreing's property, Herongate, leased by the Hon Henry Petre, c 1844. Toetoe and flax dominate the foreground.

Alexander Turnbull Library, National Library of New Zealand, Te Puna Mātauranga, A-188-013

[2] Petre, H.W., *An Account of the Settlements of the New Zealand Company*, Smith, Elder & Co., London, 1842.

[3] Swainson, M., Letter to Mr and Mrs Parkes, G. Swainson, Palmerston North.

before the Petres moved in, the house was flooded after heavy rain, causing the young bride to say, 'We propose having perches made in the drawing room ready for the next flood.'[4]

There was another heavy flood on 19 August and a canoe had to be used between the stables and the house. In the same flood Molesworth, living higher up the valley, woke up to find his bed floating.[5] A week later the Petres moved to the Hutt:

> Left the house at 1p.m. – my piano a large cart of furniture topped with chickens, rabbits, pheasants, turkeys and dear old peacock in a large basket with a piece of linen bound round his body to preserve his tail.[6]

Petre immediately began to prepare more land for grass and corn while Eleanor began to lay out the garden in front of the house. At the beginning of October, she sowed flower seeds and planted moss roses donated by Colonel Wakefield – great treasures indeed – especially when cabbage plants emerged along with the flower seedlings! By the end of November, Eleanor Petre, exasperated with the climate, remarked:

> Patience is a virtue one needs to possess in a degree in this windy country. Yesterday it destroyed my flowers. I despair of keeping anything alive that is more than one inch above the ground. Henry ploughed all day.[7]

Eleanor Petre enjoyed growing familiar flowers, but she was also observant, and described many native plants – the native fuchsia, harakeke flowers, and others. She enjoyed the horticultural shows immensely and exchanged seeds and plants, as many others did, regardless of their social standing.

The Petres continued to live at Herrongate, but when Francis Molesworth died in 1846, they purchased part of his land at Woburn (Block 21) and in 1848 had J.H. Percy build them a house in a clearing in the bush. The house had two glass-fronted bay windows and a glass conservatory.[8] William Trotter was asked to develop and maintain the garden. (We take up Trotter's story in detail later this chapter.) In 1855, the year of the big Wellington earthquake, the Petres returned to England, and the house together with 46 acres of land was sold to Daniel Riddiford from the Orongorongo station for £2,400.

Francis Molesworth

Cornish-born Francis Alexander Molesworth was only 22 years old when he arrived in New Zealand on the *Oriental*. He was the younger brother of Sir William Molesworth, a Director of the New Zealand Company, Member of Parliament for East Cornwall, and later Secretary of State for the Colonies. The family seat of Pencarrow, north of Bodmin, had been

---

4 Petre, Eleanor, Diary 1843, Alexander Turnbull Library
5 Petre, ibid.
6 Ibid.
7 Ibid.
8 Although in the 1880s a small glassworks in Auckland produced lamp glasses, water bottles, jugs, etc, all other glass was imported from England or America until the 1930s. Stewart & Co advertised stocks of plate, rolled plate, ground, ornamental, and coloured glass in the 1879 *Wellington Almanac*. Conservatories began to appear in Wellington from 1848.

F.A. Molesworth, Newry, Port Nicholson, N.Z., *watercolour by W. Mein-Smith, September 1844. The wooden house, with its steeply sloping shingled roof, had been brought out ready to erect. The forest trees and undergrowth around the house have been cleared as a precaution against fire. Wheat is ready for cutting. There are glass frames for cucumber and melons, and circular flower beds. The garden is well stocked with fruit trees and other plants from England.*

Alexander Turnbull Library, National Library of New Zealand, Te Puna Mātauranga, A-263-007

the home of the Molesworths since the sixteenth century. Its garden was thought to be one of the most beautiful in England.

Sir William had begun the garden at the age of 21. It was particularly rich in rhododendrons and conifers. Plants from Pencarrow came to New Zealand in the care of James Bryant, who was brought out on the *Duke of Roxburgh* with his young wife to keep house and help Francis develop his property in the new land. Among the trees, shrubs, and other plants were some camellia seedlings in little boxes.[9] These camellias, together with those brought out by T.J. Drake on the *Aurora,* were the first introduced to Wellington.

Francis Molesworth purchased several Town Acres in Wellington,[10] but for his Country Acres he had an eye on a beautiful tract of land about two miles up the east bank of the Hutt River. In October 1840, he was successful in securing Blocks 21 and 22 there as his Country Acres. He immediately proceeded to clear a few acres for cultivation.[11]

On 30 October 1840, he wrote to his mother:

> I have got my own two country land sections which I have commenced clearing for potatoes. By the by, the whole of the seeds (with scarcely an exception) which I procured from Forest and Black are bad, none having come up. That is a severe loss in this place as it is impossible to replace them at any price. Get William to write to F. and B. about them and tell them to send me out another batch for nothing but to mind not to put in any potatoes in with them as that is the reason of their being rotten.
>
> I do not expect to get more than 5-6 acres cleared and planted for a crop this season. By next August I hope to have at least 50 ready for planting with potatoes. If I find by this summer's

[9] Petre, H.W., *An Account of the Settlements of the New Zealand Company*, Smith, Elder & Co., London, 1842.

[10] Wakefield, E. Jerningham, *Adventure in New Zealand abridged*, Whitcombe & Tombs, 1955.

[11] According to 'Earliest New Zealand', the R.J. Barton Journals, and the correspondence of the Reverend John Butler, Molesworth chose an old garden let to Mr Read and cultivated by the local Māori, who were not exactly pleased to leave it for the land set aside for them by the New Zealand Company.

> experience that a paying return is to be had by agriculture I intend to purchase 200 acres adjacent to my own so as to make a decent sized farm of 400 acres.[12]

Two weeks later, Molesworth advertised for labourers to clear the land. On Boxing Day 1840, Harcourt Richard Aubrey wrote:

> My cousin Francis Molesworth is living where the town was first intended to be built at a place called Petone, eight miles from Wellington on the River Hutt. The land is considered more fertile than at the place now fixed on, but being subject to inundation it was quite unfit for a large settlement.[13]

Two years later, in February 1842, William Bayly, after visiting the Hutt, wrote to his parents: 'There were at a distance two farms, Francis Molesworth and another gentleman had many acres of wheat tilled and looking well.'[14]

Molesworth harvested 15 to 18 tons per acre of kidney potatoes in March 1842. At £6 per ton, this not only refunded the capital employed but also yielded a profit.[15] The *New Zealand Gazette and Wellington Spectator* reported in May that:

> on Tuesday the *Lady Leigh* commenced our export trade by taking to Sydney 20 tons of very fine potatoes, grown by Mr Molesworth upon the Hutt. Mentioning the Hutt we understand that 15 tons potatoes to the acre have been obtained and that a small patch of wheat upon measurement showed the crop to be equal to 90 bushels to the acre.[16]

The bounty of the Hutt Valley was already evident. Experience showed that the thickly timbered land on this alluvial soil was not only superior to other land but also that the price of the sawn timber helped pay for the expense of clearing it. Some settlers acquired farms of 20–30 acres which were leased at a peppercorn rent for two to four years. The tenant became both sawyer and cultivator, felling, lopping, burning, and growing potatoes, certain of a respectable independence after a few years. The absentee proprietors got their land cleared by foregoing high rents, and in some cases they authorised their agents to grant leases of up to 21 years.[17]

Roads were opening up the valley. In April 1842, John George Cook wrote:

> I found Molesworth living on the banks of the Hutt, which as you know is about eight miles from Wellington from whence there is now a good road, and ardently engaged in all his agricultural pursuits, clearing, sowing, cropping and reaping the well-earned fruits of his judicious foresight. Everyone without thought, when he first mentioned his bold determination of plunging into the heart of a New Zealand forest, predicted his ruin; he having calculated the chances better than his advisors, had resolution enough to set manfully to work, and although his expenditure and outlay in clearing must have been heavy at the outset, I believe has been amply repaid.

NEW ZEALAND GAZETTE AND BRITANNIA SPECTATOR

SATURDAY, Nov. 14, 1840

CONTRACT TO CLEAR LAND on the HUTT – The undersigned is prepared to give out immediately on contract, from fifteen to twenty acres, to be cleared, on the banks of the Hutt opposite to the piece of land cleared by the late Mr Eaton. The clearing to include falling, lopping, logging, and burning all the timber the proprietor may require. For further particulars, apply to F.A. MOLESWORTH

November 12, 1840

---

12 Ward, Louis E., *Early Wellington*, Whitcombe & Tombs, 1928.

13 *New Zealand Journal*, 1841.

14 Bayly, William, yeoman, Letter, February 1842, Emigrants' letters fromWellington, Nelson and New Plymouth, Alexander Turnbull Library.

15 *New Zealand Gazette and Wellington Spectator*, 5 March 1842.

16 *Ibid.*, 7 May 1842.

17 Patterson, op. cit.

Mill – Newry Flour Mill

The undersigned are prepared to receive wheat to grind at the following prices, viz.

Wheat ground & dressed
1/- per bushel
Wheat ground and not dressed
9d per bushel

No smutty wheat ground unless previously passed through the smutting mashing for which there will be an additional charge of 2d per bushel. Signed Molesworth & Ludlam, Newry

September 12, 1845

> **His example has been followed by other agriculturists and the valley of the Hutt is now occupied by a busy race of clearers and improvers. I do not think that one can estimate too highly the efforts of this really useful man – others have talked, he has performed.**[18]

The skills that Francis Molesworth had learnt at home were very useful in the new colony. He in turn sent his brother seeds or plants (it is not clear which) of various local species that he had collected with the help of his friend and neighbour Alfred Ludlam. Among them were the New Zealand fuchsia (*F. excorticata*), ramarama (*Lomphomyrtus bullata*), the red kowhai (*Clianthus puniceus*), totara (*Podocarpus totara*), and the karaka (*Corynocarpus laevigatus*).[19]

When the Horticultural Society was formed at the end of 1841, Molesworth was elected Vice President, with Colonel Wakefield as President. At the first show in January 1842, Molesworth won first prize for potatoes and carrots, and he continued to win prizes at the horticultural shows for the next couple of years.

On 21 June 1843, Eleanor Petre wrote in her diary:

> **Mr Molesworth's place is perfect, the corn nearly ripe. We walked about his garden and through a large field of potatoes in our riding habits and so on to the barn where they were thrashing the corn.**[20]

When visiting Molesworth's garden in September 1843, she commented on his fine garden enclosed by a thorn hedge, the only one in the colony. In December that year, Molesworth held the first strawberry and cream feast in Wellington, promising each visitor a quart of strawberries! Green peas and new potatoes were on the menu and afterwards guests were invited to pick blackcurrants and cherries.[21]

The painting on page 22 by William Mein-Smith shows Molesworth's farm with a backdrop of as yet untamed bush and stumps. The etching below by Brees shows a cluster of buildings with a flour mill, a

Mr Molesworth's farm at the Hutt. ***This etching by S.C. Brees shows Molesworth and Ludlam's flour mill.***

Brees Album of Etchings

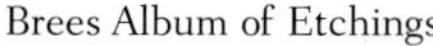

[18] Cook, John, Emigrants' letters from Wellington, Nelson and New Plymouth; *New Zealand Journal*, 16 April 1842.

[19] Smith, Irvine, *Streets of My City*, A.H. & A.W. Reed, 1948.

[20] Petre, Eleanor, Diary, 21 June 1843, Alexander Turnbull Library.

[21] Petre, Eleanor, Diary, September 1843, Alexander Turnbull Library.

Baron Alzdorf's on the Hutt, Wellington. *Watercolour by S.C. Brees, painted sometime between 1842 and 1845.*

Alexander Turnbull Library, National Library of New Zealand, Te Puna Mātauranga, B-031-001

joint venture between Molesworth and his neighbour Ludlam (of which more later).

Around the time the mill was nearing completion, Molesworth suffered a serious injury while felling a tree. He returned to England where he died, aged only 28, in August 1846. The young settlement was deprived of one of its most promising settlers. As well as being a foundation member of the Wellington Horticultural Society and a leading exhibitor, Molesworth was a committee member of the Cattle Company, formed in 1840; he had established a cattle farm at Miramar, importing blood horses from Australia and riding them at race meetings; and he was associated with the first export of potatoes from the Wellington Province and the first flour mill in the Hutt.[22]

> To Agriculturists
>
> SALE, a small quantity of very superior seed wheat, also a small quantity of seed without husk, both grown in the valley, Hutt, and warranted of the first quality. A variety of garden seeds, the produce of the Colony. For particulars, apply to
>
> C.E. Von Alzdorf, Petoni, or to
> E. Davis, at Messrs Hanson and Alzdorf's, Wellington
>
> 1841

Baron Charles Von Alzdorf

Baron Charles Ernest Von Alzdorf, German born and unmarried, arrived on the *Adelaide* in March 1840. As might be expected, every social occasion included the Baron. He secured land at the Hutt and, while he developed it, he acted as an agent in partnership with lawyer R.D. Hanson. His name does not appear on land titles, but it seems that he lived and farmed on leased land at the Hutt.[23]

The *New Zealand Britannia and Spectator* for 17 October 1840 carried an advertisement: 'Town acres and sections advertised for sale. Apply Hanson and Alzdorf'.

In 1841, Alzdorf offered locally-grown wheat for sale – a mere 16 months from the date of his arrival, and a remarkable achievement.

He exhibited wheat – over 5 feet 5 inches high and with full, large ears – together with peas and onions at the first Wellington Horticultural Society Show held on 24 January 1842. He also exhibited the Colony's first apples, four of them, taken from trees imported from London, for

22 It was not all plain sailing. According to Patterson, although Molesworth's property was promoted as the Company's 'model farm', by the time of his death in the mid-1840s the farm had incurred heavy operating losses.

23 Patterson, B., personal communication, May 1996.

which he received a special prize.[24] Until recently, it has always been difficult to obtain new season's apples in January, though Alzdorf's apples may well have been cooking apples.[25]

Other fruit trees were also proving to be successful in Wellington. Robert Stokes, first Secretary of the Wellington Horticultural Society, wrote in October 1842, 'Some peaches, figs, apples and other fruit trees procured last season from Sydney, will I think produce fruit this year as they now have an abundant show of blossom.'[26] These plants would have been acclimatised to the Southern Hemisphere, so Alzdorf's achievements in fruiting apple trees from England in such a short time is even more interesting.

Troubles with local Māori surfaced in August 1842. Alzdorf wrote:

> 'Breda'
> August 22nd 1842
>
> To George White Esq.
> Magistrate
> Petone
>
> I call upon you for intervention between the Natives and my men – the Maories have split into fencing poles the very trees I had cut down by my men to fence off what they call their ground and they are now taking possession of my own clearings. I shall not have on my place not even enough room which is expected from the floods to build a safe pigstye on this place as a farm is ruined. If you have no power to protect the first pilot in farming in this settlement or have the goodness to send a constable immediately to Wellington and if you cannot effect any remedy I shall be obliged to cease with my works and consider this place as nothing further than my residence and I trust that some party or other will indemnify for the enormous outlay I have made and the losses I shall have to meet.
>
> Yours respectfully,
> Charles Von Alzdorf

Alzdorf lays claim to being the 'pilot' farmer in the settlement, and he possibly was, but his contribution to horticulture and agriculture ended that year.[27] By 1843, he had built a hotel on part of Town Acre No 491, Lambton Quay. It was a one-storey building constructed of brick, clay, and wood and contained a Russian vapour bath. Justice H.S. Chapman thought the bath was a luxury and considered building one for himself since it was so simple and inexpensive.

The Baron's hotel was badly damaged in an earthquake in 1848. He replaced it with a two-storey building, which opened in 1852. By the Act of Session, 14 September 1854, he was given New Zealand citizenship, backdated to 1 January 1841.[28] He was killed by collapsing brickwork in the earthquake of 24 January 1855, thirteen years to the day since he first exhibited his four apples.

---

24 *Encyclopaedia of New Zealand*, Vol 1, 1897.

25 The late Dr McKenzie, Pomologist, DSIR, Havelock North, thought so. Dr D. McKenzie, personal communication.

26 *NZ Journal*, 1843.

27 Ward, Louis E., *Early Wellington*, Whitcombe & Tombs Limited, 1928.

28 *New Zealand Spectator and Cook Strait Guardian*, 25 January 1855.

Alfred Ludlam

Alfred Ludlam had spent some time in the West Indies before becoming interested in the New Zealand Company while visiting London in 1839. Paying a deposit for his land orders, he asked Henry Moreing, who was sailing in advance of him, to choose two town sites on his behalf. Moreing chose Section 169, on the corner of Ghuznee and Willis Streets, and the adjacent Section 171 on Ghuznee Street.[29] Ludlam arrived on the ship *London* on 12 December 1840.

By October 1841, Ludlam was manufacturing and advertising bricks for sale.[30]

The advertisement merited an editorial:

> We have seen a sample of the bricks made by Mr Ludlam, and consider them to be excellent quality. English bricks have been sold at five and even seven pounds per thousand, and the present price is four pounds. It will be seen by an advertisement in our paper, that Mr Ludlam offers his bricks at three pounds per thousand, and we understand will dispose of them at a lower price if he receives sufficient encouragement. We are assured that it is cheaper to build a house of bricks at fifty shillings per hundred. It would be a waste of time to enter upon a statement to show the superior appearance, economy, and healthiness of a house built of the former, rather than that of the latter material. We do hope that Mr Ludlam and others who are engaged in a manufacture of so much importance, will receive sufficient support to induce them to furnish the market with an abundant supply at moderate prices.[31]

The advertisement continued to run until at least 9 March 1842, although by this time others were also making bricks.

For his Country Acres, 'Bricks' Ludlam chose Section No 18 at Woburn and Section No 35 on the north-west side of Karori Road. He never lived in Karori. Instead, he went to Woburn, which had been cleared and successfully sown with wheat.[32] In 1845, the Union Bank is shown as owner, and Ludlam paid the purchase price of £127 by June 1847.[33] Ludlam and Molesworth became friends, and it seems that Ludlam was on his land well before the recorded date of purchase. Together they collected native plants and sent them back to England.

Ludlam was keen and energetic. He worked hard to clear the ground, planting wheat and potatoes. He secured the services of the professionally trained William Trotter (whose story is told later in this chapter). As we have already seen, Ludlam and Molesworth went into partnership to build a mill. In October 1845, William Swainson wrote:

> Hutt windmill finished. It belongs to Molesworth and Ludlam – cost an immense amount of money and they grind wheat at 1/- per bushel which is considered cheap here. Mill is built in the farm yard and will work a four horse threshing machine at the same time.[34]

[29] Ward, Louis E., *Early Wellington*, Whitcombe & Tombs Limited, 1928.
[30] *New Zealand Gazette and Wellington Spectator*, October 1841.
[31] *New Zealand Gazette and Wellington Spectator*, October 1841.
[32] Block 18 had originally been chosen in 1839 by another settler, Harry St Hill, for Mr Halswell.
[33] 1851 Land Claims of New Zealand Company, National Archives.
[34] Swainson, W., Letter to Swainson, G.W., July 1847, G. Swainson, Palmerston North.

BRICKS

Bricks on sale by the undersigned at 50s per 1,000. Terms – cash on delivery at the kiln.
A Ludlam
Willis Street,
29 October

Alfred Ludlam.
Botanic Garden Archives

BRICKS

BRICKS on sale by the undersigned at 60s. per 1,000. If taken in quantities of 15,000 a reduction of 10s. per 1,000 will be made.
Terms – cash on delivery at the kiln.
A. Ludlam
Willis Street,
January 12, 1842

Te Aro Beach, 9 March 1842

BRICKS

FOR SALE at 60s. per thousand. Apply to J. Pimble, at the Sydney Street Brick and Tile Works, at the rear of Colonel Wakefield's residence.
Terms – cash on delivery at the kiln

Molesworth's and Ludlam's mill was completed at the beginning of 1845. The *New Zealand Spectator and Cook Strait Guardian* reported on the celebration of the event on 11 January:

> On Tuesday, the last day of the year, a ball was given at Newry on the river Hutt, by Mr Ludlam to his numerous friends and acquaintances, to celebrate the completion of a large barn and the first windmill erected in that district. The barn which is larger than the Lodge Room at Barrett's Hotel, was very tastefully decorated with native shrubs and flowers; at one end was a large star formed of roses and which, backed by the dark green of the karaka leaves, had a very pretty effect. The supper was laid out in the mill and comprised all the delicacies of the season. Dancing commenced at nine o'clock and was kept up with great spirit until four in the morning, when the guests departed after having spent an evening of great enjoyment, in which nothing was omitted by their host that could contribute to their amusement. The mill, which it is expected will be ready to commence grinding the beginning of next month, is built in the most substantial manner of the wood of the district, and will be furnished with two pair of stones. It reflects great credit the energy and enterprize of the spirited proprietor, and will no doubt be of the greatest advantage to the district, and, we hope, a source of great profit to its owner. Many of the guests from Wellington remained the following day, to visit the improvements in the Hutt and to partake of Mr Ludlam's hospitality. The wheat which is now in full ear looked remarkably well, and when it is stated that this the fourth and in some parts, where the land was first cleared, the fifth crop of wheat in *succession*, we think, we adduce one of the strongest possible facts in proof of the fertility of the district. We were very much pleased with the appearance of some hops in the garden which were growing most luxuriantly and which afford the most convincing proof of the capabilities of the district for becoming the top garden of New Zealand, if care is taken to provide due shelter from the south east wind, by leaving belts of wood in clearing round those spots intended for the cultivation of this plant.

The *New Zealand Spectator and Cook Strait Guardian* for 26 April 1845 published an article by Ludlam on the cost of bringing in land at the Hutt. In the same paper on 12 July 1845, however, some of these figures were queried by Henry Jackson. Ludlam, like most of the other settlers, gave up growing wheat and potatoes, pasturing sheep and cattle instead. He acquired a reputation for his good farming methods and steady selection of good class stock.

Francis Molesworth's accident and subsequent departure was a blow to Ludlam. With William Trotter's help, Ludlam took on the management of Molesworth's garden for a while and he employed James Bryant, Molesworth's manservant, as sawyer and gardener on his own property. Bryant stayed with Ludlam until 1856. (We take up his story again in Chapter 5.)

By the middle of the decade, after a promising start, relations with the local Māori deteriorated, and land wars with local Māori were affecting the Hutt Valley. This had an effect on the confidence of the early settlers, and Ludlam was no exception.[35] At the beginning of 1846, William Swainson wrote to Walter Mantell:

---

[35] Swainson, W., ibid.

The newly built house of Alfred Ludlam set amongst the remaining native forest, painted in 1850 at the time of Ludlam's marriage. The house was built by J.H. Percy and cost £1009.3.10 plus £47.1.3 for extras. The house was badly damaged in the 1855 earthquake, mainly from falling chimneys. Watercolour, F.D. Bell.
Hocken Library

> The Hutt looks wretchedly – houses empty, fences broken down, roads over fields and through crops – and all the traces and effects of military despotism i.e. martial law. I am now the only 'Gentleman Settler' for the Riddifords have gone, Stebbings is going and most of the settlers above me have gone to other districts .... I have been confined to the house this winter and I am almost tempted to look out for a milder and dryer locality .... Ludlam is thinking of selling his farm in small allotments and returning to England .... Mr Garrett who took Mason's farm has quitted it and returns to England. In short, the agricultural population of the Hutt is fast disappearing so that when we have our lands there will be no-one to use them.[36]

Conditions in the valley did eventually improve. In 1850, William Swainson told his son Geoffrey that Ludlam had gone to Sydney to fetch his wife. About the same time Henry Petre was building a 'very pretty and gentlemanly small house' compared with Ludlam's, which 'towered over all in semi-gothic semi-modern pride, casting into shade the surrounding cottages'. Edwin Daniels was also building a 'great house'.[37]

Ludlam married Fanny Minto, third daughter of Lieutenant Colonel Gibbs, in Sydney in October 1850.[38] F.D. Bell's watercolour shows their newly built home at Woburn set against the remains of forest.
The large glasshouse visible in many of the later photographs was built at the same time as the house. The garden is newly planted, and nikau palms frame the drive and front steps. (There are many more visible in later photographs, and judging by their trunk size, they must have been planted

[36] Swainson, W., to Mantell, W., 18 January 1846, Mantell Collection, Alexander Turnbull Library.

[37] Swainson, W., Letter to Swainson, G.W., 31 February 1850, G. Swainson, Palmerston North.

[38] *Wellington Independent*, 30 October 1850.

A grove of nikau palms, c 1885.
Hutt City Library

when this painting was done). Nikau feature prominently in the photographs of the 1880s and they are still prominent today.

In July 1851, the property was extended with the purchase of 97 acres of Block 22 from Francis Molesworth's estate.[39] A Mr Pope rented the remaining three acres, which were still attended to by Trotter.

Well watered by the Hutt River and blessed with rich alluvial soil, Ludlam's garden and farm became renowned. From the beginning, he imported many plants. An analysis of his order from Camden Nurseries in Sydney in 1848 shows that apples, pears, plums, and cherries were still most important, with apricots, peaches, and nectarines at the trial and error stage. A number of *Viburnum* species, roses, and one *Crinum* complete the order.

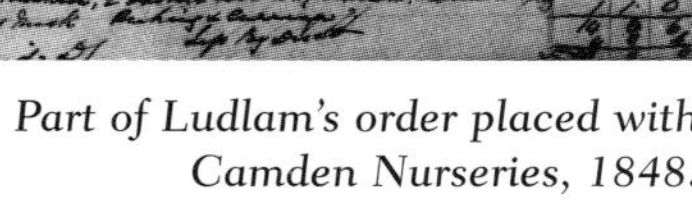

Part of Ludlam's order placed with Camden Nurseries, 1848.

Ludlam's Order Placed With Camden Nurseries 1848

7 Red Quarendron apples, 7 Cornish Gilliflower (apples)
7 Golden Harvey apples, 7 White Spanish Reinnette (apples)
7 Golden Reinnette apples, 7 ?, 7 Marie Louise (pears)
7 Chaumontelle (pears), 7 Napoleon (pears), 7 Crassane (pears)
4 Gansels Bergamottes (pears), 3 Beurre nance (pears), 7 ? @ 2/-
4 Amber Heart cherry, 2 Black Heart cherry, 2 ?
4 Bigarean, cherries, 2 Medlars 14 ? @ 2/-
2 dbl. Bloss. cherry peach, 1 Campden superb (peach), 1 Merchant Campbelli (peach)
1 Crimson Newington nectarine, 1 Red Roman nectarine, 1 Elruge nectarine
1 Moor Park apricot, 1 McKay, 1 Hemskirk apricot, 1 ?
3 Blue gage plums, 3 Green gage plums, 3 Golden drop plums
3 Viburnum japonica, 3 Viburnum chinensis, 3 Viburnum aspinoides
2 Viburnum obovatum, 1 Viburnum rugosum, 1 Erythrina of Campden
3 Podocarpus, 1 Crinum capense 2/6, 2 Rosa odorissima 3/-
2 Rosa dbl. Banksia, 2 Rosa odorata alba, 2 Rosa perditta, 2 ? Duprey
2 Rivers musk. Packing & carriage 2/-

By 1854, besides sheep and wool, Ludlam was exporting apples to

[39] 1851 Land Claims of New Zealand Company, National Archives.

Port Philip in Australia, for which he received 1¾ pence per bushel.

In 1865 Ludlam wrote an important essay on the cultivation and acclimatisation of plants for the Dunedin Exhibition.

> In forming my garden I planted the places I intended for groups of trees and shrubberies thickly with native shrubs, which in 2 years afforded ample shelter for the protection of young plants. As I obtained different varieties of plants I cut away the insides of these plantations and planted them in the place of the native shrubs, but not removing more than was sufficient to allow of sun and air to the young plants. Every year I cut away more as the plants grew until at last in many places none of the original shrubs are left.[40]

Ludlam was not only a farmer but also a lover of plants in a country just opened up for the first time to settlement, and curious about what would or would not grow. His essay describes his experiences with growing the different genera and species. Of *Escallonias*, for example, he says:

Escallonia florabunda	Grenada	Hardy
Escallonia grandiflora		Hardy
Escallonia organensis	Oregan Mountains	Hardy
Escallonia montevidensis	Montevideo	Hardy
Escallonia densa	South Chile	Hardy

> Handsome flowering shrubs, particularly the last, which was introduced into the colony by Mr W.B. D. Mantell. Its close habit of growth, dark glossy green leaves, and bright crimson flowers, render it a great addition to our gardens. It grows very quickly.[41]

Conifers planted by Ludlam in the 1860s and 1870s are features in the lawn c 1895.

Hutt City Library

[40] Ludlam, A., 'Cultivation and Acclimatisation of Trees and Plants', *Transactions of the New Zealand Institute*, Vol 1, 1869. A similar paper, by fellow settler Thomas Mason, from further up the valley, was published in the *Transactions* at about the same time.

[41] Ludlam, A., 'Cultivation and Acclimatisation of Trees and Plants', *Transactions of the New Zealand Institute*, Vol 1, 1869.

He gives good descriptions of how to grow azaleas, camellias, and roses. Besides *Crinum capense*, which he had ordered from Camden in 1848, he now has the species *C. scabrum*, *augustum*, and *pedunculatum*, together with three called *macleaii*, *niobe*, and *Helen*. (These last three may be varietal names.)

Ludlam had about 50 varieties of *Camellia japonica*. Eighteen of those mentioned in Ludlam's paper of 1865 were discussed by Professor E.G. Waterhouse in the *New Zealand Camellia Society Bulletin*, in July 1961.[42] The list included the following varieties:

White	Red
C. japonica alba plena	*C. japonica coccinea*
C. " " " *leila*	C. " " " *clio*
C. " " " *imbricata alba*	C. " " " *marina*
C. " " " *fimbricata alba*	C. " " " *splendens*
C. " " " *calliope*	C. " " " *ianthe*
Variegated	Pink
C. japonica presii	*C. japonica welbankiana*
C. " " " *rosa mundi*	C. " " " *picta*
C. " " " *variegata plena*	
C. " " " *lysanthe*	
C. " " " *donckelarii*	

Some plant introductions were too successful. The *New Zealand Gazette* office had advertised sorrel seed in November 1841. In his 1865 essay, Ludlam had this to say:

> I have a few words to say to the destruction of that pest of all pests, 'Sorrel', one which appears to flourish all the better for the attention it receives, in digging it up and carefully collecting its roots. During that last few years, I have tried many of the recipes to get rid of this enemy to the garden, but to no purpose; at last I thought I would try constant hoeing during the summer, which I have done for two seasons, and found it answer well; I simply hoe the ground very shallow on a dry day so soon as the weed makes it appearance, a few hours hot sun dries it up. This plan I have found the most effective one I have tried, for many beds are quite free from it, and in every place it was so treated, it is fast disappearing.[43]

Typically, Ludlam was also looking to the future:

> In concluding this paper, I may be allowed to hope that the information contained in it will lead to a more general cultivation of the Coniferous Trees in this country. I am quite aware that many of the rarer varieties are not so easily obtained in this colony. To those wishing to procure them, I would say, you can procure most of them from the nurseries in Australia. It has always been a matter of deep regret to me that the Government of the Colony, in former years, did not establish a Botanical Garden for the collection and propagation of trees and plants from different countries. Had such been done, New Zealand might now possess one of the finest public gardens, which would be a credit and pleasure to its inhabitants, and a source of utility in providing them with plants of a beautiful character. Perhaps, when peace is once more restored to the Northern Island, we may hope to see some advance made in that direction.[44]

---

[42] Waterhouse, E.G., 'Early Camellias in New Zealand', *New Zealand Camellia Society Bulletin*, Vol 2, No 3, July 1961, Alexander Turnbull Library.

[43] Ludlam, 1869, op. cit.

[44] Ludlam, 1869, op. cit.

Both of Ludlam's recommendations came to pass. In 1869, Ludlam introduced a Local Bodies Bill to Parliament for the formation of the Colonial Botanic Garden. Large plantings of conifers made on the Town Belt in the 1880s are a distinctive feature of present-day Wellington.

Ludlam collected plants and shrubs from all over the country as well as from Australia, China, the Himalayas, and Europe. Oranges and the Lisbon lemon grew well outdoors and first fruited in 1869. At the Christchurch Interprovincial Exhibition in January 1873, Ludlam exhibited lemons that had been grown outdoors from eight-year-old trees. They commanded attention.[45] By the 1870s, there were reputed to be 8,000 plants and 3 tons of bulbs growing on the estate. In 1877, the year of his death, there were 10 acres of pleasure gardens, 8 acres of orchard, and 17 acres of lawns. A wide drive lined with camellias and hydrangeas backed by darker-leafed native plants swept up to the two-storeyed house.

Alfred Ludlam retired in 1875, and visited England with his wife, who died there. He returned to New Zealand and died in 1877.[46]

Funeral Notice

A Ludlam

The funeral of the late Mr Alfred Ludlam took place on Monday afternoon. The hearse left the residence of Mr McNab, Thorndon, at half-past 3 o'clock, and was followed by a large number of people, amongst whom were several members of Parliament, including the Speakers of both Houses of Representatives adjourned in the afternoon out of respect of the memory of the deceased.

Evening Post

Leave McNab's residence

Hobson Street, Monday 12th, 3.30

Died 8 November 1877

Obituary

Another of the pioneers of the colony has passed away – Mr Alfred Ludlam – whose name is intimately associated with the progress of the provincial district of Wellington, and who represented for many years the Hutt in the General Assembly, and also in the Provincial Council, of which he was at one time Speaker. It was only a few weeks ago that Mr Ludlam returned to New Zealand from a visit to the Home country, where he had the misfortune to lose his wife. The deceased was amongst the many useful colonists whose circle is gradually narrowing. To him Wellington is principally indebted for the Botanical Gardens, which, although far inferior to what they should be, form nevertheless an agreeable recreation ground, the want of which would be much felt, and which in the course of a few years will, it is to be hoped, be made in reality what they are in name. The site is one admirably adapted by nature for the purpose; and its selection shows both taste and judgement, in which Mr Ludlam excelled. He also contributed largely at his own expense to stock this domain with choice and rare trees and plants, and on his own estate at the Hutt his love for horticulture was displayed to great advantage. If to quote a somewhat trite but true maxim, "He is a good patriot who makes two blades of grass grow where one grew before," Mr Ludlam is extremely deserving to be classed in this category, and amongst the gradually narrowing circles of "old identities" the loss of the deceased will be much felt.

Evening Post

15 November 1877

After his death, it was feared that Ludlam's garden would be broken up, but at the last moment James McNab bought the property with the intention of making it a commercial enterprise. When 'McNab's Gardens' opened to the public, it became a popular Wellington tea garden. (There is more on tea gardens in Chapter 8.)

If a drive is taken around Ludlam Crescent, Woburn Road, Wai-iti Street, and Nikau Grove today, some vestiges of the old gardens and some

[45] *Lyttleton Times*, 6 January 1873.

[46] Fifty years after his death, the *Evening Post* published a comprehensive summary of Ludlam's achievements under the title 'Makers of Wellington'.

of the old trees and nikau palms can be seen. Trees planted by Ludlam can be seen in a number of properties. Some noted by Burstall are:[47]

INDIGENOUS NOTABLE TREES
Agathis australis, Kauri. American Embassy, Woburn Road, Lower Hutt. Dbh 22 in; height 42 ft in 1969.

Metrosideros excelsa, Pohutukawa. Bellevue Hotel, Woburn Road, Lower Hutt. Girth at 3 ft; 22 ft; height 54 ft; spread 50 ft in 1969.

EXOTIC NOTABLE TREES
Araucaria heterophylla (syn. *A. excelsa*), Norfolk Island Pine. American Embassy, Woburn Road, Lower Hutt. Registered 1990 Notable Tree R.N.Z.I.H. Height 30.0 m; girth 4.20 m; width 12.50 m.

Araucaria bidwillii, Bunya-Bunya Pine, Queensland. John G. Wade, 29 Wai-iti Crescent, Woburn, Lower Hutt. Ddh 36 in; height 73 ft in 1969. Tree removed after 1986. (Fig. 35).

Cedrus deodara, Himalayan Cedar. Bellevue Hotel, Woburn Road, Lower Hutt. Dbh 29 in., height 59 ft, spread 58 ft, in 1969. A very old, poorly sited tree. There are many good younger trees in this locality.

Liriodendron tulipifera, Tulip Tree, Eastern U.S.A. American Embassy, Woburn Road, Lower Hutt. Registered 1990 Notable Tree R.N.Z.I.H. Height 25.0 m; girth 4.57 m; width 30.0 m.

Quercus robur (syn. *Q. pedunculata*), Common English Oak, Europe and Asia. Commonwealth Convenant Church Home, 29 Wai-iti Crescent, Woburn, Lower Hutt. Dbh 30 in; height 52 ft; spread 70 ft in 1969. Previously the Riddiford estate.

Tilia x *europaea* (syn. *T. vulgaris, T. cordata* x *platyphyllos*), Common Lime. Bellevue Hotel, Woburn Road, Lower Hutt. Diameter at 3 ft; 42 in; height 47 ft; spread 54 ft in 1969.

Ulmus procera, Common Elm, W. Central and N. Europe. Commonwealth Covenant Church, 29 Wai-iti Crescent, Woburn. Diameter at 5 ft, 37 in., height 72 ft, spread 70 ft, in 1969. Part of the old Riddiford estate.

A visit to one of these properties is an experience to be remembered, especially the sight of such exotics as a large Malaysian rubber tree, a ginkgo, and a large golden bamboo *Bambusa arundinaceae*. In 1865, Ludlam wrote:

> The bamboo if it could be grown in this country would prove useful for many purposes. The large one, I much fear, would be too tender. I have tried plants at *different* times and now have one which has been 12 months in the ground without making any growth. It is still alive and I have some hopes it may shoot up this season. In New South Wales, a district visited by harder frosts than any I have seen here, it grows to a fair height with strong canes.[48]

Could this be the same plant that finally did shoot up, forming a magnificent clump of golden canes over a century later? If so, Ludlam would have been delighted.

The story of Ludlam and his property, Newry, would not be complete without a brief resumé of his achievements and his outstanding service to Wellington in its formative years. He was a foundation member of the Wellington Horticultural Society, his name is connected with the early history of the Bolton Street Cemetery, and he was a pallbearer at both Colonel Wakefield's and Te Puni's funerals. In 1849, Sir George Grey appointed Ludlam to the nominated Legislative Council of New

---

[47] Burstall, B., Mensuration Reports, Notable Trees, Forestry Research Institute, unpublished.
[48] Ludlam, 1869, op. cit.

Munster, but he resigned after 12 months. In 1853, he was appointed Superintendent of Police. In the same year, he held a Hutt seat on the Wellington Provincial Council, where he served until 1861, including once as speaker. From 1865 to 1875, Ludlam represented the Hutt in the General Assembly. From 1867, he served on the Board of the New Zealand Institute and from 1869 on the Board of the Botanic Garden. He served in the Militia during the New Zealand Wars, attaining the rank of Major in 1868.

William Trotter

William Trotter, formerly gardener to J.T. Brook of Fletchwick House, emigrated to New Zealand on the recommendation of the horticulturist J.C. Loudon. He arrived in Wellington May 1843 and within 12 months had leased a few acres bordering the Okautu branch of the Hutt river. From the position of his property as shown in the map, the ground was low-lying and not heavily forested. Trotter wrote to his old mentor Loudon describing the land on which he had settled:

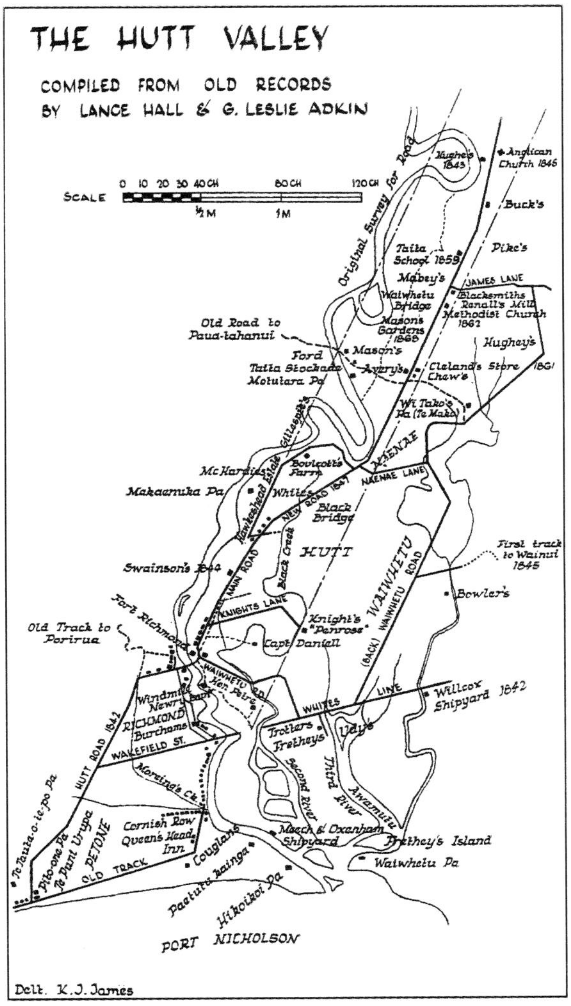

> I have taken a few acres in the valley of the Hutt where I intend to establish a fruit garden and Nursery. It is one of the sweetest spots that ever was beheld by the eyes of man. The beautiful River Hutt enclosed part of it and this is belted by a range of mountains which are covered by the most splendid trees from 50'-150' high and out of respect for you have named it Loudon's Vale ....
>
> We have had two horticultural shows since I have been here and at which I have been a judge both times. It surprises you to see what the place produces although it is only four years old.[49]

By 1848, only a shelter belt of native plants near the river and a few stumps remained of the native vegetation. Trotter hoped in time to remove the stumps.[50]

Settlers were quick to recognise Trotter's horticultural skills. While still managing some of Molesworth's property, he also took on Ludlam's property for a period of time.

Trotter was an innovative plant propagator:

> There is a beautiful native Ribes here which grows 40–50 ft high on which I have budded both the gooseberry and currant both of which have taken well and are growing amazingly. ...I have also budded the pear on the whitethorn which is doing well. In fact budding and grafting may be carried on all year round.[51]

In January 1848, he wrote in the *Gardener's Chronicle*:

> I suppose you saw in my former letter about my succeeding so well in budding and grafting fruit trees especially pears on whitethorns which I assure you make handsome trees. I have a row of apple trees before my front door about 15 months old, fully 4 feet high and

This map of the Hutt Valley shows the position of the land leased by Trotter, on the southern side of White's Line. The location of other settlers' properties are also indicated.

Once Upon a Village, *David D. Miller*

[49] *New Zealand Journal*.

[50] *The Gardener's Chronicle*, 1848, p. 493.

[51] Nairn, Robert, Banks Lecture, *RNZIH Journal*, 1932.

> branching out into splendid heads. There are also trees of my working which bore apples this year. We have splendid crops of fruit this season considering the age of the trees over at Molesworth and Ludlam's garden, which has been under my care since I came to the Hutt. I was obliged yesterday to thin out the apples on two to three of the trees as they were hanging a good deal too thick. We have a nice little vinery. I planted the vines 15 months ago, and I never saw anything grow on so rapidly and make such fine wood, and there are a few bunches on them this year which will be exhibited at the Horticultural Show – the first grapes grown in the Colony.
>
> I have some splendid melons and cucumbers coming on. We have a beautiful soil and a beautiful climate.

By 1848, Trotter had planted 400 fruit trees, which included 40 varieties of apples, 20 of pears, and good varieties of cherries and plums, all obtained from England. They were planted out following the plan of the Hampton Court labyrinth, with apples and pears being trained as espaliers so that they and the grape vines would ultimately run into each other, forming a fine hedge all round the walls.[52] This in turn was surrounded by a painted paling fence.

That year, Trotter superintended the formation of Henry Petre's garden around his new house built on part of Block 21 of the Molesworth estate, as shown in the map at the beginning of the chapter, on page 17. [53]

Trotter's own garden continued to be bountiful. In 1851, a report said:

> The fruit trees have born abundantly this year. Mr Trotter picked a pear from one of his trees the other day which weighed 28½ ozs, it was of delicious flavour and was much larger than any he had seen of the kind .... He states that New Zealand is one of the finest fruit growing countries in the world.

Trotter's gardening diary from 1 January 1850 to April 1861 is held in the Alexander Turnbull Library. It gives a day-by-day description of planting and garden work. Trotter was a professionally-trained Victorian gardener, and his garden showed it. The vegetables he grew were potatoes, turnips, celery, asparagus, onions, carrots, oats, peas, beans, cucumber, cabbage, French beans, broccoli, turnips, maize, cauliflowers, and Indian corn. Fruits grown were strawberries, gooseberries, raspberries, rhubarb, apples, melons, cherries, pears, currants, and peaches. Plants in the flower garden included roses and tobacco.

Like other settlers, he sold excess produce, but Trotter did not operate a nursery in the true sense of the word (as Alan Hale maintained), and he is not therefore New Zealand's first nurseryman.[54] Trotter spent a great deal of time planting and harvesting potatoes, as he had done back in England. This suggests that there were fewer potatoes available from the local Māori than there had been ten years earlier. Trotter stored his potatoes in a deep pit.

He must have been very busy, not only managing Ludlam's property

---

52 *Gardener's Chronicle*, 1848, p 493.

53 *Gardener's Chronicle*, ibid.

54 Hale, Alan, *Pioneer Nurseryman*.

and Molesworth's for Mr Pope but also maintaining the level of work on his own account. An indication of this hard work comes from a letter of 11 January 1850:

> My wife and youngest son are up every morning gathering gooseberries for Wellington by half-past 4 o'clock. We must have had at least 1,500 quarts this season .... I thought of Old England on New Year's Day ... here we were, from morn till night, selling ripe gooseberries – I had hundreds of people from Wellington to visit me that day.[55]

These days the harvesting of gooseberries and black and red currants is thought to be too much work for the majority of home gardeners!
On reaching adulthood, Trotter's sons took up 25 acres of land at Taita, and it seems that his energy was from then on directed to creating a special garden with them.[56]

Thomas Mason

Thomas and Jane Mason were married on 16 November 1840 at Bishophill, York. Three weeks later, they sailed for New Zealand aboard the *Olympus*. Thomas, aged 23 and a Quaker, had purchased three land orders from the New Zealand Company, each of 100 acres, for £300 sterling. Compared with the quarters allocated for assisted immigrants, Jane and Thomas were indeed fortunate – their cabin was 11 feet by 18 feet with two nice-sized windows astern.

On 20 April 1841, the ship anchored in the harbour, and Mason was given leave to pitch his tent on shore the following day. As the valley survey had been finished, it was not long before Māori helpers made a small clearing and erected a thatched wattle and daub cottage for them on their own land further up the valley. The Company later provided a wooden cottage. In this utterly isolated place, the Masons' first child, John, was born on 14 August 1841.

Thomas Mason (1903).
Botanic Garden Archives

Bordering the river, Mason's land was mostly covered with heavy totara forest. Many of the trees were huge, at least over 200 years in age, some 100 to 150 feet high and three to eight feet in diameter. Survival was paramount. The impenetrable forest had to be cleared before cattle could graze and crops could be sown.

Mason wrote to his uncle just six weeks after their arrival, asking for vegetable and flower seeds.

> Please send me some seeds of asparagus, Siberian crab, onion, red cabbage, and other seeds of good vegetables with a few hardy flower seeds as [well] ..., dianthus, and a few rose tree seeds and some hawthorn.[57]

He requested potatoes and vegetables in his second letter, and also asked for oak and ash trees in order to brighten up the sombre green of the landscape. On 10 August 1841, he wrote:

---

55 Trotter, W., Letter 11 January 1850 to E.G. Wakefield, Macclesfield, in Ward, Louis E., *Early Wellington*, Whitcombe & Tombs Limited, 1928, p 493.

56 *Gardener's Chronicle*, ibid.

57 Mason, T., Letter to his uncle 8 June 1841, Alexander Turnbull Library.

The wattle-and-daub thatched cottage built for Thomas and Jane Mason, Hutt River, 1841.

Courtesy of Alan Mason

> Have put in a few seeds and some potatoes. I have got as many sorts of native potatoes as I could and intend trying which is best. I have sown some seeds but roots are better if anyone is coming please send me a few and any other good varieties as you may happen to have. 2–3 potatoes of a sort is sufficient. I should like also if you have the opportunity of sending them – some acorns, ash seed and Siberian crab. Also a few of the best varieties of onion and if possible to be got some broom corn – a sort of maize.

The English potatoes were harvested in 1842, with a good yield, while strawberry and raspberry plants raised from seed were ready to plant out. The soil was a rich alluvial deposit of sandy loam eight to eleven feet deep and resting on gravel, affording good drainage. Violent gales swept the valley from the north-west and south-east.

Mason continued to bring land into cultivation until an outbreak of disturbances with local Māori over a quantity of potatoes that had been stolen. As a Quaker, he was unable to take up arms. Problems had been occurring from November 1841 but came to a head on 3 March 1845. Concerned about the prospect of war and the state of Jane's health, Mason took his family to Hobart, where he is said to have founded the Friends School.

Other settlers in the area also moved away or into Wellington for several years. According to William Swainson, a Mr Garrett took over Mason's farm, but many properties in the valley appeared abandoned.

In a letter to his son Geoffrey dated 28 July 1847, Swainson wrote:

> I had a long letter from Mr Mason the other day who is still in Hobart Town without any intention at present of returning to the Hutt. In him we lost the most valuable settler of the district, plain indeed in his manners but kind and considering in his disposition with great experience and great prudence, above all with a thoroughly Christian temper in every social intercourse and domestic relation.[58]

In the same letter, Swainson mentioned that even Alfred Ludlam was thinking of quitting the colony.

Things did eventually improve and in 1850 Mason returned. He brought with him eucalyptus seeds and a selection of apple trees that would form the nucleus of his orchard. In the following year, 1851, he added a further 150 fruit trees of various kinds and varieties – apples, pears, peaches, plums, cherries, apricots, Siberian crab, walnut, Spanish chestnut, almond – together with a supply of small fruits, rhubarb, etc. Gooseberry plants were obtained from Ludlam at Woburn and grapevines were imported from Sydney. It is uncertain whether the fruit trees came from Hobart or Sydney. Mason also mentions a 'macadamised' road passing through the land, a stone's throw away from the house.[59]

When the eucalyptus seed germinated, the young gum trees were planted around the periphery of the property, from which the property subsequently took its name. In 1853, a third substantial house was started on the property, but there was some delay when their carpenter decamped for the gold diggings in the middle of building the house. Like

---

[58] Swainson, W., Letter to G.W. Swainson, G. Swainson, Palmerston North.

[59] Mason, T., Letter to his uncle, Alexander Turnbull Library.

Mason's Garden, Hutt Valley, c ***1875.***
Watercolour by John Atherton Horsfall.

Alexander Turnbull Library, National Library of New Zealand, Te Puna Mātauranga, B-079-029

all the houses in the valley, this one was built on posts up to one and a half feet above the ground, on account of the floods.

Mason and his family established the first regular meetings for Quaker worship in the district. Usually it was just the family, but on occasions Friends from Wellington joined them. Fellow Quakers Frederick Mackie and Robert and Sarah Lindsey spent some months with the Masons at The Gums in 1853, and Mackie sketched the Māori whares on the property.[60] 'The little meeting,' wrote Frederick Mackie, 'buried as we are in the wilderness, was a season of refreshment and comfort'.[61]

Initially the Masons were one of three settler families in a district that was somewhat distant from Wellington, but from where all requirements and stores had to be obtained:

> The goods were brought in a row boat up the bay from town to the mouth of the river, and thence were carried on men's backs through miles of rough bush track. Starting from home at 2 a.m. and finding their way through the forest by lighted torches of totara pine, the return journey from Wellington was not usually accomplished until 9 or 10 p.m. long after darkness had set in. Mrs Mason's piercing 'cooey', and her husband's equally vigorous response could be distinctly heard re-echoing through the sombre silent forest for fully an hour and a half before he gained the river bank opposite the whare where the canoe stood ready to ferry the goods and himself across the river.[62]

In 1853, according to Mackie, there was 'an excellent road along the margin of the bay with two horse vans running daily. It was a romantic drive.' He noted flax, karaka, toetoe, and native fuchsia as plants

---

60 The Quaker Journals of Frederick Mackie on his tour of the Australasian Colonies1852–1855, published as *Traveller Under Concern*, Hobart University, 1973 and *TheTravels of Robert and Sarah Lindsey*, ed. Robert Lindsey, London, 1886 provide valuable illustrations.

61 Mackie, F., *Traveller Under Concern*, 1973.

62 Jones, William, *Quaker Campaigns in Peace and War*.

prevalent in the area, and described helping with the harvest:

> This morning I joined Thomas Mason in the wheat field, reaping. His Maori labourers soon discovered that I had never handled a sickle before. The wheat, owing to the wet summer is a good deal blighted.

At the end of 1854, Mason had 30 acres of wheat and oats and 18 cows, but he came to realise that the climate in the Hutt Valley was not suitable for growing grain. Pasture was more profitable, so he concentrated on raising sheep and cattle.[63]

Thomas Mason's homestead at Taita, c 1900.

S.R.M. Jenkin's Collection, Alexander Turnbull Library, National Library of New Zealand, Te Puna Mātauranga, F- 36239-1/2

By 1867, Mason was harvesting 10 tons of good keeping apples. One stone pippin yielded 8 cwt. of fruit. It was said that the whole of Wellington was supplied with rhubarb, tomatoes, and apples from his property, with drays leaving at regular intervals several days a week. Manure came from horses, sheep, and pigs he had imported from Sydney. Letters from 1860 make the first reference to the importation of plants and seeds from the English firm Backhouse & Son.

In the beginning, young plants were often damaged by rats or wild pigs, while severe frosts (such as those in August 1875) and bad storms took their toll. The area under cultivation covered about 12 acres – orchard, lawns, kitchen garden, flowers, and shrubs.

From 1870, when he was 52 years old, for the next 30 years, Quaker Mason, as he was familiarly known, concentrated on building up his collection of plants. In 1871, Mason asked his uncle whether catalogues were available from Backhouse & Son or from Edwards. In the same letter, he said:

> I have upwards of 100 fine kinds of roses and 60 camellias besides azaleas and rhododendrons, all of which flourish here. Some camellias are upwards of 7 feet and have been in bloom for five months. The garden is my recreation.[64]

---

[63] Mason, T., Letter to his uncle, Alexander Turnbull Library.

[64] Ibid.

Every year he imported more plants. There were hundreds of named roses; bulbs; hydrangeas; treasures from America such as the tulip tree *Liriodendron tulipifera* (45 feet in 1896); the cork oak, *Quercus suber* (35 feet in 1896); 30 varieties of the Chinese tree peony, *Poenia mouton*; bamboo; plantains; lilies; ericas; perennials; and annuals. There were at least 60 varieties of *Camellia japonica* and 46 varieties of rhododendron. Mason's letters of 1885 mention four more, namely '*Rhododendron grande*', 'Arab', John Waterer, and 'Princess Mary of Cambridge'.

The Gums became known as the finest garden in the southern hemisphere. Eight gardeners were employed on a regular basis, increasing in busy times to 15 or more. There were over eight miles of box hedging, fascinating summer houses to sit in and relax, and the paths were wide enough for Mrs Mason, who suffered ill heath, to accompany her husband around in a little dogcart.

In November 1896, Mason read a paper before the Wellington Philosophical Society, 'An account of the plants growing at "The Gums", Taita, 1,500 species in all'. Climate and some spring growth rates are recorded. The list is alphabetical, so climbers, annuals, trees, and other

Thomas Mason's garden and homestead, Taita, c 1912.
Hutt City Library

Hutt City Library

A glimpse into the garden showing the box hedging.
Hutt City Library

A path winds through the bush.
Hutt City Library

Summer house, Mason's Garden, c 1906. Box hedging can be seen in the foreground.
Hutt City Library

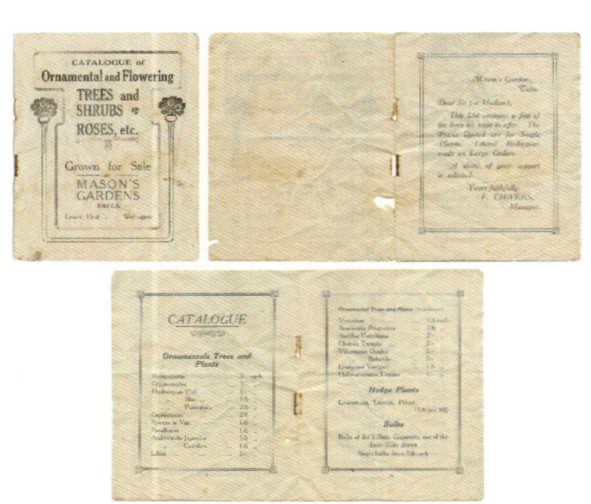
CATALOGUE of
Ornamental and Flowering
TREES and
SHRUBS
ROSES, etc.
Grown for Sale
MASON'S
GARDENS
CATALOGUE

Plant catalogue for Mason's Gardens (Mr Chivers, Manager), c 1910.

Hutt City Library

plants are not differentiated.[65] A supplementary list was published in 1903, the year Mason died.[66] The lists, itemising an incredible collection of plants, confirm that Thomas Mason was indeed a remarkable horticulturist. The list includes 25 species of *Magnolia*, 29 species of *Pinus*, 17 species of *Quercus*, 16 species of *Cupressus*, 25 species of *Iris*, and 41 species of *Erica*.

Many famous people visited The Gums, including Professor Wilson from Harvard University and, in 1896, the British nurseryman J.H. Veitch of the Royal Exotic Nursery. Veitch referred to the large collection of *Abies*, *Cupressus*, and other genera in an article entitled 'Traveller's Notes'. Many individual species were mentioned by name.

> The wide range and varied conditions under which the above named plants are found in nature, clearly point to there being many less favoured spots for the formation of a general garden than Welling-ton, New Zealand. Likewise it is not a question of the mere existence of so many species, for almost without exception all are in excellent condition, since Mr Mason does away with those that do not please the eye by any defect in vigour and health, claiming to be purely and simply a gardener, seeking no gratification from the mere possession of species.[67]

Veitch also commented that both the Tasmanian Blue Gum (*Eucalyptus globulatus*) and the Western Australian jarrah (*E. marginata*) had assumed the proportions of forest trees. By the time of his visit, an inner sheltering boundary of coniferous trees had been established.

The Gums was probably at the height of its glory when Mason died in 1903. He was a gentle, reserved man, deeply religious, but could be firm if the occasion demanded. He was extremely generous, giving struggling families fruit and vegetables until they could grow their own, donating plants to the Wellington Botanic Garden, and giving away seeds and cuttings generously. Mason would send wagonloads of flowers into the city or to the Hutt town for any special event.

When Alfred Ludlam died in 1875, Mason had replaced him as a nominated Member of the Board of Governors of the New Zealand Institute. He was Chairman of this Board when he died in 1903. He was also a member of the Botanic Garden Board and was its Chairman in 1891 when the Botanic Garden passed to the Wellington City Council. It is not surprising that some of the trees in Mason's and Ludlam's gardens – *Quercus suber*, *Liriodendron tulipifera*, *Abies pindrow*, *Abies pinsapo*, to mention a few – are also to be found in the Wellington Botanic Garden.

After Mason's death, the property passed to

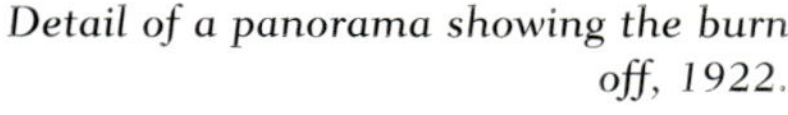

Detail of a panorama showing the burn off, 1922.

Museum of New Zealand Te Papa Tongarewa

[65] *Transactions and Proceedings* NZI, Vol XXIX, 1889.

[66] *Transactions and Proceedings* NZI, Vol XXXV, 1903.

[67] Veitch, J.H., 'Traveller's Notes, 1891–1893', Mason family papers, in the possession of Alan Mason, Fielding.

Subdivision plan of Thomas Mason estate, 1922.
Hutt City Library

his eldest daughter, and through her to her son, Thomas Wilford, later Sir Thomas. Wilford tried desperately to keep The Gums going, but the upkeep was too expensive. The Government was asked to preserve it as a national trust, and when this failed, Wilford tried to get the Hutt Borough Council to take it over as public grounds, but to no avail, though Mason had been a Hutt Councillor, Council chairman, and MP for the Hutt for 20 years. The property was bought privately and for a while became known as 'Mason's Tea Gardens'. Many Wellingtonians visited, but it was too far from both the Hutt town and Wellington city to attract sufficient numbers of people to pay for the upkeep on the property. (It still required six full-time gardeners.) Mason's Tea Garden suffered the same fate as all the other Wellington tea gardens of the time.

Eventually, the property was surveyed for building sites, with care taken to preserve as many features as possible. The end of this unique garden came on 22 May 1922 when the 'Avalon Estate' was auctioned. The auctioneer's brochure is beautifully illustrated, conveying some idea of the garden's layout.[68] The boundary trees were felled and burnt, and photographs taken from the western hills show the smoke that filled the valley for weeks.

Registered Notable Tree, the Weeping Pagoda Tree, Sophora japonica 'pendula', *7 Avalon Crescent, Naenae, September 1999.*

J. Nauta, Museum of New Zealand C.T.15695/8-10

Registered Notable Tree, Quercus suber, *Avalon Crescent, September 1999.*

J. Nauta, Museum of New Zealand C.T.15695/34

REGISTERED NOTABLE TREES

2 Avalon Crescent, *Quercus suber*. Cork Oak. In 1984 height 17 m; width 10 m; girth 3.30 m.

7 Avalon Crescent, *Sophora japonica 'pendula'*. Weeping Pagoda Tree. Only old specimen known in New Zealand. In 1979 height 4.0 m; width 7.0 m; girth 1.06 m.

7 Avalon Crescent, *Fraxinus excelsior 'pendula'*. Weeping Ash. In 1979 height 10.0 m; width 17.0 m; girth 2.60 m.

7A Avalon Crescent, *Magnolia campbelli*. In 1979. height 14.0 m; width 15.0 m; girth 2.05 m.

Avalon Crescent, *Castanopsis cuspidata*. Gold Leaf Chestnut very rare in New Zealand. In 1979. Height 10 m; width 15 m; girth 3.99 m.

NOT REGISTERED

4 Avalon Crescent, *Liriodendron tulipifera*. 45 ft in 1896; 60 ft high; 10 ft circ. 1990.

6 Avalon Crescent, *Sequoiadendron giganteum*. Big Tree. *Wellingtonia*. Height 65 ft in 1990.

6 Avalon Crescent, *Podocarpus totara*. Totara.

9 Avalon Crescent, *Liriodendron tulipifera*.

12A Avalon Crescent, *Quercus suber*. Cork Oak.

18A Avalon Crescent, *Ginkgo biloba*. Height 30 ft in 1990.

22 Avalon Crescent, *Quercus robur Quercus canariensis*. Spanish Oak.

68 Auctioneer's Brochure, 'Mason's Avalon', Hutt City Library.

Some treasures still remain and, as with Ludlam's property at Woburn, there is still a feeling of the past about the homes which have been built on Mason's estate. But since 1922 there has been further subdivision, and many important trees are still being lost, such as a totara and a liriodendron that were felled in the late 1990s.

The Lower Hutt City Council is responsible for looking after the trees. While some of them are registered on the RNZIH Notable Trees Scheme, the entire area could carry a covenant of 'Historic Horticultural Significance', as has been done, although in different words, by the Wellington City Council for part of the Donald estate in Karori. By this means, the surviving traces of box hedging, camellias, hollies, ginkgo, Cantuas, bananas, and many other legacies of the past might be preserved.

William Swainson F.R.S. F.L.S.

Portrait of William Swainson engaged in ornithological research, *oil on canvas by George Henry Harrison, c 1836.*

Alexander Turnbull Library, National Library of New Zealand, Te Puna Mātauranga, G-499

William Swainson was a talented artist as well as a prominent naturalist. He was also a soured and disappointed man who had failed to earn a living from his natural history books, twice failed to obtain a post at the British Museum, and made enemies because of his difficult temperament. He was still in mourning for his first wife, Mary, when he decided to emigrate to New Zealand in 1839. He had no previous experience of farming, and this decision ultimately did nothing to restore his fortunes.

In June 1839, he registered his application for five land orders. In July, his name appeared as a member of the committee of the first colony of New Zealand, alongside that of Francis Molesworth, George Duppa, Edward Betts-Hopper, and Henry Petre.[69] Swainson paid a deposit on the land and applied for a free passage. The Chairman of the Company, Dr Evans, after consultation with the Secretary, John Ward, granted Swainson a 75 per cent rebate because of his special qualifications. Together with his second wife Ann and four of his five children from his first marriage, he left England on the *Jane* in December 1840, arriving at Wellington on 24 May 1841.[70] His daughter, Mary Swainson, was surprised to see as many as three to four hundred houses in the settlement. The *New Zealand Gazette and Britannia Spectator,* June 1841, noted:

> Among the passengers by the 'Jane', from London, we find the name of W. Swainson, Esq., the eminent naturalist, well known to the world through his numerous talented productions. We have heard with pleasure that in all probability Mr Swainson will give the district of Port Nicholson the benefit of his first researches into the varieties in the several branches of natural history to be met with in the islands of New Zealand. It is uncertain at present which Mr Swainson will select, Port Nicholson or Porirua, as his place of residence.

On his arrival, Swainson immediately rented and subsequently bought Mr Watt's Thorndon house, settling his family and belongings in it over the next few weeks. High Cliff,[71] named after the cliff on which the house was perched, was exposed to south-east and north-west winds

---

69 Parkinson, P., *Relics in the Antipodes, William Swainson, 1789–1855.*

70 For an account of this voyage, see Swainson, F. and Natusch, S., *William Swainson, F.R.S.*, limited edition, 1987.

71 High Cliff was in Hobson Street, near the Katherine Mansfield birthplace.

and, being badly built, was very cold. A fellow passenger sold Swainson a small pig, and peas and cabbages were sown even before all their cargo from the *Jane* had been unloaded. A cow and a heifer bought at a sale on 23 June joined the four resident hens, while more cabbages, broccoli, celery, and potatoes were planted. Such were the exigencies of life in the new colony. Using his acquaintance with William Hooker at Kew, Swainson wrote asking for seeds, roots, and plants.

During his nine months' stay at High Cliff, Swainson fenced in a flower garden to protect their first flowering plants, planted a vegetable garden, and established a shrubbery from plants taken from the nearby ravine. Jonquils and daffodils had already flowered, the tulips and white lilies were expected to follow.

By the time two Horticultural Society shows had been held, Swainson had become a Foundation member. Swainson's daughter Mary sent a parcel of seeds home to her grandparents and had discovered the juiciness of the native konini berry *Fuchsia excorticata*, which she likened to the flavour of the cherry; as well as manuka tea and the edible fruit of the bush lawyer species of *Rubus*. Konini berries were used as the filling for tarts, with the occasional addition of bush lawyer berries. The fencing of wooded reserves tends to confirm Heaphy's remark that the land around this part of Thorndon was not heavily forested. The Swainsons employed a young maidservant, a boy to mind the cows, another to fetch water and scrub potatoes, and a charwoman twice weekly.

Hawkshead from the orchard. Pencil sketch by William Swainson.
Hutt City Library

Young cabbage tree – Our cows, Hawkshead 1847. *Pencil and sepia wash by William Swainson.*
Alexander Turnbull Library, National Library of New Zealand, Te Puna Mātauranga, A-187-049

Once Swainson had settled his family in their Wellington house, he turned his attention to his Country Acres in the Hutt. He built a small cottage on the land, calling it Hope Cottage. Using this as a base, he started the clearing and sowing of his 300 acres.[72] By September 1842, seven acres had been cleared and sown in wheat.[73] Next, a house was

---

[72] Map, Hutt Valley, 1840–1940, Hall, L. December, 1940.
[73] Swainson, M., Letter to Mr and Mrs Parkes, G. Swainson, Palmerston North.

built, and the family moved there in July 1843. The original cottage became the detached kitchen. The property was called Hawkshead, an ancestral name from a property at Lake Windermere. The homestead was near the river and subject to flooding.

Settlers with land aimed to be self sufficient, since food was not exactly cheap. Swainson's eldest daughter Mary, in a letter to her grandparents from December 1842, itemised the following

Bread	5½ d/ 2lb Loaf
Pork	9d. lb
Moist sugar	7d. lb
Loaf sugar	1/1d. lb
Fowls	8/- 10/ each
Beef	10d. & 1/1d/ lb
Mutton	6d
Currants	4/1 lb
Potatoes	1d. lb or 1/1d. for a 12lb Flax kit

Currants were very expensive, hence the use of konini berries.[74]

Swainson continued felling and clearing his land, protecting where possible those trees that as a naturalist he appreciated and enjoyed. About seven to eight hours were spent outdoors daily. Hedges were planted and an orchard established.

During the flood of September 1844, the river flowed over the flowerbeds and walks at Hawkshead, and was one and a half inches deep in the hall of the house. Swainson struggled on with his farming. His section produced wheat, which sold at 8/- a bushel, barley, and two crops of potatoes. However, even as early as 1846, he said it was no use farming except for their own supply since labour costs were too high.

But there were no doubts about his gardening ability. At the Horticultural Show in December 1844, Swainson was a prize-winner for a collection of twelve annuals and another of native seeds, even though the river had flooded his house and flowerbeds a few months earlier. In the summer show of 1845, he won a prize for an exhibit of gooseberries and figs.[75] Kate Chapman of Homewood in Karori wrote to her aunts in England in September 1845 that:

> There is a general custom here with a few who have good gardens to distribute newly obtained seed, then if one or two succeed better than others, the plants from the seed are redistributed. I gave one parcel to Mr Swainson – a distinguished naturalist, author of the volumes on Lardners Cabinet Encyclopaedia and who is now a New Zealand settler on the river Hutt. He told me he had never seen seeds so well preserved.[76]

Mary Swainson was a keen gardener too. On 8 October 1845, she described her garden in front of the house, perhaps the first layout described for a Wellington garden.

> The garden is now looking very well, and everything beginning to look green ... it has a sort of fence formed by trees that have been felled and not burnt off. It is now partially covered with ferns etc. and

---

[74] Swainson, M., Letter to Mr & Mrs Parkes. G. Swainson Papers.

[75] *New Zealand Spectator and Cook's Strait Guardian*, July 1845; ibid., March 1845.

[76] Chapman papers, Alexander Turnbull Library.

> where the trees are low, logs of wood are laid on them so I have a fence about four feet high. There is a border all round, and then a footpath at the edge. The square piece in the middle is to be grass. There is a tree fern in the middle, and I have four small oblong beds cut out, which I did myself. One is full of anemones, and the others of bulbs.[77]

In January 1843, before their move to the Hutt, Swainson had had an altercation with the well-known local chief Taringakuri, who had erected a pā on the bank of the river, claimed the land, and started felling trees.[78] Māori discontent was simmering; on 3 March 1845, further up the river, Māori carried away a quantity of potatoes from Thomas Mason.

Martial law was proclaimed in the Wellington district. Swainson served as an officer in the Militia in charge of 'friendly natives'. He felt nervous, as Hawkshead lay between Fort Richmond on one side and Boulcott's farm on the other, and was contemplating moving to Taranaki.[79]

In July 1847, Swainson revised Mary's front garden. By planting hedges of hawthorn and blackberry, he hoped to have blackberry pudding the following year. On 28 July 1847, he wrote to his son in Auckland:

> All the ground in front of the house is now laid out in proper beds and almost filled with 200 gooseberry and currant trees, six feet apart so that our vegetables can be grown between. I have planted hedges of hawthorn and blackberry to shelter the increased number of fruit trees. I hope to put in three fine peach trees nailed against the house. There is also a young passion flower and two fig trees. In front of the house are two more figs, another passion flower, a vine, and two climbing roses.

William Swainson's sketch of Mary Swainson in England in 1836. Mary married Major Marshall in New Zealand in 1850.

Privately owned, Alexander Turnbull Library, National Library of New Zealand, Te Puna Mātauranga, A-260-036

Swainson, regarded as the colonial naturalist, was given vegetable and fruit seeds by Colonel Wakefield in return for a collection of native plant seeds gathered from the bush.

In February 1848, fire destroyed half of Hawkshead house, its store, six months' provisions, all the agricultural implements, and money to pay for the coming harvest.[80] It seems to have started in the chimney, which was built of clay and wood, catching the thatched roof and destroying the detached kitchen and sitting room. A severe flood in 1850 washed the barn door away. Swainson's vision of being a gentleman colonist was becoming less and less likely.

He became more and more involved with writing and with his scientific observations, but the latter always centred around the quinary system of classification, which by this time was no longer used by most scientists. He never skimped on time given to drawing. He published his fern Exiccatum, *The Ferns of New Zealand*, thought to be the first of its kind. It was advertised in the *Wellington Independent*, 15 March 1851:

> Ferns of New Zealand. First part of this interesting collection from Mr Lyon, Willis Street either in large folio or in foolscap. Price 12/6.

Shells brought out from England were finally unpacked and arranged, local specimens augmenting the collection. Other collections made

77 Swainson, M., *Gazette*, No 11, p 1137, G. Swainson, Palmerston North.
78 Swainson, G. and Natusch, S., *William Swainson*, limited edition, 1987.
79 Ibid.
80 Ibid.

included plants and seeds for St John's College, Auckland, where his son was a pupil.

Swainson's 'Notes on Gardening' were published in the 1848–49 *New Zealand Evangelist*. He wrote the Gardeners' Calendar in the *Wellington Almanac* of 1851. He drew on his first-hand knowledge of growing plants in New Zealand, and his remarks for January and those on the transplanting of native plants were probably the first of their kind given for Wellington.

Plants specifically mentioned in the 1851 Almanac were:

> **Fruits** Mespilus (Medlar), plums, raspberries, grapes, figs, Cape gooseberry, peaches grafted cherries, strawberries (including white alpine).
> **Shrubs** *Camellia japonica*, roses, *Ribes sanguinea*, *Ribes* 'rosea', silver wattle or mimosa, furze, and *Ilex europea* (holly).
>
> **Perennials** Coriopsis, daisy, primrose, dahlias, *Chrysanthemum indicum*, violets, *Asphodelus lutea*, *A. fistulosis*.
>
> **Bulbs** Narcusus double white, jonquil, double daffodils, anemones, ranunclulis, hyacinths, *Fritillaria persica*, white lilies, tiger lilies, Cape bulbs, Iris, *Gladiolus fulgens* (pure red), *Ixia patens*, *Iris nervosa*, *Gladiolus natalensis*, tulips.

A case of plants and seeds Swainson had ordered from London in July 1845 was lost on the barque *Tyne*.[81] *Fritillaria persica*, mentioned in the 1851 Almanac, was ordered from Loddiges,[82] to whom Swainson had already sent a parcel of New Zealand plants and seeds:

> My kind friends the Loddiges have sent me a most valuable collection of seeds, plants, many of the former I can distribute at once, and of the latter I hope to do so in the autumn but I shall not throw these pearls before swine – in other words I will only give to those who would really value and preserve them in public gardens and should form part of St John's College and if this is to be done effectually, I will with much pleasure make up a selection of all that I can spare. Pray mention this to your Bishop.[83]

As time passed, Swainson's disillusionment grew. Work on the property, his own work on the farm, his writings, his drawings, and his collections brought him little financial return. According to Brad Patterson:

> Swainson continued to ponder, and pontificate throughout the 1840s. It was to little effect. By the early 1850s, practically destitute he was claiming that New Zealand had been nearly fatal to him. His holding of 300 acres had been reduced to a mere nine acres.[84]

Believing his financial woes would be solved in Australia, he sailed for Sydney on the *Acheron* in May 1851. While waiting for his South Australian papers, he unsuccessfully offered his services as botanical draughtsman to the Government of New South Wales. However,

35

GARDENERS' CALENDER.

By William Swainson, Esq., F.R.S.

"A Garden is the purest of human pleasures."—So says the immortal Bacon, the greatest philosopher that the world has produced, since the days of Aristotle. It is one of those few pleasures that can be equally enjoyed by the prince and the peasant. Its enjoyments are of that peculiarly mixed nature, which is most conducive to the constitution of man. They can only be truly felt by Labour; which, although a curse upon our fallen race, *in form*, has been converted, by our Beneficent Creator, into a blessing—*in fact*. The mind and the body are alike benefited. The first is soothed, the latter strengthened, and both of these effects produce that calm and healthy enjoyment of life, which neither wealth, nor power, nor station can possibly impart. Its physical effects on the human frame, as a healthy exercise, are very remarkable; inasmuch as if any one class of men were singled out as long lived, that class would be Gardeners. I could cite numerous instances in proof of this assertion; but it would be superfluous. Let any one try the experiment of working in his garden one half hour before breakfast, and he will find his health improved, his appetite increased, and his enjoyment of both augmented.

January.

Flower Garden.—The flower garden still continues, if properly managed, to exhibit a profusion of varied and richly coloured flowers, almost equal to last month. For although the lovely white lillies, nearly all the Cape bulbs, the Iris's, and the roses finished flowering the last week or ten days of the old year, the new is ushered in with all the many coloured dahlias, and three or four spotted species (or varieties) of *Gladiolus Natalensis*. The Tiger Lillies are also now in full perfection. All these require to be regularly watered during the hot dry weather, usually experienced in all this month. Most of the summer annuals have passed, but a succession of very many of them may be secured by sowing the seeds immediately they become ripe, and thus, the young plants, having full time to grow, will come into flower early in the spring. This plan of immediate sowing flower seeds, saves much time, particularly in rearing the perennial sorts, and they invariably attain greater luxurance than those sown in the spring. The different varieties of *Chrysanthemum Indicum*, succeed the *Dahlias*, and these with one or two *Coriopsis*, are the only late autumnal flowers we yet possess in the Colony.

Fruits.—All the small fruits in the Hutt valley, are in perfection from the end of December to the early part of January. But in Wellington they ripen much earlier. The grape blossoms early in the year, and figs ripen the end of this month. The Cape gooseberry, if not injured during the winter, will now be covered with ripe fruit, the produce of *last* year's flowers, but of those that are produced *this* year, only a few of the earliest ripen towards the end of autumn. Hence it is that such small crops of this delicious fruit are grown at Wellington, or in any similarly exposed situation, for one cold S.E. wind is sufficient to kill all the unripened fruit, and even the branches, which then only spring up again the following summer. This fruit is cultivated in various parts of Mexico, Carolina, &c., and is known everywhere, save here, by the name of *winter cherry*; why it should be called Cape gooseberry, we know not, for it is not found wild in any part of Africa, but only in America and its Islands.

In this mild climate, transplanting may be successfully performed nine months in the year, particularly if the change of the Moon brings rain. This operation, which inexperienced persons think very easy, is yet one that generally requires great care and delicacy. It is the slender fibres, and not the thicker branches of the roots of a plant by which it is chiefly nourished: and the more these are preserved uninjured, the less will the plant itself be affected by its removal; this is the cause why a ball of earth should invariably be preserved round all choice plants, more especially those of Australia and New Zealand, as these, more than all others, are the most difficult to remove, as the numerous failures in and round Wellington bear ample witness. On the other hand, if proper care is taken, success is almost certain. In general it may be taken as a rule, that the younger the trees, intended for removal, the better they will succeed. Native shrubs for this purpose, therefore, in ordinary hands, should never be more than three inches high, and a ball of earth must be left around each, sufficient to enclose all the tender fibrous roots.

It may be as well to notice, however, that these remarks are not applicable to the *Karaka* tree, or native laurel; whose broad shining, beautiful leaves form such an ornament to the shrubbery. The vitality of this plant is so great, that the natives, being remarkably fond of the fruit (now quite ripe) make plantations of it, in many parts of the northern districts, by cuttings of the old wood, not thinner than the little finger. We heard that this custom was very prevalent at Taranaki, and having made some experiments last year, we can vouch for its correctness.

Another exception is the native tree *Fuchsia excorticata*, as well as all the arborescent species introduced here: thick cuttings of two year old wood take root so rapidly, that if they are used only

Pages from the 1851 Wellington Almanac.

Alexander Turnbull Library, National Library of New Zealand, Te Puna Mātauranga

81 *New Zealand Spectator and Cook Strait Guardian*, July 1845.

82 Successful nursery firm established in Hackney in 1790. It reached its greatness under George Loddige, who became director in 1826. He developed an arboretum at the nursery, adopted the Wardian case, and developed the market for conservatory plants. The firm declined after 1846 due to increasing air pollution. The leading nursery in London became James Veitch in Chelsea, a branch of the successful business in Exeter.

83 Swainson, W., Letter to G.W. Swainson, 15 April 1848, G. Swainson, Palmerston North.

84 Patterson, B., op. cit..

Fern Grove by Lucille Frances Swainson, April 1857. This was drawn two years after William Swainson's death. It features specimen trees on the lawn, central planting in what appears to be a lawn with a path around it, and a backdrop of bush.

Alexander Turnbull Library, National Library of New Zealand, Te Puna Mātauranga, A-188-033

through his friend La Trobe in Victoria, he was offered a similar job there at a salary of £350 per annum plus expenses.[85] Swainson subsequently wrote a report, based on the old-fashioned quinary system of classification, that was forwarded to William Hooker at Kew, who remarked:

> If I was pleased with your report, I cannot say that I gave to our Secretary for the Colonies an equally flattering account of Mr Swainson on the Gum Trees!!!. In my life I think I have never read such a series of trash and nonsense. There is a man who left this country with the character of a first rate naturalist (though with many eccentricities) and he goes to Australia and takes up the subject of Botany of which he is as ignorant as a goose.[86]

Swainson's adherence to the quinary system of classification was his downfall. He returned to Wellington, and shortly afterwards his beloved daughter Mary died. The 1855 earthquake demolished the Hawkshead house, but Swainson still maintained his interest in gardening. Plants and bulbs were salvaged to nearby Fern Grove and he wrote: 'No other outdoor recreation is so delightful to me.'[87]

On 6 December 1855, at the age of 67, William Swainson died of bronchitis. It was 15 years since he had emigrated. His wonderful drawings of early Wellington are invaluable, as are his exquisite illustrations of birds and shells, and other studies of fauna and flora. Along with many other settlers, he failed to make a fortune by growing grain. Had fate been kinder, Swainson might well have been 'the father of an indigenous natural history of New Zealand'.[88]

Swainson was never happier than when he was sketching. He was a talented draughtsman and observer of nature. He initiated ornithological techniques for which he should be remembered with respect. He

Elm trees that originated from William Swainson's property Hawkshead. April 1999.

W. Shepherd

[85] 1852 Gov. Botanist La Trobe, Melbourne Library.
[86] Ibid. Hooker was quoted in the *Victorian Naturalist*, Vol. 44: 65, 1927.
[87] Swainson, W., Letter to G.W. Swainson, 15 April 1848, G. Swainson, Palmerston North.
[88] Patterson, P., *Relics in the Antipodes, William Swainson 1789–1855.*

Thomas Cotter's dairy farm, Silverstream, Watercolour by Christopher Aubrey, c 1890. Conifers planted in the 1870s are well established, while the native bush has retreated to the hills behind. The well-formed picket fence contrasts with the post and rail one. The entrance path to the home is designed according to the fashion of the time, encircling a bedding display.

Alexander Turnbull Library, National Library of New Zealand, Te Puna Mātauranga, C-030-016

brought the art of natural history lithography to a high standard, and his work, especially after 1830, is highly regarded.[89] But all that remains of Hawkshead today are the elm trees at the corner of Magar and Rutherford Streets. Fortunately they are registered on Lower Hutt's District Scheme.

The legacy of the dream

What actually happened in the Hutt contrasted strongly with the optimism of the 'Emigrants' Song' and Wakefield's dream of a checkerboard of fields edged with thorn, or gorse hedges enclosing field upon field of waving corn. No one cultivated the vine or the olive, as advocated by Henry Petre. Instead, there was an untidy patchwork of partly cleared sections, stumps of trees, swampy ground, primitive bridges, and log fences.

A village had grown up about the 'Aglionby Arms', but Wakefield's attempt to subdivide and form a central village on Block 4 at Petone to serve surrounding estates failed dismally. With the passing of time, and thanks to the uplift from the 1855 earthquake that drained the swamps, conditons became easier, but of the settlers we have considered, only Mason and Ludlam could be said to have succeeded in what they set out to do. Nonetheless, all of them did well with their gardens and plants. Ludlam and Mason made significant contributions to nineteenth-century horticulture in Wellington, including the Botanic Garden, and Swainson with his *Gardener's Almanac*. William Trotter

[89] William Swainson, F.R.S., F.L.S., 1789–1855, A Comm Exibition, ATL, 29 September to 25 November 1989.

Market gardening at the Hutt, c 1890s.
Hutt City Library

and James Bryant moved from being dependent on the estate system to a comfortable independence.

After 1845, the early emphasis on grain growing in the Hutt Valley was succeeded by ancillary agriculture.[90] By 1853, Mason had become convinced that the climate was unsuitable for wheat. Both he and Ludlam turned to pastoralism.

In the 1890s, dairying and market gardening grew rapidly in importance. By 1900, the Hutt Valley was the market-gardening area for Wellington. Māori, the early providers for the settlers, continued to supply the Wellington market. Of the 45 Hutt Valley vendors licensed to sell in Wellington in 1872, a third were Māori. The Chinese began to move into market gardening in the 1880s, and a number of plant nurseries, including Coopers Seeds (see Chapter 7), were established in this fertile and flat valley. In 1940, it was estimated that 447 acres were in market gardens.

The plant nurseries flourished until the latter part of the twentieth century, when the land became too valuable to be used for this purpose. Today, nurseries in the Valley no longer supply locally-grown plants.

Urbanisation increased rapidly, with planned settlements mushrooming from the late 1930s to the mid 1950s. Large areas in the Valley were covered with state houses on quarter-acre sections, each with a vegetable garden. Domestic vegetable growing has declined markedly in the 1980s and 1990s.

The gardens of Ludlam, Mason, Molesworth, and Swainson stand out in prefiguring the region's landscape today. All but Mason were foundation members of the Wellington Horticultural Society. Trotter was a judge at two early shows and Alzdorf was an exhibitor. Mason, living further up the Valley and away in Hobart during the Wars, was a little later in participating in public affairs.

---

[90] Patterson, B., op. cit. 1992.

*Willow Bank, the house and garden of Sir William Fitzherbert in Melling, c 1876. by James Bragge. The 26-acre property was first settled in the early 1850s. The garden features beautiful tall willows on the boundary, a hedge, and a lawn with specimen trees, including a monkey puzzle tree (*Araucaria imbricata*), a cabbage tree, a macrocarpa, and a* Pinus radiata.

Hutt City Library

The Hutt's contribution to Wellington's Botanic Garden

One aim of the Horticultural Society was the formation of a Botanic Garden. These Hutt settlers and others of a similar persuasion never lost sight of this aim, and in 1869 Ludlam successfully introduced the Botanic Garden Bill to Parliament. Both Ludlam and Mason were great benefactors to the Garden, as well as serving as Board members, although they lived some considerable distance from the it.

Two other Hutt Valley settlers were closely associated with the Botanic Garden. One was William Fitzherbert (later Sir William) who, as Superintendent for Wellington, was an *ex officio* member of the Botanic Garden Board. An 1875 photograph of Willow Bank, Fitzherbert's home near Melling, shows that he was in close touch with Ludlam and the Government's conifer seed distributions that had commenced in 1870. Three young conifer trees are featured – a radiata pine, a macrocarpa, and a monkey puzzle, the latter a Chilean conifer.

It was a fourth resident of the Hutt, John Duthie of Balgownie in Naenae, who helped to disestablish this Board. Duthie was Mayor of Wellington when he introduced the Vesting Act to Parliament in 1891. Photographs of Balgownie in the 1890s show an outstanding property, beautifully landscaped with a carpet bedding feature, rose beds edged with Buxus, a pond complete with a boat and swans, as well as a small stand of radiata pine and other conifers. Today, Balgownie, with its backdrop of nineteenth-century

[Right] This simple shingle-roofed cottage, built in 1841, has been delightfully upgraded with a conservatory room and a newly designed garden.

Hutt City Library

[Left] The original post and rail fence shows through the branches of what appears to be a thorn hedge surrounding Isaac Cooley's home.

Hutt City Library

Balgownie, looking down to the garden below, c 1900.

Hutt City Library

[Left] Balgownie, looking down to the garden below, c 1900.

Hutt City Library

[Right] Balgownie in 1999, near the Laura Ferguson Trust Home, as seen from the Melling bridge. Both properties are surrounded by conifers planted over 100 years ago.

J. Nauta, Museum of New Zealand C.T.15695/40-42

conifers, is situated next to the Laura Ferguson Trust Home.

Hutt Valley settlers made an extraordinary contribution to the Wellington Botanic Garden, though they thereby lost the opportunity of having a Botanic Garden in the Hutt. As we have seen, financial constraints prevented the two private botanic gardens, Ludlam's and Mason's, being purchased and they were eventually subdivided. Around 1900, Hutt inhabitants began to focus on the Valley itself. A horticultural society formed in about 1902 is still in existence today, but despite the ideal climate for horticulture there is no botanic garden, and the market gardens are gone.

Today, the Hutt Valley (including its industrial areas) is softened by trees and shrubs, some deciduous. Native flora is encouraged on the western hills and also at Percy's Reserve, which plays a similar role to the Otari Native Botanic Garden at Wilton. It is a managed landscape, described by Walter Cook as 'an economic and cultural landscape based on agriculture, horticulture and forestry, and no longer displaying the harshness of the 1860s'.[91]

The latest trend is for larger gardens in country areas, along the Akatarawa Road, in Whiteman's Valley, and also at Ohariu.

---

91 Cook, Walter, 'The Great Transformation: an artifact to be proud of', unpublished text of a talk given in Petone, 1998.

Chapter 3

COUNTRY ACRES AROUND LAMBTON HARBOUR

The previous chapter described the land taken up by the early settlers of the Hutt Valley, beyond that grey beach at Petone, and the plants and gardens they established there. As in the Hutt Valley, the country acres to the south of the new settlement of Wellington, at the southern end of the harbour, encompassed some flat land. Instead of a river given to flooding there was a lake. The area to the west and north of the settlement, now the suburbs of Karori, Kelburn, Wilton, Wadestown, Ngaio, Khandallah, and Johnsonville, was hilly, with little flat land. There was little forest around the edges of the harbour itself, but almost everywhere was exposed to the wind.

Watt's Peninsula

Watt's Peninsula, originally called Motu-kai-rangi by the first Māori settlers,[1] is about four square miles in extent and was joined to the rest of Wellington by a low isthmus. It was named after James Watt, who was the first European to land cattle there. In 1840, approximately 1800 acres of steep hills devoid of timber surrounded a swamp and a freshwater lake, Roto Kura, that covered about 700 acres.[2] Here Francis Molesworth, James Coutts Crawford, the Reverend Vesey Hine, and Edward Jerningham Wakefield were the main settlers to obtain land.

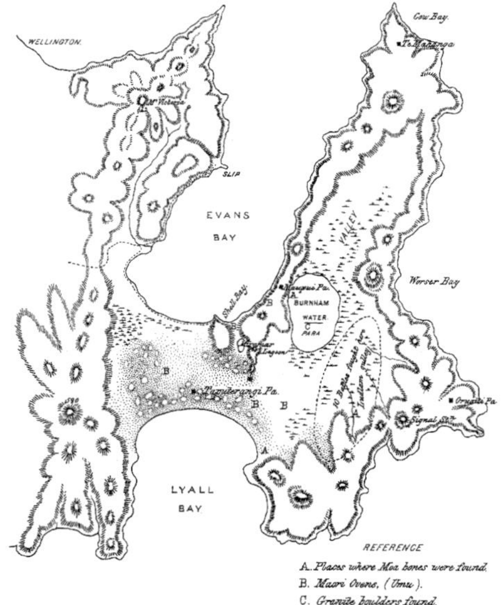

Plan of the Miramar Peninsula, *drawn by J. Buchanan, c 1870. From* Transactions & Proceedings of the New Zealand Institute, *Vol V, 1872.*

In a paper delivered to the New Zealand Institute in 1872, the Colonial Museum botanist, John Buchanan, described the plants found on the peninsula.[3] Such an account of an area of Wellington's indigenous flora is rare indeed – the only other detailed account, written by Buchanan in 1875, was for plants in the Wellington Botanic Garden.[4]

It would seem from Buchanan's article that the settlers on the peninsula did not encounter large timber trees, though stumps of totara piles found in what had been the defence works of Maupui Pā had probably come from the area. The remaining bush, devoid of large trees, was confined to gullies on the northern part of the peninsula. Among the plants listed, Buchanan recorded the now rare dry scrubland plants *Discaria toumatou* (matagouri or wild Irishman)[5] and *Carmichaelia australis* (a native broom). The presence of *Knightia excelsa* (rewarewa) and *Freycinetia banksii* (kiekie) may signify that the area had recently been forested.

James Crawford arrived in Wellington from Australia, but not as a New

---

1 McKinnon, Malcolm (ed.), *New Zealand Historical Atlas*, Auckland, 1997.

2 Crawford, John, 'Miramar Peninsula', *Transactions & Proceedings of the New Zealand Institute*, Vol. V, 1872.

3 Buchanan, John, 'Plants Found on the Miramar Peninsula', ibid.

4 Shepherd, W. and Cook, W., *The Botanic Garden, Wellington: A New Zealand History 1840–1987*, Millwood Press, 1988.

5 Matagouri today is found widely in the South Island. It once flourished as far north as the Wanganui, Manawatu, and Horowhenua areas. Following settlement, it was thought to have become extinct in the North Island. In 1996, the plant was found again at Bulls in the Manawatu (*The Dominion*, 21 June 1996).

Zealand Company settler. He had served in the British Navy, and when he took his discharge at the age of 21 he sailed to Sydney, where he obtained an engagement to help drive some cattle to Adelaide. He then came across to New Zealand and was at Port Nicholson about the time of the arrival of the first New Zealand Company settlers.[6]

Crawford purchased land at Watt's Peninsula from the New Zealand Company. He returned to Sydney in March 1840, where he bought horses and cattle to stock his prospective cattle farm Glendavar. With Francis Molesworth's co-operation, Crawford quickly promoted the formation of a cattle company. New Zealand flax (*Phormium tenax*) was the dominant plant in some parts, and Crawford helped form an association to consider ways of dressing flax for export.

Crawford went to England in 1841, and came back to New Zealand in 1846, full of new ideas. He saw the future of the peninsula as a collection of tenant farms specialising in dairy stock, poultry, and market gardening.[7] Since he was not a New Zealand Company settler, Crawford was not indoctrinated by Company visions of the country as a 'Pacific granary', and he made no attempt to grow grain. But he extended his property, purchasing land from Francis Molesworth's estate.

In 1847, Crawford spent a considerable sum of money tunnelling through solid rock to drain Burnham Water, as the lake was now called, into Evans Bay, and then proceeded to drain the remaining swamp. At first, the drained land was very sour, as the sandy parts were in need of organic material. As the land was drained, grass seed was sown. It was estimated that the drainage and cultivation cost £3,000.[8] However, Crawford was prevented from developing further plans for the peninsula by the Reverend Vesey Hine and E.J. Wakefield, who refused to part with their lands.

Glendavar, home of J.C. Crawford, c 1845. Burnham Water is in the centre and Cook Strait is visible in the distance.

Alexander Turnbull Library, National Library of New Zealand, Te Puna Mātauranga, A-229-009

Crawford again left the country, this time very depressed and unable to see a future for Glendavar. He returned in 1857 and expanded his farm, but lived in town. His knowledge of agriculture, engineering, and geology served him in good stead as a Governor of the New Zealand Institute. For the years 1866–78, he was Sheriff of Wellington.[9]

In 1872, Crawford delivered a paper to the New Zealand Institute detailing the Peninsula's geological and archaeological history. In this paper, he renamed the Peninsula 'Miramar', meaning 'behold the sea'. In 1884, he

[6] *Dictionary of New Zealand Biography*, Vol I.

[7] Patterson, B., 'The Grain Mirage', *Stout Centre Review*, May 1992.

[8] *Transactions & Proceedings of the New Zealand Institute*, Vol XI, 1878–79, p. 530.

[9] *New Zealand Dictionary of Biography*, Vol I.

described his land holding on the Peninsula:

> The forest had been destroyed possibly by the advent of man and had been replaced by swamps and a lake (Burnham Water) in the centre. The swamps supported a vegetation of raupo, flax etc... Roots of large trees are found in its bed, in situ ... imbedded timber from the old forest is excellent firewood, and as in clearing the ground for ploughing it must be removed, all trace of its previous existence will disappear during the next few years.[10]

[Left] Māori gardens and whare at Karaka Bay, near Worser Bay, 1879.

Henry Wright Collection, Alexander Turnbull Library, National Library of New Zealand, Te Puna Mātauranga, F-9027-1/4

[Right] J.C. Crawford drained Burnhan Water in 1849, creating an ideal habitat for flax. A flax industry had developed by the time this photo was taken in the 1900s.

S.C. Smith Collection, Alexander Turnbull Library, National Library of New Zealand, Te Puna Mātauranga, G-24889-1/1 , PAColl-3082

Along with James Crawford's drainage, the development of the flax industry on Watts Peninsula owed a great deal to Luke Nattrass, a flax miller, agent, and artist who first came out to New Zealand in 1836. Sent by Lord Derby and Lord John Russell to report on the country, Nattrass returned to England in 1839 with information on the possibility of a flax industry.

Nattrass found New Zealand flax growing plentifully near Lyall Bay and Watts Peninsula, and he returned to New Zealand with a number of men from Ireland who were skilled in the dressing of flax. He established a flax mill on the Peninsula and, thanks to his experimentation and the skill of his workers, he gained an award at the Paris Exhibition for the fineness of the fibres produced. He also imported a set of hand machines for dressing flax by the Donlan process, but from 1844 to 1860 flax continued to be mostly hand dressed by Māori workers.

Nattrass invented a mechanical and chemical process for making fibre from flax and applied for a patent in 1871. By 1873, he and others had brought success to one of New Zealand's earliest industries. The Miramar flax mill was one of thirty in operation exporting 6,000 tons of fibre a year.[11]

In about 1843, the whaler and trader James 'Worser' Heberley settled at Worser Bay on the East coast of Watts Peninsula, on land owned by his wife's family, who helped him build a house. From here, he acted as pilot for the ships coming into Wellington Harbour. In 1849, an official pilot was appointed and a pilot station was established in Tarakena Bay facing Cook Strait.

In 1866, a new pilot station was built on seven acres of land at Worser Bay made available by James Crawford. In 1894, a caretaker was placed in charge.[12] Today, the house is the sole surviving building, and it carries a C

Miramar Flat, looking south from Crawford's Farm paddocks to Lyall Bay, c 1900.

H.M. Christie Collection, Alexander Turnbull Library, National Library of New Zealand, Te Puna Mātauranga, G-19085-1/1, PAColl-4055

[10] Crawford, J.C., 'Changes in the Hataitai Valley', *Transactions and Proceedings of the New Zealand Institute*, Vol XVII, 1884–85, pp. 342-5.

[11] Kenneally, J.M. and B.M., *On the Edge of our City*, 1984.

[12] Ibid.

Classification from the Historic Places Trust. The photo is important for what it shows of the garden in this rather isolated and exposed part of the Peninsula.

The land adjoining the Miramar Peninsula – from Evans Bay through what is now Kilbirnie to Lyall Bay – was flat and, until the 1890s, mostly sand dunes. It was here in 1841 that Smith and Revans established a dairy farm, seeing a positive future for dairy products rather than grain. The farm was close to the Town Belt Reserve, which separated this area from the Newtown Town Acres.

(Left) Pilot's Cottage, Worser Bay, c 1880s, with a low hedge, shrubs, and what seems to be rows of plants.
Lent by Ann Moffat

(Right) Miramar Peninsula, looking south over Mount Crawford Prison to Miramar, Lyall Bay, and the airport.
Photo, Lloyd Homer, IGNS, CN.11041A

Lyall Bay, c 1900, showing extensive sand dunes.
S.C. Smith Collection, Alexander Turnbull Library, National Library of New Zealand, Te Puna Mātauranga, G-45212-1/2, PAColl-3082

Kelburn

Little has been recorded of Kelburn's original plant cover. The eastern parts of both Blocks 28 and 29 were covered with kanuka and manuka, which extended as far as The Terrace. When Wellington was surveyed, a 13-acre strip of land was set aside for a botanical garden. In 1847, a tract of Town Belt land measuring 52 acres 2 roods 37 perches, adjacent to the 13 acres, was given in compensation to the Kumototo Māori under the McCleverty Awards. A sketch accompanying the Deed shows Māori cultivation extending over parts of both Blocks 28 and 29.

Early photos and records for the Botanic Garden show the extent of kānuka-mānuka cover on its upper reaches.[13] The same vegetation extended

[Left] Map attached to the Deed that gave Kumototo Māori the land from the Town Belt. Blocks 28 and 29 are shown, as well as Māori cultivation.

down to The Terrace.[14] How much else of Kelburn may have been similarly covered is not known.

In the early 1860s, a settler named Moxham began farming Block 28. There was forest on some of it, and kānuka-mānuka in the upper area along the boundary of what would later become the Botanic Garden. Along this boundary, Moxham planted a gorse hedge. It was a costly mistake, for the gorse spread rapidly and became a nuisance to the farm and later the Botanic Garden. The 1875 map for the Botanic Garden calls the path in this area of the Garden 'Gorse Path'. The name is still used, and recently gorse was found growing near the boundary of the North Terrace pines.[15]

In 1896, Upland Farm was roaded and subdivided into quarter-acre sections, each with a frontage of approximately 55 feet. Judging by contemporary photographs, there was little specialised design evident in these turn-of-the-century gardens, which seem not to have had vegetable gardens. This was probably due to the steep sections, with the houses being placed towards the rear, probably to take advantage of any view. Today, many of these properties have been subdivided even further, but trees and shrubs now soften the once harsh landscape.

[Top] Block 29, Upland Farm, c 1880. The windshorn conifers probably came from the adjacent Botanic Garden.

Alexander Turnbull Library, National Library of New Zealand, Te Puna Mātauranga, G-3932-1/2

[Bottom] A view across to Northland from Grove Road that shows bush running from Mariri Road to the Glen and Botanic Garden, 1902. The conifers on the Glenmore slope are well established.

---

13 Shepherd, W. and Cook, W., op. cit.

14 Kilmister, Alfred, Manuscript, Alexander Turnbull Library.

15 Author's observation, 1992.

Karori Valley

> The Karori Valley consists of 2500 acres. It commences about two miles from Wellington thence running in a south-westerly direction to the coast near Cape Terawhiti. The valley is covered with forest, but less densely than those previously described and here is to be found the finest timber of the vicinity of Port Nicholson. From one spot in this valley counted fifty trees around me that would each make a top for a large vessel.
>
> **Charles Heaphy.**[16]

The men who surveyed Karori had a difficult time taking their straight lines through somewhat dense forest. One surveyor said, 'Karori is a horrid place' as he struggled with the survey in Parkvale Road.[17] Rimu forest ran all the way down from Church Hill to Parkvale Road, and kahikatea was predominant in the low-lying areas.[18] In the region of Friend Street, there were several kahikatea of considerable size, while on the opposite side of the main road around Campbell and Beauchamp Streets, matai dominated the forest canopy.[19] Kilmister maintained there were only odd trees of tōtara in Karori, yet his son sawed one 5 ft in diameter.[20] In 1844, Chapman said that his land was not too heavily timbered, but that there were magnificent rimu, mataī, tōtara, kahikatea, rata, rewarewa, and hinau trees in parts of it. Younger tōtara, presumably from Karori, were given to the Botanic Garden in 1874/75 by Robert Donald.[21]

[Left] Bridge over Kaiwarra Stream near Old Devil's Bridge. Karori Road, c 1867. *W.T.L. Travers,*

Fieldes Collection, Victoria University of Wellington

[Right] Karori Road, photographed in the 1870s by William Berry.

Onslow Historical Society

The road to Karori followed a track that went from the top of Tinakori Road, over what was known as Baker's Hill, down to the Kaiwharawhara Stream at the junction of what is today Chaytor Street and the Old Karori Road. Here a bridge, Devil's Bridge, was constructed as early as 1842. It was replaced several times. Photos taken by W.T.L. Travers in the late 1860s and William Berry in the late 1870s show the density of bush in the area, but most of it had been removed by 1895. In the early years, the road was only suitable for horses and was always difficult, especially in the wet weather.

With no Māori living in the area, the Company was able to release

16 Heaphy, Charles, *Narrative of a Residence in Various parts of New Zealand.*

17 Patrick, M., *From Bush to Suburb, Karori 1840–1980*, Karori Historical Society, 1990.

18 Rimu *Dacrydium cupressinum*, kahikatea *Dacrydium dacryioides*, matai *Prumnopitys taxifolia*, totara *Podocarpus totara*.

19 Patrick, M., op. cit.

20 Kilmister, Alfred, Manuscript, Alexander Turnbull Library.

21 Shepherd, W. and Cook, W., op. cit.

sections to intending settlers fairly quickly. John Yule, a Scotsman and cabin passenger on the *Bengal Merchant*, which arrived on 20 February 1840, chose Section 36, lying between what is today Donald and Campbell Streets. Yule was quick to clear some of his land. In December 1841, keeping for himself 20 acres of the highest land as suitable for dairy farming,[22] he subdivided the remainder into three 25-acre blocks and one 5-acre lot, which were described as having:

> a large portion cleared and bushed, and ready for burning and receiving crops and with its rightly valuable timber, fertile and level soil, and with an abundant supply of water.

The 5-acre block that Yule had subdivided, where Karori Normal School is today, was purchased by a Mr Tyser. Two-and-a-half years later, Judge H.S. Chapman leased this block along with Tyser's unfinished house. The meticulous records that Chapman left enable us to have a very clear picture of life in the bush in that first decade.

The 100-acre sections at Karori laid out by the New Zealand Company with the names of early owners.

From Out of Bush to Suburb by Margaret G. Patrick

Chapman and Homewood

Chapman, who may have been the author of Henry Petre's booklet, 'The Settlements of the New Zealand Company',[23] was the editor of the pro-Company *New Zealand Journal*. In 1842, he was appointed Judge of the Supreme Court for the southern division of New Zealand. Together with his wife Kate and young son Harry, he sailed for New Zealand on the *Bangalore* in June 1842.

Kate was seven months pregnant when they arrived, so it was not long before Chapman found and rented the land and house in Karori. Chapman arranged with Tyser to complete the house in lieu of rent, although not in the extravagant way originally envisaged by its owner. The Chapmans quickly settled into their new home, planting the seeds they had brought out with them and cultivating a vegetable garden, for Chapman was a prudent, cautious man when it came to all financial matters. In June 1844, he wrote:

The Honourable H.S. Chapman, Judge of the Supreme Court, New Zealand, *lithographed from a portrait by T. Lawrence.*

Alexander Turnbull Library, National Library of New Zealand, Te Puna Mātauranga, B-039-010

> I have peas in pod, broadbeans in blossom, whilst cherry and other fruits have not yet lost their leaves. The garden operations now going on are such as would be done in mild weather in March in England. We are sowing cabbage and small salading today and transplanting cabbages and Brussels sprouts. Our clover sown 6 June is appearing.
>
> We have laid out a portion of the garden as a nursery for fruit and other trees to be ready to move to our future house. We have apples, pears, peaches, plums, cherry filberts, walnuts, currants, goose-berries, ash, oak, furze, laburnums, acacias, broom, straw-berries and other trees, shrubs and plants.

What a remarkable collection of plants acquired just two years after leaving England! The letter continued:

> I lost all my plants on board the *Bangalore*. They were fifteen months in boxes (Wardian cases) and although they were flowering at sea, the hot sun at Sydney and a month at Auckland destroyed them. I have been more lucky with some just received by the 'Bella Marina', I have just got them into the ground all are well except the gooseberries of which only one is live. This is strange as the 36

---

22 Yule sold this when he left Wellington in 1852. (See Robert Donald, Chapter 8.)

23 This is the view of Patricia Burns in *Fatal Success*, Heinemann Reed, Auckland, 1989.

currants all alive. I have also filberts, six walnuts, and three mulberries, all well, also about 40 grape vines in addition to the twenty-four I had before .... Our nursery also contains some English Ivy plants, — furze, whitethorn and some flowering shrubs.

In November 1844, Chapman wrote: 'You know I have been looking out for a piece of land to establish ourselves on, I'm very difficult to suit.'[24] He wanted a property not too close to town, not leasehold and not in dispute

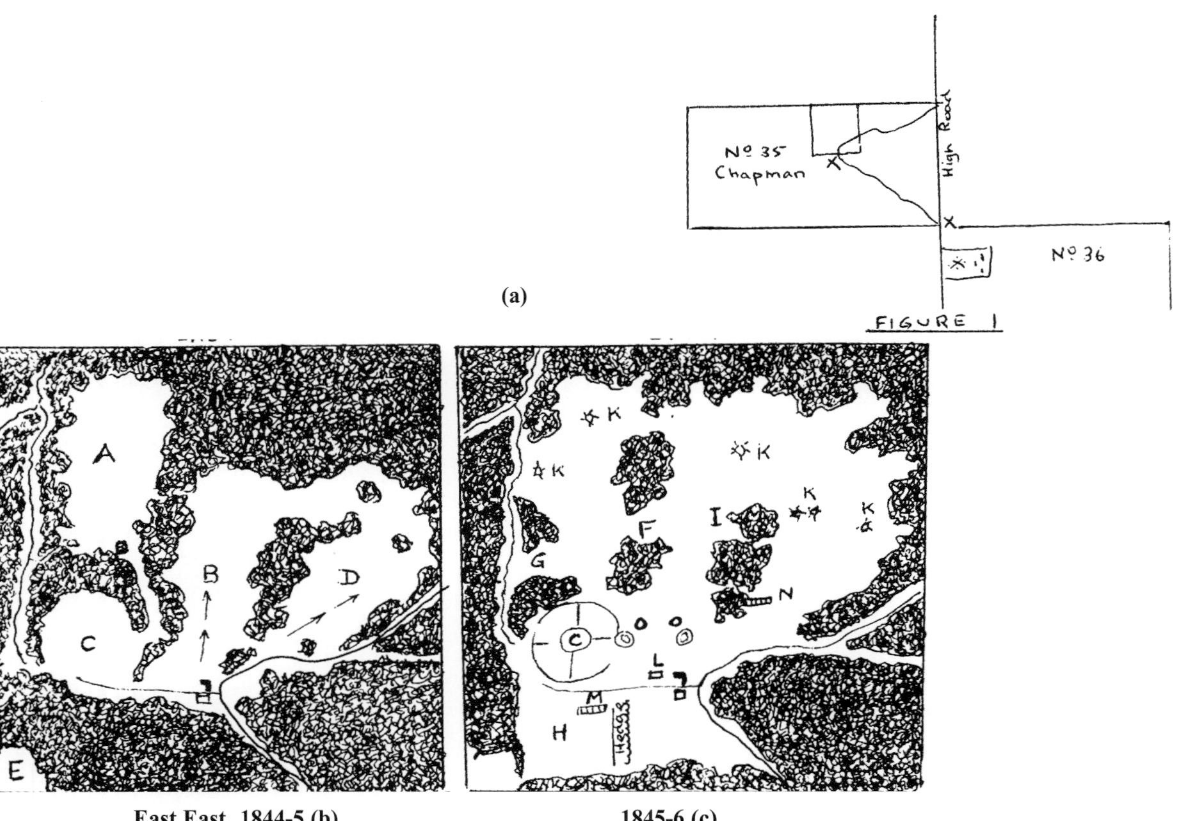

Chapman's sketches of his property Homewood, redrawn from the original.

Alexander Turnbull Library, National Library of New Zealand, Te Puna Mātauranga, MS-Papers-0053-11B

with Māori or others. It had to have good soil and rural beauty. He found what he required in Karori, buying Section 35 for £325 from Alfred Ludlam.

Chapman's papers and letters for the years 1844–52 describe how his house, farm, and garden emerged from the forest. Homewood, as the property was called, came to be regarded as a model farm, rather like Francis Molesworth's property at the Hutt. Chapman expected that the farm would ultimately become a fully economic unit and, should he have to move suddenly, he expected to be able to recoup all his capital expenditure.

Chapman kept his father fully informed of his plans for Homewood. Three of his sketches are important. The first shows the rented 5-acre block in relation to the new 100-acre purchase, while the second and third show the clearings and extension of these as the design for future garden and buildings started to take shape.

---

[24] Records of the property Homewood have been well preserved and are held in the Alexander Turnbull Library. Unless otherwise stated, all the information given here is drawn from these records or from Beryl Smedley's book, *Homewood*, published in 1980.

(**a**) shows a square of 10 acres (i.e. 10 chains by 10 chains) which is the portion of the section occupied by the clearing. The plot X is where we now live. The roadway from X to X has been partly made to cart timber and is completed from the W corner of the section, nearest to our house, to the clearing by a wide 'line' or path way through the bush. The eastern portion of the projected road is not cut – when we can spare a day we shall cut a 'line' so as to be passable for a horse, and so as to ascertain a good line of road.

(**b**) shows this year's clearing. **A** was the first clearing about an acre and a half. It is planted with potatoes, cabbages and turnips. In May it will have a second grubbing and burning and will be sown with wheat. **B, C** and **D** are subsequent clearings. They have been burnt off (a little before we intended by an accidental fire) and will be grubbed and will receive crops of various kinds between this time and May. **C** is the head of the gully – a hollow like a shallow saucer. It is to be Kate's parterre. From it the gully deepens and a run of water has its head close by. The further bank of the gully is abrupt – this side is a gentle slope where a second run of water is marked is a pretty cascade over rocks with beautiful banks and a pool below. The edges of the woods are killed by fire, but enough has been left to enable me after cutting away the dead trees to preserve a beautiful park-like effect with some truly magnificent trees. The site of the house is marked in red. The front is N.E. and the arrows pointing towards **B** show the direction of a beautiful and extensive prospect across the Kai WarraWarra valley to the Porirua Road 2 miles distance and thence from hill to hill about 10 miles further. In the direction of the other arrows I can see the blue hills through the trees on the other side of the harbour. I think it not unlikely we shall open out a view of the sea and part of the harbour. I think we are sufficiently elevated above the Tinakori range for this result. I reckon **A, B, C** and **D** make about 6 acres, **E** will be 2 or 3 more. You will of course understand that the dark pats are wood. The section is in fact all forest except where I have cleared. From the spot where the house will most likely stand to the eastern boundary line is a slope – indeed the ground slopes in all directions – very gently at the back. Across the gully, as I have said, is a bank which is a good shelter towards the N.W.

(**c**) shows how the spot will get opened out by a second or third grubbing. **F** is a fine clump of enormous White Pines (Kahikatea) which are uninjured. It will be much smaller than it now is as the fire has got in and killed more than half of the trees but enough remain. **G** is where we think of placing the stockyard with cow houses, pig styles, sheds, poultry houses etc. H as well as I can judge will be a good spot for the kitchen garden. In two years these 6 or 8 acres will be in grass except the gardens, and the land for tillage will be part towards the high road and part on the western side of the clearing. To ascertain the direction in which we look, turn to your map of the district. in the district marked Kai WarraWarra you will see the government domain marked in pink: below it you will see a winding road through 5 and 6. if you draw a pencil line from the middle of the section 35 to the road in No. 5 you will see the valley and stream and hills across which we look. Beyond the road in clear weather we see even the Porirua 'heads' ....

In (**c**) I have made a few references. You are aware that the stumps must remain for several years i.e. until the lateral roots are cut off and decay and get gradually obliterated so that the stump can be easily topped over. The expense of clearing away the stumps at first would be ruinous – the attempt has in fact ruined many an Englishman in America. To give you an idea of the difficulty of getting rid of stumps there is one in our present garden 10 feet in diameter at three feet from the ground with large lateral roots some of them extending 6 or 7 yards from the tree. These roots are easily cut off and destroyed in the process of cultivation but the stump must be submitted to. I have scattered a few about Fig. 3 marked **K.** They may soon be made ornamental – some may be converted into seats – others into flower stands and other covered with creepers. The rest are chopped at and otherwise ill treated until they decay. Three years will get rid of many – some will last Harry's life!

At **I** I shall have a greenhouse and at **M** will be the frames. **N** will be a latticed place for our guinea fowls and **O** two large flower stands. Glazing for frames here costs 8d per foot, in England it costs 1/4. Kate has been successful lately with her cuttings and nursery generally in preparation for the new garden. The round basin **C** will be thoroughly cleared for her by April – the proper time for transplanting there are only two or three stumps and none above two feet in diameter so that they will go about the end of the second year.

The site of the stockyard is not quite determined on. I shall prefer some where about the back of the house but the spot marked **G** has the great advantage of a run of pure water with such a fall that we can do what we please with it: even now the accumulation of rubbish has formed it into a succession of dammed pools as marked in blue, the gradual line of descent being marked red.

While operations on Block 35 were getting under way, Chapman continued to build up stocks of plants ready for the move across the road. Shortly after the purchase of the block, Chapman told his father:

Our ground is now producing and we have ceased to buy many things which previously were making demands on the pocket. I have 2 acres of new land, planted and sown with potatoes, cabbages, turnips, peas, all of which will be off in May so as to allow wheat to be got in.

Homewood, facing north, c 1870s.
Homewood, British High Commission file

The family in England were constantly being asked to send seeds, especially those contained in pulpy fruit – currants, gooseberries, mulberries, strawberries. The fruit was squashed between layers of blotting paper or cotton and posted off to New Zealand when dry. Young Harry Chapman called it 'the smash technique'.

If there were a surplus of seed on arrival, it was distributed or exchanged among the experienced gardeners, including William Swainson, the naturalist. This was evidently a common practice. Chapman exchanged a filbert tree for one dozen briar roses with Francis Bradey, while Bradey gave Chapman three dahlias. Besides the berry fruits mentioned above, lilac, three sorts of broom, laburnum, two sorts of acacia, bladder senna, and alders were raised from seed.

In December, anticipating the move to the new property, Chapman ordered a crate of garden pots, sixty to the case, from Sydney to take the many plants being raised. There were three sizes of pots – small size were 1/- per dozen; 48s, a larger size, were 1/6; and 32s cost 2/6. 'They were no cheaper in England,' said Chapman. He also asked his father for grasses that would be suitable

[f]or his high undulating land – meadow foxtail, crested dogstail, sheeps fescue, meadow fescue, hard fescue, sweet vernal, smooth stalked meadow, rough stalked meadow, English lucerne, and for lawns short blue meadow seed.

By the spring of 1846, all plants had been transferred to the new property.

We have transferred all the remainder of the fruit trees and a great number of English shrubs from the seed you sent and others. We have an immense number of roses and we have skirted a pretty piece of native bush standing at the terminus of our garden with brooms, lilac, hollyhock, mallow, foxglove, elder, bramble, furze etc. all of which will group well with the native shrubs.

Painting of Homewood by C.D. Barraud, 1849. Johnston's Hill is in the background. The drive winds up to the house past tall trees hung with rata vines, epiphytes, and ferns.

Alexander Turnbull Library, National Library of New Zealand, Te Puna Mātauranga, F-21070-1/2

As early as August 1842, the *New Zealand Gazette* had predicted that Karori would not become a grain-growing area. Settlers sowed small areas in wheat, oats, or barley for their own use. In June 1845, Chapman had two acres of wheat, which he calculated would yield enough flour for a year, and nearly three tons of straw that would be made into manure. Chapman's letter to his father 30 January 1846 was very optimistic:

> **The harvest here will be splendid. The Hutt lands will yield 45 bushels per acre and the bush and hill country 30 bushels.**

The Chapmans moved into their new home by 24 August 1847. Midwinter flowers at Homewood in 1848 included *Fuchsia globosa, F. coccinea, F. riccartonii, F. youelli,* a rose, pansies, antirrhinums, hollyhock, scarlet verbena, sweet William, sweet scabious, tobacco full of bloom and seed, scarlet geranium, Chinese primrose, yellow lupine, and an unknown shrub from the Cape. In August that year, Chapman ordered 10,000 hawthorns from Hobart Town for only 14/- per 100.

> **I only want 5,000-6,000 so I disposed of the rest. Last year I paid 15/- a hundred for a few. 14/- per 100 is less than the price in England. I shall plant hedges in all directions. I have also got 2,000 sweet briar plants for £1 to make garden hedges as wind breaks.**

Illustrations of Homewood in 1850 and in 1880 include trees from the original forest. Chapman counted the annual rings in a cross section of various tree trunks at one stage, estimating that hardly any were over 400 years of age – a rimu gave a count of 302 years, a white pine 186 years, and other species 224 and 225 years. His wife, Kate, said that the bush, with the supple-jack's hard, tough, looping stems, was so thick it was hopeless to attempt to make a way through the forest without bill-hook and compass.

At the very top of Johnston's Hill, a stunted windshorn miro contrasted markedly with the normal growth of similar trees down below. The centre of

Eligible Freehold Property for Sale

FOR SALE, the Property of Mr JUSTICE CHAPMAN, called HOMEWOOD, situated at Karori, 21/2 miles from the Court House. The Estate consists of 118 1/2 acres of land, of which about 30 acres are more or less cleared, (some perfectly stumped and in meadow) in such manner as to produce a picturesque effect, by preserving belts of Trees and opening distant prospects.

There is a good House of 10 Rooms, with a 3 roomed Cottage, Barn, & c., within an enclosed yard; together with Stockyard, Milking Sheds, and other Outbuildings. There is also a Well of good Water, with Forcing Pump and every convenience for a family. The Garden is extensive and ornamental, and is well stocked with Fruit Trees.

It forms a very complete residence for a family, is capable of great improvement at a moderate expense, and will be sold a bargain. A large portion of the Purchase Money may remain on Mortgage.May be viewed at any time.

Apply to

|Mr JUSTICE CHAPMAN,
Homewood,
Mr BRANDON,
Solicitor, Lambton-Quay
Wellington, January 16, 1851. [sic]

the section was not as heavily timbered as the rest and so this was where clearing of the property began. Chapman attempted to form a park to retain some of the larger trees by sowing grass underneath, but over the years these trees were gradually removed, especially when land was sold off.

When Chapman learnt he was to be appointed Colonial Secretary at Hobart Town at the end of 1850, Homewood was advertised for sale.

Chapman did not recoup all his outlay, as he had hoped. In finalising his accounts prior to leaving Wellington, he estimated a shortfall of several hundred pounds in his investment in the property. In March 1852, the family left New Zealand. Chapman returned in 1864, when he was appointed Judge of the Supreme Court, at Dunedin.

Today, Homewood stands in just over two acres of grounds. Two totara, one by the front porch, may be seedlings from the original forest. Its story is taken up again in Chapter 5.

Karori Road, looking south over a ten-acre block that was originally part of Section 36, c 1893. Campbell Street shows a remnant of Campbell's farm with Wright's Hill slopes in the background. The house in the foreground was later owned by W. Choat. Macrocarpas and camellias in this photograph are still there today.

Alexander Turnbull Library, National Library of New Zealand, Te Puna Mātauranga, F-22973-1/2, PACoII-6001-03

The vales of Karori

Until 1888, the Karori Valley was mainly a farming community. Cattle- and sheep-farming were the preferred occupations, with settlers growing only enough wheat to grind for their own needs. Parakeets were as troublesome as they were at the Hutt.[25]

The romantic word 'vale' seems to have been favoured for property names – Karori Vale, Campden Vale, Park Vale, Eden Vale (this last being later known as Donald's Tea Garden). F.W. Hurst, a foundation member of the Horticultural Society, was well established at Campden Vale by 1851, selling fruit trees and other plants.

Another settler, S.D. Parnell, worked as a carpenter for Chapman while establishing his own farm unit. His diary tells of his buying, selling, and mating his first precious cattle with owners from all over Wellington as herds were slowly built up. He even mentions mating his animals with Riddiford's at the Hutt. Similarly, his stock of fruit trees was built up by exchanging seed and budwood from settlers such as Hurst, Woouldom, Chapman, and others.[26]

---

[25] Kilmister, Alfred, Manuscript, Alexander Turnbull Library.

[Left] *Stephen Lancaster with some of his family in his first home, built c. 1859. The dormer window and verandah details were typical of this style of home built around the 1860s. The plants in the garden are hard to determine.*

Karori Historical Society collection, Alexander Turnbull Library, 846891/2

Stephen Lancaster's first home is on the left and his second home, Chesney Wold, is on the right, 1870. The bush on the hills behind is being burnt off, and a paling fence now secures the boundary of Chesney Wold.

Lady Smedley Collection, Alexander Turnbull Library, National Library of New Zealand, Te Puna Mātauranga, F-84688-1/2, PAColl-5277-1-07

It is from diaries such as Parnell's that the difficulties of those early years become apparent, as well as the interdependence of settlers from all walks of life, maintaining contact with each other and continually exchanging items of value.

Stephen Lancaster, a quarryman from Accrington, built his first home on Karori Road, down towards what is now Karori Park, shortly after his arrival in 1859. Lancaster, who became the borough's first mayor, built several homes. In 1866, he built Chesney Wold, a short distance from his first home.

From 1893 to 1898, Katherine Mansfield's family, the Beauchamps, rented Chesney Wold from Stephen Lancaster. Two of Mansfield's well-known stories, 'The Dolls' House' and 'Prelude', are based in Karori. 'Prelude' describes a child, Kezia, arriving at Chesney Wold for the first time, 30 years after it was built:

> When she opened [her eyes] again they were clanking through a drive that cut through the garden like a whip lash, looping suddenly an island of green, and behind the island, but out of sight until you came upon it, was the house. It was long and low built, with a pillared verandah and balcony all the way round. The soft white bulk of it lay stretched upon the green garden like a sleeping beast. And now one and now another of the windows leaped into light. Someone was walking through the empty rooms carrying a lamp. From the window downstairs the light of a fire flickered.[27]

In a very early story, Mansfield wrote: 'In the days of our childhood we lived in a great old rambling house planted lonesomely in the midst of huge gardens, orchards and paddocks.'[28]

In 1900, shortly after the Beauchamps left Chesney Wold, the house was altered and a portion of the veranda on the east side glassed in to form a conservatory.

As the years went by, further alterations were made to Chesney Wold. Land was sold off and in 1969 the house was divided into two flats. Today, Chesney Wold, now at 372 Karori Road, has been returned to one residence, but it bears little resemblance to the original house built in 1866.

The notes put together in 1932 by Alfred Kilmister, a descendant of John

Chesney Wold c 1867, soon after it was built, showing the layout of the carriage entrance way, the perimeter planting of trees, the remaining trees from the original bush, and the slope of the forest-clad hills on the far side of Karori Road.

Museum of New Zealand B.12441

[26] Parnell, S.D., Diary, Alexander Turnbull Library.

[27] Mansfield, Katherine, 'Prelude', in *The Stories of Katherine Mansfield,* edited by Anthony Alpers, Oxford University Press, Auckland, 1984, p. 228.

[28] Mansfield, Katherine, 'About Pat', in Alpers (ed) ibid., p. 5. According to Alpers, the 'Pat' of the title was Patrick Sheehan, the Beauchamps' handyman at Chesney Wold from 1893-1898 (ibid., p. 545).

The stylised garden at Chesney Wold after the second alteration in 1900s. There is now a formal box hedging to the drive and clipped shrubs in one bed.

Margaret Kivell Collection, Alexander Turnbull Library F.1738551/2

Kilmister, an early Karori/Makara settler, together with the letters of Judge Chapman and the diary of Parnell, add to our understanding of conditions encountered by the pioneers. John Kilmister was a cooper and brewer by trade. Conditions in Gloucestershire, where John had worked on a farm for several years, were so unpromising that he decided to emigrate to New Zealand. He arrived with his wife Frances and son John on the *Lady Nugent* in March 1841. The family stayed in the Government Depot for the first ten days, before moving into a clay and mud hut at the top of Bolton Street.

Like many of the newcomers, John could turn his hand to most things. He pit-sawed timber for the first house built in Khandallah, then he moved for a short time to the Hutt after the 1848 earthquake. From here, pit-sawn timber was used to build his next home on The Terrace, where he established a small farm breeding goats, which he sold in milk for a guinea per head. Next, he bought a farm on Tinakori Hill and, after the burn-off, dug the soil between the stumps to sow wheat. He chopped some soil into small round mounds, planting one potato in each.

Kilmister worked hard. Timber for Walter Mantell's house was pit sawn near Wilton's bush and carried by hand to Sydney Street. Kilmister helped with road building, and acquired land in Johnsonville, where he grew wheat. In 1855, his son, now aged 19, began working for 5/- per day on the commencement of the Makara Road. John junior soon bought 750 bush-covered acres over the big hill behind Karori Cemetery for 10/- per acre. To build his four-roomed cottage, he pit sawed a totara five feet in diameter.

There were wild cattle and pigs in the bush – animals descended from those first cattle left to fend for themselves in unfenced areas. John spent 25 years clearing and fencing this land. Seventy years later, the totara fence posts and hinau rails were still serviceable. John junior reared 10 children before returning to live in Wellington. His father died in 1904, aged 96.

The Kilmisters' ownership of land was widespread and included land at south Karori, the hills north of Parkvale Road and above the cemetery, and, more recently, on hills above Wilton's Bush. The decision to emigrate in 1840 had been beneficial, even though it had demanded extremely hard work.[29]

In the midst of the economic recession of the 1880s, Graham's 100-acre Block 34 (east

Podocarpus totara, *64 Homewood Avenue. Its measurements in 1981 were height 15 m, girth 5.5 m, width 15 m.*

J.Nauta, Museum of New Zealand C.T.15698/15-17

Myoporeum laetum, *ngaio, Lemnos Avenue, November 1999.*

J.Nauta, Museum of New Zealand C.T.15702/34-37

[29] Kilmister, Alfred, Manuscript Section, Alexander Turnbull Library.

of Yule's Block 36, Karori) was subdivided into a dozen or more small cultivated lots. These were let out to tenant farmers. Crops, including wheat, were planted and there was pasture for cows. It all gave the impression of a village. Shortly afterwards, when new roads were formed linking Ponsonby Road to Cooper Street, Karori was proclaimed a borough.

The Karori tunnel was opened in 1900, and that steep climb up over Baker's Hill was no more. Steadily, all this time, the bush was being cleared. This had included the pit sawing of the rimu stand on the northern side of Karori Road and its shipping to California for £1-1-0 per hundred feet.

The large mataī at 12 Homewood Avenue has been placed on the District Scheme. Surrounding properties feature sizeable cabbage trees, and there is a substantial ngaio in Lemnos Avenue. A tall mamaku tree fern in Friend Street is a reminder of the time when the whole area was covered in native bush.

Friend Street, Karori, looking west to grazing land, 1999. A lone 100-year-old tree fern is a reminder of the forest that once covered the valley.

J. Nauta, Museum of New Zealand

Registered Notable Trees in Karori are:

Podocarpus totara. 64 Homewood Avenue. 1981, height 15.00, girth 5.5 m, width. 15 m measured at 1.4 m. Oldest tree of its type growing in a home garden in Wellington city area. (Fig. 94).

Dacrycarpus dacrydioides. 10 Homewood Avenue. 1993, height 12 m, girth 1.65 m, width 140 measured at 1.4 m. A Stand 10 trees, an outstanding contribution to setting of nearby dwellings.

Ilex aquifolium. 15 October 1867. 22 Donald Crescent. 114 years old. 1982, height 9.5 m, girth 1.06 m, width 12.00 m at 1.4 m. Probably oldest and largest holly tree in Wellington.

Wilton

The bush in the area that is now known as Wilton was a mixed forest of rimu, mataī, kahikatea, miro, hinau, and northern rata. Māori cultivations were recorded on the north-facing slope near Otari.[30] Native pigeons, kākā, tuī, and weka were shot in great numbers and later wild pigs and cattle roamed the area.[31] Prior to 1847, Ngāti Tama claimed traditional occupational rights over the Otari area. Although the initial land sales went through in 1839, only 43 of the country lots allocated to Māori were taken up by them.[32] Ownership of the land in this early period is complex, and involved that given to Māori under the McCleverty awards.[33]

It was not until 1859, by which time most Māori had left their settlements at Kaiwharawhara, Pipitea, and Kumototo, that Samuel Maxton was issued with a Crown Grant, Country Section 1 in the Kaiwharawhara

Wilton farm, showing homestead, pasture, and remaining bush, c 1906.

Lent by Wilton family

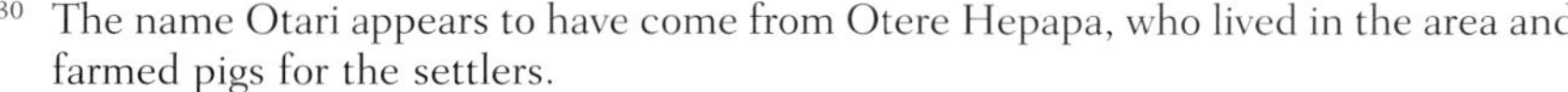

[30] The name Otari appears to have come from Otere Hepapa, who lived in the area and farmed pigs for the settlers.

[31] Kilmister, Alfred, Manuscript, Alexander Turnbull Library.

[32] *Management Plan 1996, Otari Native Botanic Garden*, Wellington City Council.

[33] McLean, Gavin, *Wellington: the First Years of European Settlement 1840-1850*, Penguin Books Auckland, 2000.

District on the northern side of Tinakori Hill. The following year Maxton sold 108 acres to Job Wilton. The block of land ran up the northern face of Tinakori Hill to meet the Town Belt.

As in the Hutt Valley and Karori, wherever the new settlers penetrated, they cut down the forest. Job Wilton was no exception, but he had the foresight to preserve and fence 17 acres of forest near his homestead. He opened this forest remnant to the public, taking care to ensure that when visitors had left all fires were put out. As the road improved, Wilton's Bush became more and more popular with visitors from town.

By the turn of the century, Wellington residents were concerned about how little native vegetation now remained. Māori who owned land in this area were willing to sell, and in August 1906 the land acquired from them was gazetted as a scenic reserve. In 1918, it became a reserve 'in Trust for Recreation Purposes and the Preservation of Native Flora'.[34] The Minister of Lands expressed his hope that Job Wilton would also ensure his land was protected.

[Left] View of the garden, looking east to the bare hills of Chartwell, 1932. The forest remnant formerly owned by Job Wilton lies in the gully to the left. The custodian's cottage is to the right, with the newly planted collection area in front.

Evening Post Collection, Alexander Turnbull Library, National Library of New Zealand, Te Puna Mātauranga, G-88441-1/2

[Right] Job and Ellen Wilton's house at Wilton Road, looking east, c 1920. The old shed on the left is on what is now Bowling Club land, but the twelve-bail cowshed and the dairy still survive. The Pinus radiata *to the left of the homestead and macrocarpa to the right came from the Wellington Botanic Garden in 1874. They were felled over 100 years later, but the stumps remain.*

Curtis, Onslow Historical Society

Meanwhile, Martin Chapman, son of Henry Chapman of Homewood, purchased some of the Wilton property with its bush remnant. When he died in 1924, 5½ acres of the bush originally preserved by Wilton was bought by the Wellington City Council for £2,300 and added to the Reserve.

In 1926, Dr Leonard Cockayne, Honorary Botanist to the Royal New Zealand Institute of Horticulture, proposed that the Reserve be known as the Otari Open-Air Plant Museum and outlined four objectives for it:

The collection of as many New Zealand species as possible; the propagation of various types of primitive New Zealand vegetation; the restoration of the forest as far as possible to its original form; and the demonstration of the usefulness of indigenous plants in New Zealand Gardens.[35]

The name was changed in 1998 to the Otari Native Botanic Garden, but in 1999 it was renamed the Otari Native Botanic Garden and Wilton Bush Reserve.

Over the years, not only has the Garden pioneered the use of native plants in our gardens but it has also become the foremost native plant garden in the country. As with Wellington's three other Botanic Gardens, it has its own

---

[34] Quoted in *Management Plan 1996, Otari Native Botanic Garden*, Wellington City Council.

[35] [Cockayne ref needed]

Management Plan. It is funded entirely by the Wellington City Council. Besides the original forest remnant, the largest of its type in Wellington, the remainder of the forest is of varying age and condition, having been disturbed in the past by Māori cultivation, followed by logging and clearance for farming. The Otari Garden has established and continues to maintain a number of native plant collections consisting of over 1,200 hybrids, species, and cultivars.

In 1998 a project was undertaken to link the two areas of the Garden, improve visitor access and educational interpretation, and generally upgrade the Reserve. The $1.6 million upgrade, funded mainly from the Charles Plimmer bequest, was completed by October 1999. The Joseph Banks entrance and the car-park entrance are now linked by a 75 metre canopy walkway spanning a deep bush-filled valley, and a new alpine rock garden has been built at the car-park entrance. The total area of Garden and Reserve is 74.9329 hectares.

[Left] The walkway that links the Otari Visitors Centre to the main rock garden and collection areas, November 1999.

J. Nauta, Museum of New Zealand

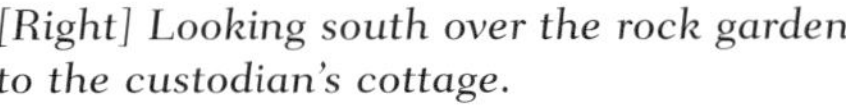

[Right] Looking south over the rock garden to the custodian's cottage.

J. Nauta, Museum of New Zealand C.T.15702/21-26

The beach at Thorndon with Wadestown hills in the background.

Alexander Turnbull Library, National Library of New Zealand, Te Puna Mātauranga, C-11895

Wadestown

The suburb of Wadestown is built on the north-eastern face of Tinakori Hill. It is one of Wellington's hilliest suburbs. From Heaphy's key to his north-facing painting of 1841, numerous potato cultivations were known to have been situated there. Brees' illustration of 1844 shows hills and some standing forest.

Bought by John Wade and James Watt, the land was the first of the New Zealand Company's country acre blocks to be subdivided. By 1841, Wadestown had been subdivided into half-acre lots, but settlement was slow because of difficulties of access. Until the 1880s, there were only a few scattered cottages, owned mainly by labourers who returned home from the town in the evenings to spend what little spare time they had clearing and cultivating the land.

Two such men were Joseph White and Samuel Retter, who bought adjoining lots at the top of Wade Street.[36] White was a keen gardener and proud of his potatoes, cabbages, parsnips, peas, carrots, onions, and turnips, which he was quick to grow. He entered his garden in the 'cottage garden

Fairlight, Wadestown, c. 1880s, before the addition of a second storey. The bush behind has not been cleared.

[Alexander Turnbull Library]

This exceptionally fine bunya bunya was planted on the original Fairlight property c 1870, before it was subdivided. The sheltered position has allowed it to reach its present size. 9 Fitzroy Terrace, December 1999.

J. Nauta, Museum of New Zealand C.T.15702/4-5

section' of the 1843 Horticultural Show and won first prize.

Until the 1880s, two larger properties contrasted markedly with the smaller cottages which dotted the hills. In 1862, on the site of 29 Pitt Street, plasterer John Hooper had his small cottage. This was later enlarged by a builder, John Beard. The next owner, a civil servant named John Davies, planted an orchard and laid out lawns with flowerbeds, as shown in the 1880s watercolour above. The property was named Fairlight.

Fairlight c. 1890s. Wadestown Road on the left.

Wellington Public Library

[36] White later became a sawyer in the Hutt Valley and increased his land holdings in Wadestown, the Hutt Valley, and the Wairarapa. Retter increased his Wadestown holding by manual work, road making, etc.

Looking from Anne Street across to Fairlight on the rear right-hand side of the picture, December 1999. The bunya bunya and hoop pine are visible alongside the lower house on the left side of photograph.

J. Nauta, Museum of New Zealand C.T.15705/34-36

Later in the same decade, E.W. Lowe added another storey, creating a striking mansion that dominated the ridge on which it was built. The photograph shows a large area in trees near the boundary alongside Wadestown Road. Two trees survive from the original Fairlight at what is now 9 Fitzroy Terrace. Both are registered as Notable Trees – an *Araucaria bidwillii*, or bunya bunya, and a large hoop pine, *Araucaria cunninghamii*.

Many of the sections from what is now Orchard Street down to Kaiwharawhara were more than half an acre. They were amalgamated in the 1850s into one unit, Highland Park Farm, by a wealthy and shrewd Yorkshireman, W.B. Rhodes. On this property in the 1860s, Rhodes built The Grange, a huge mansion that dominated the skyline.

The Grange on the skyline of Wadestown, c 1867, by W.F.E. Liardet.

Mitchell Library, Sydney

An 1869 oil painting of the house looking north to what today is Mt Kaukau shows a flight of steps leading up to what was possibly a lawn with a fountain. The perimeter planting of trees seems stylised compared with a photograph taken early this century.

Taken from the opposite direction in the 1860s, the picture overleaf shows the fountain on the left and a well laid-out vegetable garden protected by what may be thorn hedges. The hills behind are well cleared of bush and stumps.

A much later photograph taken from Wadestown Road shows the now mature grounds surrounding the house and the entrance off Wadestown Road.

The Grange, Orchard Street, Wadestown, looking north to Mt Kaukau. Oil painting by Nancy Tilbury, 1869.

(Left) The Grange soon after it was built, 1868. The fountain shown in the Tilbury painting is on the left. The vegetable garden is sheltered by hedges, possibly thorn.

Rhodes Album, Alexander Turnbull Library, National Library of New Zealand, Te Puna Mātauranga, F-110510-1/2

(Right) The Grange from Wadestown Road, c 1890. Mature trees show wind sheer. Rhodes was interested in camellias. Some pines surround the property, but do not appear to have been planted as a perimeter planting inside the boundary hedge as shown in the Tilbury painting.

Alexander Turnbull Library, National Library of New Zealand, Te Puna Mātauranga, F-30772-1/2

In 1904, there was a lower entrance at the junction of Newman Terrace and Grant Road, and an easement next to Stowe over a small strip of land down to the beach and Rhodes' wharf. The property's suitability for use as Government House was examined in 1907, but was ruled out as being too expensive. Katherine Mansfield's parents then occupied the house. Following its damage by fire, The Grange was demolished in 1929, the property subdivided, and Orchard Street was formed.

Country Acres to the North: Ngaio to Johnsonville

As in the Hutt Valley, Karori, Wilton, and Wadestown, settlers on the northern hills of Wellington (from present-day Ngaio through to Johnsonville, Glenside, and Ohariu Valley) experienced difficulties with access and isolation. With little flat land cleared, the first years were hard, especially when families had to toil up steep, rough tracks with their goods and provisions.[37]

The first road from Wellington to Porirua followed the route of a Māori track from Kaiwharawhara across Paerau Hill, down to what is now Box Hill, and on to Johnsonville. It was known as the Bridle Track. Another track ran from Ngauranga, joining the Bridle Path at Johnsonville, and continuing northwards as the Porirua Road.

All three tracks passed through Māori potato gardens dating from the early nineteenth century. In his key to his 1841 painting from Clay Point, Heaphy notes numerous potato gardens on the Wadestown hills and two on the Tinakori slope. Most were the gardens of Te Atiawa, except around Kaiwharawhara where Ngāti Tama, a tribe from north Taranaki, had a small

---

[37] The Onslow Historical Society, which formed in 1971, has rendered an invaluable service publishing a quarterly magazine and, in 1983, the book *Wellington's Northern Suburbs*. New information comes to light continuously, enriching what is already known. Unfortunately, details of gardens and garden plants are not generally recorded, diaries are few, and much of our knowledge is based on photographs, sketches, and paintings. Fortunately, the area is rich in early illustrative material. The map drawn by J.P. Bent[h]ell and used as the frontspiece to *Wellington's Northern Suburbs* is reprinted here with the permission of the publisher Millwood Press. It details many of the places referred to in this chapter. With his lens, scientist, lawyer, and early photographer W.T.L. Travers captured invaluable scenes of pioneering in this area in the 1860s as New Zealand's virgin bush was destroyed forever. Artists such as G.F. Angus, William Swainson, and his daughter Mary Marshall have left even earlier records.

Native potato grounds, c 1840. Watercolour by Owen Stanley. Ngauranga Māori were understandably reluctant to give up the cultivation on land which is today Mandalay Terrace, Khandallah.

Royal Society of Tasmania and Tasmanian Museum and Art Gallery

kāinga. The pictorial record and descriptions for these potato gardens in Wellington is poor, except perhaps for Owen Stanley's somewhat impressionistic watercolour of Ngauranga Māori potato gardens in the area of today's Mandalay Terrace.

The Bridle Path was improved in the early part of 1841, but it was still far from satisfactory. The tenants of Daniell's Trelissick Farm formed a track on the east side of the valley up to the top of the ridge, what is now Cockayne Road. This road, Old Porirua Road, still exists; narrow, winding, and steep even today. One early settler wrote of the need, '... to brave the dangers of the road, the very narrow side cuttings up the Kaiwarra Hill, where a false step might precipitate you and the horse you rode into the fearful depths below'.

The Glen in Kaiwharawhara was the home of Major Marshall and his wife Mary, the eldest daughter of William Swainson. Shown here as a solitary property, it was not isolated for long, as settlers continued to move into the area. Mary was keenly interested in her garden. In 1850, she wrote: 'We have been busy planting bulbs, the African gladiolus and Ixias become perfect'.

Mary inherited her father's ability to draw, and managed to capture for posterity the ambience of bushman's cottages on the slopes above Porirua Road.

Cottages similar to those sketched by Mary were later described by

The Glen, Kai wara-wara, *sketch by William Swainson, 1856. The home of Mary Marshall and her husband.*

Privately owned, Alexander Turnbull Library, National Library of New Zealand, Te Puna Mātauranga, A-189-022

[Left] The beginning of the Porirua Road with mill, cottage, and Schultze's flour mill, c 1860s.

Photo, W.T.L. Travers, Nelson Provincial Museum]

[Right] Ngauranga Gorge Road, 1860s. The scarred landscape following removal of the bush.

James Bragge, Museum of New Zealand

Wooden Cottage, Porirua Road, *sketch by either Mary Marshall or William Swainson, c 1840s.*

Private Collection, Alexander Turnbull Library, National Library of New Zealand, Te Puna Mātauranga, F-19223-1/2

Ngaio's first known house, on the site of Perth Street, c 1860. It was known as 'Murray's Place' after the man who leased Trelissick farm.

Alexander Turnbull Library, National Library of New Zealand, Te Puna Mātauranga, F-10409-1/2

Elsdon Best:

> Across the space of long years comes the vision of the wattle and daub chimneys, the slab huts, the weatherboard cottages, of the days when the old Bush Legion was in camp. Back over the weakening wires of memory looms up the log-strewn clearing, the black desolation of the new 'burn', the primitive home of the pioneer.

What was thought to be the oldest house in Ngaio may have originally started as one of these simple cottages. Situated near what is today Perth Street and enlarged over the years, it was photographed in the 1880s, and gives some idea of the hardships experienced by many settlers in those early years. It contrasts with houses built nearby, such as Crofton and Chew Cottage.

Sawmills were operating in Ngaio by 1843. Juliette Daniell, daughter of Captain Daniell,[38] the owner of Trelissick Farm, describes what the area was like when sawmilling began:

> We went to live at Upper Kaiwarra, where a small house was built on a property of about 300 acres. Some of the beautiful 'bush' had been cleared and the spot occupied by **Māoris** before it was purchased from them. The surroundings were very lovely – the hills covered with a magnificent forest, and the sound of the rushing Kaiwarra streams could be heard through the trees. About half-a-mile distant, sawmills had been erected. We could go to them by a path cut through the 'bush', and it was a great delight to watch the cutting of the timber there, and to see the dams made to keep back the water for use in the sawmill.

Once the bush had been removed from around the houses, they were exposed to the winds, blowing through the stumps of the fallen forest. The stumps were gradually removed, but the land appeared even more ugly, bare, and windswept. There was an urgent need for shelter. Settlers planted thorn hedges and hollies until the late 1860s, when macrocarpa and pine seed from California became available.

A photograph of Daisy Hill Farm taken at the turn of the century shows Robert Bould's home in Johnsonville protected by pines, planted thirty years or more previously. The pastureland is fenced but devoid of shelter.

This picture of Daisy Hill Farm shows the reality of the cleared land, typical of the Wellington area. Turnbull Thomson's painting of 1856 from Khandallah, looking towards Pipitea Point, or William Fox's of 1857, depicting neat farms and cornfields separated by gorse or thorn hedgerows, are

[38] The Daniells moved to the Hutt early in 1849.

misleading. They showed an idealised landscape, not what actually existed.

In time, the many quaint clay-walled cottages and wooden shacks built in the 1840s were replaced by more substantial homes. The land surrounding two of these in Ngaio – Crofton and Chew Cottage – was photographed by Travers in the 1860s, still with fallen trees and stumps around. These houses, both now over 140 years old, are important landmarks from the past. They do not contribute a great deal to garden design by today's standards, but they were typical of Wellington, with its difficult climate and topography.

Daisy Hill farm, Johnsonville, c 1900. A bare landscape softened by the Californian pines planted in the 1870s.

McBride, Onslow Historical Society

Crofton, now 21 Kenya Street, was built in 1857 by William Fox, later Premier of New Zealand. Fox soon moved closer to town, and in 1862,

Map drawn by J.P. Benthell in 1931 shows districts of Wilton, Ngaio, Khandallah, Johnsonville, and Ohariu.

Courtesy of Onslow Historical Society Inc.

This photograph shows sawyers' cottages and a new barn in the area where John Chew built his house, near where the Ngaio Town Hall is today. W.T.L. Travers, c 1860.

Nelson Museum

Wellington from Khandallah, 1856. Painted by John Turnbull Thomson, First Surveyor General of New Zealand.

Hocken Library, Otago University

View towards Pipitea Point from near the present Rama Crescent, c 1857. Watercolour by William Fox.

Hocken Library Dunedin

CHURCH OF ENGLAND GRAMMER SCHOOL, KAIWARAWARA

PRINCIPAL – WALTER LAWRENCE MARTIN, ESQ.
Late of H.M. 15th Regt.

THIS School is intended for Education more particularly of the Children of Parents belonging to the Church of England, but it is open to all who conform to its Rules.

The course of Instruction will comprise the Bible and Prayer Book, Ancient and Modern Classical Languages, History and Geography, Arithmetic and Mathematics.

No pupil will be received who cannot read and write fairly.

TERMS:-

Tuition . . . .£15 a year
Board . . . .£50 a year

To be paid Quarterly in advance to the account of the 'Kaiwarra Grammar School' at the Union Bank of Australia.

A Quarter's notice is required before the removal of a Boarder.

Wellington, 31st Jan., 1868. Advertisement New Zealand Spectator & Cook Strait Guardian.

31 January 1863

Crofton as an exclusive boys school, c 1860, by W.T.L. Travers. The remaining forest is visibly smaller than it was in an earlier photo, before the house was extended.

Nelson Museum

Pines and a newly planted macrocarpa hedge date this photo of Crofton by W.T.L. Travers to the 1870s. Young men and women are engaged in playing tennis and croquet.

Nelson Museum

Crofton became a Church of England boys' boarding school attended by the sons of many leading families. Considered for a time to be Wellington's Christ's College, its raw surroundings were a far cry from similar English-style schools.

In 1875, shortly after the photograph at the top of the page was taken, the school closed, mainly because Wellington College had opened and it was closer to the city. Crofton reverted to a private home and was occupied by the Berry family. The open verandah was glassed in and a chimney removed.

[Left] Crofton with well established garden, drive, and sunroom, c 1890s.

Holmes family, Onslow Historical Society

[Right] Mary and John Holmes in their summer garden at Crofton, 1910.

Lent by Ann Moffat

The house changed hands and the jeweller Wilson Littlejohn, later the first Mayor of Onslow, became the new owner of Crofton. A wide drive now led up to and alongside the front of the house and there was a well-kept garden. In 1895, the property was subdivided and land surrounding the homestead sold off in fourteen building lots.

The next owners were John and Mary Holmes. John's brother Lancelot had earlier been the pilot living in the pilot's house in Worser Bay. Both families were interested in their gardens. Although the property suffered at the hands of later owners, it has now been lovingly restored.[39]

[39] A complete visual record of a house, such as the series of photographs of Crofton, from 1861 to the present, is rare.

The Chew house as it appeared about 1861. It has a shingle roof and open verandah, which contrasts with the iron roof and closed verandah of today. The surrounding bush in this early picture indicates the house's isolation. It had only its own timber mill for company in this part of Ngaio, which was known then as Crofton. Some shrubs have been planted along the roadside boundary.

Dominion

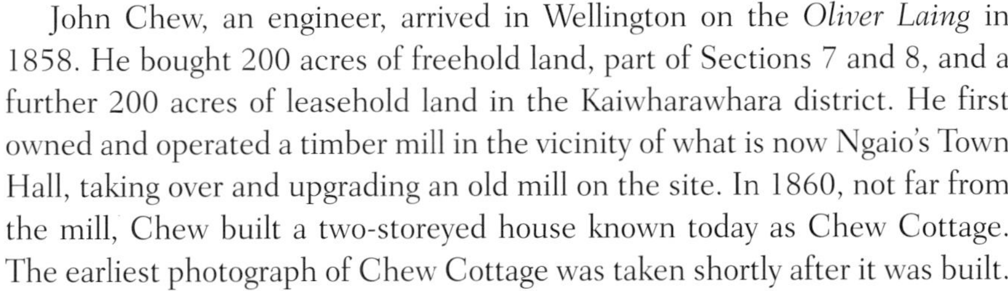

John Chew, an engineer, arrived in Wellington on the *Oliver Laing* in 1858. He bought 200 acres of freehold land, part of Sections 7 and 8, and a further 200 acres of leasehold land in the Kaiwharawhara district. He first owned and operated a timber mill in the vicinity of what is now Ngaio's Town Hall, taking over and upgrading an old mill on the site. In 1860, not far from the mill, Chew built a two-storeyed house known today as Chew Cottage. The earliest photograph of Chew Cottage was taken shortly after it was built.

The house was very exposed. Pines were planted on the boundary in the 1870s to give some protection from the prevailing nor'westerly winds. The garden today is charming, with one tree, an unknown variety of pear, dating back to last century.

Houses built in the Onslow district in the latter part of the nineteenth century and featured here indicate that the pioneering days were over. Conditions were easier, houses larger, and attention could now be given to the gardens. Very few gardens were exceptional, because of the continual struggle with the lie of the land, the climate, and the need for shelter. The photographs of houses in Khandallah all (except for George Clark's) have conifers, two have thorn hedges, and one even shows what appears to be kānuka-mānuka vegetation on the hills. In some cases,

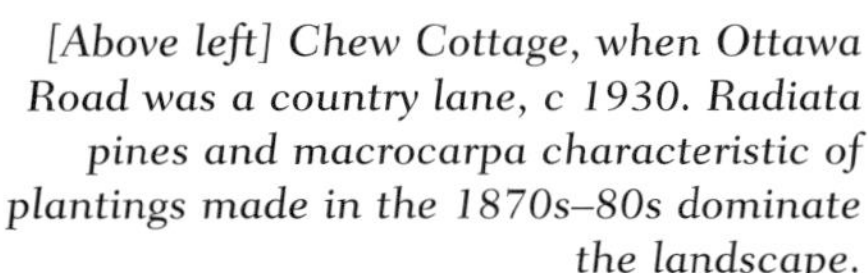

[Above left] Chew Cottage, when Ottawa Road was a country lane, c 1930. Radiata pines and macrocarpa characteristic of plantings made in the 1870s–80s dominate the landscape.

Judy Siers collection, Maurice Crompton-Smith

[Above right] Chew Cottage, when structural alterations were made and the verandah removed, c 1900. The garden is overgrown and plants unrecognisable.

Judy Siers collection

[Opposite] View of Chew Cottage from the road today. The chimney has been removed.

J. Nauta, Museum of New Zealand C.T.15795/1-4 or 41-44

[Top left] Donisthorpe, 12 Kenya Street, Ngaio, after reconstruction and landscaping. The centre portion was built in 1895 for a carpenter, James Kinneburgh. The wings were designed by architect Schwarz in 1906 for Arthur Newbold, who named the house. The Wellington City Council has it listed as an historic home.

Onslow Historical Society

[Top right] Khandallah House, 35 Burma Road, was built in the 1850s, shortly before Chew Cottage. This delightful garden was lost when the spacious colonial house unfortunately burnt down in 1910. This photograph was taken c 1890.

Onslow Historical Society

[Bottom left] 5 Kohima Drive, built in the 1880s. Taken from the railway embankment, the photograph shows hawthorn hedges along Old Porirua Road, now Burma Road; pines from the 1870s–80s; and the remains of bush behind; c 1907.

Stuart album, Onslow Historical Society

[Bottom right] George Clark's house, 78 Clark Street, Khandallah, c 1888. Hedges are visible, as is a vegetable garden with bush behind.

Onslow Historical Society

extensive planting of radiata as hedges proved to be inappropriate, causing nuisance as the hedge grew.

Wyatt House, No. 42 on the Old Porirua Road, is interesting. In 1863, William Wyatt purchased approximately six acres of Section 3 from Dunbar's estate. On a steep slope, the house, a two-storey building with a Georgian façade, was built the next year, with access for a horse and trap entering from the west corner of the property. In the 1870s, a tanner at Kaiwharawhara, Carter Hodges, bought the property, remaining there until about 1925. Hodges established an interesting garden, as photographs show, becoming more of a farmer than a tanner. Some fruit trees, lilac, bluebells, and bulbs, all relics from this time, continue to bloom here each spring.

Wyatt House, c. 1940. View of the front of 'Wyatt House' after the top balcony had been removed and the porch built over the front entrance.

Newlands collection, Onslow Historical Society

Johnsonville and Ohariu

Like other areas in Wellington, the country acres of Johnsonville and its frontier extensions Ohariu Valley and Porirua did not yield to systematic

[Left] Carter Hodges in his garden, 42 Old Porirua Road, c 1900.
Onslow Historical Society

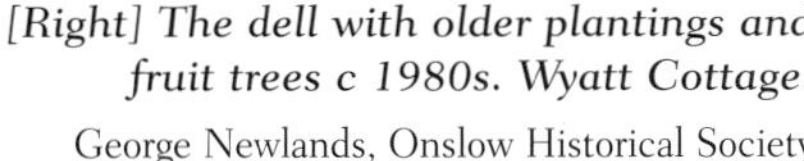

[Right] The dell with older plantings and fruit trees c 1980s. Wyatt Cottage.
George Newlands, Onslow Historical Society

farming and cropping, as envisaged by the New Zealand Company and many of its absentee owners. No one foresaw the gullies, ravines, rushing streams, dense bush, and native reserve land, nor the narrow, steep tracks that had to be negotiated before these country acres could be reached. Few settlers were wealthy enough to be large-scale employers. First-class passengers were young, had come to New Zealand to make their fortunes, and had limited money to pay wages. Steerage passengers were therefore directly affected by the financial limitations of the capitalists.

Because of financial constraints, the 100-acre blocks sold by the New Zealand Company in the Johnsonville and Ohariu area were soon broken up. Owners sold or leased small lots to immigrant labourers. Speculative buying and selling, often initiated by absentee owners, prevented many of the poorer immigrants from purchasing land. Even so, the small family farm developed here as it did in the Hutt Valley, Karori, and elsewhere.

Frank Johnson, who arrived on the *Adelaide* in March 1840, chose Section 11 on the west side of Old Porirua Road, now Johnsonville Road, for his 100-acre country block. With a sawmill established and some of the bush felled, it soon became known as Johnson's Clearing and later as Johnsonville. Johnson also bought Section 24, a mile further north, but this was cut up and the smaller parcels of land sold.

Looking north along Johnsonville Road, c 1904. St John's Anglican Church, among the trees in the distance, is to the left of the Old Porirua Road.
S Head Collection, Alexander Turnbull Library, National Library of New Zealand, Te Puna Mātauranga, G-7448-1/1

[Left] Bush settler's whare, with a well-planned survival garden, January 1856. Pencil and wash by William Strutt.

Alexander Turnbull Library, National Library of New Zealand, Te Puna Mātauranga, E-453-f-011-1

Halfway along the track between Kaiwharawhara and Porirua, Johnson's Section 24 became the centre of a small clearing, initially called Halfway. Today it is known as Glenside. Anthony Wall, an agricultural labourer, and his wife Susan bought eight acres of Section 24 from Johnson, and the house they built on the property was known as Halfway House. From a sketch made a few years later, it resembles two thatched cottages joined together.

Twelve months after settling on their property, in December 1842, Susan described the remarkable progress they had made in such a short time, including removal of forest.

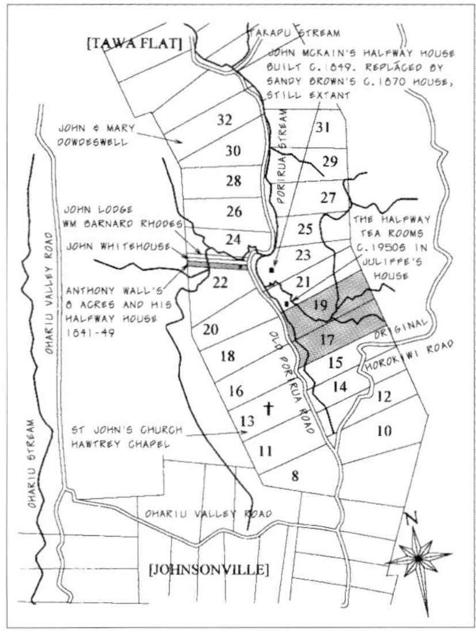

Drawn from an 1870 Department of Lands and Survey map, this shows Section 24 at Halfway. Drake's Sections 17 and 19, closer to Johnsonville, are seen in relation to the area.

From Anthony Wall by B. Kay

> My Dear Sisters,
>
> ... we are sited on our own little farm ... wee got too cows and a cow calf, wee have a good stock of poultry and wee kill our own pork. Wee have plenty of potatoes and all sorts of vigitable growing whisch wee shall find a great help to our family for wee have ... them all to buy from the natives and potatoes and all sort of vigitable are very dear at present. Wee have got potatoes a fortnight ago, there is plenty of cabbage and peas and all sort of vigitable ready to cut now .... I am selling fresh butter at 3 shillings a pound, new milk at 8 pence pr qurt, eggs is 2 shellings a dozen, fresh beef 9 pence pr lb, mutton the same, pork is sixpence, flour about 3 shillings a stone .... I hope in a short time we shall grow our own wheat.[40]
>
> The livestock had been exported from Sydney and the cows referred to were Longhorns, costing £8.10s at auction. Clearing the bush was not easy.[41]
>
> The trees after being cut have to be lopped and logged and all, including every twig, put into a pile and after a few days burnt. A huge dead rata had logs piled around it before firing – the fire generated so much heat that it penetrated the ground, burning the roots so that the tree eventually toppled. We have now cleared a triangular space 60 yards long fronting the road.

House [where] we halted halfway to Pororua August 28, 1849, *sketch by Martha King.*

Alexander Turnbull Library, National Library of New Zealand, Te Puna Mātauranga, A-100-001

[40] Kay, Barbara, *Anthony Wall, Settler of Porirua*, Wall family 150th family reunion, 1996.

[41] An 1848 unpublished census shows A. Wall having five acres in crops and four cattle.

Drake's homestead (Section 19).
Lawson Robertson

> **The house will stand on a slight rise about 20 yards back from the road with the dark background of the forest behind it. The open space I will divide between kitchen garden and garden separated by the path leading up to the house.**

Besides clearing his own land, Anthony Wall, like many working immigrants, went out labouring for 6/- per hour. His 11-year-old son accompanied him, working for half that amount.[42] Conveniently situated at Halfway, the Walls offered accommodation and food to many weary passing travellers. The road gradually improved, and by 1848 gardens, cottages, and clearings appeared on both sides of the road as the forest receded.

There were many settlers like Susan and Anthony Wall. The isolation of these small family units in the dense dark green bush is well portrayed in William Strutt's 1856 watercolour.

As in other areas, children outnumbered adults. Returns for the Porirua district in 1844 gave a population of 44 males, 35 females, and 154 children. In cultivation were 61 $^{5}/_{12}$ acres in wheat, 15 acres in barley, 22 $^{5}/_{8}$ acres in green crops, and 7 $^{3}/_{4}$ acres in grasses. By 1870, Johnsonville's population was still less than 200.[43] The hills were still forested, but houses were becoming more substantial than the two-roomed wattle and daub dwellings that had been built at first. When the railway line was built in 1878/79 it transformed the area physically, socially, and economically.

Eton-educated Thomas Drake, a keen gardener, arrived on the *Aurora* on 22 January 1840. Thomas and Selina Drake had not only the most comfortable cabin on the *Aurora* but they were the only ones on that voyage to bring out a prefabricated house.[44] They had a knowledge of plants and, according to a descendant, Thora Parker, brought with them camellias and rhododendrons from the Himalayas.

---

[42] Kay, Barbara, op. cit.

[43] Pearson, David, *Continuity and Change in a New Zealand Township*, George Allen & Unwin, 1980.

[44] Thomas Drake, descended from John Drake, brother of Sir Francis Drake, was the eldest son of Captain John Drake of the East Indian Company. Educated at Eton, he worked in a London bank before deciding to emigrate to New Zealand.

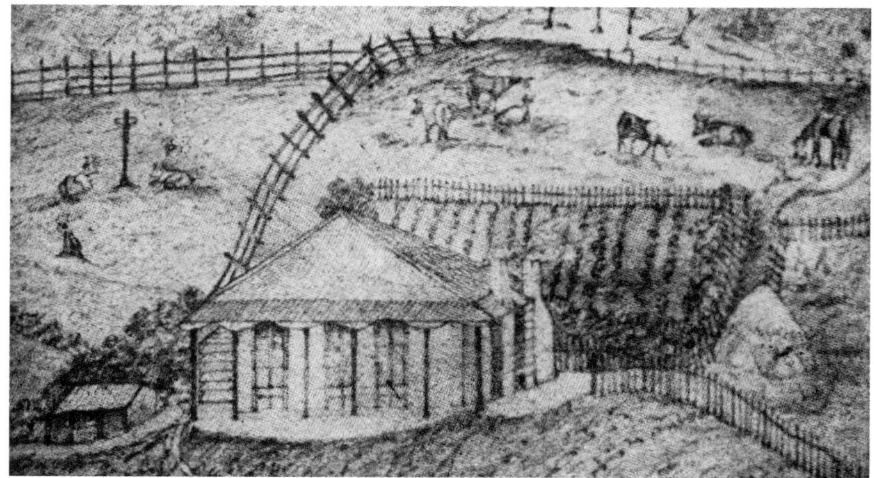

Glenside, Broderick's house, which was later demolished for the Tawa Flat deviation. Sketch loaned by Broderick family.

Onslow Historical Society

The Drakes were allocated Town Acre 467 on The Terrace and a year later Country Section No 19 along Porirua Road, just north of today's Johnsonville. They erected their prefabricated house on their Town Acre, on the site of the present Wellington Club.

In 1843, Selina Drake's sister Anne arrived in Wellington with her husband Creasey Broderick. Drake sold 26 acres on the north of Section 19 to his brother-in-law, and in 1847 the two families decided that together they were in a position to start farming their land north of Johnsonville. Both families built clay cottages until such time as Drake's prefabricated house could be removed from The Terrace and brought out from Wellington by bullock wagon – a difficult feat over the narrow road from Kaiwharawhara.

Drake later purchased more land, increasing his holding to 357 acres, which in time carried over 350 sheep. But it is not Drake's farming success that concerns us here, but his gardening. In the 1880s, a grandson wrote:

> Grandfather had made a wonderful garden, it seemed to extend for miles with a small creek with many rustic bridges where small trout could be seen. All of grandfather's time was spent there, and a lot of time of his employees. Plants and shrubs came from India sent by uncles stationed there, includ-ing Rhododendrons, and Azaleas, from Darjeeling, the foothills of the Himalayan mountains, the summer resort of those forced to live there. They had been cared for on great grandfather Drake's ship and were over a year in transit.[45]

Rhododendron ponticum *planted on Thomas and Selina Drake's property, possibly before 1900. This photo was taken c 1997.*

W. Shepherd

The Governor of the day visited Drake, as did members of the New Zealand Institute (now the Royal Society of New Zealand). From 1870–84, Drake donated plants to the Wellington Botanic Garden.[46] His donation in 1874–5 included macrocarpa seed (*Cupressus macrocarpa*). Old macrocarpa are still found today around his property. Drake was the donor to the Botanic Garden, not a recipient of conifer seed. Where did this macrocarpa seed come from? Do any of the Botanic Garden trees come from this seed? Macrocarpa was established in New Zealand by the 1860s, particularly in Canterbury. Did a New Zealand Institute or government member visiting Drake after 1865 bring a gift of macrocarpa seed? Or did Drake's brother-in-law, Creasey Broderick, obtain some seed from Monterey when participating in the Californian gold rush?

---

[45] Parker, Thora, *And Not to Yield*, David Bateman, 1987.

[46] Shepherd, W. and Cook, W., op. cit..

Earp's Bucket Tree, 1954.
M.D. King

After Drake's death in 1889, his son Walter managed the property for his widow. By that time, it was running 500–700 sheep. Later, most of the land was sold to the Crown, which broke up the Paparangi Estate, as it was known, and the land was sold off in the form of small farm units.

Today, the Wellington City Council owns the land immediately around the site of the old Drake home, which burnt down some years ago. Little remains of the original garden – a few large hollies, an elm tree, macrocarpa, young rimu, a few kōwhai, and notably a large rhododendron. The latter is a fine form of *R. ponticum*, a rhododendron not from the Himalayas. Blackberry, Old Man's Beard, and other invasive weeds cover most of the property.

There is a macrocarpa on Section 37 in Tawa, close to Johnsonville, which is particularly noteworthy and unusual. Of uncertain age but well over 100 years, it is registered as a Notable Tree. Known as 'Earp's Bucket Tree', its shape probably began through the pruning efforts of the young emigrant Frederick Westbury, employed by Earp in the 1880s. William Earp arrived in 1854 and by 1864 had cleared enough land to run 100 sheep. His house,

Bradey papers.
Alexander Turnbull Library

FREEHOLD PROPERTY.

Votes for the County of Surrey.

THREE HOUSES AND LAND,

And a Plot of Building attached,

WITH ROOM TO BUILD A DOZEN HOUSES, IF REQUIRED.

The Houses are New and Brick-built, in a most neat and substantial Manner, with an intention to keep, and not to Sell. They are very valuable, as they will not want Repairing for many Years.

LAND TAX REDEEMED, WITH GOOD TITLE.

No. 1, containing Five Rooms with good Fixtures, a capital enclosed Yard and Garden, 150 feet deep, surrounded with Green Privet Edges, Fruit Trees, &c.

No. 2, Ditto.

No. 3, A Shop, with Circular Front, containing Six Rooms, with good Fixtures, and a Shed, with Garden 150 feet deep, well stocked with Fruit Trees, and surrounded with Green Privet Edges. There is an excellent Pump of Spring Water.

A PLOT OF LAND, laid out as an Ornamental Flower Garden, fronted with a most excellent Fence, and well stocked with Fruit Trees, Flowers, and Vegetables. This is a fine opportunity for small Capitalists, as each Lot may be purchased separate, or all in one Lot, by Private Contract, by applying to Mr. Bradey, on the spot.

They are situated in POMEROY STREET, OLD KENT ROAD, in a new and fast rising Neighbourhood, where every foot of Land is fast rising in value, is well situated for Letting, being the first Street leading from the two great Roads - the Old Kent Road and the Peckham Road - in a very pleasant and Healthy Neighbourhood, commanding a fine View of the Surrey Hills, known as BRADEY'S PLACE, the Property of Mr Bradey, Boot Maker.

They can be inspected from Nine in the Morning, till Seven at Night. – Principals only will be treated with.

BRADEY,

BOOT MAKER, OLD KENT ROAD,

Returns his sincere Thanks to his Friends and Customers for the Liberal Patronage he has received for nearly Twenty Years, and informs them that he has Wholly Removed to

No. 3, Bradey's Place, Pomeroy Street, Old Kent Road, Hatcham.

HE HAS ALSO OTHER PROPERTY FOR SALE, VIZ.–

A Capital 8-Day Clock, a large Chimney Glass, a good Mahogany Sideboard, a Mahogany Wardrobe Bedstead, Tables, and other useful Household Furniture.

J. B. has also for Sale a Stock of Well-made BOOTS and SHOES, of his own making, of all Sizes, and Leather of the best Texture.

These are all to be Sold at Prime Cost; any one Pair is worth Two Pair of Sale-made ones, and will be Sold at as Low Prices. Any Gentleman or Person wishing for a Pair, by sending a Note, will have them sent to their Houses to try on. Every thing set forth in this Bill will be Sold very Cheap, as J. B. is going Abroad as soon as he can dispose of his Property, and get his affairs settled.

ALSO,

A GREAT AND CHOICE COLLECTION OF DAHLIAS,

Including a great Number of the First Show Flowers in the World.

Also, PINKS, PICOTEES, and a Collection of other FLOWERS.

Capital named Double Dahlias, commencing at *4d.* per Plant.– Any one addressing a Note, as above, can have a Collection sent to their Houses.

N.B. If not speedily Disposed of by Private Contract, will be offered shortly to Public Competion by Auction.

called Boscobell, was built in the 1860s by James Taylor. The house has now gone, but the Bucket Tree is a remarkable landmark.

Bradey's Town Acre, Newtown, Block 932.

Francis Bradey of Porirua

Francis (Frank) Bradey, born in Tamworth, England, in 1793, was the grandson of a former Chancellor of Ireland. At the time of his emigration to New Zealand, he was a well-established boot-maker and horticulturist in Old Kent Road, Hatcham. The two advertisements opposite indicate that besides the brick house and garden well stocked with fruit trees and surrounded by privet hedges, there was an extra block of land laid out as an ornamental flower garden. Bradey specialised in growing dahlias and picotee pinks.[47]

He paid for his land orders in August 1839 and, together with his family, arrived at Port Nicholson on the *Adelaide* in March 1840. In 1841, he returned briefly to England on the same ship as Henry Petre. Both appeared well satisfied with the new colony and in 1843 both men returned. Bradey was in demand for his boots. His diary for 3 June 1844 says, 'Gardened all day – bootmaking by candlelight'. A pair of boots sold for £1.[48]

Bradey's property in Newtown Block 932, between Adelaide Road and Hanson Street, was called Tamworth Cottage.

A great deal of time was spent sowing and harvesting potatoes. On 30 August 1844 Bradey planted a hedge of high shrubs around the garden and in the following month he planted for shelter a hedge of sweet briars across a little garden. When Mr Hart of Aldridge the Solicitors called he commented: 'You have the prettiest laid out grounds of anyone in Wellington.'

There were a number of well-known visitors to the garden including Wilkinson and Judge Chapman. They exchanged plants. For a filbert tree from Chapman, Bradey gave 50 broccoli plants, polyanthus, a dozen sweet briar roses, and four rhubarb plants. Later, he gave Chapman three dahlias. From St Hill, Bradey bought two cherry trees, four currant trees, two multiflora roses, and two unidentified flowering trees for the princely sum of fivepence.[49]

Boot-making seems to have become secondary until June 1846, when this announcement (at right) appeared in the paper.

CHEAP BOOTS

F.H. Bradey having commenced business once more in the boot trade begs to announce to numerous friends and former patrons that after a few more preliminaries he will be prepared to supply his customers with an article in his former original and unrivalled style.

A great supply of colonial made water tight, elastic sides and bluchers on hand at reduced prices.

Francis Bradey
Next door to Nelson Hotel
Lambton Quay

June 11 1846

It would seem that he was operating on part of his Lambton Quay Town Acre. That same year, on 13 December, a new *Wellington Almanac* came out which, Bradey hoped, would 'sustain its past reputation for usefulness'.

Bradey was anxious to claim his Country Acres in the Porirua district. But because of the disputes over land ownership with the local iwi in Porirua, Bradey's land order of August 1839 was not signed until 27 April 1847, and at last he was able to start farming.[50]

Pit-sawn timber from the property was used to build his two-storeyed house in what is today part of Whitby. It burnt down accidentally in 1949.[51] Bradey kept his business going in Wellington, living in Mulgrave Street during

---

47 Bradey MS Folders 1 & 2, F., Bradey collection, Alexander Turnbull Library.
48 Ibid.
49 Ibid.
50 Ward, Louis E., *Early Wellington*, Whitcombe & Tombs, 1928.
51 *Paremata Story*, Paremata Residents' Association.

the

NEW-ZEALAND LAND COMPANY.

Certificate of Selection.

No. 777.

I, the undersigned Principal Agent of the New-Zealand Land Company in New-Zealand, do hereby certify, that, in pursuance of a Land Order, dated at London *the* First *day of* August *1839. Number* One Thousand and Twentyfive *the Lands hereinafter mentioned, that is to say** the Preliminary Country Section No 37 on the Surveyor General's Plan of the District of Tukapu being bounded on the North by No 36 and 38 on the South by unsurveyed land on the East by No 39 and on the West by No 33.

* Here insert a full description of the Land according to the Surveyor-General's Map.

have been chosen and selected by H C Kettle for Francis Brady *of* Wellington New Zealand

This Certificate is accepted by the said Francis Brady *as conclusive evidence of the selection, and also as an actual delivery of the Possession of the Lands.*

Dated at Wellington *the* Twenty seventh *day of* April 1847.

Registered in the Colonial Land Office by me, David Lewis *Principal Clerk.*

W. Wakefield *Principal Agent.*

[By courtesy Mr. Charles Bradey, Duck Creek.

Fig. 30A.—"Pahautanui." Reproduction of a Certificate of Selection or Land Order, dated 1st August, 1839.

New Zealand Land Company Certificate of Selection No 777.

week, but spending weekends on his country property, which he and his sons developed into a productive farm. One son, Alfred, stayed on at Tamworth Cottage in Newtown, while Frederick worked the Porirua block.

There is little evidence of Bradey's gardening activities after he obtained title to his Country Acres. Horticultural Society Shows were in abeyance through the 1850s and did not revive until a combined Agricultural, Horticultural and Pastoral Show was staged in November 1862, by which time Bradey was 70 years of age. Bradey died in 1872, but his sons and grandsons continued farming until the property was subdivided. No sketches or photographs of his Newtown property have been found, but three of his tools hang in a privately owned Wellington spa room along with an extensive collection of other items used in early colonial days.

Wellington Independent, 25 August 1857

The Bonnie Blooming Hawthorn

FOR SALE, 100,000 two year old PLANTS, @ 30s per 1000. Apply to

ALFRED BRADEY,
Tamworth Cottage,
JOHN HOUGHTON,
Willis Street, or to
FREDERICK BRADEY,
Porirua Harbour.

21 August 1857

James Bryant

James Bryant and his wife, as mentioned in Chapter 2, originally came to New Zealand to work and keep house for Francis Molesworth. Bryant had been foreman gardener at Pencarrow, the home of Molesworth's oldest brother. After Francis Molesworth's death, Bryant was employed as sawyer and gardener by Alfred Ludlam until about 1856. For the next four years he leased a large garden and orchard. Unable to obtain it freehold, he moved to Johnsonville, at first splitting shingles, then taking over the Ames Hotel at Johnsonville in 1860.

Frank Bradey's tools, dating from 1840.
J. Nauta, Museum of New Zealand C.T.15696/123-124

James Bryant.
Onslow Historical Society

Bryant and his sons worked all around the Ohariu area, plying the various skills needed in the district until Bryant purchased half of Section 25 Ohariu. Here the family developed Huia Farm. A simple cottage was built from their own pit-sawn timber, with a veranda added later. Even the bricks for the chimney were made from clay on the property.[52]

The Bryant family felled and burnt the bush and sowed wheat between the logs and stumps. Once pasture was established, they ran and milked a herd of cows. The butter pats they made had a rose design on top and were sold to private customers in Wellington. Bryant also ran sheep and sold their wool. Eventually, the property extended to 3,000 acres, carrying 1,700 sheep and 300 cattle, and the Bryants were Ohariu's 'wool kings'.

Bryant died in 1902. His will, written just before his death, described him as 'James Bryant, gentleman'. He had been successful in New Zealand,

James Bryant and family in front of his cottage, Huia Farm, c 1876. (Mrs Bryant died in 1877.) Built in the 1860s, the timber for the cottage was pit sawn and bricks were made on the property. The roof was shingled, and the window panes were small. The verandah shown here was a later addition. It had taken 36 years from his time of arrival in New Zealand for Bryant to reach this level of independence.
Onslow Historical Society

and was no longer subservient to the class system of his birth. The humble gardener who brought camellias out from Cornwall in 1840 had done well.

Hard manual work such as splitting shingles, felling bush, sawing timber,

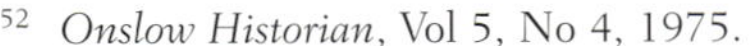

52 *Onslow Historian*, Vol 5, No 4, 1975.

Home of William and Josephine Bryant (née Bassett), c 1900. The pines and macrocarpas in the background and foreground were planted in the 1870–80s and are now large trees. The shrub on the left lawn could be a camellia.
Onslow Historical Society

making bricks, and erecting fences, does not allow much time for gardening, even for a professional gardener such as James Bryant. The next generation in Ohariu Valley was more fortunate. The three cottages are similar in style, with roses visible outside the Kilsby home.

[Left] Home of Jim Kilsby and family, c 1890s. Jim Kilsby was a son of Ohariu timber miller George Kilsby.
Onslow Historical Society

[Right] Alfred and Margaret Best (née Hume), c 1890s. G. Best was an well-known early settler in Ohariu Valley. The garden is not as well developed as the Bryants' or Kilsbys'.
Onslow Historical Society

The Stebbings at Pine Hill

Pine Hill Farm at Halfway (Glenside) was established by Benjamin Stebbings in 1863. The original cottage, although altered over the years, was occupied by the family until 1951. It was demolished in 1974.[53]

Stebbings's only son, Henry, married in 1906. From that marriage, there were twin girls, Eva and Eileen, born in 1907 and a son, Leonard. Trees were among Eva's earliest memories of her childhood at Pine Hill. If Eva's recollections are accurate, the macrocarpa and pines would have been planted in the 1870s and 1880s:

Pine Hill, Glenside, just prior to demolition, 1974. The huge macrocarpa in the front garden was referred to by Eva.
Onslow Historical Society

> My earliest memories of Pine Hill are of trees, as a tiny child I remember looking out the back door and being entranced by the layers and layers of moving green as the branches of tall trees moved in the wind. My father and grandfather planted trees everywhere round the home section both for beauty and for shelter. Two trees stood out above all others. One was a huge macrocarpa that stood in the front garden and was used by generations of magpies for their early morning carolling. The other was a tree of the pinus variety. My father called it *Pinus alypensis*[54].... It was a magnificent tree and grew in the lower orchard. The needles were much shorter than those of the radiata and more of a grey-green, with much smaller cones. From the hill above the orchard this tree looked like an enormous round grey-green pin-cushion. Unfortunately it had a short life with innumerable branches growing out of it. In time dead needles, wind blown rubbish and soil collected there and caused the tree to start rotting. In an extra heavy gale it split completely in half and soon afterwards the remains had to be felled.

Eva gives details of the orchard that are especially interesting. Estimating that there were 70 trees, she listed the following apple varieties:

(E early, C cooking, K keeper).

E	Irish Peach*		Jennington*	CK New England Pigeon C
C	Yorkshire Greening (Alfrieston)*		Northern Spy*	
C	Codlin*		Mayton's Red	
C	Brabant*		Russet*	
	Maidens Blush*		Tom Pitt	
	Peasegood*	CK	Beefington	* Mentioned in Thompson's *Gardener's Assistant*.

She singled out currants – red, black, and white – for special mention, remembering vividly currant pies and the crushed berries sprinkled with sugar and covered with cream – delectable!

Pine Hill was divided into four blocks, and each block, according to Eva, contained some native bush. A stand of olearia beside a stream was mentioned, the only group on the farm.[55] The exact date of the name Pine Hill is unknown, but it appears to have been in use by 1891, when the conifers that had been planted in the 1870s had become a dominant feature in the landscape.

Country Acres come to town

As the nineteenth century ended, the change from bush settlement to suburbia was becoming evident. Each valley in Wellington had perhaps been more like an American or Australian frontier town than the peaceful English meadows nostalgically remembered by the settlers. The reality was much more like that shown in the Daisy Hill photograph or the 1930s photograph of Papanui station, a coastal hill country farm. Cleared of bush, the steep hills were scarred by erosion. The only green came from the pines and

---

53 *Onslow Historian*, Vol 22, Nos 1 and 2, 1992.

54 *Pinus halipensis*. Listed by J. Buchanan 18/8/79 as making rapid growth and suitable for New Zealand. Shepherd W. and Cook W., op. cit.

55 Stebbings, Eva, *Onslow Historian*, Vol 22, Nos 1 and 2, 1992.

Papanui station, Ohariu, c 1930. A scarred, bare landscape relieved only by pines and macrocarpas planted in the 1880s.
Onslow Historical Society

Hills behind Ngaio returning from pasture land to native forest.
J. Nauta, Museum of New Zealand

macrocarpas planted in the 1880s.

The first substantial homes began to appear in the 1850s. Chapman led the way as early as 1847 in Karori, Ludlam in 1850 at the Hutt, William Fox in Ngaio in 1857, John Chew also in Ngaio three years later, Rhodes in Wadestown in the 1860s, and Stebbings at Glenside in 1863. The houses of the wealthy began to exhibit conspicuous displays of flower beds and well-manicured lawns, while tradesmen and wage earners with smaller

Eagles' farmlet, Ngaio. Vegetable growing, particularly of potatos, still continued on smaller sections in the 1920s.
Onslow Historical Society

State houses, Bould Street, Johnsonville, 1944. Built on large sections, vegetable gardens were common.

John Pascoe Collection, Alexander Turnbull Library, National Library of New Zealand, Te Puna Mātauranga, F-1181-1/4

Perched for a view on very steep sections, these State houses in Homebush, Khandallah, were exposed to all winds. Gardens, especially the vegetable plot, became almost non-existent.

Onslow Historical Society

houses used their sections for the growing of produce.

Apart from the properties already mentioned, and those in the next chapter, there was no proliferation of outstanding gardens. Horticultural societies were established in the suburbs and subdivisions continued. The advent of state houses in the 1940s, each on its own large block of land, made another kind of impact on the landscape. Home-growing of vegetables on the quarter-acre section was common, except where houses were perched on very steep sections.

Many of these large sections have since been subdivided. Infill housing in both city and suburb has reduced the size of gardens, which are often replaced by ornamental courtyards, decks, and indoor plants. These are all extremely attractive and plant nurseries are full of customers replacing seasonal plants for these small areas.

Supermarkets with a huge range of vegetables on sale discourage the home grower and skills are being lost. Within the bounds of the old Homewood 100-acre block, for example, there are only a handful of owners who still grow vegetables – the author is one of them! How would Chapman view this state of affairs today?

PLAN
OF
THE TOWN OF
WELLINGTON
PORT NICHOLSON
the First and Principal Settlement
of the
NEW ZEALAND COMPANY
14th August
1840
LAMBTON HARBOUR
MOUNT VICTORIA
MOUNT ALBERT
MOUNT COOK
TINAKORE

Chapter 4

THE TOWN ACRES

SETTLERS' GARDENS

The 1,100 town acres laid out for settlement at the southern end of the harbour by surveyor Mein-Smith and his team covered the flats of Thorndon and Te Aro, and the slopes along The Terrace. Mein-Smith was required to provide open space. He did the only thing he could, and reserved the inner faces of the steep hills surrounding the limited area of flat land. This public open space was called the Town Belt, as it is still known today.[1]

The surveyor's grid for the sections was laid over all, irrespective of Maori pa and gardens, hills, gullies, and swamp. The plan did not allow for jetties or quays, but instead for an area of the Te Aro swamp to be developed as an inland anchorage (on the site of the present Basin Reserve), with the entrance channel running between Kent and Cambridge Terraces. These were to be the boulevards required under the Company's instructions for the layout of Wellington.

For the few informed settlers who may have aspired to English landscape design as promoted by Capability Brown and Humphrey Repton, with its sweeping lawns or pasture interrupted with groups of trees or shrubs, the reality of the topography, the limited area of flat land, and the wind must soon have squashed their grand intentions.

The Survey Map of 1841 is an excellent reference, showing the swamp and proposed Basin, the Town Belt, the 1,100 one-acre sections, Native Reserves, and Government Reserves. Clay Point (now known as Stewart Dawson's corner) was a small promontory on the shoreline that divided the Thorndon Flat from the larger Te Aro Flat. The Terrace, which ran along the hillside above the beach, was broken at the Kumutoto ravine, around the present-day Woodward Street, and was bridged at a later date.

The sections on the upper side of Tinakori Road and those on The Terrace were sloping, but the Māori gardens on the lower side of Tinakori Road were low lying. The town acres along The Terrace and in Thorndon were covered mainly in manuka and kanuka, those at Te Aro were covered in either fern, flax, or raupo. Settlement on the town acres was therefore much easier than on heavily forested country acres. Settlers' houses were first built along The Terrace, the Thorndon Flat, and the northern part of Te Aro Flat.

Development of the sections lagged in the swampy areas and also, because access was difficult, in Oriental Bay and Newtown. These parts of the town went ahead only after the 1855 earthquake had raised the land.

At first all travel between the Hutt Valley and the new town at Thorndon was by boat. Dicky Barrett ran a cutter, the *Harriett*; a Mr Wright ran a ferryboat; Captain Daniells' boat carried passengers and cargo. Otherwise, it was a case of walking, which was possible only at low tide because of the streams to be forded at Ngauranga and Kaiwharawhara.

(*Opposite*) Plan of the Town of Wellington, Port Nicholson, *1841, Mein-Smith. Wellington was the first and principal settlement of the New Zealand Company. Government sites are pink, Native Reserves green. From* Maps, Plans and Views Relative to the Colonisation of New Zealand, 1840-1842.

Museum of New Zealand Te Papa Tongarewa

[1] See Chapter 9.

Landslip caused by earthquake near Wellington New Zealand Jan 1855, *watercolour by Charles Emilius Gold.*

Alexander Turnbull Library, National Library of New Zealand, Te Puna Mātauranga, B-103-016

There was considerable danger in travelling by boat. On 25 August 1840, around the time the decision was taken to establish the new site for Britannia, a tragedy occurred when a boat from the new settlement capsized 100 yards from the beach at Petone in a fierce southerly. Of the 12 people on board, Frank Bradey, boot-maker and horticulturist, was one of only three survivors.[2] The *New Zealand Gazette* of 29 August 1840 stated that Mr Wright's boat was the only properly equipped boat in the harbour. So urgent was the need for better access between Petone and Wellington, as the town was now called, a road was completed that linked the two the next year. The *New Zealand Gazette* of 9 October 1841 said:

> **The road from Wellington to Petone is now completed and perfectly easy to be gone over by vehicle. Mr G. Phillips with his dray and team of bullocks has had the honour of being the first to travel over it which he did two or three days ago and arrived here with flying colours.**

At best, the tracks and roads in the developing township were extremely primitive, and the track along the foreshore was dependent on the tides. It took a large earthquake to provide a solution to the latter problem. A big earthquake in 1848 severely damaged or destroyed buildings, but the one in 1855 (estimated at a massive 8.2 on the Richter scale) effected major changes to the landscape. One of them, a slip that partially blocked the existing road, was recorded at the time.

---

[2] Ward, Louis E., *Early Wellington*.

With the whole of the western shoreline of the harbour having been raised a metre or so on average, there was now sufficient room for a wider road from Wellington to the Hutt. There was no longer a need for a retaining wall along the Lambton Harbour waterfront and Oriental Bay. The swampy land at Te Aro was lifted up and drained, which meant the proposed inland anchorage was no longer possible. The Hutt Valley, too, underwent changes, with the draining of swampy land and the extending of the Petone foreshore.

The houses and gardens that developed in Wellington were the product of various influences: the climate and soil, the hilly terrain, and an immediate need to produce vegetables and fruit. Many early sketches emphasise the kitchen garden. There is little written information on the gardens, but from the pictorial records it is evident that English terms such as 'gardenesque', 'picturesque', and 'naturalistic' were not applicable.[3] Gale-force northerlies, salt-laden southerly storms, and the topography were, and still are, the principal designers of Wellington's houses and gardens. Wellington architect Bill Toomath maintains that Wellington is one of the most difficult places in which to build.[4]

Fashion came later, when features such as drives, paths, fences, ponds, fountains, rockeries, sunken gardens, patios, ferneries, herbaceous borders, and herb gardens became possible. Nonetheless, the plants mentioned in settlers' letters and diaries were not only those necessary for survival or for their sentimental value but were often the latest in fashion, for example, roses, calceoleria, agaves, camellias, and rhododendrons.

A flat town acre allowed ample room for the house, a kitchen garden, an orchard, and grazing for a horse and a cow. Fox's panorama (below) shows there was no shortage of timber for the fences. The limited number of town

Section of Panorama of Wellington Harbour 1846 by *William Fox. Above the shore development are houses along Wellington Terrace. Neat timber fences surround the geometrically laid-out gardens of cottages in Thorndon.*
Hocken Library, Otago University

3 'Picturesque' was a fashion of the eighteenth century; a 'picturesque' garden was laid out to look like a picture. 'Gardenesque' style developed in reaction to the picturesque: the garden was designed to contrast with its surrounding landscape. Arbours, trelliswork, parterres, and bedding-out schemes were all features of the gardenesque garden.

4 'You have the steep and often loose terrain. You have the great amount of wind to brace against and you have the rain that can drive vertically up some hillsides .... There is a drama to the landscape dominated by that harbour which we all stretch and perch to see.' Toomath, Bill, *The Landscape*, 1987.

Henry Wright and Reginald Wright in the garden of Henry's house in Britomart Street, Berhampore, 1892. The height of the trellis work in the background indicates the need for shelter.

Henry Wright Collection, Alexander Turnbull Library, National Library of New Zealand, Te Puna Mātauranga, G-66324-1/2

[Below right] View looking up Hawkstone Street to the beginning of Karori Road and Mr Brandon's house, 1847. On the right is Wickstead's four-roomed English-built cottage with veranda, and with peas, beans, turnips, parsley, spinach, beetroot, and mignonette in the garden. Next to it, partially obscured, is the Cadets' College, which housed survey cadets of the New Zealand Company. St Hill's gothic cottage, with carved bargeboards and finials, appears above these. The house and kitchen garden on the left of the road belonged to Mr Joah Wakefield.

S.C. Brees, Alexander Turnbull Library, National Library of New Zealand, Te Puna Mātauranga, A-109-031

[Below left] This watercolour by S.C. Brees shows a cottage, with a kitchen garden in the rear, on the slopes below the court buildings, c 1843.

Alexander Turnbull Library, National Library of New Zealand, Te Puna Mātauranga, B-031-009

acres, the wind, and the hilly nature of the area invited early subdivision. Except where the resulting sections were tiny, such as Lorne Street, Haining Street, and Saunders Lane, the kitchen garden and orchard continued to be important, though on a smaller scale, as shown in an 1892 photograph of Henry Wright's Berhampore garden.

The kitchen garden in Britain was highly evolved by the end of the nineteenth century. The growing of fruit and vegetables was essential, and it is the Victorian kitchen garden that was transported to New Zealand. Early kitchen gardens in Wellington were extensive, as is evident from the diaries of Chapman and Parnell in Karori, Trotter at Lower Hutt, and Bradey in Newtown.

Trotter and Bradey spent many hours on their potatoes. Other root crops, such as parsnips, swedes, turnips, beetroot, and carrots were soon established, along with green vegetables, such as beans, peas, cabbage, cauliflower, lettuce, leeks, celery, spinach, and, of course, rhubarb. A remarkable variety of seed was available from agents as well as the *Gazette* office. A few settlers built cold frames and 'lights' to take cucumbers and melons until they realised they could be grown outdoors. Orchards and small fruits were established and, when living conditions became easier, there was the luxury of the flower garden. It took some time, and after considerable subdivision, before fashion dictated that front and side gardens were for ornamental use only, leaving the back for the vegetable garden.

Although familiar varieties of vegetables were available, failures were common, mainly owing to poor storage on the long voyage out from Britain or delays in on-shipment from Sydney. Viable onion seed was extremely difficult to obtain. Many fruits – strawberries, gooseberries, apples, pears, peaches, plums – were introduced as seed, so there were innumerable varieties, some good and some worthless. Early selection and, in particular, the exchange of budwood among the settlers soon provided better varieties.

The settlers used traditional techniques. Soil was trenched and spade dug, refuse was composted, and there was plenty of animal manure to improve the soil. There was no revulsion about using human waste in gardens in Victorian and Edwardian times. Night soil, mixed with soot and ashes, sometimes known as 'native guano', was available in the 1850s from

5 See Chapter 7.

6 Taylor, Nancy M. (ed.), *Journal of Ensign Best*, Government Printer, 1966.

nightman-gardeners such as Henry Woouldom.[5]

In the young colony, the necessity for survival occupied all, even temporary residents such as Lieutenant Best, who had arrived in June 1840 with 30 soldiers to control the 'rebel settlers'. Best procured a dwelling of sorts near Pipitea Pa, at the junction of where today Hobson, Davis, and Moturoa Streets converge. He stayed until February and spent most of his leisure time working. He made handles for tools, ground chisels, cut down a tree for fencing, and broke up the ground in front of the house. By 26 August, he was able to say that his garden was fairly well stocked and, except for two gates, the fence was finished. It was very windy and he was afraid the strong winds would injure the plants.[6]

Brees' cottage, looking down Hawkstone Street, c 1845. There is a large subsistence garden with small shrub area in front of the house. A kahikatea, spared the axe, remained a landmark for many years. The fence on the left enclosed Hill's house and fields.

S.C. Brees, Alexander Turnbull Library, National Library of New Zealand, Te Puna Mātauranga, B-031-021

Robert Stokes, the Secretary of the newly-formed Horticultural Society, visited Sydney and brought back plants. By August 1842, not only was he growing plenty of vegetables but he also had rhubarb, strawberries, raspberries, gooseberries, red, white and black currants, apricots, figs, several varieties of plums, apples, and pears. Not everyone could visit Sydney, but vegetable seeds were readily available and the interchange of plant material increased after the Horticultural Society was formed at the end of 1841.

Te Aro Flat, c 1843. The houses of Strang and Stokes are on the extreme right, fronting on to Woolcombe Street, later known as The Terrace. Scrub in the foreground and behind Woolcombe Street also covered The Terrace slopes (and Mount St Cemetery) as far as Te Aro Valley.

S.C. Brees, Pictorial Illustrations of New Zealand

In Thorndon, Colonel William Wakefield's garden was both a utility and a demonstration garden, showing newcomers what would grow in the new settlement. Prefabricated in England, his house was erected on the rise where Parliament stands today, with its entrance facing Sydney Street East. Brees noted the large selection of plants and the neat and tidy garden, even though

Colonel Wakefield's residence, Wellington, c *1845. Engraved by Henry Melville from a drawing by S.C. Brees, London, 1847. A peaked roof supports a veranda with forked branches. The use of tree limbs as rustic posts for the veranda was a fashion established by Decimus Burton in his work for the London Zoo. A smaller attached cottage lies to the rear. Wellington Terrace houses are on the left, with manuka scrub above the road as well as in the foreground.*

Alexander Turnbull Library, National Library of New Zealand, Te Puna Mātauranga, A-109-032

The position of the Government Domain, surrounding streets, and the Town Acres of Thorndon.

Thomas Ward, Survey Plan, 1891

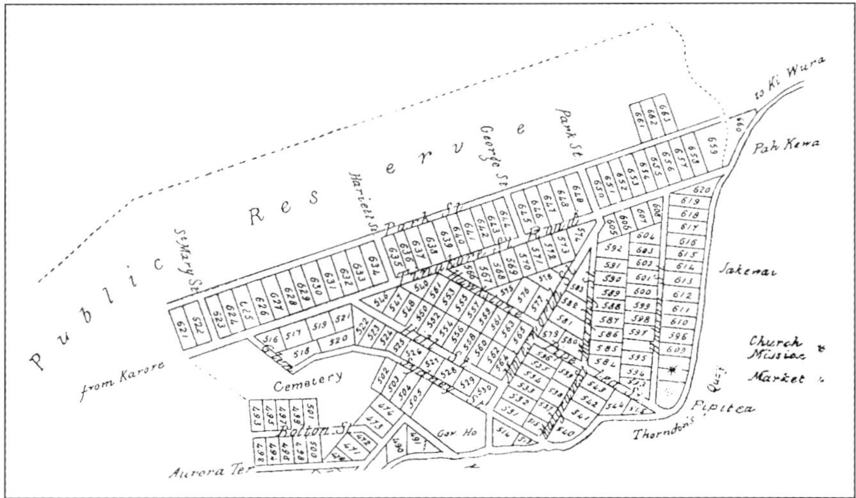

it was exposed to the winds. In 1842, Henry Petre observed that Wakefield had successfully raised English oaks from acorns. Wakefield was generous, and gave cuttings and plants for their own gardens to many new arrivals. The white moss rose was a favourite given to many, including Eleanor Petre.

The Prime Minister's House, looking south over the kitchen garden, c 1890s. Tinakori Road is in the foreground.

Museum of New Zealand Te Papa Tongarewa 1273

An extensive kitchen garden is shown in the 1880s on town acres at 630 and 631 Tinakori Road, which later became Premier House.

From the beginning, social class and economic factors played a part in shaping and determining the gardens around Wellington's homes. Wakefield's garden on the Government Domain and St Hill's attractive Hawkestone Street home with garden, orchard, and stables contrast markedly with small cottages such as Stock's in Abel Smith Street, although we don't know how extensive his garden was. The raupo thatch on cottages like Stock's was outlawed during the 1840s because it was a fire hazard.

In 1850, en route to Canterbury, the Godleys occupied a rented property not far from the Government Domain for a brief time. Charlotte Godley described the garden as follows:

> It is very pretty with sweet-briar, honeysuckle clove pinks, and white moss roses and other real English plants scarcely out of flower and over run with fuchsias which make hedges almost .... There is a kitchen garden too so that we have been eating our own cabbages, horse-radish and lettuce and there are lots of watercress in the stream close by.

When Mrs Eyre and Mrs McCleverty gave her a bunch of violets in the spring, Charlotte wrote cheerfully: 'The room is sweet and besides has two nosegays of wallflowers and stocks.'[7] Charlotte's letter is so optimistic one could be forgiven for imagining that Wellington was a beautiful place, somewhat along the lines of an attractive English village:

> It is I suppose rather characteristic of an English colony that the gardens here are full of English plants and trees. We have in this garden for example fuchsias, roses (including white moss roses which don't seem to do very well) sweet-briar, (clove) pinks, honeysuckle, daffodils (just now coming into flower) ... and one oak, about 8 feet high.[8]

Te Aro Flat, c. 1858. This photograph by A.H. Stock was taken three years after the 1855 earthquake. The area is no longer swampy. The simple cottages and houses correspond to Charlotte Godley's observations of 1850, but there is an encouraging amount of greenery. St Peter's Church, built in 1857 on the corner of Willis and Ghuznee Streets, is conspicuous.

Alexander Turnbull Library, National Library of New Zealand, Te Puna Mātauranga, F-34971-1/2

Two years later, in 1852, John Shaw echoed Charlotte Godley's optimism, saying that many of the houses formed delightful residences with pretty gardens in front.[9] Ten years later, in 1862, Edwin Hodder remarked that the town abounded with tasteful houses, mostly wooden with gables and green verandas, surrounded with gardens in which the Australian plants acacia, blue gum, and mimosa trees flourished.[10] Australian plants provided much-needed shelter.

The cottage and its garden

Of necessity, the majority of Wellington's early homes were cottages in scale and in character. As the nineteenth century progressed, they continued to be used and added to, and new ones built, often alongside the larger, newly constructed houses of the wealthy.

The simple one- or two-roomed cottage or cabin is both old and universal. It has been made of every material – raupo, wood, cob, slab, or wattle and daub. The basic plan was easily added to, with a lean-to at the back or the attachment of another similar unit. A veranda added to the front was often partially or completely glassed in later.

In 1850, Walter Mantell's simple cottage in Sydney Street West occupied two town acres of land and in time a well-developed garden surrounded an expanded cottage.

The photograph of Te Aro Flat c 1858 shows simple cottages and houses. The Aro Street sections were narrow, with rough paling fences, but by the 1870s most of the cottages had neat, extensive vegetable gardens at the rear, with flowers and shrubs in the front. Each was completely different from the next, but there was not one 'Cottage Garden' in the modern sense.[11]

Walter Mantell's sketch of his cottage in Sydney Street, 1850, in relation to Tinakori Road. The timber for the cottage was cut by John Kilmister near Wilton's bush and carried on his back to Sydney Street. Original sketch in letter from W. Mantell to R. Mantell, 9 Oct 1850.

Alexander Turnbull Library, National Library of New Zealand, Te Puna Mātauranga, F-117572-1/2

By the time Wellington became the capital in 1865, Hawkestone and Hill Streets had mellowed, many cottages had been enlarged, and the gardens were well laid out. As the population moved outwards, cottages were built

7 Godley, Charlotte, *Letters from Early New Zealand*, 27 August 1850.
8 Godley, Charlotte, op. cit., 12 September 1850.
9 Shaw, John, *A Tramp to the Diggings: Being Notes of a Ramble in Australia and New Zealand in 1852*, London, 1852.
10 Hodder, Edwin, *Memories of New Zealand Life*, London, 1862.
11 See Chapter 5.
12 See Chapter 7.

[Above] Cuba Street, 1864. Shingled cottages with picket fences built close to the footpath. The gardens have shrubs up to fence height and seem full, and there are probably vegetable gardens at the rear. The cottage on the left is the house and factory of Edward Dixon, Ginger Beer Manufacturer. The youth holding a rifle is a reminder of the militia in those days.

Alexander Turnbull Library, National Library of New Zealand, Te Puna Mātauranga, F-60601-1/2

[Above right] Cottages on the slopes of Mt Victoria, c 1870s, overlooking Te Aro Flat and foreshore before the reclamation of this part of the harbour. There is room for a garden round the cottages, but only a few of those on the left have trees and shrubs.

Museum of New Zealand Te Papa Tongarewa

on quite large blocks of land. Cottages ranged from the desirable to the unattractive, with or without gardens, as the photographs show.

[Right] Te Aro reclamation, looking west, c 1880s. Some of the cottages in the foreground have neat utility gardens, but they are under pressure from encroaching city businesses and industrial buildings. The back yard is dominated by clothes lines, vegetables, woodshed, and privy (often on the back boundary). There are a few trees and a hedge in the properties in the foreground. The rough wooden fences date from the first period.

Wellington City Council

A raw Wellington landscape: Holloway Road. off Aro Street, c 1880. After the bush was cleared, Wellington's hills and valley decided the position of the houses and the dimensions of the open space. Gardening was difficult and in many cases minimal. The house in the left foreground has a lawn and shrub border on either side of steps up to the house.

J.N. Taylor Collection, Alexander Turnbull Library

Also C.T.15696/37-42

Possibly Tinakori Road, c 1875. This shingle-roofed cottage is rough fenced to protect the garden from the cows. Annie Bramley, wife of the Botanic Garden's Custodian, is seated.

Museum of New Zealand Te Papa Tongarewa B.16209

A cottage with steps to the veranda, 205 Ohiro Road, Brooklyn, c 1880–1890. Designed to suit the section, the planting is simple. The service area at the back is screened by a trellis.

Museum of New Zealand Te Papa Tongarewa, B.14262

The residence of Louis Christeson and family, Willis Street, Wellington, c 1895. Part of the veranda has been glassed in. For Wellington, this was an exceptionally well-designed garden, with a variety of roses and other flowers. The circular path gives an air of formality. Details of the back garden are shown below.

Harkness Collection, Alexander Turnbull Library, National Library of New Zealand, Te Puna Mātauranga F.619161/2

In Louis Christeson's garden, near the conservatory, with a drive and carriage in the background.

Harkness Collection, Alexander Turnbull Library, National Library of New Zealand, Te Puna Mātauranga, F-62476-1/2, PAColl-4953

View of the rear of Louis Christeson's house in Willis Street.

Harkness Collection, Alexander Turnbull Library, National Library of New Zealand, Te Puna Mātauranga, F-62475-1/2, PAColl-4953

Inside the conservatory at the rear of Louis Christeson's house.

Harkness Collection, Alexander Turnbull Library, National Library of New Zealand, Te Puna Mātauranga, F-62480-1/2, PAColl-4953

A Newtown house, c 1890s, 'perching for a view'. There is a shelter belt of conifers in the foreground, fencing, and some planting.

Henry Wright Collection, Alexander Turnbull Library, National Library of New Zealand, Te Puna Mātauranga, G-66337-1/2, PAColl-5032

Villas and mansions

By the end of the second decade, as the colony became more established, wealthy settlers and those whose fortunes had prospered vacated or replaced their humble dwellings, building grander homes with more extensive grounds.

There was not a great deal to distinguish the gardens of villas and mansions from those of the cottages. The larger houses built in the city were akin to those seen in other parts of New Zealand, but climate and topography decided the garden. Deciduous trees did not flourish. In steep suburbs such as Brooklyn and Kelburn, the villa gardens developed in a way that was uniquely Wellington. Houses perched or stretched to see the view. Semi-detached houses were quite common and a few terraced houses were built.

All were set in a bare landscape that gave a harshness to nineteenth-century Wellington. An 1860s sketch for a superior cottage-style residence was drawn against barren Town Belt hills. When built, it was set alongside a two-storey villa with a side entrance. The hills behind were stark. More substantial homes began to appear in the 1860s and 1870s, but the surrounding hills remained bare until well into the twentieth century.

The lodgings of John Pearce on Wellington Terrace, c 1850. A well-fenced, well-formed garden with sloping hill behind. The garden arch is the earliest yet located. Ink and watercolour by John Pearse.

Alexander Turnbull Library, National Library of New Zealand, Te Puna Mātauranga, E-455-f-039-4

The Terrace

The town acres on The Terrace were amongst the first to be settled, and with only manuka or kanuka to be removed they were relatively well developed by the 1850s. Halfway along Thomas Drake, who had arrived on the *Aurora*, had erected a kitset house on his town acre. By 1850 John Kilmister had established a small goat farm. Sketches and photographs show superior cottages and villas towards the northern end of The Terrace, with well-developed gardens.

Town acres 440 and 441 in Woolcombe Street, as the southern end of The Terrace was originally known, were fortunate choices for Robert Stokes and Robert Strang, as both men were interested in gardens. Their sections were situated in a hollow near the present-day intersection with Ghuznee Street, where the bush covering the Brooklyn Hills and Te Aro Valley gave way to manuka-kanuka scrub. It was fairly sheltered from the north-west,

Looking down The Terrace towards Thorndon, just above the Woodward Street intersection, c 1880s. The widening of the road has left the houses above the road with damaged fences. Cattle driven along this road made it more unpleasant in wet weather. The bare Tinakori hills are in the distance.

Alexander Turnbull Library, National Library of New Zealand, Te Puna Mātauranga, F-35521-1/2, MS-Papers-0148-111A-075-e

Southern end of The Terrace, known originally as Woolcombe Street, c 1870s. Ghuznee Street is on the left opposite Robert Stokes' house and garden on Town Acre 441. The bush on the far hills has gone and so too has the manuka/kanuka along The Terrace.

Ward's *Early Wellington*

with good soil at the bottom of the slope. The land would have been easy to build on, and the large sections, warm and sheltered, lent themselves to open spaces, lawns, borders, and gardens rich in horticultural treasures.

By 1842 Stokes had not only established many fruit and vegetable varieties but also a wide selection of ornamental plants obtained mainly from Sydney – magnolias, camellias, daphne, oleander, honeysuckle, jasmine, roses, elder, privet, and passionflower.[13]

Strang had arrived on the *Bengal Merchant,* bringing seeds, including tree seeds with him. Strang's daughter married Donald Maclean and his property, Dalmuir, later came into Maclean's possession, while Stokes's property, called St Ruadhan, was eventually owned by Sir Donald's son Douglas (later Sir Douglas), who was born at Dalmuir in 1852. Douglas Maclean thus became owner of both properties.

[Above] House and garden at the intersection of Bowen Street with The Terrace, 1854. There is a paling fence, a shrub frontage, and a utility garden to the right. The tree on the left may be a eucalypt; other plants are indeterminate.

Richard Taylor Papers, Alexander Turnbull Library, National Library of New Zealand, Te Puna Mātauranga, F-44662-1/2

[13] Ward, Louis E, *Early Wellington*, Whitcombe & Tombs Ltd, 1928, p. 319.

Views of Robert Stokes' property, St Ruadhan, in the 1920s

[Below] Native trees, palm, and flowers with a garden seat around an oak tree in the garden of St Ruadhan, the house belonging to Sir Douglas Maclean, c 1923. Note the Victorian use of plants bordering the lawn.

Alexander Turnbull Library, National Library of New Zealand, Te Puna Mātauranga, C-16678-1/2, PA1-o-615

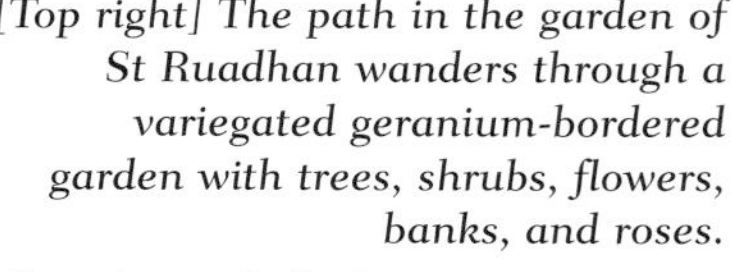

[Top right] The path in the garden of St Ruadhan wanders through a variegated geranium-bordered garden with trees, shrubs, flowers, banks, and roses.

Alexander Turnbull Library, National Library of New Zealand, Te Puna Mātauranga, C-16675-1/2, PA1-o-615

[Centre right] The path to a classical bolster-shaped sundial in the garden of St Ruadhan, the reverse view to the picture above.

Alexander Turnbull Library, National Library of New Zealand, Te Puna Mātauranga, C-16676-1/2, PA1-o-615

[Bottom right] The front path of St Ruadhan, leading to The Terrace. A luxuriant garden with native cabbage tree.

Alexander Turnbull Library, National Library of New Zealand, Te Puna Mātauranga, C-16674-1/2, PA1-o-615

In the 1870s, next door to Dalmuir, George Denton built a two-storeyed house he called Fernhill. (Strang and Stoke had moved on by this time.) Denton was a member of the New Zealand Philosophical Society and Secretary of the Acclimatisation Society. At Fernhill he bred trout and kept birds brought out from England – blackbirds, thrushes, starlings, and finches – that were subsequently liberated in Wellington. For two years after the house was built, Denton employed a man to plant trees. The photograph here gives no indication of any trees surviving from the original bush, so perhaps the nikau and the rata seen in the 1990s were transplanted here in the 1870s.

George Denton's son William, born in 1867, inherited his father's love of nature. In his turn, he continued planting, especially native plants, many of which came from the Tararua Ranges:

> At the back of the house a spring wells up and has been diverted into a little trenched rivulet that half circles the yard. Here mosses, ferns and curious alpine plants creep or bend according to their kind and different varieties of ponga ferns shade them. Twisty steps turn in a maze in the bush that slopes up the hill. Here almost every tree or shrub is different and each one has a story that Mr Denton can relate with accurate knowledge.[14]

Not all were native plants. A 1923 illustration shows conifers behind the house and on the adjoining Town Belt.

Neither William Denton nor his sister married. In the 1950s, the Denton family gave 37 acres in Highbury to the City Council, to be known as the George Denton Park. When William died, money was left for the botanical improvement of Wellington College grounds, with the residue given to the Wellington City Council for beautifying Wellington by botanical means. The Denton Trust, as it is known, has funded and continues to fund a number of beautification projects in Wellington.[15]

Photographs taken in the 1920s of the wonderful gardens at Dalmuir, St Ruadhan, and Fernhill show that the properties, together with the plantation on Section 48 of the Town Belt, would have made a wonderful inner-city park. But Wellington was not ready for such ideas, and today two blocks of apartments, the Maclean Flats, occupy the land. Fernhill was lived in until

[Above left] Fernhill and garden, c 1923. Conifers can be seen in the background. The lawn is just visible, surrounded by belts of mature trees and shrubs.

Adkin Collection, Alexander Turnbull Library, National Library of New Zealand, Te Puna Mātauranga, G-23392-1/4, PAColl-0844

[Above right] Looking down the main path from Fernhill to The Terrace and across to Mount Victoria, c 1895, twenty years after the house was built.

Alexander Turnbull Library, National Library of New Zealand, Te Puna Mātauranga, F-20120-1/2

[Above] Fernhill, c 1873. The house was built to the rear of Town Acre 439, next door to Robert Strang's Dalmuir, with a drive at the side. The positioning was to capture a view of the harbour. The surrounding land is bare of scrub or native vegetation but seems to have a great deal of gorse. The deciduous trees on the lawn are edged with shrubs. The steep slope of an earth terrace leads down from the house. The land to the rear was later planted with conifers, and a wooden picket fence added.

Alexander Turnbull Library, National Library of New Zealand, Te Puna Mātauranga, F-18820-1/2

[14] New Zealand Historic Places Trust file on Fernhill.

[15] The Denton Trust also assisted with the publication of this book.

Watercolour by Charles Iggleston, signed and dated 1868. It shows Captain Sharp's house and garden on The Terrace near Salamanca Road, looking north towards the Hutt Valley. Circular flower beds were fashionable in Britain and elsewhere.

Alexander Turnbull Library, National Library of New Zealand, Te Puna Mātauranga, C-119-022

the 1990s, when both it and the nikau palms were moved. A 30-tonne crane with a special cradle was used to transfer the nikau, and great care was taken to avoid damaging their fragile roots, but they did not survive the move. Like most of the large mansions built in early Wellington, Fernhill, St Ruadhan, Dalmuir, and their gardens are now only a memory. Only Fernhill's rata, a listed tree on the District Plan, remains.

Large houses with greater design evident in their gardens began to be built along The Terrace from the 1860s, after Wellington had become the capital.

Looking north from Aurora Terrace, with Parliament Buildings, Government House, and the Museum on the extreme left. The house in the foreground has well-formed paths, dividing hedges, a rough paling fence, a fenced service area, and some kanuka.

National Library of New Zealand, Te Puna Mātauranga B.14867

The residence of George Moore on The Terrace, opposite Aurora Terrace, c 1890s. It is a substantial home, with a glassed-in conservatory/veranda, set in a garden planted with deciduous trees, cabbage trees, and a eucalyptus.

Museum of New Zealand Te Papa Tongarewa B.14635

Elibank, the home of Walter Turnbull, on the corner of The Terrace and Bowen Street, c 1860. The planting at the corner of Museum Street and Sydney Street is in the foreground.

W.J. Harding Collection, Alexander Turnbull Library, National Library of New Zealand, Te Puna Mātauranga, G-532-1/1, PAColl-3042

Elibank c 1890s. There is a picket and paling fence, with steps down from the house to a well-tended lawn and what appears to be a fruit garden, with a peach and gooseberries.

Alexander Turnbull Library, National Library of New Zealand, Te Puna Mātauranga, F-25225-1/2

Willis, Abel Smith, and Webb Streets

Wellington's first Mayor, George Hunter, arrived on the *Duke of Roxburgh* in 1840. He bought several town acres on upper Willis Street, which he ran as a small farm, known as Hunter's Hill. It included MacDonald Crescent and Dixon Street, running back to The Terrace. He later gifted the vegetable garden to St John's. This sheltered part of Willis Street was soon a residential area for the well-to-do. By 1848, it boasted a footpath that was not to be used by horses or cattle. Trees flourished here.

Although many of the city's older inhabitants can recall some of the outstanding homes and gardens of wealthy citizens in this part of Te Aro Flat, the pictorial record is poor. Fortunately, a few photographs remain.

Inverlochy House, built in 1878, occupied the block bordered by Vivian and Abel Smith Streets on the north and south, and Willis Street and The Terrace to the east and west. Carriages could turn off Abel Smith Street, and pass through imposing entrance gates to travel along an avenue of pines and sycamores, past the mansion and around to the stables, utility garden, orchard, and vinery, to the back gates on Vivian Street. The avenue, no longer tree-lined, is now known as Inverlochy Place. An imposing residence, Inverlochy was built for Thomas Kennedy MacDonald, a prominent Wellington citizen who later became a City Councillor and a Member of Parliament. The grounds were spacious and extremely well laid out, with,

[Left] Dr Fell's home, c 1890. Heavy timber beams form terraces for plants on the steep section. There are deciduous trees, an ornate wrought iron front fence, timber steps, and gate.

Fell Collection, Alexander Turnbull Library, National Library of New Zealand, Te Puna Mātauranga, PA1-q-075-10

[Above right] Willis Street, 1889. The picturesque home of Dr Walter Fell, designed by Clere and built in 1887, is perched behind the buildings fronting on to the street. There is timber terracing and steep wooden steps up to the house.

M. Bogle Collection, Alexander Turnbull Library, National Library of New Zealand, Te Puna Mātauranga, F-29692-1/2

[Left] Inverlochy House as it was in the 1870s. Features include a garden plinth with urn and a monkey puzzle tree. One fountain can be seen to the left of the entrance steps. There is a young Norfolk Island pine on the extreme left.

Courtesy of the *Evening Post*, Photo 6687, 1987

somewhat unusually for the times, a certain amount of garden ornamentation. The garden was at its peak in the 1890s.

There were two conservatories and, in front of the house, three fountains, two of which still can be seen today. The recession of the 1880s exacted its toll and in the 1890s MacDonald was forced to sell Inverlochy House. It was first divided into two flats, then, with later additions, into nine apartments. In 1980, due for demolition, it was saved by the concern of citizens. Williams Development Holdings, the owners, gave the building to a citizens' trust that converted the building into an Arts Education Centre. The cost was around $200,000. The Stout Trust donated $40,000, the Wellington City Council $8,000, while the Trust used around $100,000 of its own funds.[16]

[Top] Avenue of pines off Abel Smith Street leading to gates of Inverlochy House.

Museum of New Zealand Te Papa Tongarewa B.1402?

[Above left] Inverlochy's rear entrance on Vivian Street. It features box edgings and a well-presented garden.

Museum of New Zealand Te Papa Tongarewa B.14027

[Above right] The orchard of Inverlochy House with vinery.

Museum of New Zealand Te Papa Tongarewa B.14023

Most of the Inverlochy land has been subdivided. A Norfolk Island pine, *Araucaria heterophylla*, and a London plane tree, both on Wellington's list of heritage trees, remind us that Inverlochy House was once set in one of the finest gardens in Wellington. A large puriri at 4 Inverlochy Place was also part of the original garden.

[Opposite left] Norfolk Island pine at 3 Inverlochy Place, December 1999.

J. Nauta, Museum of New Zealand Te Papa Tongarewa C.T.15701/1-5

[Opposite right] Two fountains on either side of the top of the main steps to Inverlochy House, December 1999.

J. Nauta, Museum of New Zealand Te Papa Tongarewa C.T.15701/7-11

[16] *Evening Post*, 21 December 1982.

18 Edge Hill, off Kent Terrace, c 1890s. The property fronted on to Kent Terrace itself, and the conifers in the foreground are part of the median planting between Kent and Cambridge Terraces. There is a protective wooden cage around a newly-planted tree. The property has paling fences cutting through older mature thorn hedges, indicating this is a recent subdivision of a much larger property. As well as the hedge, the paling fence on the left separates one flowering bush from two similar ones. The wind sheer from the nor'westers has distorted both the hedge inside the fence and the conifers. The Town Belt hills behind the house are fenced, but the land is bare and parched. The eastern side of the city was much drier than the western side.

Henry Wright Collection, Alexander Turnbull Library, National Library of New Zealand, Te Puna Mātauranga, G-20674-1/2

Kent Terrace and Newtown

The land on the eastern side of town was considerably drier than that in the west because of its exposure to the prevailing north-westerly winds. Conifers planted on the Town Belt in the 1870s thrived in the harsh conditions. Conifers were also planted along the median strip between Kent and Cambridge Terraces and, as in other parts of the city, in many private properties too.

As time went on, larger houses gradually replaced the early cottages in Newtown. In 1896, Henry Wright, who had lived in Britomart Street, Berhampore, from 1877, moved into a larger house in Mein Street, Newtown. An accountant, Wright had had some experience as a ranger on Little Barrier Island, and was a talented photographer and a specialist gardener. His tropical plant collection was gifted to the Botanic Garden in 1928, eight years before his death.[17]

Thorndon

From the beginning of Wellington's settlement, Thorndon Flat fell into several parts: the commercial, Government, and cemetery land; the residential area; and the Maori cultivations between Grant and Tinakori Roads. Most desirable were the town acres in the residential elevated areas of Hill and Hobson Street and Tinakori Road with their views of the harbour. From the 1850s, wealthy business people built large houses here, first in Hobson Street and Fitzherbert Terrace, and then further afield.

[Below] Sydney Street, looking south to house of James Hector, which was built adjoining the Colonial Museum, c 1865. Walter Mantell's property is to the right. Curving paths separate the several planting areas, and there is a rough paling fence. Elibank is in the background. The new Government House has not yet been built.

Museum of New Zealand Te Papa Tongarewa B.10881

17 *Evening Post*, 21 December 1928.

[Right] Museum Street c 1880, showing James Hector's house and garden enclosures fifteen years after it was built. The garden has maturing conifers in one area, hedges, roses, shrubs, and a small hedged (walled) area that is possibly growing vegetables. A climber softens the veranda, which is partially enclosed. The rough paling fence has been replaced by a modern, capped paling one.

Museum of New Zealand Te Papa Tongarewa B.9781

[Below] The view from Wadestown, with Grant Road in the right foreground, c 1871. It shows a cottage in Tinakori Road, and the Princess Hotel on the corner of Murphy and Molesworth Streets. The large house in Hobson Street to the far left was built for W.M. Bannatyne (Town Acre 613). Many trees have been established in this area.

A.P. Ferguson Collection, Alexander Turnbull Library, National Library of New Zealand, Te Puna Mātauranga, F-29084-1/2, F-29819-1/2

[Below] Similar view c 1877. Pendennis, on the corner of Grant Road, has replaced two earlier cottages. Houses are being built along Fitzherbert Terrace, with a central planting of pines visible. Four military cottages face Grant Road.

Alexander Turnbull Library, National Library of New Zealand, Te Puna Mātauranga, F-3682-1/2

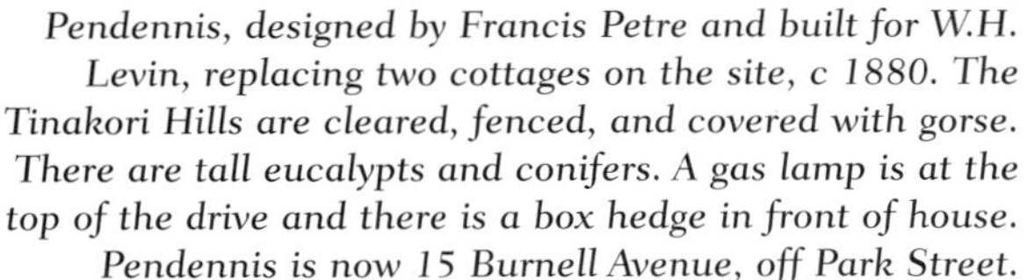

Pendennis, designed by Francis Petre and built for W.H. Levin, replacing two cottages on the site, c 1880. The Tinakori Hills are cleared, fenced, and covered with gorse. There are tall eucalypts and conifers. A gas lamp is at the top of the drive and there is a box hedge in front of house. Pendennis is now 15 Burnell Avenue, off Park Street.

Alexander Turnbull Library, National Library of New Zealand, Te Puna Mātauranga, G-20597-1/1

The view from Pendennis, 1878. A lamp is at the top of drive to Tinakori Road. Pipitea Point and part of the Railway Station is on the left. The house in the left foreground, once owned by Joseph Joseph, is now in Burnell Avenue.

Burton Brothers Collection, Alexander Turnbull Library, National Library of New Zealand, Te Puna Mātauranga, B-349-10X12

Built in 1858, this property, now 52 Hobson Street, is one of the oldest in Thorndon. It was occupied by Charles John Abraham, Bishop of Wellington, in 1861, subsequently by the artist John Turnbull Thompson, first Surveyor General of New Zealand, and in 1877 by G.M. Waterhouse. The house, which faces the harbour, had a large lawn, probably used for croquet, surrounded by a shrubbery. Little land surrounds the house today.

Artist J.T. Thompson, courtesy R. Bush and R.G. Gilbert

The imposing town house of John Johnston (of Homewood), Fitzherbert Terrace, c 1880s. It was designed by Thomas Turnbull in 1878 with a formal garden layout. A pair of lancewoods have been planted with future landscape effect in mind. The house was demolished in the 1930s, and the Thorndon tennis courts are now on the site.

Alexander Turnbull Library, National Library of New Zealand, Te Puna Mātauranga, F-52959-1/2

In 1907, after Katherine Mansfield's return from London, the Beauchamps moved into their fourth home, at 47 Fitzherbert Terrace, now the site of the American Embassy. A row of pines was planted down the middle of the street in the 1880s and removed in the 1930s to create the Katherine Mansfield Memorial Garden.

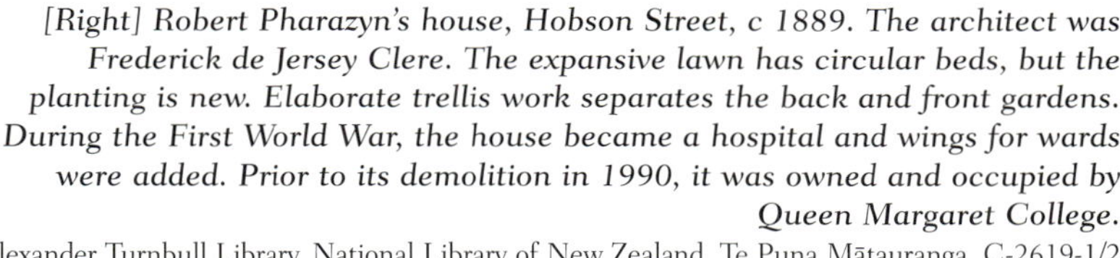

[Right] Robert Pharazyn's house, Hobson Street, c 1889. The architect was Frederick de Jersey Clere. The expansive lawn has circular beds, but the planting is new. Elaborate trellis work separates the back and front gardens. During the First World War, the house became a hospital and wings for wards were added. Prior to its demolition in 1990, it was owned and occupied by Queen Margaret College.

Alexander Turnbull Library, National Library of New Zealand, Te Puna Mātauranga, C-2619-1/2

Pines planted in the 1880s frame 47 Fitzherbert Terrace, the fourth home of the Beauchamps, c 1920s.

Alexander Turnbull Library, National Library of New Zealand, Te Puna Mātauranga, F-2583-1/2

Preparing the site for Katherine Mansfield's Memorial Park. Removal of the pines, 1932.

Evening Post Collection, Alexander Turnbull Library, National Library of New Zealand, Te Puna Mātauranga, G-89801-1/2

[Top left] Felling pines outside 47 Fitzherbert Terrace, September 1930.

Alexander Turnbull Library, National Library of New Zealand, Te Puna Mātauranga, C-24719-1/2

[Top right] Preparation and design for Katherine Mansfield Memorial Park, 1933.

Evening Post Collection, Alexander Turnbull Library, National Library of New Zealand, Te Puna Mātauranga, C-3213-1/2

[Left] Katherine Mansfield Memorial Park entrance, 3 August 1951. A memorial tram shelter was presented to Wellington by her father after her death, but was removed when the motorway was formed. A less imposing memorial has been erected opposite Katherine Street.

Evening Post Collection, Alexander Turnbull Library, National Library of New Zealand, Te Puna Mātauranga, F-67392-1/2

[Right] Elm trees in Katherine Mansfield Memorial Park, 1997. A view looking north-east across the park, which has been enlarged by an extension over the northern part of Fitzherbert Terrace.

W. Shepherd

[Top left] Wellington Harbour from the garden of No. 2 Tinakori Road by Sarah Greenwood, 1861. A lawn edged with shrubs overlooks Thorndon Baths to the hills of Mount Victoria. A path appears to pass above the lawn.

Alexander Turnbull Library, National Library of New Zealand, Te Puna Mātauranga, F-126308-1/2

[Top right] Thorndon Baths before the formation of The Esplanade. Thorndon Quay runs along the shore. Hobson Street properties on the upper side of Thorndon Quay have well-formed gardens. One on the left has what might be a young box edging with border of plants behind, both edging a perennial border. Some plants appear to be named. The unformed road may be Davis Street. Photograph by H.W. Davis.

Mrs E. Ellis Collection, Alexander Turnbull Library, National Library of New Zealand, Te Puna Mātauranga, F-52961-1/1, PACOLL-3083

Leonard and Jane Stowe's house Tiakiwai, originally No 2 Tinakori Road, and still extant, was built in the 1860s on a rise above the Thorndon beach near the pa of Pakuao, partly on Maori Reserve Land. There were imposing entrance gates on the site of the present Cottleville Terrace store. Jane Stowe (née Greenwood, from Motueka) was a keen gardener and well-known artist. In the spring of 1869, she wrote to her sister Anne: 'Our garden has never looked so gay – the monthly roses a sight, lilacs, laburnums, scarlet passion-flowers, tulips, Persian lilacs and native clematis.' From the house, steps led down through a shrubbery to a lawn, edged with shrubs, that overlooked the Thorndon Baths and harbour.

Stowe was subdivided in 1930, and today the former orchard is on the property of 21 Stowe Hill. Three of the original pear trees remain, one of which is a golden pear. The present owner of Stowe maintains that there are Maori middens in the area and that wild kumara come up in all parts of the garden, including the rose bed. There is a stump of a very large eucalypt behind the house on the left, while a very large elm was removed from the front garden.

Residence and garden, c 1860s, Tiakiwai. Leonard Stowe was Clerk of the Legislative Council.

Alexander Turnbull Library, National Library of New Zealand, Te Puna Mātauranga, F-137406-1/2

Stowe, 1870-1880. A second storey has been added and a back wing to the left. Steps lead down to a lawn.

Privately owned, Alexander Turnbull Library, National Library of New Zealand, Te Puna Mātauranga, F-137409-1/2

At one stage when the section was freehold and clear of Maori Reserve status, Lombardy poplars were planted along the front and on one side boundary. Besides the pear trees, perhaps one of the most interesting plants is a camellia attributed to Barney Rhodes. He had an interest in a narrow strip of land running from his property in Wadestown, alongside Stowe, down to the beach and his wharf. Today the house is divided into two flats, and lovingly cared for by the present owner.

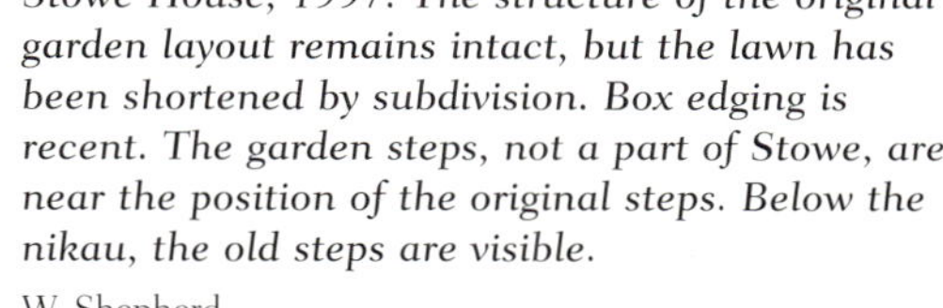

Stowe House, 1997. The structure of the original garden layout remains intact, but the lawn has been shortened by subdivision. Box edging is recent. The garden steps, not a part of Stowe, are near the position of the original steps. Below the nikau, the old steps are visible.

W. Shepherd

[Below left] Tinakori Road with cleared Tinakori Hills in background, c 1870. The Wellington home of Judge Johnston and his wife, before they left for Christchurch. There are circular beds in the lawn and a most unusual wooden planter on the edge of the lawn. There is a conservatory, picket fence and gate on the right, and a solid paling fence on the left.

Alexander Turnbull Library, National Library of New Zealand, Te Puna Mātauranga, F-111452-1/2

[Below right] Watercolour by William Mein-Smith, c 1850s. The house and conservatory in Tinakori Road are similar in style to Ludlam's Woburn home, which was built about the same time. The house has a post and rail fence. The bush on Tinakori Hill has only been partly cleared, and the burnt trunks of forest trees can be seen. This may have become Joseph Joseph's home, still extant in Burnell Avenue.

Alexander Turnbull Library, National Library of New Zealand, Te Puna Mātauranga, A-034-022

75 Tinakori Road, part of Town Acre 568, the home of the Beauchamps after they left Karori in 1898, this was a large mansion that was pulled down to make room for the motorway. The taupata hedge is growing inside a wooden fence with three entrances. The macrocarpa dates from the 1870s.
J.M. Hardwicke Collection, Alexander Turnbull Library, National Library of New Zealand, Te Puna Mātauranga, F-8615-1/4, PAColl-5297

Fernbank, Tinakori Road, c 1878, where Elsdon Best spent his school days. The shingle-roofed cottage has been added to by attaching a gothic cottage with carved barge boards. There is a small front garden, a sloping bush section behind, and possibly a lawn to the side.
Onslow Historical Society

There were other noteworthy properties along Tinakori Road. Katherine Mansfield describes the street at it was in the early years of the century:

> Our house in Tinakori Road stood back from the road. It was a big, white painted square house with a slender pillared veranda and balcony running all the way round it. In front from the veranda edge the garden sloped away in terraces and flights of concrete steps – down – until you reached the stone wall covered with nasturtiums that had three gates let into it – the visitors gate, the tradesmen's gate, and a huge pair of old gates that were never used .... Tinakori Road was not fashionable; it was very mixed. Of course there were some good houses in it, old ones, like ours for instance, hidden away in gardens.

In the 1880s, Alfred Boardman, manager of the South British Insurance Company, bought land in Patanga Crescent, building a large house at No 31 around 1892. Captain F. Holm of the Holm Shipping Line bought the property about six years later, calling it The Anchorage. The property remained in the Holm family until the 1970s. The garden was beautiful, like St Ruadhan on The Terrace, and in a favourable position, sheltered by the Botanic Garden hill above today's Anderson Park. Some land around The Anchorage has since been sold and built on. However, a few plants tell of its former glory – an 1883 pear tree, a rhododendron, and a large pohutukawa that is registered as a heritage tree on the District Scheme.

[Left] Multi-storey houses, Tinakori Road. Drawing by Hilda Walker. The villa has adapted to the steep narrow sections with little space between the houses. Designed by Rob Roy MacGregor in 1903, they were as much a feature then as they are today.

[Above] Thorndon, Sydney Street West. Drawing by Hilda Walker. An historic precinct with a mix of houses covering the bare hillsides that were shown in Mantell's sketch of 1850.

Perching and elegant, this mansion, Blundell House, needs no plants to embellish it, except for a short hedge between the gazebo and the lawn with bird bath.

Burton Bros, 1890s, Museum of New Zealand Te Papa Tongarewa

[Below top] Ribbon development along the main road in Newtown, c 1908–13. The houses have a small front garden, no side gardens, but little room at the rear. Hutson's brick and tile factory is in the centre of the picture.

S.C. Smith Collection, Alexander Turnbull Library, National Library of New Zealand, Te Puna Mātauranga, G-19664-1/1

[Below bottom] Odlin's housing estate, before the advent of the motor car, c 1910. The subdivision of steep hills means that access was difficult and the house was often placed to the rear of section. It was the era of the zigzag path and the terraced garden.

Postcard, Museum of New Zealand Te Papa Tongarewa B.12452

Suburban villas and their gardens

Some late nineteenth- and early twentieth-century two-storey villas with land around them were attractive and free-standing. Front gardens may have been small but there was room for side gardens.

In some areas such as Newtown, ribbon development of villas along a main road left little or no frontage or land between the houses. Ground behind the house was often limited. Some settlers would have had memories of terrace houses – joined together, built of brick or stone, close to the road, and with open space or garden behind each house. Semi-detached houses, built of wood (sometimes sharing an internal brick wall) were common in Mount Victoria, where there was a shortage of flat land. Corrugated iron was often used for the inside walls of houses that were close together.

Where the land was steep, as in Tinakori Road, five-storey terrace houses were built, very characteristic of Wellington, with gardens made on whatever land was left.

In the developing hill suburbs of Brooklyn and Kelburn, when hillside sections were subdivided and then built on, access dictated the style of the garden. The advent of the motor car and the need for a garage complicated the picture even further.

[Above] The roof garden of 17 Manners Street, c 1890s. Potted plants include New Zealand flax.

Beverley Shore Bennett Collection, Alexander Turnbull Library, National Library of New Zealand, Te Puna Mātauranga, F-173031-1/2

Perching too but in another way was an inner-city roof garden in Manners Street in the 1890s, belonging to Robert and Mary Martin. Outside the conservatory, the illustration shows the couple admiring their garden of potted plants.

Photographs of people working in their gardens are hard to find. Fortunately, a charming picture of Golder Cottage, taken in 1900, has survived. Built in Upper Hutt in 1875, the original three-bedroom cottage was later extended in the front. The property today carries a Category II rating from the Historic Places Trust. Irene Wilmhurst, Golder's grand-daughter, remembers a large vegetable garden with herbs, roses, dahlias, and geraniums growing up the side of the chimney, a circular planting of grape hyacinths around a tree, and a white camellia. There were apple, pear, and lemon trees, a red plum, gooseberries, raspberries, black currants, and a large yard where the hens were kept at the bottom of the garden.

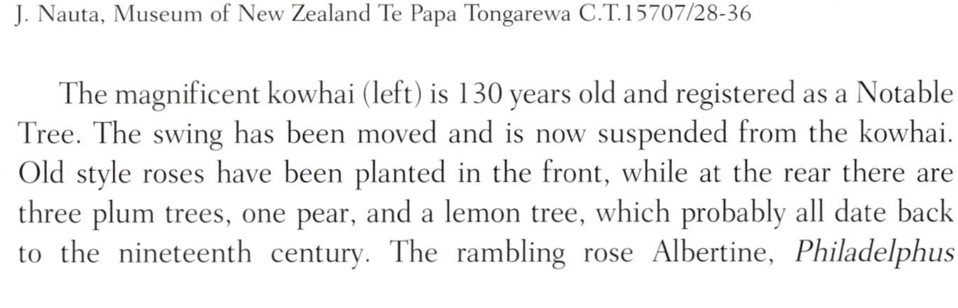

[Above left] Golder Cottage, built in 1875 on a 100-acre country block in Upper Hutt, c 1880.

Golder family

[Above right] Golder Cottage extended, c 1900. Bert Golder is hoeing, Agnes is wanting to push Ellen in the swing. William Golder, at the corner of the house, talks to grandfather Alexander Martin, his brother Tom, and Vincent and Mary.

Golder family

[Left] Golder cottage, 1999. On the left is an historic kowhai tree with swing.

J. Nauta, Museum of New Zealand Te Papa Tongarewa C.T.15707/28-36

The magnificent kowhai (left) is 130 years old and registered as a Notable Tree. The swing has been moved and is now suspended from the kowhai. Old style roses have been planted in the front, while at the rear there are three plum trees, one pear, and a lemon tree, which probably all date back to the nineteenth century. The rambling rose Albertine, *Philadelphus coronarius* or mock orange, a lilac, and a wisteria contribute to the ambience of this delightful home and garden from the past.

Apart from fences and conservatories, structural features are not obvious in these pictures. Fences made from manuka branches were common in parks such as Newtown and the Botanic Garden. Towards the end of the century, however, wrought iron fences and local pottery, urns, and figures, were available.

Manuka fences and ornamental arch, Botanic Garden, 1904. The path edgings are of Buxus.

Watt Album, Alexander Turnbull Library, National Library of New Zealand, Te Puna Mātauranga, F-80403-1/2

The fountain played and the goldfish swam in the pond, c 1963. An unusual fountain featuring the figure of a Maori woman with feathered cloak. Moore House, Johnsonville, shortly before it was destroyed.

Onslow Historical Society

Peter Hutson & Sons' Wellington Pottery Exhibit, New Plymouth Exhibition, December 1904.

Auckland Weekly News, 12 January 1965

Wrought iron fence, wooden gate, and posts. Detail from Dr Fell's Willis Street house.

Alexander Turnbull Library

Flood waters in Saunders Lane, now Little George Street, March 1893. From 1898, Harold Beauchamp and his family lived in the big house on the hill (background, centre left), which faced on to Tinakori Road. As an example of speculative housing for struggling workers, two Town Acres, Nos 643 and 644, were developed together, with little space for gardens. The Māori had found the area good for growing but, as the photo shows, it was no site for housing.
Alexander Turnbull Library, National Library of New Zealand, Te Puna Mātauranga, F-1348-1/2-MNZ

Wellington as the capital

In the 1860s and before, Wellington was a sprawling, shabby village, sometimes dusty, sometimes muddy, and with an ugly backdrop of bare hills after the forest had been cut down. The decision to bring central government to Wellington in 1865 acted as a catalyst for commercial building in the city centre, and for house building and subdivision in the inner suburbs of Mount Victoria, Te Aro, and Thorndon. By the 1870s, there were church spires on the skyline, an attractive Government House, Parliament House, the Colonial Museum, a hospital, and many other substantial buildings. In spite of the depression in the 1880s, subdivision continued in the suburbs.

Yet the wind never ceased and the Town Belt largely remained bare. In 1910, Count Hochberg described the gardens as bare of trees, with the few flower beds smothered with dust.[18] In spite of the rather imposing town buildings, there was only a token of greenery in Victorian Wellington. It would be another fifty years before there was extended use of plants in the inner city.

Until the underground sewers were built, for many years the layout of gardens was dictated by the position of the privy and the wash-house, which were detached from the house. Water was drawn from a well in the back yard. Properties with 55-foot frontages fell generally into one or the other of the designs shown below.

Where sections had been divided into small lots for speculative housing for the poorer, as in Lorne Street (off Cambridge Terrace), or Haining Street (off Taranaki Street), there was no land available to garden. Low-lying Lorne Street, with 30 houses to the acre, all without drainage, became a cesspool.

Subdivision was intense in parts at the northern end of the town too, in

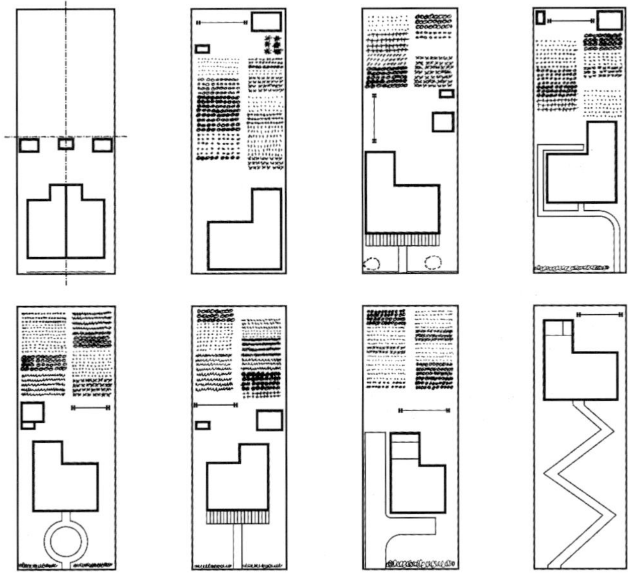

Typical layouts of house, outbuildings, gardens, and paths for the 50–55 ft frontage sections created by the subdivision of the Town Acre Section. Drawn by Martin Hill, 2000.

[18] Hochberg, Count Fritz, *An Eastern Voyage: The Journal of the Travel of Count Fritz Hochberg through the Empire, in the East and Japan,* London and New York, 1910.

Thorndon Flat, looking across to Oriental Bay and barren slopes of Mt Victoria, c 1905. Hobson Street is to the left, showing T.C. William's house (now Queen Margaret College). Fitzherbert Street has large homes. To the right, densely packed houses surround Molesworth and Murphy Streets.

A.E. Birch Collection, Alexander Turnbull Library, National Library of New Zealand, Te Puna Mātauranga, F-67401-1/2, PAColl-1781-001

Saunder's Lane off Tinakori Road and in Aorangi Terrace. Charles Mills, a builder, bought town acre 638, south of Saunder's Lane, erecting workers' cottages, mostly leasehold. Poplar Grove, as it was called, sloped steeply down from Tinakori Road and had severe drainage problems. By 1891, it had eleven houses on it, yet the surrounding town acres were still being used for grazing and the growing of produce.

Subdivision was similarly intense in the Molesworth–Murphy Street area. This area was devoid of greenery, contrasting markedly with Hobson and Fitzherbert Streets, where hollies, gums, wattles, poplars, sycamores, oaks, and fruit trees had softened the landscape.

Te Aro Flat from Mt Victoria, looking west towards the Town Belt and Fitchett Farm, c 1875. There is planting along Kent and Cambridge Terraces. Intense subdivision can be seen between Webb and Vivian Sts, and overcrowding in Lorne St. The nursery for Coopers Seeds is visible in Taranaki St.

Burton Bros., Museum of New Zealand Te Papa Tongarewa

Imposing central city buildings in Victorian Wellington with little or no greenery: apex section between Lambton Quay and Featherston Street, c 1900. A small fenced garden beside the drinking fountain donated by the politician John Martin does little to soften the severity of the buildings. Unsealed roads made it dusty in summer and muddy in winter.

Alexander Turnbull Library, National Library of New Zealand, Te Puna Mātauranga, F-15856-1/2

Willis Street, c 1904 – a street of trees. Bamford's 'cottage of content' is at the extreme right in the foreground. Hunter's Corner (Webb Street) is behind the cart. St Peter's Church can be seen in the distance.

Ward's Early Wellington

Upper Willis Street, 1997. Webb Street is to the left above Quality Inn. Three oak trees protected on the District Scheme are over 100 years of age.

W. Shepherd

Pohutukawa (Metrosideros excelsa) *on The Terrace, an historic tree registered on the District Scheme and as a RNZIH Notable Tree, c 1998.*

W. Shepherd

The greening of Wellington

From the beginning of the twentieth century, successive Park Directors began introducing trees and shrubs, first to inner-city streets, and later to the suburbs. This gradual greening of the city, with shelter gained from higher and closer buildings, results today in a vivid yellow-green spring display in city and suburban streets and street frontages as deciduous trees from Europe burst into leaf. Not only do these trees soften the landscape and the man-made structures but they also blend harmoniously with kowhai, tall mamaku, cabbage trees, and other indigenous plants, contributing to the distinctive ambience of Wellington. Tree-lined Aro Street, planted with kowhai and the Australian *Agonis flexuosa*, is so different from the street shown in Bragge's panorama of the 1870s. Throughout the city, plants from all over the world mingle with those native to New Zealand. After 160 years of settlement, the vegetation is distinctive – something to nourish and cherish. Important trees must be placed on the District Scheme, while some are suitable for registration as Notable Trees under the Royal New Zealand Institute of Horticulture. The three oak trees at the top of Willis Street, for example, registered as Notable Trees under both schemes, are now all that remain of what was once a street of trees. Planted more than a century ago, they remind us of the homes and gardens that were once here, and soften this commercial corner of the city.

In other parts of the city there are oaks, hollies, elms, gums, pines, and macrocarpas to be seen, as well as cabbage trees, totara, ngaio, mamaku, and flax, remnants or seedlings from the original indigenous vegetation. Pohutukawa do extremely well here, but as they are not endemic to the Wellington region, only the oldest are significant, such as the Notable registered pohutukawa outside the Wellington Club on The Terrace.

Of the houses illustrated in this chapter, very few have survived to the present day. Yet by recording them here, their part in central Wellington's evolving landscape is acknowledged.

Chapter 5

GARDENS OF SPECIAL SIGNIFICANCE

The gardens of the residences occupied by top-ranking public officials are generally laid out and maintained by professional gardeners. As the capital city, Wellington has a number of these properties, and their gardens have been influenced not only by climate and topography but also by the styles and fashions of the time, as well as changes made by each new incumbent.

Watercolour from Eccleston Hill, c 1849. St Paul's Church is on the right. In the centre is Government Reserve, with William Wakefield's house and its well-laid-out garden with ponds. Wakefield died in 1848.

Alexander Turnbull Library, National Library of New Zealand, Te Puna Mātauranga, A-090-007

First Government House, Thorndon

For some time before his death in 1848, Colonel William Wakefield's house was known as Government House, although strictly speaking, until central government came to Wellington, this term applied only to the Governor's house in Auckland. On his death, Wakefield's house was extended for the Lieutenant-Governor's use and completed by February 1849, when a ball was held in the new suite of rooms.[1]

Bernard Collinson's 1849 sketch in Chapter 1 clearly shows the extended house with its well-laid-out grounds. A note on the sketch says 'Government House formerly Colonel Wakefield's', while the house on the left of the sketch is labelled 'A. Domett's house'. In another drawing, Collinson extended the view of Government House to show its relationship with St Paul's Anglican Church, the distant pa of Te Aro, Mount Cook, buildings all along Lambton Quay, and The Terrace. A similar sketch by C.R. Read seems to show Domett's house, with its glass-house/conservatory and vegetable garden, as an adjunct to Government House.

The first Government House, formerly Wakefield's house. Pencil sketch by C.R. Read, 1849. The house looks out on to well-designed, tiered ornamental gardens, circular bedding displays, and paths. A separate house on the property has an attached glasshouse. The extensive vegetable garden on undulating land is well fenced. Hill Street is in the foreground.

Mitchell Library, New South Wales

An 1855 Lands and Survey plan of the garden, studied in conjunction with an 1849 watercolour from Eccleston Hill, reveals the layout and appearance of this most important house and garden. Its position was certainly exposed. There were three ponds – two were close to Sydney Street and a third one was lower down, beneath the flagstaff and guns. The Waipirau Stream from Glenbervie and Sydney Streets flowed into these ponds and found its outlet to the sea at the corner of Bowen Street and Lambton Quay. Flower gardens and an orchard were situated above the upper pond, and vegetable gardens and paddocks faced what is now Museum Street.

---

[1] Ward, Louis E, *Early Wellington*, Whitcombe & Tombs, 1928.

[Above left] Colonel Wakefield's house, with the new rear extension built when it became the home for the Lieutenant Governor, c 1849.

Alexander Turnbull Library, National Library of New Zealand, Te Puna Mātauranga

[Above right] The Wellington Club, formerly Baron Von Alzdorf's Hotel, Lambton Quay, c 1871. Note the new Government House alongside Wakefield's original house. From Life and Recollections of New Zealand Colonist, *Vol 3.*

Alexander Turnbull Library, National Library of New Zealand, Te Puna Mātauranga, F- 32000-1/2

As early as 1863, it was realised that a new Government House and General Assembly building would be required when the government moved to Wellington. In 1865, the area from Park Street to Cottleville Terrace lying between Grant and Tinakori Roads was bought for this purpose, and His Excellency the Governor was informed that the House would undertake to vote all such sums of money as would be required for the new buildings.

Perhaps anticipating a need for weekend or more rural accommodation, the government also bought Mr Jackson's property at Lowry Bay, intending to upgrade the property. On Alfred Ludlam's advice plants were ordered from Ferguson in Sydney for both Lowry Bay and the town garden, as this letter to Frederick Weld shows: [2]

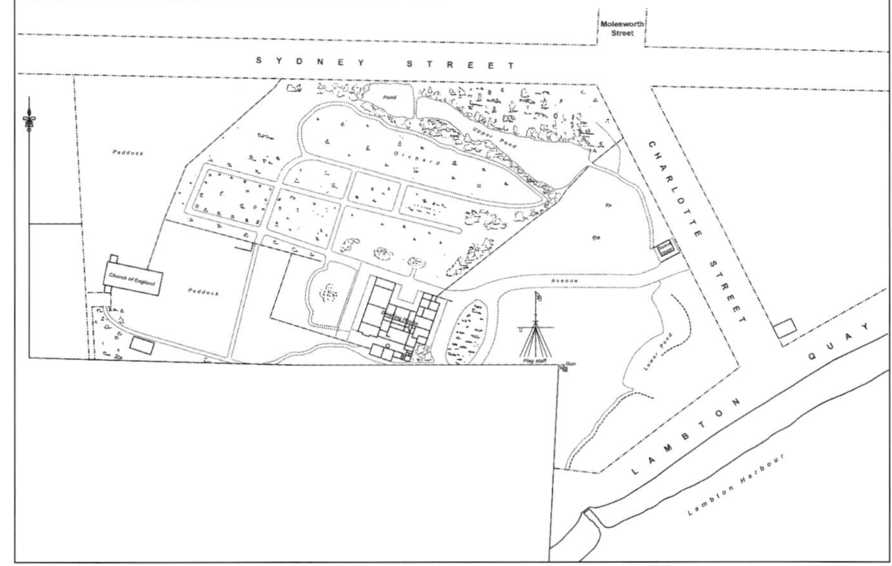

Plan of Government House garden, c 1855. The garden with its three ponds is well laid-out. A wooden fence separates the entrance drive from the garden, which is itself fenced from the paddocks.

Lands & Survey Department XI, F.41855

List of Plants for Domain at Lowry Bay and Town Garden

Newry
Monday April 3rd
My Dear Weld,

I send you two lists of plants one for the new Domain at Lowry Bay and the other for Town Gardens. I have selected trees and plants that are quite hardy or nearly so – if you send for these they would form a good foundation for the future. I avoided naming any Camellias, Roses, Azaleas etc. – you should forward the lists to Ferguson by the

[2] National Archives 65/816 in I.A.I. 65/1279. Weld was Prime Minister from November November 1864 to October 1865.

mail on the 7th so as to ensure his sending an early pick from his collection. And they should not be delayed being sent down later than the May steamer. In order to prevent unpacking in Wellington of those plants intended for Lowry Bay they had better be packed separately. I propose sending you a box of apples by old Knight's cart tomorrow. He will leave them at Wise's Hotel, so you must enquire.

Yours ever, in haste

A. Ludlam

Watercolour by J. Pearce, 1852–56. Jackson's property in Lowry Bay was bought in 1865 for development as the Governor's residence.

Alexander Turnbull Library, National Library of New Zealand, Te Puna Mātauranga, E-455-f-036

The majority of fruit trees Ludlam ordered are mentioned in Thompson's *Gardener's Assistant*, a book with which early settlers were familiar. Most of the pines selected, except for *Pinus insignis*, were Mediterranean. At 5/- each, insignis pine and macrocarpa were still relatively rare. One plant was ordered for the city and two for Lowry Bay.

Invoice of 4 boxes 1 bale of plants – supplied

F. Ferguson to the Government of New Zealand

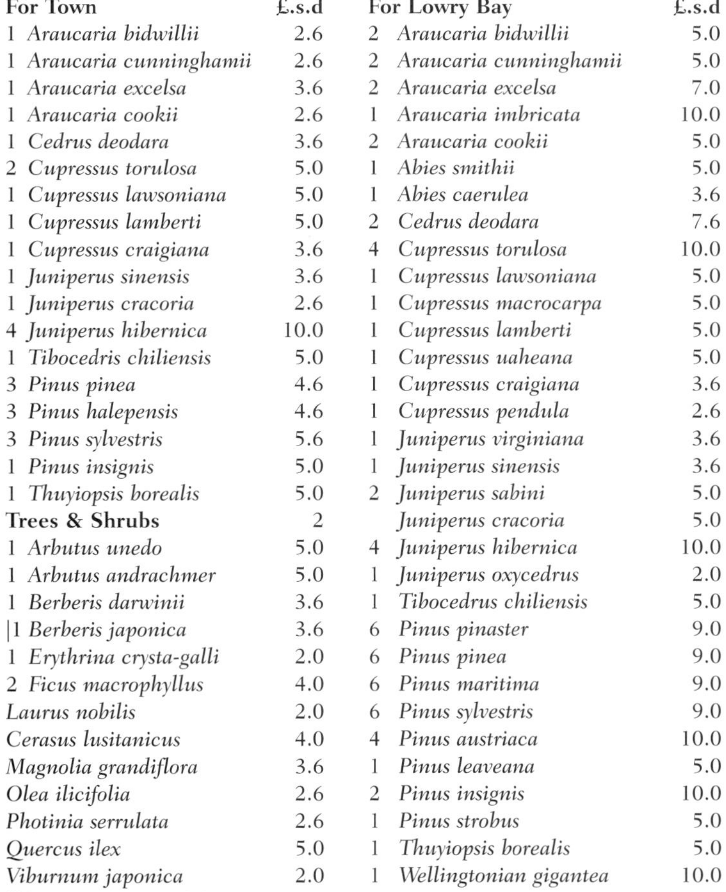

For Town	£.s.d	For Lowry Bay	£.s.d
1 *Araucaria bidwillii*	2.6	2 *Araucaria bidwillii*	5.0
1 *Araucaria cunninghamii*	2.6	2 *Araucaria cunninghamii*	5.0
1 *Araucaria excelsa*	3.6	2 *Araucaria excelsa*	7.0
1 *Araucaria cookii*	2.6	1 *Araucaria imbricata*	10.0
1 *Cedrus deodara*	3.6	2 *Araucaria cookii*	5.0
2 *Cupressus torulosa*	5.0	1 *Abies smithii*	5.0
1 *Cupressus lawsoniana*	5.0	1 *Abies caerulea*	3.6
1 *Cupressus lamberti*	5.0	2 *Cedrus deodara*	7.6
1 *Cupressus craigiana*	3.6	4 *Cupressus torulosa*	10.0
1 *Juniperus sinensis*	3.6	1 *Cupressus lawsoniana*	5.0
1 *Juniperus cracoria*	2.6	1 *Cupressus macrocarpa*	5.0
4 *Juniperus hibernica*	10.0	1 *Cupressus lamberti*	5.0
1 *Tibocedris chiliensis*	5.0	1 *Cupressus uaheana*	5.0
3 *Pinus pinea*	4.6	1 *Cupressus craigiana*	3.6
3 *Pinus halepensis*	4.6	1 *Cupressus pendula*	2.6
3 *Pinus sylvestris*	5.6	1 *Juniperus virginiana*	3.6
1 *Pinus insignis*	5.0	1 *Juniperus sinensis*	3.6
1 *Thuyiopsis borealis*	5.0	2 *Juniperus sabini*	5.0
Trees & Shrubs	2	*Juniperus cracoria*	5.0
1 *Arbutus unedo*	5.0	4 *Juniperus hibernica*	10.0
1 *Arbutus andrachmer*	5.0	1 *Juniperus oxycedrus*	2.0
1 *Berberis darwinii*	3.6	1 *Tibocedrus chiliensis*	5.0
1 *Berberis japonica*	3.6	6 *Pinus pinaster*	9.0
1 *Erythrina crysta-galli*	2.0	6 *Pinus pinea*	9.0
2 *Ficus macrophyllus*	4.0	6 *Pinus maritima*	9.0
Laurus nobilis	2.0	6 *Pinus sylvestris*	9.0
Cerasus lusitanicus	4.0	4 *Pinus austriaca*	10.0
Magnolia grandiflora	3.6	1 *Pinus leaveana*	5.0
Olea ilicifolia	2.6	2 *Pinus insignis*	10.0
Photinia serrulata	2.6	1 *Pinus strobus*	5.0
Quercus ilex	5.0	1 *Thuyiopsis borealis*	5.0
Viburnum japonica	2.0	1 *Wellingtonian gigantea*	10.0
Viburnum sinensis 2.0			

For Lowry Bay only

	Plant	Price
	Arbutus unedo	5.0
	Arunda donax variegata	2.6
	Berberis atropurpurea	2.0
	Berberis Darwinii	3.6
	Berberis japonica	3.6
	Erythrina camidensis	2.0
	Escallonia floribunda	2.0
	Escallonia grandiflora	2.6
	Fagus sylvaticus/copper	5.0
	Ficus macrophyllus	4.0
	Forsythia suspensa	1.6
	Gynerium argentium	2.0
	Ilex cornuta	2.0
	Laurus nobilis	4.0
	Cerasus lusitanicus	6.0
	Ligustrum japonicum	2.0
	Magnolia grandiflora	3.6
1	*Magnolia conspicua*	
1	*Magnolia purpurea*	2.0
1	*Olea fragrans*	2.6
1	*Photinia serrulata*	2.6
1	*Prunus triloba*	
2	*Quercus ilex*	5.0
2	*Quercus cerris*	4.0
1	*Viburnum arboreum*	2.0
1	*Viburnum Japonicum*	2.0
2	*Viburnum opulus*	2.0
1	*Viburnum plicatum*	2.0
1	*Viburnum rugosum*	2.0
1	*Viburnum suspensa*	2.0
1	*Weigela rosea*	2.0
1	*Weigela amabilis*	2.0

Cherries

Morella
Amber Heart
May Duke
Bleeding Heart
Biggareau
White Heart
Black Heart
Black Eagle
Heart of Midlothian
12 Trees at 1/6 each

Peaches

Royal George
Camden Excellent
Royal Kensington 12
Late Admirable 4
Newington
Noblesse
Fenton de Venus
Barrington
Shanghai

Pears

1 Chaumontelle
1 Jargonelle
1 Marie Louise
1 Windsor
1 William's Bon Chrietin
1 Swans Egg
1 Winter Nelis
1 Glout morceau
1 Summer Bergamot
1 Orange Bergamot
1 Beurre de Roi
1 Beurre de Capiaumont
12 Trees at 1/6 each

Plums

1 Coe's Golden Drop
1 Coe's Late Red
1 English Damson
1 Early Pedrigon
2 Green Gage
2 Orleans
1 Reine Claude
1 Violette Hative
1 White Magnum Bonum
1 Yellow Magnum Bonum
1 Purple magnum Bonum
1 Incomparable
14 Trees at 1/6 each

Nectarines

Hardwick
Elruge
Red Roman
13 Trees at 1/6 each

Apricots

Moor Park Apricot
2 Trees at 1/6each

Figs

White Genson
Green Ischia
Singleton Perpetual
Brown Province
6 Trees at 1/6 each

Vines

Muscat of Alexandria
Red Frontignan
Royal Muscadine
Black Hambro
Trees at 6d each
Packing cases at 7/6 each

Olives

Finest French Olives at 2/6 each

*Where prices are hard to determine in the original they have been omitted.

Nearly three weeks later, 21 April 1865, Weld ordered further deciduous plants from Nelson's nurseryman Hale.

100	Birch Silver	6	Maple English
50	Birch Weeping	6	Maple Scarlet
100	Oaks 2 yrs old	6	Scarlet Oak
50	Sycamore 2 yrs old	6	Alder
25	Elm Broad Leaves	24	Mountain Ash
25	Elm English	6	Common Ash

Second Government House, Thorndon

Government House was built in 1871, this photograph was taken in the 1880s. The site is now occupied by the Beehive. The Town Belt behind is leased for farming. The Colonial Museum is in the left rear. There is a formal drive with gas light, shrub borders with a number of conifers, and a rough paling capped fence.
Museum of New Zealand B.16968

The properties at Lowry Bay and Tinakori Rd were not developed, and the latter was sold in 1873. Instead, in 1871, a new Government House, designed by William Clayton, was built on the site of the present Beehive, above Wakefield's house. It was an imposing and gracious Italianate-style building with a conservatory attached, and Sir George Bowen was the first Governor to live there. The grounds were landscaped, and a coach house and stables for ten horses were erected on the corner of Museum and Sydney Streets, opposite the house of James Hector.

In 1907, a fire demolished Parliament Building, and Government House was taken over for the use of Parliament. A single oak remains from early plantings in the grounds of the second Government House. Situated in Museum Street and registered as a Notable Tree, it serves as a reminder of those early days of the colony, when Wakefield was successfully raising young oak trees from English-grown acorns on this site.

[Below left] Government House and grounds with bedding displays, c 1900.
Postcard

[Below right] Quercus robur, registered Notable Tree, Museum Street, Wellington, 1997.
W. Shepherd

Third Government House, Dufferin Street, Newtown

The present Government House with glass conservatory, c 1920. There is formal bedding above the drive.

Alexander Turnbull Library, National Library of New Zealand, Te Puna Mātauranga, F-117623-1/2, PAColl-6075-22

In 1910, a new vice-regal residence was built in Dufferin Street, Newtown, on the site of the former Mount View Asylum. Claude Paton of the Government Architect's Office designed the two-storey wooden building in the half-timbered Elizabethan style. The house is set in spacious grounds with a northern elevation, looking out over a large lawn. The formal entrance faces south. In 1993, it was classified Category I by the New Zealand Historic Places Trust.

[Right] Government House, Newtown, 1911. Built on the site of the lunatic asylum, it is surrounded by approximately 50 acres. This view shows the layout of grounds to the rear.

Alexander Turnbull Library, National Library of New Zealand, Te Puna Mātauranga, F-32208-1/2

[Above] Brick entrance gates to Government House, the Guard House, and formal bedding displays on the left and right of the drive, c 1912. Wellington College is just visible on the hill to the left.

Alexander Turnbull Library, National Library of New Zealand, Te Puna Mātauranga, F-112430-1/2

The early layout of the grounds can be seen above. A small section of the fifteen-foot-high wall of the Mount View Asylum was kept intact, 30 feet in length on the eastern boundary and 10 feet on the south end. Built by prison labour from bricks made in the prison brickworks, many of the bricks show the arrow motif that can also be seen in the bricks of the Mount Cook barracks in Tasman Street. Graffiti on some of the bricks includes a Dutch scene of a windmill and a house with a picket fence. This relic from the past is now registered as Category II by the New Zealand Historic Places Trust.

During the Depression of the 1930s, the Governor-General Lord Bledisloe encouraged the unemployed to develop garden plots in the grounds. Government expenditure was tight and the grounds became run down. In 1935, Bledisloe's successor, Lord Galway, sought to rejuvenate the garden. Alfred Buxton, a Christchurch landscape architect, had just completed Homewood for Benjamin Sutherland. It was suggested that he tender for the erection of a wall, the levelling of the ground, and the establishing of lawns for Government House. Nine plans, more elaborate than any other set of Buxton's plans, were submitted. They included a formal sunken garden with ornamental ponds and a proposed private garden.[3]

[Above left] Portion of asylum wall and gate, Government House, December 1999.
J. Nauta, Museum of New Zealand Te Papa Tongarewa
C.T.15698/3-6

[Above right] Drawing on asylum wall, December 1999.
J. Nauta, Museum of New Zealand Te Papa Tongarewa C.T.15698/30-42

The Private Garden Space

Proposed private garden, Government House, Wellington.
Alfred Buxton & Sons Christchurch, 1935

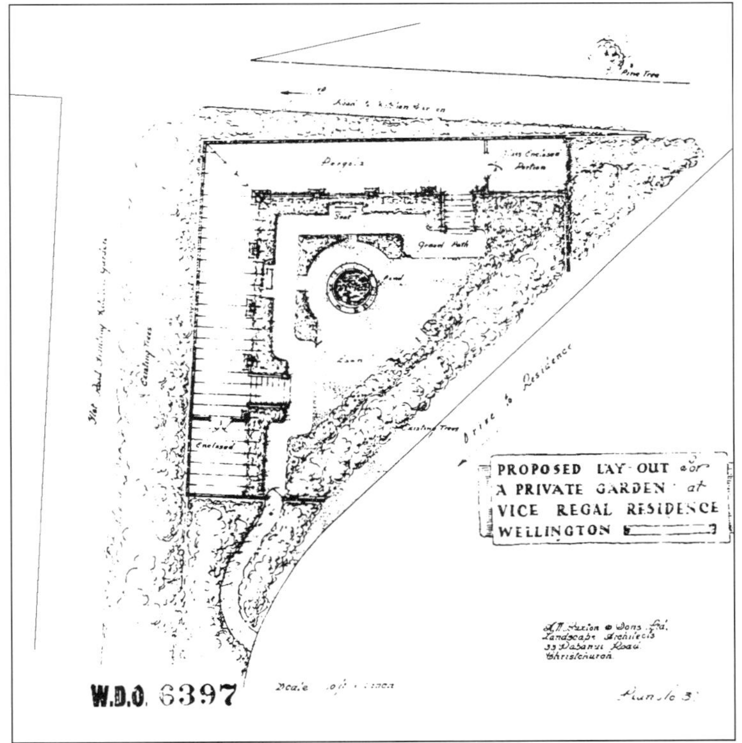

A ground plan of a proposed private garden on the left-hand side of the drive, Government House, Wellington. Glass was to have enclosed portions are at either end.
Alfred Buxton & Sons Christchurch, 1935

[3] Tipples, Rupert, *Colonial Landscape Gardener*, Lincoln College, Canterbury, 1989.

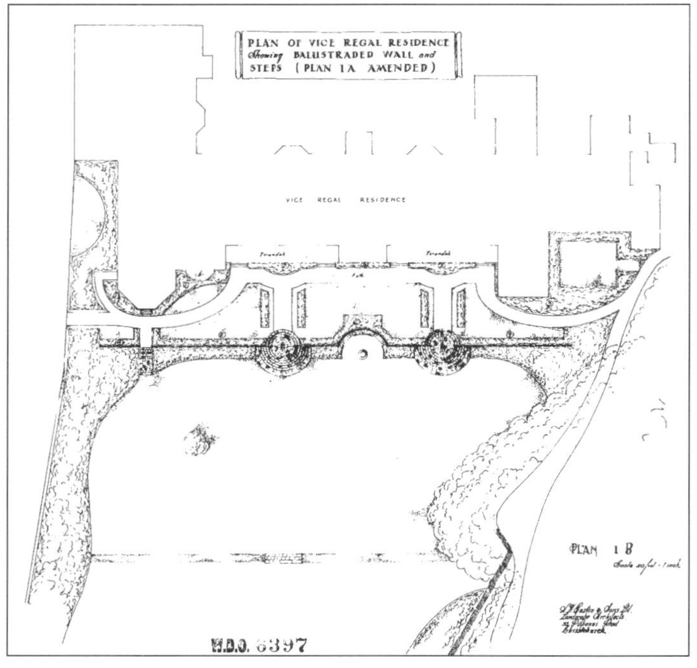

Amended plan for terrace, wall, and steps down to the main lawn, which is on two levels.

Alfred Buxton & Sons Christchurch, 1936

Newly planted rockery, lawn with flower beds, c 1925.

Alexander Turnbull Library, National Library of New Zealand, Te Puna Mātauranga, F-18232-1/1, PAColl-3739

Formal Garden – The Public Space

The plan for the sunken garden was modified. Buxton's tender for the erection of a stone wall, steps to balustrading, levelling of the ground, and establishment of the lawns was £2,699. But, although the price was considered reasonable by the Ministry of Works, the plans were never executed, priority being given instead to improving the glass-houses, the boiler system, and the shade house for the rather more modest sum of £774.

Buxton's plans may have influenced the garden layout nonetheless. For example, the seat to the left of the drive with shrubs behind it seems to invite one into a private garden, as Buxton had planned. Similarly, the veranda steps leading down to a path edging a small lawn terrace, which in turn leads down to the main lawn, edged with large shrub borders, has some affinity with Buxton's revised plan.

Formal sunken garden with ornamental ponds, shrub border, and background wall. Plan for Government House, Wellington.

Alfred Buxton & Sons Christchurch, 1935

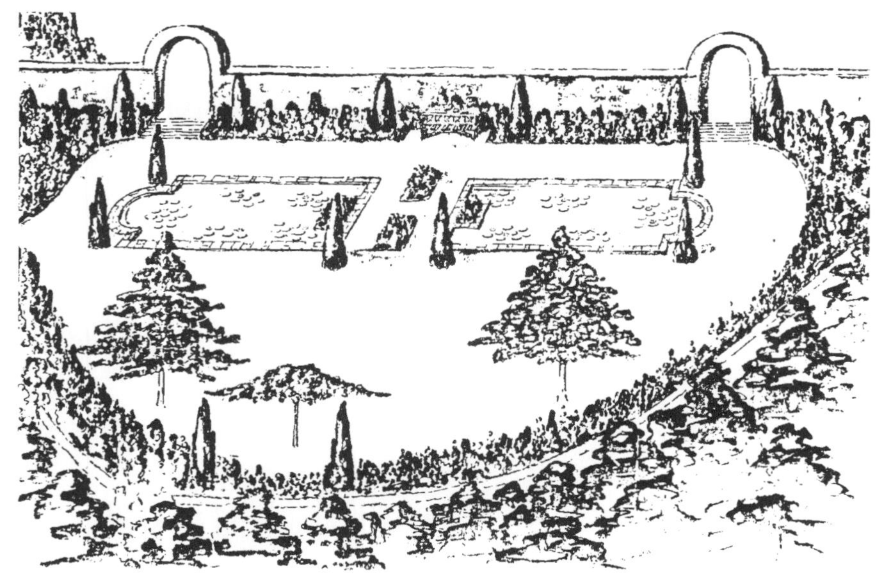

The structure of the garden remains unchanged, but details vary, as in any garden. For example, the newly planted rock garden shown above has gone, the trees lining the drive have matured, while the formal beds in the main lawn have also been removed.

Today's Governors-General are New Zealand citizens. Though they are more familiar with New Zealand plants and gardens than their English predecessors, that does not necessarily mean they understand Wellington's climate

Border to main lawn and concrete mowing-strip, looking south, Government House, December 1999.

J. Nauta, Museum of New Zealand C.T.15698/17-26

and its demands. In the 1980s, during Sir David Beattie's term of office, Government House was refurbished. The garden too underwent changes. Extensive planting of both exotics and native trees began, and some of the sheltering pines on the south and west, planted in the 1870s, were unfortunately removed.

The Reeveses followed the Beatties. Lady Reeves continued to work closely with major plantings carried out by the gardening staff. The line of pohutukawas along the drive to the house continues to give protection to the long border of perennial plants edging the lawn. Framed by climbing roses, steps from the house lead down to the large lawn, bordered on the north and west by perennials and shrubs. The grounds to the east and west are sheltered by the trees planted over 120 years ago.

In the 1960s, Ministry of Works' head gardener James Stirling found it difficult to grow flowers satisfactorily at Government House. A more recent supervisor, Bruce Nisbet, believed that more trees, lifting and filtering the wind, would help create a sheltered micro-climate, though because of the lie of the land, wind would always be a problem. The pohutukawas along the drive give some protection in spring and summer to azaleas, magnolias, camellias, spring bulbs, and the summer flowers – plants that give beauty and charm to this garden.

Dame Catherine Tizard made the house and garden accessible to all. The incumbents at the time of writing, Sir Michael and Lady Hardie-Boys, are taking a keen interest in the garden and are consulted by the contractors and a panel of well-known horticulturists. But the garden's exposure to wind will continue to challenge the gardeners and the need for functional open space.

At the end of the 1980s, the Ministry of Works' 90-year management of this property ended. A document of 1989 called the 'White Paper on the Vice Regal Suite' formalised the future funding and organisation of this government estate, and by 1990 the garden was managed on-site, not from a downtown office. The contract for work in the garden is now let out to closed tender, renewable after three years but tendered out again after six years. This change, bringing with it a known budget, has been beneficial

Parterre edged with Corokia 'Red Wonder', Government House, December 1999.

J. Nauta, Museum of New Zealand C.T.15698/27-32

Dwarf conifers on a slope, Government House, August 1999.
J. Hobbs

to the property as a whole and the garden is developing a special character that suits its public function and cultural history.

Management of Government House grounds today, apart from the lawns, is almost completely organic. English and other exotic plants continue to be featured, but more New Zealand native plants are used. Plants such as the Australian *Anigozanthus* (Kangaroo paw) at the main gate have been replaced by native *Carex*, flax, and Marlborough daisy. Visitors walking from the car park on the south to the main entrance to the house pass a well-designed and eye-catching bed of native plants, while native trees, especially kowhai, and other plants feature along the southern border of the lawn. Trimmed *Corokia*, 'Red Wonder', has been used as low hedging from the ballroom entrance along the side of the house, in place of the more traditional *Buxus sempervirens*. Outside the conservatory, the *Corokia* forms the outline of a European parterre design, replacing the customary box hedging.

Native border looking south, White Chatham Island forget-me-not, Government House, December 1999.
J. Nauta, Museum of New Zealand C.T.15698/25-29

This particular garden has to look good all year round when viewed from both the drive and within the conservatory. The site is asymmetrical and extremely windy. The design separates the area into two 'rooms', divided by hedge. In the southern 'room', there are three box-edged circular beds, featuring golden totara. A central rectangular shape in the northern 'room' displays a low terracotta 'begging bowl' set among a bed of Chatham Island forget-me-nots with an edging of *Buxus*. Outside this central feature are four standard plants of the pink-flowered *Rhododendron yakushimanum*. This striking formal display, blending New Zealand and European plants, fits a European design appropriate for a home once occupied by dignitaries from Britain. The small path on the north of the parterre features two beautiful white *Clianthus* bushes, while at the entrance to the main lawn opposite are two saluting ceramic figures reminding all of the official nature of the property.

Since 1990, the borders to the main lawn have received special attention. Edges have been modified and bordered with mowing strips. The north-west border, with its spotty planting of strong pink spring-flowering shrubs inherited from an earlier period, has been calmed by the introduction of white-flowering shrubs. The border on the east inside the pohutukawa has been completely replanted to include plants such as the blue-green *Carex trifida* and other grasses that move with the wind.

The northern slope below the main lawn has been planted in dwarf conifers that are eye-catching from the main drive and, by filtering the wind upwards, will in time possibly provide more shelter for the lawn above. Sir Michael Hardie-Boys has suggested planting the north-west face of this slope with Australian and South African plants. Already *Erica cerinthoides*, with its striking red flowers, is succeeding. The site is ideal and the concept excellent, given the many international figures who visit this garden.

On the left side of the drive, a little quirkiness brings a smile to the face – a recent planting of a group of the large glossy-leafed *Meryta sinclarii*, 'a puka forest', has its own ceramic 'puka family' standing in the shade of the tree's beautiful large leaves – the ceramics are the work of an Island Bay potter.

The 'Puka' family stand among a planting of young Meryta sinclairii*, Government House, August 1999.*

J. Hobbs

Above the puka forest lies the secluded Asylum Garden, somewhat reminiscent of Buxton's private garden. A long lawn is bordered on the east and a small part of the south by the Asylum wall remnant, which is now softened with a few climbing roses. At the southern end of the area is a small enclosed swimming pool.

Since 1990, the general work at Government House, besides the plantings, has included the realignment of steps, changes to curbing, the sealing of paths, the forming of walkways, and the creation of focal points to encourage visitors to explore further. After ten years of redevelopment, the grounds have now entered a maintenance phase. With the personal interest and involvement of the Governor-General and his wife, a dedicated trained staff, and empathy on the part of all for the special nature of this place, the benefits of this work are now apparent. In another decade, the property will celebrate its centennial and, while not yet administered as an historic garden, it is developing as a garden of special significance, an important Wellington garden on a difficult site.

Premier House, 260 Tinakori Road

Sections along Tinakori Road were popular with the new settlers. According

Tinakori Road, Town Acre 630, Wellington, showing Levin's house in the foreground, c 1847. Engraving by H. Melville after an original by S. Brees.

Alexander Turnbull Library, National Library of New Zealand, Te Puna Mātauranga, PUBL-0020-20-2

Town Acre 632, Tinakori Road, c 1860. Town Acres 630 and 631 are on the left (the Levin/Collins property). A Crown Grant was given to James St Hill in 1853 for Town Acre 632 at a time when Edward Gibbon Wakefield lived in the house. When Wellington became the capital in 1865, the Lieutenant Governor moved from Government House to this house. In this photograph a serpentine drive winds up to the cottage; today the present building (which replaced this cottage) is completely hidden by trees and shrubs.

Alexander Turnbull Library, National Library of New Zealand, Te Puna Mātauranga, F-31728-1/2

to Ward, Thomas Tate chose Town Acre 630; George Hunter, Town Acre 631; and Michael Seymour, Town Acre 632.

From an early date, Nathaniel William Levin had the use of number 630 and by 1847 had built a substantial cottage on it. In 1852, he acquired a Crown Grant for the section next door, number 631, and in 1854 a Crown Grant for 630. In 1862, Levin sold both properties to Richard Collins, a member of the recently formed Town Board, who added a southern wing with matching veranda. In 1865, Collins sold the house and sections 630 and 631 to the Crown for £2,909. From then until the present day, except for a period of forty years, it has been known as the Prime Minister's house or Premier House.

Town Acres 630 & 631. First Ministerial residence, c 1860s. The south wing is Collins's addition to the earlier Levin building.

Museum of New Zealand Te Papa Tongarewa B.12674

By 1873, when Julius Vogel was Prime Minister, a further substantial alteration transformed the house into a two-storey building with a conservatory on the north-east face.

Further additions to the house were made in 1926 while Gordon Coates and his family of five daughters lived there. When head gardener Abraham Robinson and his family were living in the servants' quarters, from 1928 to 1936, a comprehensive plan for the grounds of Premier House was drawn up by landscape architect Frederick Tschopp of the Works Development Office.

For many years, the Works Department ran its nursery from the flat land inside the Tinakori Road frontage on the left-hand side, where the lily pond is marked on the Tschopp plan. From the recollections of Mr Lesley Robinson, much of the Tschopp plan was implemented. Robinson, the son of Coates' head gardener, was 13 when he lived at 260 Tinakori Road. In later years, he recalled the garden:

> My main impression in those early days was the amount of bloom in the gardens. As you came in through the northern gate, the main gate, there were kauri trees, pohutukawas and ferns and further up the driveway, English yews and ornaments. On the left side of the main gate were seed propagation trays and there were dahlias, chrysanthemums and asters in red, white, pink, purple and yellow.
>
> The southern entrance was the tradesman's entrance. On both sides of the path there was a mass of blue and purple cinerarias, and then the lawn verge. In the triangle where the two paths met were camellias, rhododendrons, azaleas, pink and white, and a huge

> magnolia. Where our sleeping quarters were ... if you had the window open, when it was blooming, you'd get a tremendous scent from that tree. It was beautiful.
>
> To the right, the path wound round to the old coach house (just south of where the smaller ministerial house is now). There was a very old coach all covered in cobwebs and dust and the stables were there.
>
> The tennis court on the western boundary of the property was sunken low with banks on either side planted mainly in lobelia and polyanthus, carnations, cineraria and ferns. They held garden parties on the lawn tennis court. Society people would come and they would have a band which played in front of the ponga fern pavilion.
>
> Behind the fernery, steps led up to the four fowl houses. They kept Bantam chicks, and White Leghorns. Even a couple of geese if I remember rightly. Yes and ducks ... duck eggs. I remember them vividly now. When a chicken was required for eating at the house, that was my job. I never liked killing them. I didn't even like plucking them. I hated it.
>
> Beyond that and extending to the south western boundary was the orchard with apple trees of all varieties, lemons, raspberry and black currant bushes, a big cherry tree and a huge pear tree we used to climb – Winter Cole.
>
> Below the orchard, still on the southern boundary was a lovely rose garden. Almost a hundred roses of all different colours. They had a few standard roses around the perimeter of a grass path, perhaps a metre wide. And then inside the path they had miniature roses, old types, building up to standard roses in the centre.
>
> On the Tinakori Road frontage of the southern end of the property was a large vegetable garden.

The Prime Minister's residence, Hill Street corner, c 1900. Part of the Collins addition on the south has been retained. The garden is well developed and the two Norfolk Island pines are clearly visible in front of the house. Gorse is establishing itself on the Tinakori Hill behind.

Alexander Turnbull Library

When the first Labour government came to power in 1935, Michael Joseph Savage did not wish to occupy such a large house. There was talk of subdividing the property by extending Grant Road through the back of the section. Two years later, in 1937, it became a dental clinic, and from 1937–76 it served as an annexe to the main dental clinic in upper Willis Street. After fluoride was added to Wellington's water supply in the 1970s, the dental annex was closed. The house was used as a crèche, until finally it was left empty and forlorn. The Ministry of Works continued to operate its nursery headquarters from inside the entrance gate and used the tennis court to grow flowers for Government House receptions. New Zealand native plants used in the 1970 Japan World Exposition ('Expo 70') were propagated here by the head horticulturist, James Stirling.

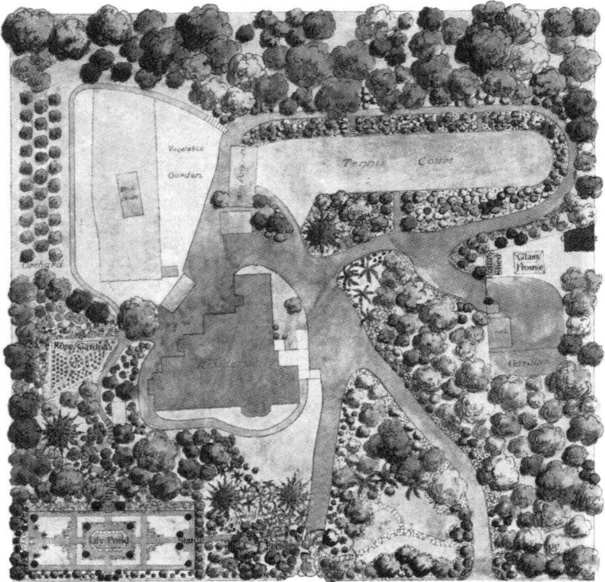

Proposed layout for Ministerial residence, F. Tschopp Landscape Architect, Works Development Office, 1930.

In the 1980s, the house was completely restored for use again as the Prime Minister's residence. The plant nursery was closed and the buildings were removed. The refurbished residence was opened by Sir Paul Reeves in July 1990, and Sir Geoffrey Palmer was the first Prime Minister to occupy it. Today, this mansion continues to function as a family home, but the ground floor rooms are used for public functions.

The garden of Premier House retains some of the plants dating from the

[Above left] Premier House today, taken from Hill Street, January 2000. The Tinakori Hill behind is in pines.
J. Nauta, Museum of New Zealand Te Papa Tongarewa

[Above right] The Garden Party, *Watercolour by Vivian Manthell, 1988.*

late 1860s and the alterations made in 1873. Of the original Norfolk Island pines, only one seems really healthy. In the 1890s, the vegetable garden was on the south Tinakori frontage, and it was still there when the Ministry of Works took over the area for its plant nursery. More recently, it has become a car park, upgraded with a perimeter planting of trees and shrubs. A gardener's shed has been erected on the site and new steps with a handrail replace the old stone steps of the Tschopp plan. The slope above is planted with native plants. The rose garden and orchard are no more, and the tennis court is a pleasant lawn. A horse chestnut (*Aesculus hippocastanum*) and a lime (*Tilia vulgaris*) are on the Wellington District Heritage list, but not the 130-year-old Norfolk Island pines in front of the house.

Premier House has hosted many functions over the years. Artist Vivian Manthell immortalised one special occasion in her water-colour, 'The Garden Party'.

Homewood, Karori

The story of the early years of Homewood, from the 1840s until Justice Chapman's departure in March 1852, has been told in Chapter 3. John Johnston and his wife Henrietta Charlotte followed the Chapmans, the purchase money coming from Henrietta Charlotte.[4]

The Johnstons had five children before they came to Homewood, and their last child was born there. Farming operations were not as intensive as in Chapman's time, but they were still maintained as far as the entrance on Karori Road. Johnston was a successful merchant, and wealthy enough by 1873 to afford a town house on sections 4, 5, 6 Fitzherbert Terrace. In 1866, the house at Homewood was extended close to the plan originally envisaged by Chapman.

Following Johnston's death in November 1887, his son Charles took over the property. Charles was Member of the House of Representatives for Te Aro from 1881 to 1887. In 1889, he was elected Mayor of Wellington. He

[4] It was Henrietta who gave the extra strip of land needed to 'tidy up' the gift of four acres given by Chapman to St Mary's Anglican Church in Fancourt Street.

lived at Homewood, improving the grounds with a great deal of planting, and making a new tennis lawn. He and his wife entertained with parties, picnics, and dancing on the lawn – all the social activities normally entered into by the early colonial gentry. When he retired as Mayor in 1891, he was appointed to the Legislative Council. He then lived in town, but holidays were spent at Homewood.

Major changes were now made to Homewood. The gate on the main road was moved to its present position, enabling the farm to be divided into four. In 1899, the old Homewood drive now became Homewood Avenue. Ten acres along the main road were subdivided and sold off between 1895 and 1899.

Little of the original bush remained. In 1902, Charles Johnston and his wife moved to their Hobson Street home while the house was altered. Over the next two years, Homewood was extensively remodelled, including the building of a circular turret and square tower, both with crenellated edgings. Part of the Chapman house was retained as servants' quarters.

Looking across the croquet and tennis lawns to Homewood in 1925. There is a large planting of cabbage trees on the left.

R.P. Moore, Homewood High Commission

The house looked out on to a new tennis and croquet lawn with pavilion, much as it does today. Below this was the orchard. The garden was charming, with primroses, daffodils, anemones, and azaleas ushering in the spring. When the croquet season opened, the string band played on the lawn, and tea was served in the pavilion.

Shortly before Charles Johnston died, he was knighted. Lady Johnston remained at Homewood for another seven years, before moving to Thorndon in 1925. In that year the photographer Moore took an interesting view of the property.

Homewood was sold for £13,500 to a contractor, Charles Pulley, in 1925. Pulley lived in the house, but sold off much of the land. By 1928, sections on the Homewood side of Homewood Avenue to Hatton Street, Waikare, and Hauraki Streets were sold. The house and remaining grounds, 2 acres 14.8 perches, were then sold to Benjamin Sutherland for £7,000, but Pulley retained Johnston's Hill.[5] The bush that Chapman had known had long gone, but from 1928 to 1957 the garden under Sutherland achieved its greatest prominence.

The orchard has been replaced by a croquet lawn, but the shelter belt of radiata pines has not yet been removed, c 1928.

Lent by Graham Sutherland

Benjamin Sutherland, founder of the Self-Help Grocery chain, developed a unique estate at Homewood, which he opened to the public on many

[5] Karori Progressive Society members, concerned about Pulley's supposed subdivision of Johnston Hill land, offered to purchase the area for use as a reserve of bush and open space. Pulley agreed to sell for £2,500. Wellington City Council paid half and the local residents the remainder. Today, Johnston's Hill Scenic Reserve and returning bush can be enjoyed by all.

[Above left] One of the waterfalls in the winter garden.

Homewood High Commission

[Above middle] Two of Platt's lions look over the fountain, c 1930s.

Courtesy G. Sutherland

[Above right] The Homewood driveway, c 1939. Macrocarpas have been planted on left-hand boundary. Magnolias, rata, and other shrubs are newly planted. Johnston's Hill is in the background.

occasions. It was an astonishing place, of a kind not seen elsewhere in New Zealand. Sutherland engaged the Christchurch landscape architect Alfred Buxton to lay out the garden, no expense spared, employing twelve to twenty men over a period of two years. A large conservatory, or 'winter garden', as it was known, was attached to the house off the dining room, facing north.

The winter garden was recalled in 1986:

> The winter garden situated between the house and the swimming pool was two-storied. Looking through the big window in the lounge there was a conservatory with the appropriate plants, then a fernery on a slightly lower level then down to the pool. Seven months was spent building the fernery which was made up of about 70 tons of rock and steel reinforcement. All the rocks were hand picked from the quarry and wired into place before being cemented in. The main waterfall fell over a path but was adjusted so that water did not fall on the path. The trees in the foreground were steel rods covered in cork bark. The looped trailers at the top were lead water pipes covered with cork with gas jets inserted to water the ferns. He waterfall fell into a pool which in turn fed three others resulting in two other smaller falls. Every waterfall had coloured lights behind and in some areas the lights were masked to represent the sun or moon reflected in the pools. There were 72 lights in the whole complex. The whole building was enclosed with different coloured glass panels and at one side there were tanks of tropical fish which could be glimpsed through the rocks and ferns. There was a glow-worm grotto at the bottom right hand corner of the complex'.[6]

Buxton designed three walled gardens, ferneries, grottoes, and glow-worm caves with pools and waterfalls. The grape house was demolished, and the house looked out to a fountain with coloured lights and two lions, cast by William Platt, guarding the entrance to the house from the tennis court. Two more lions were placed near where the drive forked. Hundreds of people visited the gardens – members of societies such as the Wellington Free Ambulance, the Wellington Swimming Centre, kindergartens, university groups. The author visited there in 1941 with the University Easter Tournament Representatives and can vouch for the impact the property made on all. Two articles written about this time describe this garden wonderland.

> To appreciate the real beauty of the Gardens one must walk along the Vista path. Turning to the right after entering the gate we come to a sunken path behind the trees on the edge of the lawn. Every few yards a different perspective meets the eye ... to the left a sunken rose garden comes into view, and in a tree shaded bower on the right is a little gnome village .... A small pond complete with fountain and

One of the four lions cast by William Platt in 1934 from drawings made by the artist at Wellington Zoo, December 1999. Of the four lions, two have two tails.

J. Nauta, Museum of New Zealand C.T.15697/14-18

[6] Letter to Graeme Sutherland from F. Neate.

goldfish next claim attention. On the bank sits the Doctor, spoon and medicine bottle in hand ready to give relief to his patient, a poor wee frog .... Continuing we happen upon a veritable farm yard settlement: pigeons, rabbits, hares, snails .... Up a tree not far away are the Chasing Cats.

On our left is open air Fernery No. 3, containing small waterfalls and a miniature bathing pool where several ladies are lying on the bank .... In all the open air Ferneries 2, 3 and 4, one is transported in fancy miles away from the hurly burly of city life to the delightful atmosphere of our unspoiled forest land.

Following the incessant sound of gay chatter, one continues on under the portico until we come in sight of the Aviaries, eighteen in all, where are gathered hundreds of birds, many of rare species and gorgeous colouring ....

The Begonia Houses present a feast of luxuriant colour ... from them one enters the lovely Winter Garden with its truly tropical atmosphere. Here are an Augusta Strelitzia with its tremendous leaves, huge Palms, and Ferns of many varieties, and the rare purple Bougainvillea. In the centre is a miniature park and ornamental pond, complete with water lilies and ducks. In the park are hundred of people listening to music being played by a band on a rotunda. This charming scene is set in a bed of maidenhair, backed with asparagus, and walled on either side with hydrangeas .... Through the foliage and great glass windows one sees right through the Grotto Fernery to the shimmering waters of the swimming pool.

In the Grotto Fernery ... one's first feelings are of wonder and awe, as having intruded in some enchanted glade .... Through crevices in the rocks can be seen waterfalls, streams and limpid pools with their mossy banks.

Taking a path to the right and crossing a rustic bridge, one comes to the Glow-worm Cave, cunningly fashioned in the hillside. At the entrance is a most charming scene. Disposed in care-free attitudes around five tiny fountains are grouped several gnomes, watching with delighted attention balls kept in play by jets of water on which are played vari-coloured lights.

Entering the Glow-worm Cave from the Fernery, one must do so very quietly, for these little creatures are extremely shy .... They light up the walls and ceiling as stars on a cloudless night ....

There were banks of hydrangeas and brilliant azaleas, and ferns, from pongas to rare types; Fernery No. 4 with its tiers of rocky shelves which give the appearance of a miniature amphitheatre; and everywhere little figures – the Bookworm, three Card players using a large toadstool for a table, a Drunkard lying under the hedge with two bottles beside him.

A rustic bridge crosses a pool containing many rare species of fish, including Japanese Fantail and Blackmoore, and wax-like water

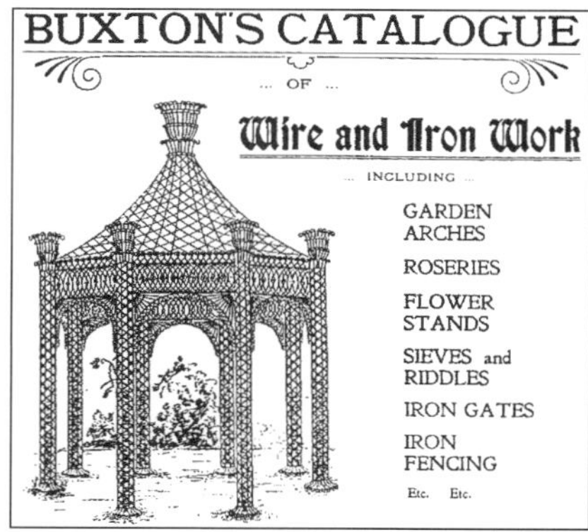

Buxton Catalogue, c 1905.

[Below left] Looking from the house down to the tennis court, the croquet lawn, and the pavilion, c 1930s. The fountain with coloured lights was in the immediate foreground, but is not visible here.

Frank Thompson, courtesy G. Sutherland

[Below right] A path leads off the main circular drive above the tennis court, c 1930s. Behind the tennis court and to the right of the pergola is the wall of one of the ferneries. There is a sundial in the foreground.

Courtesy Mrs J. McKay

[Above left] Homewood, looking across the Japanese Garden and its Buxton designed bridge and background walls, c 1980s. The square and crenellated edge to the balcony are from the 1904 alterations. The billiard room alteration is more recent.

Homewood British High Commission

[Above right] A serene house in a serene setting, Homewood, December 1999. The present British High Commissioner's wife, botanical artist Mrs Sue Williams, admires features from the past such as the two totara trees and the lions, together with the relatively new armillary sphere sundial set in a formal bedding display.

J. Nauta, Museum of New Zealand C.T.15697/4-28

lilies. More gnomes and frogs abound here and on the edges of the large lawn.[7]

When Jean Sutherland was married on 19 January 1938 the *Evening Post* said:

> It was a windless afternoon, clear and sunny. The flower-beds were a brilliant sight against the background of English and native trees, and a rose-coloured carpet stretched from the rockery steps to the two big weeping elms in front of which the ceremony took place.
>
> In the hall of Homewood rose-tinted hydrangeas were massed against the stairway and large flat bowls of white agapanthus gave a bridal note to the decorations.

No mere photographs can evoke the ambience of the unique Buxton/Sutherland garden of Homewood during the 1930s and 1940s.[8]

In 1957, Mrs Sutherland heard that the British High Commission was looking for a residence for the High Commissioner and offered Homewood for sale. The property had become too much for her, and much of the garden was run down. In October 1957, and owing much to the insistence of Lady Mallaby, wife of the High Commissioner, the British Government bought the property for £45,000.

Redecoration of the house and refurbishment of the garden were necessary. The winter garden, too hard to repair, was pulled down. Some ferneries and grottoes were removed, and many of the trees, fences, and shrubs replaced, particularly after the *Wahine* storm of 1968. Alterations, redecoration, and replanting continue as subsequent High Commissioners and their wives occupy Homewood.

In November 1999, Homewood was the venue of a special garden party hosted by Robert and Pat Alston to celebrate the fiftieth year since a British High Commissioner first occupied the house. The house and croquet pavilion, registered Category I by the Historic Places Trust, together with the

View of the totara framing the front entrance to Homewood, December 1999.

Photo. J. Nauta, Museum of New Zealand C.T.15697/19-24

[7] Programme, Open Day, Free Kindergarten, 30 November 1937.

[8] For those wishing to know more about Homewood and its families, the reader is directed to Beryl Smedley's excellent book *Homewood*. This account is focused on the garden, some of the information coming from Smedley's book, some taken from the Chapman papers at the Alexander Turnbull Library.

garden, continue to be used to offer hospitality for charitable and community occasions, as they were from the time the Johnstons acquired the property. As a legacy from the past, the two totara, seedlings from the original bush, continue to grow and have carried over into the new millennium. The property and these trees are special, not only for Karori and its residents, but for the city as a whole.

Gardens around historic homes

Gardening is both an art and a science, a social history, and a rich store of a way of life. In New Zealand, garden history is still in its infancy and has not taken off as it has in Australia, our nearest neighbour.

In the latter part of the twentieth century, interest in Wellington's architectural heritage gathered momentum as efforts were made to save and preserve some important city buildings. An appreciation of older houses in both city and suburb followed, with a consequent boom in renovation and recreation of old housing stock. Polished floors and Edwardian-styled rimu furniture evoke memories of the past, but restyling of the interior with modern kitchens and bathrooms and vibrant colour schemes result in vastly superior houses giving not only comfort but also workable ease to present owners.

The re-establishment of authentic gardens around these houses has received little attention. However, the preservation and restoration of three historic residences in Wellington – Antrim House, the Katherine Mansfield Birthplace, and Nairn Cottage – have involved discussions and decisions on what to do with their gardens.

The three houses are very different. The Nairn Street cottage was built in 1857 by a builder and his wife. The Katherine Mansfield Birthplace was a simple villa of the 1880s, the home of a young married couple whose middle daughter would become a famous writer. Antrim House was built in 1904 to exhibit the status of a wealthy businessman with a large family. Its grounds were maintained by a professional gardener. The Beauchamps' garden and that at the Nairn Street cottage were adequate, and secondary to the activities of young children.

Research into the garden at Antrim House for the years 1905–30 suggests that the garden, while not so grand as the house, complemented and enhanced its dignity and respectability. This was not the case for Mansfield's Birthplace at the time of her birth, nor for Nairn Cottage. These differences between the three properties have influenced the re-establishment of their gardens today.

Antrim House, Boulcott Street

Designed by William Turnbull and built for Robert Hannah in 1904, this striking Italianate-styled house is now the headquarters of the New Zealand Historic Places Trust, who have registered it as Category I. A Yorkshireman, Sam Scott, was employed as part-time gardener. Evidently he was happy to repeat the same theme year after year, which is not surprising for those times, when the custom was to use plants in bedding displays in front of perennial or more permanent background shrubs. They were very striking in the summer.

Antrim House and its garden, with an ornate fence and entrance gate, not long after its completion, c 1910. Young plants that are staked on account of the wind include cabbage trees, holly, magnolia, rhododendrons, fuchsias, carnations, sweet William, and bedding begonias. Five beds, circular and square, are inserted into the lawn. Edged with a similar planting to that around the main beds, they follow the bedding plant fashions of the time. The right-hand boundary of the property adjoins that of Plimmer House. The houses behind are on The Terrace.

S.C. Smith Collection, Alexander Turnbull Library, National Library of New Zealand, Te Puna Mātauranga, G-23048-1/1, PAColl-3082

In 1940, fire damaged Antrim House – it was being used as a hostel at the time. Photographs taken then show the same flower beds in the lawn, but the trees and shrubs had grown up along the drive and inside the front fence. Both grounds and house received attention following the fire. In 1947, when the United States Government considered purchasing the property, the illustrated record still shows the carpet bedding in the lawn, but in front of the house is a neatly clipped hedge with holly tree on the left corner and tall cabbage trees behind.

The city was slowly encroaching and absorbing Boulcott Street. By 1951, the area had become shabby and Antrim House was but a shadow of its former glory.

In December 1987, Antrim House was purchased by the government for use as the headquarters of New Zealand Historic Places Trust. The house was beautifully restored, while the garden came under the care of the Wellington City Council's Parks Department. The department's landscape architect, Ron Flook, designed its refurbishment with concern for its maintenance. The garden does have a suitable relationship with the age of the house. The holly and cabbage trees at the corner of the drive have been retained and the shape of the borders recreated to match the original layout. To the right, the old conservatory now functions as an office, and in the space between that and the house a parterre was designed to complement the house and demonstrate the garden fashion of the time. To the rear of the house, some old magnolias received attention.

Box edged beds enclosing roses, Antrim House, 1997.

W. Shepherd

Backing on to Antrim House and the steep sections on The Terrace, is its neighbour, Plimmer House. Built in 1868, it is a small gentleman's residence in Gothic Revival style with steeply pitched roof, tower, and rusticated weatherboards.

[Above left] Original siting of Plimmer House, c 1911, with its charming garden.

Museum of New Zealand

[Above middle] Plimmer House, with apartments on The Terrace intruding, 1967. The house was moved forwards on the section in the 1980s and is a well-known restaurant today.

Alexander Turnbull Library, National Library of New Zealand, Te Puna Mātauranga, F-27012-1/2

[Above right] Plimmer House, now separated from Antrim House by the commercial building behind, November 1999.

J. Nauta, Museum of New Zealand C.T.15701/22-25

Isaac Harold Plimmer bought this attractive property adjoining Antrim House in 1911. One lady remembered the huge *Diosma* bush which 'scented the whole street .... There were beautiful camellia trees, moss roses, violets, primroses, bluebells and other spring bulbs'. In the 1960s, an apartment block was built behind both Antrim House and Plimmer House. Plimmer House changed hands and in the 1980s was moved forward on the section, most of the garden being lost in the process.

Katherine Mansfield's Birthplace, Te Puakitanga, 25 Tinakori Road

Te Puakitanga – 'first place of the story teller' – is a property of historical literary importance that is open to the public. Owned by the Katherine Mansfield Birthplace Society, the house has been sensitively restored, even down to replicas of the original wallpapers, and furnished with furniture of the 1880s. (Mansfield was born in 1888.) The garden, likewise, has been planted using plants that were fashionable at the time. The property is situated near the site of High Cliff, the home of William Swainson, and not far from Pakuao Pa, where Stowe's house Tiakiwai was built.

The author was asked to examine the garden in 1987, shortly after the property had been acquired by the Society. The garden was disappointing, with little of significance except for the roses, which were subsequently identified as being from the 1940s. There were two karaka, a karo, a side bed of acanthus, a few arums, and other miscellaneous plants. The report recommended that the management should decide on a policy for the garden's future. Suggestions from various groups of horticulturists were discussed.

The creation of a garden for the Katherine Mansfield Birthplace highlights many of the problems associated with or encountered internationally in the management of gardens around historic homes. For example, when the

The seaward end of Tinakori Road in 1867, showing the uplift after the 1855 earthquake. A road runs along Thorndon Quay from Pipitea Point, with Hobson Street houses and W.M. Bannatyne's house predominant in the centre. Stowe House, not visible, was above Dr Featherstone's house, later the Caledonian Hotel, on the right. The two gullies cutting across the flat are clearly visible.

Museum of New Zealand Te Papa Tongarewa B.14596

The bridge from Hobson Street to Tinakori Road, c 1883. Tinakori Hill is in the background.
William Berry

garden itself is not historic, what are the choices? If there are large trees and original views are obliterated, what is sensible – leave the trees untouched because they are part of the property's history, trim the trees, or remove the trees? If a property was originally laid out before the advent of the car, should it return to that era? What plants should be chosen? What is the planting plan? Maintenance costs have to be considered – labour costs, manures, pruning, weeding, spraying.

In the case of Antrim House, Ron Flook solved the problem of maintenance in the courtyard between Antrim House and its parking area by designing a series of box-edged beds to surround and shelter selected rose varieties. It is a turn-of-the-twentieth-century period design. Maintenance is minimal, but its relation to that particular house is fiction.

Large trees requiring removal were not a consideration with the Katherine Mansfield Birthplace, but the cost of establishment of the garden, and its maintenance, were vitally important. It was decided to make the garden representative of the years 1880–1900, with plants that could be obtained in Wellington then.[9] The Beauchamps were young and not wealthy when they lived there. Moreover, they were still establishing their family, so the garden needed to be suitable for young children.

The garden has gradually evolved along pragmatic lines. There has been time to incorporate plants mentioned in Mansfield's writings, as was always intended, and to add plants likely to have been grown during the period chosen. Volunteer botanist Wendy Tolley manages the garden. It is authentic in some ways, not authentic in others, but it captures the mood, the period, and the writings of the author, providing today's visitors with a garden that satisfies their desire for literary references. It complements the current use of the house, no longer a family home but a museum and biographical memorial. Two karaka trees have been retained. They were probably planted well after the Beauchamps' time, but karakas were mentioned by Mansfield in 'The Garden Party' . 'They were so lovely with their broad gleaming leaves and their clusters of yellow fruit.'[10] The side hedge shown in the photograph has long gone.

The birthplace of Katherine Mansfield. The property's hedge was later replaced by the paling fence that is there today. There are pines growing in the gully behind the house.
Museum of New Zealand Te Papa Tongarewa

A swing bridge once linked Hobson Street with Tinakori Road, crossing a gully, and according to Mansfield, the gully was filled with tree ferns. In the 1960s, the gully and some of the back section of No 25 were taken to form the motorway. Appropriately, *Dicksonia* tree ferns are being established in a corner by the back fence. A kowhai has been planted in the front, a link with kowhai growing so well further up Glenmore Street, but it is inappropriate to replant *Pinus radiata* on the rear boundary, although originally there was a row of these along the top of the gully behind the house. The archaeological work to establish the original layout of the garden has been thorough and meticulous.

Mansfield was only five when she left her birthplace in Thorndon to live in Karori, so her recollections of her first home are remarkable. Her writings

---

9 As research for this book proves, by 1870 and except for the latest varieties, the majority of plants were obtainable in New Zealand, and could have been available in Wellington.

10 'The Garden Party', *The Stories of Katherine Mansfield*, ed. Antony Alpers, Auckland, OUP, 1984, p. 488.

include vivid impressions of her country and the houses she lived in, together with their surroundings – sand, sea, wind, bush, running water, trees, and garden flowers. The garden at No 25 she remembered as:

> Small and square with flower beds on either side. All down one side big clumps of arum lilies aired their rich beauty, on the other side there was nothing but a straggle of what children called 'grandmother's cushions'.

The garden is small and square still, with a narrow gravel path around two sides of the lawn.

The left-hand bed inside the gate features the perfumed quartered lavender rose 'Reine des Violettes'. A white *Wisteria sinensis alba* covers the once unattractive paling fence on the left between the two karaka trees. The bed behind the porch, once filled with acanthus and arums, has the beautiful white rose, the rugosa hybrid 'Blanc double de Coubert'. The arums are still there. Inside and tumbling over the front fence is *Rosa banksiae lutea* and the deep-purple quartered moss rose 'William Lobb'. Many of the roses have been donated.

There is a strong accent on annuals, whose seeds are collected, cleaned, and packed by Tolley, and sold to visitors to the house. Slowly, shrubs and perennials are forming a permanent background to seasonal flowers, which Tolley says will help minimise the upkeep. Native plants have not been excluded: near the *Dicksonia*, the Chatham Island forget-me-not, *Myosotidium hortensia*, *Arthropodium cirrhatum* (renga renga), and the climber *Clematis paniculata* have been included.

Readers requiring further information about the house or garden should apply to the Katherine Mansfield Birthplace Society Inc.

Katherine Mansfield's Birthplace, December 1999.

J. Nauta, Museum of New Zealand

Brick-edged gravel path between lawn and border, October 1999.

J. Nauta, Museum of New Zealand
C.T.13705/37-39

Nairn Street Cottage, 68 Nairn Street

The Nairn Street Cottage, built in the 1850s by William Wallis, is registered in Category II by the New Zealand Historic Places Trust. It is an excellent example of an early working-class cottage. Some features, such as the veranda, the iron roof, and the wash house, are later additions or alterations.

Before emigrating, Wallis lived just north of London. Originally apprenticed to a builder, it is believed that from 1853 he worked for Sir Joseph Paxton in London. His building experience was gained in the Crimea, working with a team of Paxton's men erecting prefabricated hospitals for Florence Nightingale. Following his marriage, he sailed for Wellington, where his skills as a carpenter and builder were in demand. He built this cottage, his first home, on a town acre in Nairn Street.[11] He succeeded so well, besides having a large family, that in 1874 he bought and built on the section next door. William died in 1911, but the original cottage remained in the family until 1977, when it was bought by the Wellington City Council at the time they were building the Nairn Street/Brooklyn Road flats.

Nairn Street Cottage, built in 1857 by William Wallis, 1999.

W. Shepherd

A cottage museum society formed in 1972 successfully campaigned for 68 Nairn Street to become a museum. Restoration work began shortly after the property was acquired by the Wellington City Council.

In an appendix to the Colonial Cottage Museum Society report for 1997 are proposed garden plans from two landscapers. Again the suggestions highlight the difficulties of restoring, recreating, or creating an historic garden.

The second house from the left is Nairn Street Cottage, viewed from the rear, c. 1890.

Built in 1857, the house was lived in by the family until 1977. Initially, as still happens, the presence of young children would have influenced the amount of land allocated for their activities and the area allocated for the garden. Gardens may be refurbished every ten years or so – as the family grows up, or as plants grow bigger, or to incorporate new ideas and new plants. Over a period of 130 years, many changes would have occurred.

The sketch indicates the position of the house on the section, the front path, small front garden, and the side path to the privy at the rear, which was serviced by the night cart. There are a number of trees and shrubs on the property, planted by family members at different times. In developing a garden policy for 68 Nairn Street, as with the Katherine Mansfield Birthplace, a number of factors had to be considered. What funds were available for development and maintenance? What is to be the purpose of the garden and its relationship with the cottage? Which period during the 130 years should the garden represent?

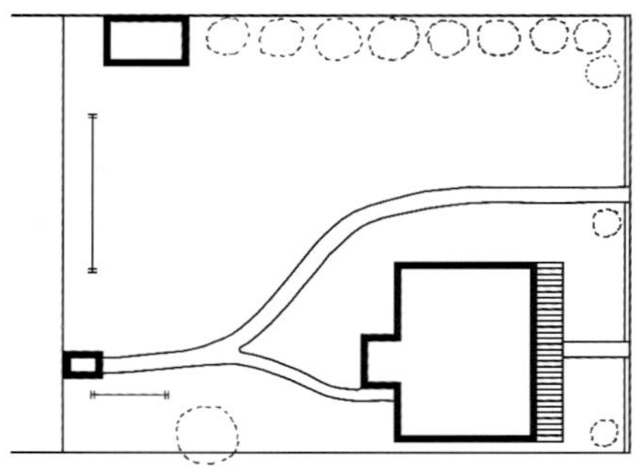

Sketch showing layout of paths and outhouses of 68 Nairn Street.
Martin Hill

Research for this book may influence the final outcome, for it is now known that one of Wellington's early plant nurseries was almost adjacent to Nairn Cottage when it was first built. The plant nursery was founded by John Watson in 1850. For a short time after 1860 the nursery, functioned as the Portobello Tea Gardens, and was run by William Mansill. Around 1873, it became a market garden owned by the German gardener Heinrich Bunckenburg (Panorama 3). The story of the nursery is taken up again in Chapter 6. Suffice to say here that in 1854, before the Nairn Cottage was built, the nursery offered a number of flowering plants for sale, including possibly the first roses in Wellington.

> A selection of hybrid, perpetual, Bourbon, Noisette and tea-scented roses, 20 varieties of geraniums, 20 varieties of verbenas, 9 varieties of Calceolaria etc. Myatt's surprise strawberry, Queen strawberry, holly, *Berberis aquifolia*, a fine hybrid rhododendron, whitehorn quick, holly, plums, pears, Medlars, Damson's etc.
>
> The roses, geranium, verbenas, and strawberries are warranted imported from England and of the finest description.[12]

In 1863, the nursery, now owned by Mansill, advertised fruit, forest trees, shrubs of every description, a collection of calceolarias, garden seeds, and plants for sale. An enlargement of Bragge's 1875 panorama [Panorama 2] shows trees around Nairn Cottage and larger trees on the nursery land. The 1890s Burton Brother's panorama [Panorama 3] has a house built on the vacant site next door to Nairn Cottage. During the fifteen years between the

[11] Wallis's sole ownership of the Town Acre has not yet been clarified, subdivision seems to have occurred in the 1850s.

[12] *Wellington Independent*, 21 October 1854.

two photographs there were many changes. Nairn Street's well-formed footpaths of the 1890s, by impinging on the original house frontages on the right-hand side of the road, had caused the removal of trees that were originally at the front of these properties.

By the 1890s, little was left of the nursery and market garden but a few trees. New houses had been built on some of the land, and Brooklyn Road had formed across the vacant lower end.

As part of the Nairn Street Cottage restoration work and using the foregoing information, Martin Hill created a plan for a garden around Nairn Cottage in 1998. It remains to be seen if any of it eventuates.

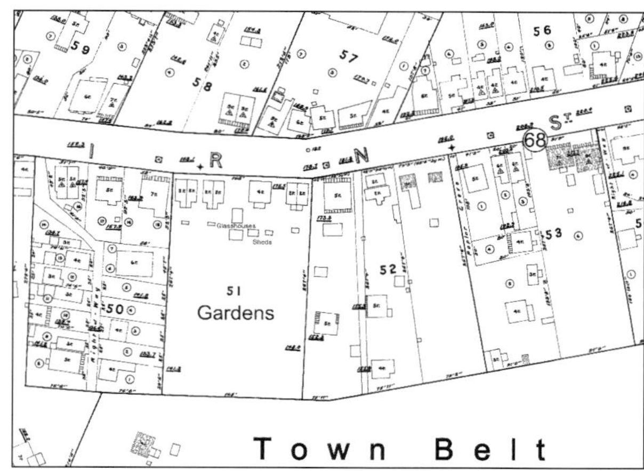

[Above] Surveyor's plan of Nairn Street, showing site of former nursery and Nairn Street Cottage in relation to the Town Belt.

Ward Survey Plan, 1891

[Above left] Thompson Street/Nairn Street/Aro Street, 1875. The newly built Kirkcaldie house at the top of Thompson Street is as yet unplanted. Nairn Street Cottage with vacant land alongside is the fourth house on the right-hand side of Nairn Street. A paling fence encloses a row of trees, and there are trees along road frontages. An extensive area of the Watson/Mansill Nursery has probably just become a market garden.

Bragge, 1875. Museum of New Zealand

[Above right] A similar view, c 1890s. A house has been built next to Nairn Cottage. Nursery land has been partially built on, and paling fences have aged.. Trees have been removed from in front of the right-hand Nairn Street properties to form footpaths. Pine trees surround Kirkcaldie house in Thompson Street.

Burton Bros Collection, Alexander Turnbull Library, National Library of New Zealand, Te Puna Mātauranga, G-4463-1/1-B

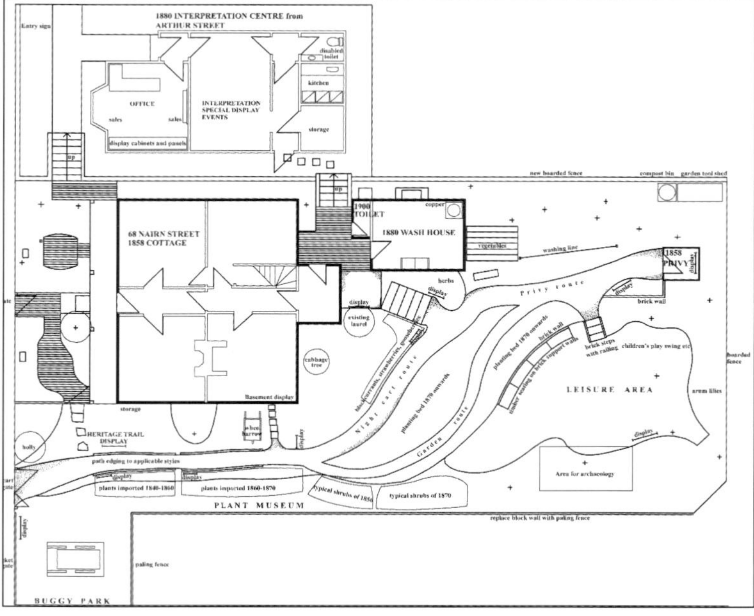

[Right] Proposed plan for Nairn Street Cottage garden layout, 1998.

Martin Hill

Chatham Island forget-me-not, N.M. Adams

Chapter 6

THE HORTICULTURAL AND A&P SOCIETIES

Twenty months after the arrival of the first ships, a group of settlers held a preliminary meeting to consider establishing a horticultural society. There was general approval for the idea. The inaugural meeting took place on 8 November 1841. 'Mr Watts, the spirited landlord of Barrett's Hotel kindly allowed the gratuitous use of his room for the meeting on Monday.'[1] The meeting was convivial. Chaired by Colonel Wakefield, Dr Featherston moved and Mr A. d'B. Brandon seconded the motion that 'a society for the promotion of horticulture in all its branches be formed and that it be called the Wellington Horticultural and Botanical Society'.

The first house built on Lambton Quay beach and Barrett's Hotel, site of the first Horticultural Society Show on 22 January 1842.

Ward's Early Wellington

Thus the first horticultural society in New Zealand was formed. The objectives of the Society were:

> 1. To promote cultivation as extensively as possible not only among the landed proprietors and immigrant capitalists but by offering premiums for the best and neatest garden to direct attention to stimulate the efforts of the working classes, to the formation of gardens and to show them the value of their leisure hours in securing the blessings of independence and in enlarging the circle of their domestic enjoyment.
>
> 2. To import considerable quantities of flowers and fruits commonly cultivated in England but which it was understood might easily be obtained in the sister colonies particularly Van Diemen's Land and to distribute them in small parcels among members at cost price.
>
> 3. To develop a Botanic Garden as soon as land was allocated.

[1] *New Zealand Spectator*, Alexander Turnbull Library, 10 November 1841.

As might be expected, prominent settlers were elected as the fledgling society's office bearers.

PRESIDENT
Colonel Wakefield

VICE PRESIDENTS
R.D. Hanson Esq.
M. Murphy Esq.
F.A. Molesworth Esq.
J.T. Wickstead Esq.

TREASURER
R. Stokes Esq.

SECRETARY
Dr Featherstone

COMMITTEE
C.E. von Alzdorf
R. Barton Esq.
Mr Henry
Dr Evans
Capt. Smith R.A.
J. Wade Esq.
H. St. Hill Esq.
Mr Hurst
Capt. Darvill
Rev. J. McFarlane
W. Swainson Esq.
Mr D. Wilkinson
R. Stokes Esq.
Maj. Baker
E. Johnston Esq.
A. Ludlam Esq.
J. Watt Esq.

With New Zealand Company support, the new Horticultural Society was intended to be a means of bringing settlers and local Māori together to grow the food that was essential for everyone's survival. Within ten days, 103 people had joined.[2] It was a promising outcome. From Colonel Wakefield down, the majority of colonists were united in the effort of developing this new environment, and establishing plants and crops from their homeland. The distinctions of gentlemen, military men, and minor nobility such as the Baron must have vanished as exhibitors and visitors enthused over the treasures on display.

The European population had been increasing steadily, with farming and grazing under way at Karori, Lyall Bay, Lower Hutt, and Porirua. The small community was confident as it celebrated its second anniversary on 22 January 1842. There were sailing and rowing matches, a hurdle horse race, rural sports, a ball at Barrett's Hotel, and other festivities. The first Horticultural Society Show was held two days later on 24 January 1842 at Barrett's Hotel. The time of the year was not favourable, being too late for spring's bounty, yet too soon for most late summer produce and flowers, but the display was evidently gratifying. Judging from the prize list, much was already being grown in the Colony.

Mr Burcham's cabbages, grown within 30 yards of the beach at Petone, were exceptionally noteworthy. One, a hybrid, weighed 21½ lb., while the other, an 'Early Fulham', weighed 12 lb. Some potatoes grown from native seed by Francis Molesworth measured as much as nine inches. Dr Featherston's dahlias were a first for Wellington, as were also Mr Hurst's geraniums, which were said to be very beautiful. Baron Alzdorf exhibited Wellington's first apples – four of them – while his wheat was over 5 ft 5 in high, with very full and very large ears. Like the apples, the wheat was a first for Wellington.

Imagine the euphoria of that first show – the pride and achievement in producing the crops, flowers, and fruits from home in this southern land. Just imagine those four apples! More importantly, the show, as intended, had

[2] *New Zealand Journal*, April 1843.

PRIZE LIST WELLINGTON HORTICULTURAL SHOW HELD 22 JANUARY 1842

For COTTAGER'S GARDEN		Gardener's prize – BEST GARDEN	
1— prize £1.10	Mr James	1st prize £1	Mr Hunt
2nd prize 15/-	Mr D. Johnston	2nd prize	D. Wilkinson

Judges R.B. Barnes Esq., F. Johnston Esq., Mr J. Jackson, Mr Henry

FLOWERS		
12 annuals	First prize	J.T. Wickstead Esq.
Seedling geranium		
Coll. Geraniums	Extra prize	Mr Hurst
Bouquet flowers	First prize	D. Wilkinson
	Second prize	Capt. Smith R.A.
	Extra prize	Maj. Baker
Dahlias	Extra prize	Dr Featherstone
VEGETABLES		
12 potatoes		
6 kidney, 6 round	1st prize	F.A. Molesworth
	2nd prize	A Ludlam
	Extra prize	Mr Burcham
	Extra prize	Capt. Mein-Smith
12 pods peas	1st prize	Mr Bannister
	Extra prize	Baron Alzdorf
6 beans	1st prize	E. Pharazyn
	2nd prize	Mr MacLagan
Kidney beans	1st prize	E. Catchpool
	2nd prize	Mr Hunt
Cauliflower	1st prize	D. Wilkinson
	2nd prize	E. Johnstone
2 turnips 2 varieties		
2 of each	1st prize	D. Wilkinson
	2nd prize	R. Stokes Esq.
	Extra prize	Maj. Baker
	Extra prize	Mr Baines
6 carrots	1st prize	F.A. Molesworth Esq.
	2nd prize	Col. Wakefield
4 lettuces 2 varieties	1st prize	A. Ludlam Esq.
2 of each		
6 onions	1st prize	Mr D. Lewis
	2nd prize	Capt. Smith R.A.
Best 2 roots beet	1st prize	H. Knowles Esq.
	2nd prize	D. Wilkinson
4 cabbages 2 varieties	1st prize	Mr Burcham
2 of each	2nd prize	E. Johnston Esq.
4 pot-herbs		Capt. Smith R.A.
Kohl rabi	Extra prize	E. Johnston Esq.
BEST SPECIMEN WHEAT		
(From the Hutt Valley)		The Baron Alzdorf
EXTRA PRIZE		The Baron Alzdorf
(4 apples)		
NATIVE PRIZE		
6 large potatoes		E. Keti, Pah Pipitea

Table 1

Petone, where Mr Burcham's prize-winning cabbages and turnips were grown. They were exhibited in the first Horticultural Show at Barrett's Hotel on 24 January 1842.

S. C. Brees, Alexander Turnbull Library, National Library of New Zealand, Te Puna Mātauranga

Horticultural and Botanical Society
The next Exhibition will take place at the Exchange, on Tuesday, March 22.
All articles must be sent before 10 o'clock, a.m.
I.E. FEATHERSTON, Secretary
Admittance to ladies' and subscribers, gratis to non-subscribers, 1s.
New Zealand Spectator, 16 March 1842

brought together 'the various classes of immigrant and local Māori' and demonstrated the range of produce that could be grown in Wellington. A winning exhibit of potatoes from a resident of Pipitea Pa is worth remembering even today. Anniversary celebrations, and this Horticultural Show in particular, were just the tonic those early settlers needed. It is not surprising, therefore, that another show was scheduled and advertised within a few weeks.

Again, it was a success. *The New Zealand Journal* of 6 August 1842 drew attention to the range of vegetables grown and concluded:

> Vegetables may be purchased in Wellington much finer and cheaper than in London and by far the greater part are produced in gardens in and around the town which have been described as barren hills.[3]

Following the success of these two shows, Robert Stokes, foundation treasurer of the Society, wrote:

> All were agreeably surprised at the collection of vegetables and other productions displayed on each occasion, embracing all the varieties in ordinary cultivation and which in point of size and quality could not be surpassed in England. Indeed many kinds of vegetables as the variety of cabbage, turnips, pea etc. grow here more luxuriantly. In the meantime the formation of newer gardens has continued steadily during the autumn and winter, fruit trees and other valuable plants being introduced. From the different enquiries which I have made I find there cannot be less than 2000 fruit trees in the Colony. The greatest part of them in the town and its vicinity but a considerable portion of them in the Hutt. The greater part of these have been brought from Sydney and Van Diemen's Land but some have been sent from England, and I am anxious to see a little greater importation from thence, as the very best varieties may there be selected. I think too much pain cannot be bestowed in procuring the best varieties as they can be safely multiplied by grafting; but if we satisfy ourselves with inferior kinds at first we shall lose much time in retracing our steps and correcting our mistakes, and the right application of time in a new colony is the *onum necessarium*. Contributions to the Wellington Horticultural Society of fruit trees and other useful plants will be of more service than subscriptions; they need not be afraid of sending too many as, after the first and principal settlement is supplied we have our friends at Wanganui, Taranaki, and Nelson to think of. Fruit trees should be of the best varieties which may be readily procured from a respectable nurseryman. Peaches, nectarines, apricots, apples, pears, plums, gooseberries, and currants are all useful and will bear the voyage.

The need for shelter was recognised and he asked for quick-sets for

[3] *New Zealand Journal*, Alexander Turnbull Library, 6 August 1842.

hedging, saying:

> The thorn I am certain would grow better here even than in England, there can be no dispute about it making the best and most lasting hedge but as yet I regret to say we have been unable to obtain any .... Any boxes of plants intended for the Society if sent carriage paid to the New Zealand House, will be duly forwarded by the Company's vessels.

Stokes's letter ended with an invaluable list of plants he was growing in his own garden:

> An ample supply of vegetables, rhubarb, strawberry, raspberry, gooseberry, black, white and red currants, the peach, nectarine, apricot and fig, several varieties of plum, several varieties of apples and pears. Also cherries, filberts, mulberries, and quinces, magnolia, camellia, daphne, oleander, passionflower, honeysuckle, jasmine, ranunculus, tulip, picotee and a very nice collection of roses, also elder, privet, watercress, a few blackthorns, a good sized asparagus bed (plants of which were raised from seed and will be ready for cutting next spring).
>
> These were mostly obtained from Sydney and I have every reason to think they will do well. Some peaches, figs, apples, and other fruit trees produced last season from the Colony will, I think, produce fruit this year as they now have an abundant show of blossom. I have also a few vines brought from England. I may mention as a curious horticultural fact that the carnation has never yet been introduced into Sydney; they have picotee but not the carnation ....
>
> I am on my way to Valparaiso on private business but while there I shall not neglect the interests of our society or the Colony, but I shall endeavour to procure such plants and seeds as may be likely to flourish in Port Nicholson, particularly the Spanish chestnut, and the Alpaca grass, a species of lucerne which I understand has been extensively introduced from Chile to the south of France and which is considered very valuable.[4]

Stokes must have combed Sydney nurseries in order to acquire this impressive plant collection. Whether he was successful in procuring and introducing the Spanish chestnut will never be known, but settlers by now were assured that this new land was fertile.

The schedule for the autumn show for March 1843 was found among Francis Bradey's papers in the Alexander Turnbull Library.

THE COMMITTEE OF THE WELLINGTON HORTICULTURAL AND BOTANICAL SOCIETY

WILL AWARD THE FOLLOWING PRIZES
AT THEIR EXHIBITIONS

***The next Exhibition will take place on** Tuesday the   day of 184-*

VEGETABLES	£ s d.	FLOWERS	£ s d.
Best 12 Potatoes, 6 kidney and 6 round	0 3 6	Best Dahlia	0 2 6
Second best do	0 2 6	Best Seedling pansy	0 2 6
Best 12 pods of peas	0 3 6	Best 6 Pansies	0 2 6
Second best do	0 2 6	Best Seedling Geranium	0 2 6
Best 6 pods of beans	0 3 6	Best 6 Geraniums	0 2 6
Second best do	0 2 6	Best 6 Roses of different varieties	0 2 6

[4] *New Zealand Journal*, Alexander Turnbull Library, 1842.

Best 6 Kidney Beans	0 2 6
Best 2 heads of Cauliflowers	0 3 6
Second best do	0 2 6
Best 4 heads of Broccoli of 2 varieties, 2 of each	0 3 6
Second best do. Do	0 2 6
Best 4 Cabbages of 2 varieties,	0 3 6
Second best 2 of each	
Second best do	0 2 6
Best 6 Carrots	0 3 6
Second best do	0 2 6
Best 6 Onions	0 3 6
Second best do	0 2 6
Best 6 Leeks	0 2 6
Best 2 root of Beet	0 3 6
Best 2 roots of Mangold Wortzel	0 3 6
Best 3 heads of Celery	0 2 6
Best 6 stalks of Rhubarb	0 2 6
Best 3 Artichokes	0 2 6
Best Sample of Wheat, of any variety	0 3 6
Best sample of Oats	0 3 6
Best sample of Rye Grass	0 2 6
Best collection of Pot Herbs	0 2 6
Best dish of Mushrooms	0 2 6
Best 3 Tomatas	0 2 6
Best 3 Capsicums	0 2 6
FRUITS	
Best 12 strawberries	0 3 6
Best 12 Cherries	0 3 6
Best 2 Peaches, 2 Nectarines, 2 Plums} for each }	0 3 6
Best 2 Apples, 2 Pears, for each	0 3 6
Best bunch of Grapes	0 3 6
Second best do	0 2 6
Best Cucumber	0 3 6
Second best do	0 2 6
Best Vegetable Marrow	0 2 6
Best Pumpkin	0 2 6

Best 3 Balsams	0 2 6
Best 6 China Asters	0 2 6
Best 12 Annuals	0 2 6
Best 4 Stocks of 2 varieties, 2 of each	0 2 6
Best 3 Bulbous Plants in flower	0 2 6
Best Auricula	0 2 6
Best Bouquet	0 3 6
of Flowers do	0 2 6
Best Device	0 3 6
Best Bouquet of Native Flowers (with} Names attached) }	0 5 0
Second best do. Do	0 2 6
Best Collection of Flowering Shrubs	0 2 6
Second best do	0 2 6
Second best do	0 3 6
SEEDS	
*Best Collection of seeds of Native Plants	0 10 0
Second best do	0 7 6
Third best do	0 5 0
Best sample of Barley, do	0 3 6
Best 3 cobs of Indian Corn	0 3 6
COTTAGERS' PRIZES	
Best 4 varieties of Vegetables of any sorts,} 2 of each variety}	0 7 6
Second best do	0 5 0
For the Cottager's Garden in the best state of Cultivation, and in the neatest order,	1 0 0
In Wellington	
For the second best Cottager's Garden, do. Do	0 10 0
For the best Cottager's Garden in the Valley of the Hutt	1 0 0
For the second best do. do	0 10 0
Best Melon	0 2 6
PRIZES FOR THE NATIVES	
For the 6 largest Potatoes	0 5 0
For the 6 second largest do	0 2 6
For the largest Pumpkin	0 5 0
For the second largest do	0 2 6

---

*The Seeds and Bouquets of Native Flowers to become the property of the Society.

N.B. __ The Judges have power to award a Prize for any article not comprised in the above schedule, which they deem worthy of one.

Cottagers (who must be Members of the Society) intending to compete for the Cottagers' Garden prizes, must give notice of their intention to the Secretary, at least fourteen days before the day of Exhibition.

Any person can become a Member of the Society, by paying 5s. annually.

All articles must be sent to the place of Exhibition before 10 o'clock, a.m., on the day of Exhibition.

I.E. FEATHERSTON, SECRETARY WELLINGTON TERRACE

The *New Zealand Journal* of 16 September 1843 carried a description of the spring show:

> Whether the long prevalence of the late dry weather was occasioned by the comet, or what not, we had evident proof, that even the scorching effects of a comet cannot check the progress of vegetation in this part of the Colony. Though our collection of flowers, owing to the season of the year, may not have been so numerous or varied as at other seasons, there was a marked superiority as to quantity and quality of all the culinary productions of the kitchen garden. We have been a constant attendant for many years at our great Smithfield exhibition at home, and we would fearlessly challenge Messrs Gibbs, Phillips, etc. to best the productions of Port Nicholson. As a whole we may say, we never saw any collection to equal the vegetables exhibited by Daniel Riddiford Esq., of the Hutt – whether for size or purity of growth, of every specimen. In short, we may fairly say, that the judges were sorely puzzled to choose the best among the good. One cabbage grown by Mr James, cottager of Wadestown weighed 41 lbs. Some excellent varieties of potatoes were exhibited, and we have no doubt, that had we been in possession, a year or two ago, of good seed, we would, ere this, have exported potatoes, planted at Christmas, which, though not full grown at the same place, viz. – on the summit of our 'barren hills', yielded at the rate of forty bushels an acre. Messrs Bowler and Smith sent a splendid specimen of barley; it unfortunately arrived after the judges had left.

Judges for the summer show held on 31 December 1843 were Earl Percy, and Messrs Fuller, Burnet, Lawson, and Lumsden. As might be expected, there were more flowers than at the first show, but prizes still went to the more influential settlers – Stokes, Johnston, Hurst, Featherston, William Swainson, Harry St. Hill, D. Wilkinson, F.A. Molesworth, Scutchings, and Captain Smith. Strawberries, gooseberries, cherries, and blackcurrants made their appearance, while among the new flowers were collections of Cape plants, balsams, double pinks, and salpioglossus. Joseph White of Wadestown took first prize for the cottager's garden with McHardie coming second.[5] Of his success White wrote:

> I got the first prize for having the largest garden, in the best cultivation, and in the neatest order. I got the first four prizes for vegetables – potatoes, cabbages, turnips, onions. My potatoes were from a few early ones that I had brought out with me. I took two cabbages; the worst head was 15 lbs. The prize for the garden is £1 and the other prizes are 3s6d each. We pay 5s a year to be a member of the Society. The show of flowers was beautiful.[6]

Shows were held 21 December 1844 and 25 March 1845. Rarities were figs grown by Swainson and mulberries by Colonel Wakefield. Swainson also exhibited cape gooseberries and pumpkin, while F.A. Molesworth showed melons and cucumbers. One cucumber shown by Mr Murphy measured 22½ inches – huge by today's standards. Hops were also exhibited, while the wheat that gained first prize weighed 66 lb. to the bushel. The same people exhibited, with the notable addition of Stephen Stockbridge in the vegetable section.

But the first Horticultural and Botanical Society had other aims besides holding shows. In September 1842, 11 months after the Society was formed,

---

[5] *New Zealand Journal*, Alexander Turnbull Library, 1842.

[6] Immigrants' letters from Wellington, Nelson, New Plymouth, Alexander Turnbull Library.

seeds and cuttings from the Sydney Botanical Garden were available for distribution to members.[7] Robert Stokes organised this shipment when visiting Sydney. The Shipping Notice of 14 September 1842 said '6 cases trees 'Brougham' from Sydney. Passengers Boulcott and Stokes'. The letter accompanying the shipment to Dr Featherstone, the Society's Secretary, read:

> Sir,
>
> I have forwarded the plants and seeds promised under the care of Mr Boulcott who has very obligingly taken charge of them and I hope they will reach you in good condition. The following is the list of plants; the seeds are named on the papers.

1 Erythrina cafra	4 Melia australis – white	4 Olive seedlings
1 Alpina nectans	cedar of NSW	1 Lime
1 Ficus macrophylla	Cederella, red cedar do.	1 Canna indica
cuttings elastica do.	1 Hibiscus mutabilis plena	1 Furcraea gigantea
2 Oak – English	1 Hibiscus Syriacus	4 Province roses
1 Nerium splendens	1 Datura arborea	1 Common china rose
	1 Hydrangea hortensis	Salix Bonaparte – cuttings
	2 Rosa multiflora, red	4 Double flowered
		pomegranate

> A quantity of white cedar seeds in the case among the plants – it is an ornamental flowering tree. Vine cuttings in the case are numbered as far as the present stock and an old catalogue enabled me but having spare room I filled up with the next best. Some may prove more valuable with you than here; even if otherwise they will not be lost as they can be grafted with better kinds; when they bear, which in your favoured climate, I have no doubt may be the case with most of them in 2 years. There are no fruit trees in this garden and few bulbous plants; of what there are I shall send you bulbs when the season arrives for transplanting they are growing now. At any future time when opportunity occurs I shall send seed or plants of anything that is likely to be of advantage to your colony.
>
> I have the honour to be, Sir,
> your most obedient servant,
> Nasmith Robertson,
> Superintendent Botanic Gardens.
> Botanical Gardens Sydney
> August 22, 1842

Stokes advised the Sydney Botanic Garden on how the plants should be packed:

> They should be packed in cases lined with zinc, so as to be airtight, the roots well packed in damp moss, and; the plants well secured from moving with the same substance; no straw should be used, as it ferments with the moisture, to the serious injury of the plants. This I have ascertained from experience, as in a collection of fruit trees I received from England by the 'Indemnity', which were nine months out of the ground from the vessel's not sailing until March instead of November, as advertised, and which were very carefully packed, those packed in moss were, from the cause above mentioned, many of them dead, and all more or less injured. It is hardly necessary to add, they should be taken out of the ground before germination commences in the spring.[8]

---

[7] *New Zealand Gazette* and *Wellington Spectator*, Alexander Turnbull Library, 14 September 1842.

[8] Sydney Botanic Garden Archives.

In 1844, Messrs Harris, the eminent Hackney nurserymen, sent a large case of gooseberry plants. Packed in earth in zinc-lined cases, few showed signs of life on arrival. The committee regretted the loss of valuable plant material for the Colony's gardens and informed the Hackney nurseryman that they believed that this method of posting plants or seeds in an airtight container could not be depended upon. Successful transportation of both seeds and plants could not be taken for granted, and the newspapers of the day reported many of the losses. There was great joy among the settlers when a successful parcel of seeds or plants was unwrapped.

Edward Gibbon Wakefield, still in England, was aware of settlers' needs and in 1845 he sent the Horticultural Society a valuable seed collection gathered from the Jardin de Plantes in Paris.[9] In this year, too, the Society's kindred organisation, the London Horticultural Society, forwarded a parcel of fruit tree seeds, which were distributed to members.

By 1847, Sir Edward Howe was able to say in the English Botanical magazine:

> **The Wellington Horticultural Society has been very prosperous having been supplied with plants from the Botanic Garden at Sydney and from Messrs Loddiges. New Zealand is admirably adapted for a horticultural or botanic garden as plants of all climates flourish in it, even better than at Sydney as they are not in the same danger of suffering from drought.**

The formation of a botanic garden was one of the Society's original aims, and it continued to pressure to have land allocated for this purpose. Hopes were realised in 1844 when 13 acres of the Town Belt were appropriated for a botanical garden reserve.[10] Some money collected for its development was held by the trustees Messrs Stokes and Woodward, but the reserve did not receive attention until 1868.[11] The story of the Botanic Garden is taken up in a later chapter.

The Wellington Horticultural Society made a substantial contribution to plant introductions to New Zealand in that first decade. Fruit and vegetables took priority, but the lists of prize-winners in the shows confirm that flowers such as dahlias, geraniums, and annuals made an early appearance, along with plants from the Cape and important food items.

Towards the end of the first decade, settlers' problems with land titles and disputes with Māori were reflected in a growing lack of interest in the Horticultural Shows. On 23 December 1850, commenting on the latest show, the newspaper said, 'This society is retrograding for the present exhibition is not to be compared with those of previous years.'[12] A dispute about picking exhibits for the show on a Sunday may have had an effect on the number of exhibitors. Stephen Stockbridge won the section for apples, while the Government Gardener, David Wilkinson, won prizes for beet, picottees, and six geraniums. Mr J. McBeth (probably James) won a prize in the cucumber class.

Although support for the Society was low, many successful exhibitors

---

[9] *New Zealand Spectator* and *Cook Strait Guardian*, 15 February 1845.

[10] Shepherd, W. & Cook, W., *The Botanic Garden Wellington*, Millwood Press, 1988.

[11] Ibid.

[12] *Wellington Independent*, Alexander Turnbull Library, 25 December 1850.

continued to develop their gardens. Stokes and Woodward resigned on 24 February 1851, but James McBeth was added to the committee. Some time after 1851, the Society became inactive and a decade passed before a further series of horticultural shows was staged.

In the interval between the demise of the Horticultural Society in 1851 and the formation of the Agricultural and Pastoral Association, Wellington grew from a village into a prosperous town. The earthquake in 1855, though destructive, raised the beach along the western side of the harbour, so the road was no longer in danger of being washed away. The raising of Lambton beach by two feet gave better drainage to Lambton Quay, and it became a proper road. On 10 June 1856 the road over the Rimutaka Range was opened, giving access to the Wairarapa.

Immigrants were arriving in the new Black Ball Clipper ships, and as people left Wellington to move inland, others came to fill their place. Carter records that there was life and activity throughout the length and breadth of the Wellington Province.[13] In 1856, the first General Assembly meeting was held in Wellington, while in 1857 the contract was let for the construction of the Government Buildings. Shops were starting to appear among the houses and gardens of the residential Thorndon and Te Aro areas. The population in 1858 stood at 3,208, with 1,625 in the Hutt and 1,216 in the surrounding county.

It is remarkable that for all Wellington's growth over this period, there was no similar expansion in horticulture as there was in Auckland and Christchurch. Horticulture was at a low point in Wellington, after a promising beginning. But according to the commentators of the time, gardens were good and in some cases quite attractive, thanks to neighbourly exchanges of plants.

The Agricultural, Horticultural and Pastoral Association

On 23 December 1861, a decade after the Wellington Horticultural Society had faded away, the *Wellington Independent* carried a notice inserted by the Agricultural, Horticultural and Pastoral Association indicating that it intended to hold a Horticultural Show about the first week in January 1862. The notice was still appearing on 30 January 1862, though no show had taken place. The organisers were probably testing community views and seeking support. The show eventually took place later that year, on 26 November.

It was a festive occasion, with the Superintendent declaring a public holiday. Many exhibitors at the shows of the 1840s were present, and memories of earlier times were recalled with nostalgia. One thousand people attended, with exhibitors including Archdeacon Stock, as well as Mr Watt with amaryllis, Mr Plimmer with oleanders and camellias, Walter Mantell with escalonia 'Brilliant', and Messrs St. Hill, Wilkinson, Plimmer, and E.W. Mills with floral work. Captain Buck showed silkworms. There were the usual vegetables and collections of fuchsias, pinks, pansies, stocks, roses, verbenas, bignonia, geraniums, forget-me-nots, and 'Bleeding Heart' (*Dicentra spectabilis*).

---

[13] Carter, C.R., *Life and Recollectionas of a New Zealand Colonist*, 3 vols London, 1866-75.

Ratification of the Association's formation followed in March 1863 and was the forerunner to the Agriculture and Pastoral Associations still surviving in New Zealand today. Bad weather affected both the attendance and the quality of the exhibits at the next show, on 21 March 1863. Judges were Messrs J.M. Taylor, R. Donald of Karori, D. Robertson, and N. Wilton. The *Wellington Independent* was impressed with

> the hues of the 'Spanish Rennet', the delicate pink of hawthorn 'Dean', the magnificent dark red of 'Black Prince', the beautifully marked 'White Alphiston', the mellow looking 'chaumontelle' and juicy, Honey-Sweet 'Marie Louise' pears.

Grapes shown were 'Black Hamburg' and 'Sweet Water' by Mr. R. Donald of Karori and Mr Minifie respectively (the latter's grown in the Queen's Hotel conservatory). Almonds were shown for the first time, as well as walnuts that were probably harvested from trees planted about 10 years previously. New Zealand spinach, tobacco, and fuchsias were on display.

In spite of the bad weather, there was high enthusiasm for a resumption of shows. A fortnight later, on 9 April 1863, a general meeting of the Association agreed

> to give full effect and vigour to their operations all over the Province with district Agricultural, Horticultural Shows to be held in Wellington, Hutt, Wairarapa, Porirua, Turakina, and Wanganui or any other part of the Province.

Messrs G. Hunter, G. Moore, J. Johnstone, A. Ludlam, R. Collins, W.B. Rhodes, James Sellars, J. Woodward, R. Stokes, and W. Spinks were elected to the committee, J.H. Wallace was appointed Secretary, with His Honour the Superintendent as President.

With committee members such as Woodward and Stokes, it is not surprising that reference was made to importing plants and developing the land set aside for the Botanic Garden. The latter remained an unfulfilled aim of the first Horticultural Society. The Provincial Government was asked

> to place the Reserve on Tinakori Road under the management of the Association with a view to the establishment of the botanical gardens and that the funds belonging to the late Horticultural Society be made available for this purpose.

Chatham Island forget-me-not, Myosotidium hortensia, *first exhibited 3 November 1863.*
N.M. Adams

Meanwhile, a further combined Agricultural, Pastoral and Horticultural Show was held on 3 November 1863, but the date was a little late for spring plants and still too early for summer. The lovely Chatham Island forget-me-not *Myositidium hortensia* made its first appearance, shown by Captain Battersbee. David Robertson, the Cemetery Sexton, staged a collection of ferns, while the Reverend Stock exhibited an unusually small fern. Other exhibitors were Captain Rhodes and D. Wilkinson, while Thomas Mason won the prize for the cactus section. Mimulus, calceolaria, azalea, auricula, rhododendron, prunus, japonica, and cineraria were among the exhibits.

A further Agricultural and Pastoral Horticultural Show was to have been held on 17 March 1864, but owing to the death of Superintendent Featherston's wife, it was postponed until the 24th. As might be expected, the delay affected the quality of the display. Judges were Trotter, McLeod, and Duncan. Vegetables were good, with the prize winners being Messrs Donald, Read, Wilkinson, Woodward, Barton, Collins, Ebden, and P. Laing. Copeland exhibited more than 19 different varieties of fruit. Gillies won a prize for Ribston Pippin apples, while Donald, Wilkinson, and Plimmer won the grape section. Robertson had a unique collection of ferns in stands constructed entirely from the trunks of tree ferns. Mansill, the nurseryman, received an extra prize for a very good collection of yew and holly.

Combined shows did not satisfy everyone. A correspondent called 'Veronica' had earlier written:

> I should be glad to see the Horticultural Society take its stand as it ought to do, separate and distinct from the Agricultural Association, that each may bring its products at the right time for the show. But while they continue to remain as one society let everyone do their best. if carried out as it should be, the Secretary should be enabled to correspond with some society in England and yearly receive from it, choice seeds for distribution among its members and to collect from here seeds and plants in return ... encourage the mechanic and working man not to take a cottage without a small plot of garden ground and increase the health of the family instead of living as some do at this time in little boxes not fit for them ... urge upon them to do their utmost to uphold this society which above all others increase the comforts of life.

The suggestion of holding separate agricultural and horticultural shows was heeded, and horticultural shows were held on 24 November, 23 December, and March 1865. The *Wellington Independent* commented that during the last year or two considerable important additions had been made in flowers and shrubs by both professional and amateur gardeners.

At the November show, around 500–600 people attended. Rhododendrons and cherries were shown by Mr Plimmer. Mason from Taita had a fine line of asparagus; flower pictures by Barraud were on display; while Robertson took prizes for roses, pelargoniums, verbenas, and fuchsias. Door takings amounted to £13.8.6.

As might have been expected, the 23 December 1864 show, just on Christmas, was a disaster and the write-up very unfavourable, although it was hoped shows would continue in the future. There were no prize cards, cloths were stained, and attendance was poor. Thomas Mason exhibited cherries and raspberries.

The next show, on 29 March 1865, was held in the Odd Fellows Hall, but there was a dearth of exhibitors and visitors, in spite of some excellent specimens of fruit, flowers, and vegetables.[14] There was a noticeable increase in apple varieties. Mansill exhibited some very fine Hallett's pedigree wheat and, together with Thomas Mason of Taita, carried away a number of prizes for their respective collections of apples of various kinds. Close runners up in the show of vegetables were Messrs Donald, Copeland, Duncan, and Jackson. This was not the season for flowers and they were scarcely worth noticing, except for Mason's bouquet of roses and Wilkinson's exquisitely beautiful fuchsias.

---

[14] The Horticultural Society revived, and splendid shows and other activities were a dominant feature of life in Wellington until the late 1970s, when it finally went into recess and was absorbed by the local branch of the Royal New Zealand Institute of Horticulture.

The Agricultural and Pastoral Show held at the same time also provided a dismal display and the prophesy was that it would go under if the standard did not improve. No shows are recorded for 1866.

Nurserymen did not participate in shows in anything like the same way as their counterparts in Canterbury.[15] In the 1860s, local nurserymen stocked forest trees, which included conifers new to cultivation anywhere, but they were not featured in the Horticultural Shows, as they were in Canterbury. At first, Wellington's needs for shelter were less than those of Canterbury, but by the late 1860s, after a mere 25 years, the settlers had created a bare, windswept landscape, and there was an urgent need for forest trees, for both shelter and firewood.

As Wellington grew, many exhibitors mentioned in early shows became prominent in other horticultural spheres. Ludlam and Mason, as we have already seen, had developed in the Hutt Valley two of the finest gardens in the country. Wilkinson, Donald, and Mansill ran Tea Gardens in Oriental Bay, Nairn Street, and Karori respectively. Donald, Mansill, and Stockbridge were nurserymen. Thomas White and J. McBeth became seedsmen.

In 1869, following the passing of the Botanic Garden Act, Robert Stokes and Jonas Woodward, foundation Secretary and Treasurer respectively for the Horticultural Society that had been formed in 1841, handed over the money collected for the formation of the Botanic Garden. Board member Alfred Ludlam had been, like Woodward and Stokes, a founding committee member of the 1841 Horticultural Society. At last the New Zealand Company's instruction to its Surveyor and an aim of New Zealand's first Horticultural Society had come to fruition.

As an endowment for the formation of the Garden, the sum handed over, £411, was inadequate for this purpose, yet it was the only money made available to the Botanic Garden Board under the Botanic Garden Act. Ludlam, Stock, and Mason became Governors of the Botanic Garden Board, contributing to the garden's initial development from its raw wilderness. Wellington citizens can be proud that their Botanic Garden links back to the very beginning of its settlement. Today, on Soundshell Lawn, an amillary sphere sundial, funded jointly by the Historical and Early Settlers Association and the New Zealand Royal Society, reminds us of this link with the past

It is not intended to trace the history of the Wellington Horticultural Society and its shows to the present day. Their early ups and downs are explained by climatic difficulties and the dates chosen for the shows, clearing land, problems with securing land titles, wars, and settlers moving on to other areas. The early prize lists illustrate just how quickly colonists discovered that the soils of their new country could produce a wide range of plants, in many cases surpassing those they had grown back in England. The Hutt Valley was particularly fertile and was helped by its somewhat more favoured position, which gave some shelter from the frequent gales and rain that periodically lash the hillsides of Wellington. By 1870, records and garden catalogues show that most plants available in the northern hemisphere were obtainable here, the Wellington Horticultural Society having played a major part in the early introductions of plants to Wellington.

---

[15] Challenger, 'Canterbury Nurserymen', *Journal of the RNZIH*, 1979.

FOR NAMES OF VARIETIES SHOWN ABOVE AND SPECIAL OFFER—SEE COLOURED PAGES.

Chapter 7

WELLINGTON'S PIONEER NURSERYMEN AND SEEDSMEN

The *New Zealand Gazette* noted in 1841 that, since the arrival of the *Aurora* in January 1840, 19 immigrants were listed as gardeners – a relatively high number. Some were labouring gardeners, a few had some professional training, while others had some familiarity with the nursery trade. According to Challenger, the meaning of the term 'gardener', 'nurseryman', and 'landscape gardener' was variable, and the overlap between them was considerable.[1] This is reflected in early advertisements. It may have been that officials in England gave preference to those prepared to offer themselves as gardeners, regardless of whether in fact they were trained. This chapter deals with those gardeners who had had some professional training, and who contributed so much to the young colony.

The first nurseryman?

According to Robert Nairn, William Trotter of Wellington was New Zealand's first nurseryman,[2] and this was quoted by Alan Hale in his book *Pioneer New Zealand Nurserymen*. Nairn's interpretation is based on a few words in Trotter's letter to J.C. Loudon of May 1844: 'I have taken a few acres in the valley of the Hutt where I intend to establish a fruit garden and nursery.' A map of the early Hutt Valley drawn in 1840 by Lance Hall shows the position of Trotter's leased land, but no evidence has so far come to light to say that this place was run as a commercial nursery – that is, as a place for selling plants. The first nurseryman was probably Carnegie of Auckland, based on an advertisement in the *Auckland Chronicle* of 1843:

FRUIT TREES

The undersigned has for SALE a few Apple, Pear, Plum, Peach Apricot, and Cherry Trees, propagated in New Zealand from the choicest stock. Also a few Roses, Willows, Foy, and Vines. The above are much superior to any imported trees, none having suffered by a long sea voyage.

D.F. CARNEGIE

Applications left at the Exchange Hotel, will be attended to.

Epsom,

Sept. 4, 1843

Auckland Chronicle, 6 September 1843

Shortly after his arrival, even though he was occupied with clearing his block of leased land, Trotter first began working for Ludlam, and subsequently for a Mr Pope, who rented Molesworth's property after Molesworth's death. Trotter was a skilled propagator, and he may well have given away budded stock plants or exchanged some plants for others, but Hale's claim for him as New Zealand's first nurseryman does not survive scrutiny.

---

[1] Challenger, S., 'Pioneer Canterbury Nurserymen', *JRNZIH*, 1979.

[2] Nairn, R., Banks Lecture, *JRNZIH*, 1932.

Wellington Nurserymen 1845-1867*

Year	Name	Plants Sold	Locality	Other Details	Reference	Agent
1847-1881	Stockbridge, S.	Mainly fruit trees, seed, native plants. Also apples and other fruits	Ohiro	Prize winner W.H.S. Consistent advertiser. Also sold fruit in season	*Wellington Almanac* 1852	John McBeth later Houghton
1850-1857	Watson, John	Blue gum seed, white thorn, England Fruit Trees & garden seeds	Willis Street Nursery		*Wellington Independent*, Aug. 25, 1850	
		Roses, geraniums, verbenas, calceolarias, strawberries, quicks, white thorn & fruit trees, rhododendron	Nairn Street, top of Willis Street	Plants imported from London. Lent money to Hislop in Christchurch in 1859	*Wellington Independent*, Oct. 21, 1854	
1850-1854	McBeth, James	Fruit trees, veg. plants, seeds	Tinakori also store Pipitea	W.H.S. Committee member Feb. 1851	*Wellington Independent*, Feb. 26, 1851 Lyttelton Times, Jan. 11, 1851	Assoc. with W.Lumsden
1851	Hurst, F.W.	Fruit trees, roses, rhubarb	Camden Vale, Karori	Foundation member W.H.S. Early prize winner for seedling geraniums	*Wellington Independent*, May 7, 1851	Mr Spinks, Herbert Street
1851-1859	Woouldom, H.	Fruit trees. Florist & seedsman	Willis Street Chimney Sweep & Nightman.	Letter in N.Z. J. asking for rhubarb plants, Sept, 1851	*Wellington Almanac*, 1863	
1852-186?	Lumsden, W.	Forest trees, fruit trees. Ornamental trees, evergreens & deciduous. Greenhouse & herbaceous plants, flower roots, veg. plants	Tinakore Nursery	Judge at 3rd Hort. Show	*Wellington Independent*, July 24, 1852	James McBeth
1853	Donald, R.	Strawberries, gooseberries, picnic grounds. Holly, conifers, native trees	Eden Vale, Karori	Tea Gardens & Nursery	*Wellington Independent*, Nov. 12, 1853	
1857-1867	William Mansill	Roses, fruit trees, hollies, ornamental trees & shrubs	Willis Street Nursery became Portobello Nursery. Ran as a Tea Garden 1860-62	Bought J. Watson's business. Continued to import	*Wellington Independent*, March 26, 1857	
1865-1990's	Cooper, F.	Seeds	Taranaki Street, Bijou Nursery, Alicetown	Centennial Publication	Cover 1941 Catalogue Alexander Turnbull Library	
1867	Robertson		Managed Portobello Nursery after Mansill's death in 1867	Landscape gardener & florist. Public Cemetery *Wellington Almanac* 1873	Rates Books W.C.C.	

***From the time of their first advertisement**

Stephen Stockbridge

Unquestionably Wellington's first nurseryman, and its most prominent in the early years, was Stephen Stockbridge. His first advertisement, for grafted apple trees, appeared in April 1847, and he continued to advertise until his untimely death in 1865. Specialising for over twenty years in fruit trees, hollies, and quicks, his nursery made a major contribution to the colony's developing gardens. His orchard was also an important supplier of fruit to the young settlement.

Listed as a 'gardener' and accompanied by his wife Mary and their five children, he arrived at Wellington on 1 May 1842 on the ship *London*. He had trained as a nurseryman at Reading, the home of Sutton's Seeds. On arrival in Wellington, he bought 40 to 50 acres of Crown Land in the Owhiro Valley for £5 per acre.[3] It had been advertised as suitable for market gardening.

The area was indeed fertile. Dr Dieffenbach noted in 1847 (the year of Stockbridge's first advertisement) that there were four sections in cultivation, 13 cultivators, 19½ acres in wheat, 25¾ acres in barley, 10½ acres green crops, and ½ acre in grass.[4]

At the horticultural show in March 1845, Stockbridge exhibited vegetables. He won the section for apples in 1850 but does not appear to have played any further part in exhibiting at shows, due perhaps to the considerable time spent in his nursery, as well as the failing public support for the Horticultural shows at this time.

Behind Stockbridge's brief advertisement of 1847, 'A fine collection grafted apple trees, 2/- each', lay much hard work. It takes a year to obtain a buddable tree, or one suitable for grafting, from seed, and four years are needed to produce a thousand plants for sale. Suitable budding material may have been imported, perhaps on plants transported in wet sacks or Wardian cases from Australian sources, or suitable budwood may have come from trees established around early Cook Strait settlements. The process of building up stock was necessarily slow for all nurseries selling fruit trees.

In the absence of plant or seed catalogues for Stockbridge's nursery, his first advertisement in the 1852 *Wellington Almanac* is significant. The advertisement emphasises that his garden seeds were 'grown in the Colony' and that his agent was John McBeth in Willis Street. In the previous year's *Almanac*, McBeth had offered 'Garden Seeds, Warranted Fresh and True to Their Kinds', but these were probably imported, since he is known to have imported seeds and plants from Hobart and from London.[5]

SURVEYOR-GENERALS PLAN
The Ohiro District

MESSRS J. AND G WADE have received instructions from the Prop-rietor to submit to public competition, at the Wellington Exchange, on Saturday, the 4th of December, at 1 o'clock precisely; Section No. 14 on the Surveyor-General's Plan, in the immediate

VICINITY OF WELLINGTON,

And only half an hours work from

THE EXCHANGE

This Section is well sheltered, and from its contiguity to the town, is admirably adapted for the residences of merchants and others, desirous of possessing a retired residence in the immediate neighbourhood of the seat of business.

Also, from the richness of its soil, it is admirably adapted for

DAIRY STATIONS, AND MARKET GARDENS

To suit the convenience of purchasers, it will be laid out in

FIVE ACRE LOTS

Plans will shortly be prepared and exhibited at the Wellington Exchange, and the Offices of the Auctioneers.

Terms, and other particulars will appear in a Hand-bill.

---

[3] The spelling Owhiro was sometimes used in early documents. Brees, for instance, described the locality in these terms: 'Owhiro valley runs from the sea at Cook's Strait to near Te Aro Flat and is known in the colony as Happy Valley.' The valley was named after a man called Whiro, and the correct spelling is once more being used.

[4] Ward, Louis E., *Early Wellington*, Whitcombe & Tombs, 1928, p. 284.

[5] John McBeth is not to be confused with another agent and storekeeper, James McBeth. John Houghton later became Stockbridge's agent.

xxxi

To Families, Country Dealers, and others:

JOHN M'BETH,

WILLIS-STREET,

HAS always on hand a large Stock of the following Articles, and receiving from Sydney by every opportunity viz. :—

Cougou Teas	Preserved Meats	English Caps
Fancy do	Lon. Sperm Candles	Tartaric Acid
Coffee	American do	Carbonate of Soda
Chocolate	Belmont do	Cream of Tartar
Loaf Sugar	China Preserves	Flour Sulpher, Senna
Crushed do:	Jams and Jellies	Grey Paper
Manilla do	Pickles, Mustard	Brown do
China do	Salad Oil, Sauces	Printing do
Java do	Vinegar,	Foolscap do
Mauritius do	Bottled Fruits	Post do
Pearl Barley	Lemon Syrup	Ink, red and black
Scotch Oatmeal	Anisee do	Crockery, a large assortment
Split Peas	Sardines	Long Brooms
Whole do	Preserved Salmon	Hearth Brushes
Flour	Anchovies	Paint do
Rice	Red Herrings	Shoe do
Sago	Pickled Herrings	Scrubbing do
Arrowroot	Bacon and Hams	Tooth, Hair, and Nail Brushes
Patent Groats	Smoked Tongues	Horse do
Pepper, Black	Eggs	Rack and Smalltooth Combs
Do. Ground	Cheese, Pt. Copper	Perfumery, a large & varied assortment
White do.	Butter, Fresh & Salt	Lamp Oil
Allspice	Ox Marrow	Sperm Oil
Mixed do	Bottled and Tin Blacking	Lamp Wick
Cloves, Mace, Ginger	Black Lead	Candle Wick
Nutmegs, Cayenne	Bath Brick, Whiting	Wheat Mills
Curry,	Bottle Wax	Window Glass
Carraway Seeds	Linseed Oil	New Zealand Produce of all kinds
Soap, Soda, Blue	Turpentine	Garden Seeds, warranted fresh & true to their kinds
Starch, Candles	White Lead	Fresh Kent Hops
Raisins, Currants	Black Paint	&c., &c., &c.
Almonds, Figs	Pitch, Tar	
Orange & Lemon Peel	Roping	
Dates, Honey	Tobacco Pipes	
Treacle, Lucifers	Meerschaums	
Tobacco, Snuff	Hall's H F Gunpowder	
Cheroots	Shot, Nos. 1, 2, & 3	
Bottled Ale & Porter		

—oo—

☞ The Prices of the above Goods are always at the lowest, and a liberal allowance made on all cash sales and prompt payments.

Wellington, January 1, 1852

xlvii

OHIRO NURSERY

S. STOCKBRIDGE

BEGS respectfully to inform the Public that he has always at his

NURSERY

An extensive assortment of the most approved varieties of

APPLES, PEARS, PLUMS, CHERRIES, PEACHES,

and other Fruit Trees.

The Apple Trees are warranted to be free from the American Blight. Also a large collection of the best sorts of Gooseberries, Currant, Raspberries, &c., all good bearers.

All orders from the different Settlements received at the approaching season will be carefully executed.

N.B.--- An extensive Stock of Vegetable and other Garden Seeds grown in the Colony.

Always on hand a great variety of Seeds of Native Shrubs.

Orders left at Mr. JOHN M'BETH'S, Willis - street, will be punctually attended to.

Wellington, January 1, 1852.

[Above left] Wellington Almanac, *1851.*

Alexander Turnbull Library, National Library of New Zealand, Te Puna Mātauranga

[Above right] Wellington Almanac, *1852.*

Alexander Turnbull Library, National Library of New Zealand, Te Puna Mātauranga

FRUIT, FRUIT, FRUIT

For SALE by the Undersigned

Good kitchen and Eating Apples at 6d. per lb. Grown free from American blight. Also, Fruit Trees about 10,000 comprising Apples, Pears, Plums, Cherries, Medlars, 1, 2, and 3 years grafted (trees-warranted free from American blight.) Asparagus, and Rhubarb Plants and Garden Seeds.

N.B. – The Pear Trees are grafted on real pear stocks, not on Quince and White Thorns, as the Quince and White Thorns do not last many years. The time for planting the above trees is from May till September. To be obtained at the Nursery of

STEPHEN STOCKBRIDGE

Ohiro

Orders left with John Watson, Chandler, at the Independent Office, Wellington, will be punctually attended to.

Wellington Independent, August 27, 1856
Repeated through to May 23, 1857

Stockbridge listed a 'great variety of Seeds of Native Shrubs' for sale, indicating both an interest in the native flora and a local demand for such seeds. He was at least ten years ahead of Canterbury nurserymen in this, if we accept Challenger's findings. '...From systematic extraction and collation of all nursery advertisements in the Canterbury newspapers before 1860 almost no attention has been made to the horticultural value of New Zealand plants in the country itself. So if one can extract principals from such limited data, it is probable that the 1860-65 period was one of broadening the base of plant material.'

Except for Hurst's advertisement in May, Stockbridge was the only other advertiser of plants

ON SALE CHEAP FRUIT TREES

Apples, Pears, Plums, Cherries, Siberian Crab, or Cherry shaped Apple and Medlars, all grafted, best sorts, at the nursery of S. Stockbridge, Ohiro, from 1s. to 2s.6d. per tree, from 1, 2, and 3 years, grafted, all free from the American blight. Orders left at Houghton's near the Post Office, Wellington, will be punctually attended to and where a sample of fruit and fruit trees may be seen.

April 8, 1857.

Wellington Independent, May 23, 1857

ORCHARD GROWN FRUIT FOR SALE FRUIT, FRUIT

The Undersigned now having formed a regular fruitery similar to those in England desires to inform the public generally that he will for the remainder of the season be enabled to supply his customers with fruit of almost every description and of the very best quality. He has now on hand a large quantity of Ribstone Pippins, now Pareils, Pearmains and other choice varieties of fruit which he is prepared to sell at reduced prices.

STEPHEN STOCKBRIDGE

Ohiro

N.B. – Orders punctually attended to. Hotels and families supplied.

Superior strong quicks at £3 per 1,000.

Wellington Independent, April 3, 1857

for 1851. He was a regular advertiser, with some advertisements running for a considerable time, for example, 'Fruit for Sale', dated 27 August 1856, was still running in May 1857.

The *Wellington Independent* mentioned in February 1863 that Stockbridge brought into town 'a quantity of remarkably fine ripe White Dutch sweetwater grapes, glasshouse grown'. Occasionally he advertised cider for sale. In 1859, two cases of apples were shipped to Lyttelton.[6]

Unfortunately, after such a useful contribution to fruit growing in Wellington, Stockbridge met with a fatal accident while on his way to Port Cooper to sell 'Quicks'. The *Evening Post* of 21 June 1865 reported:

> A sad accident occurred about 8 p.m. yesterday evening which resulted in the death of a well known member of the community. It appears that Mr Stockbridge, Nursery Gardener of this city, intended to go to Christchurch in the *S.S. Rangatira* and that he was walking along the wharf to go on board when owing to the darkness of the night he missed his footing and was precipitated into the water. Succour was at hand and an instant search instigated without avail. This morning the body was discovered lying on the beach at Kai Warra Warra and an inquest was held this afternoon.
>
> Inquest-Meeting at Crown and Anchor on the body of Stephen Stockbridge the jury returned a verdict of accidentally drowned and attributed the accident to the absence of proper lights on the Queen's Wharf'.

***Evening Post,* June 22, 1865**

Mrs Stockbridge continued the business with the help of her sons until her death in 1881, when the nursery was closed.

FRUIT TREES FOR SALE

Apples, Pears, Plums, Cherries, Gooseberries, Currents, Quicks, Laurels, Holleys, Fruit Trees very strong to be sold very cheap, apply to Mr John Houghton, Willis Street or to Mr Stephen Stockbridge, Ohiro Nursery near Wellington.

Wellington Independent, April 13, 1861 to July 8, 1862

Repeated April 22, 1863 to December 1864

Also May, 30 1865 to December 22, 1866

---

6 *Wellington Independent,* 6 May 1859.

WILLIAM LUMSDEN begs to intimate to the gentlemen of Wellington, that from a long practical experience in all the different branches of Horticulture, in the principal Gardens of England and Scotland, he would be happy to tender his services in the laying out of grounds, by contract or otherwise. For reference, please to apply to E. Park, Land Surveyor.
N.B – Flower and fruit gardens laid out on the most approved plan.

New Zealand Gazette and *Wellington Spectator*, November 17, 1841.

William Lumsden, James McBeth, and the Tinakore Nursery

The advertisement left appeared in the *Wellington Spectator* about the same time that moves were under way for the formation of the Horticultural Society. Lumsden, listed as a gardener, arrived on the *Oriental*. In 1845, he was living in Wadestown, and in 1848, still listed as a gardener, he was in Lambton Quay. Little is known about him and any training he had, but there was an early recognition of his talents in the colony, and he was judge at the third Horticultural show in December 1842.

By the end of the first decade, sufficient land had been cleared for the colonists' immediate purposes. The time was right for the establishment of nurseries, and several were formed around the same time. Three years after Stockbridge's first advertisement, the 'Wellington Nursery Tinakore' was advertised. It seems there was a connection between Lumsden, the agent James McBeth, and the beginning of the Tinakore Nursery. The *Wellington Independent* of 28 August 1850 reported under shipping news that the *Munford* from Hobart Town carried 3 crates of trees, 6 packages of fruit trees, 2 packages of seed, and 1 case of garden seeds. This cargo was itemised in the same newspaper, thus telling us today what varieties of fruit trees and vegetable seeds James McBeth imported from Hobart in 1850.

FRUIT TREES AND GARDEN SEEDS

JAMES McBETH will received per Munford shortly to arrive from Hobart Town, the following fruit trees, from 1 to 2 years old selected by a person* well acquainted with the climate and wants of the district of Wellington and through the advice of one of its experienced professional men**.

May Duke Cherry
Bigarreau Cherry
Black Heart Cherry
Black Eagle Cherry
Noblesse Peach
Magdalene Peach
Nectarine (various)
Apricot Moorpark
White Magnum Bonum Plum
Red Magnum Bonum Plum

Jargonelle Pear
Gancel's Bergamotte Pear
Swan's Egg Pear
Muirfowl Egg
Black Currant
White Currant

White heart Cherry
Amber heart Cherry
Morello Heart Cherry

Royal George Peach
Newton Peach
Medlars
Mulberries (various)
Orleans Plum
Yellow Gage plum
Green Gage Plum
Chaumontelle Pear
William Bonchretian Pear
Maria Louisa Pear
Collmar Pear
Red Currant

ALSO THE FOLLOWING SEEDS

Blue Gum Seed
Early Frame Pea
Early Warick Pea

Blue Prussian Pea
Racehorse Pea
Knights Dwarf Marrow Pea

---

* Thomas Mason from Taita was living in Hobart at this time and it seems likely that he selected the fruit trees.

** Lumsden, if the sequence of advertisements is studied, fits the description of the local adviser.

Early Charlton Pea	Woodford Dwarf Marrow Pea
Queen's Early Dwarf Pea	Imperial Dwarf Marrow Pea
Broad Windsor Bean	Taylors Long Pod Bean
Early Magagan Bean	
Strasburgh Onion	Early Horn Carrot
Blood Red Onion	Alterinham Carrot
White Spanish Onion	Long Red Carrot
Globe Onion	French White Carrot
James Keeping Onion	Sea Kale
Silver Skin Onion	Cabbage Lettuce
Early Dwarf York Cabbage	White Cross Lettuce
Large York Cabbage	Turkey Rhubarb
Battersea Cabbage	Giant Rhubarb
Red Dutch Cabbage	Gigantic Asparagus
Sugar Loaf Cabbage	Vegetable Marrow
	Tomatoes
Radish (various)	Brussels Sprouts
Early Cauliflower	Early Dutch Turnip
	Early Stone Turnip
	Yellow Maltese Turnip
Early Malta Broccoli	Manchester prize Cucumber
Miller's Dwarf Broccoli	Long Prickly Cucumber
Chapel's Cream Broccoli	Shorty Cucumber
Purple Cape Broccoli	White Cucumber
Blood Red Beet (Mitchel's)	Giant Parsnip
White Clover Seed	

The next reference to the Wellington Nursery Tinakore appeared two months later in the *Wellington Independent* on 26 October 1850.

WELLINGTON NURSERY TINAKORE

JAMES McBETH begs to intimate that the following are now ready for sale:-

Cabbage & cauliflower plants	Cherry trees in garden pots
Cucumber	Tulip and anenome roots
Melon	Rhubarb plants

Specimens of the flowers now to be seen at his store Pipitea

WELLINGTON NURSERY TINAKORE

JAMES McBETH begs to intimate that the following are now ready for sale:-

Jargonelle Pear	Chaumontelle Pear
Gancel's Bergamotte Pear	William Bonchretian Pear
Swan's Egg Pear	Maria Louisa Pear
Muirfowl Egg	Collmar Pear
Black Currant	Red Currant
White Currant	

JAMES McBETH, Wellington Nurseryman whose business is under management of a person of great professional experience both at home and for 10 years in Wellington offers garden seeds and fruit trees.*

Lyttelton Times, January 11, 1851

For the rest of 1851, Stockbridge was the only advertiser, but on 24 July 1852 the advertisement opposite appeared and ran until September 1854: Recently-established fruit trees were a saleable commodity in those days!

W. LUMSDEN Nurseryman and Florist. Begs most respectfully to inform the inhabitants of Wellington and the neighbouring settlements that he has for sale an assortment of:-

Forest, fruit, and ornamental trees
Evergreen and deciduous shrubs
Bulbous flower roots
Asparagus, sea kale, rhubarb, cauliflower, cabbage, celery, and ordinary plants.

Plantation and Pleasure Grounds contracted for; and planted in the most judicious manner, according to the diversity of the soil and situation so as to produce effect with utility. William has been commissioned to sell a very superior assortment of apple trees, now growing in one of the best gardens in Wellington – such an opportunity is seldom to be met with by those who are desirous of having a crop the first year after planting. Also an assortment of gooseberry bushes in full bearing.
Fruit trees warranted free from blight or any other diseases.
Wellington Nursery,
Tinakore Road,
July 20, 1852.

Wellington Independent, July 24, 1852

* Again, one could conclude that Lumsden fits the description of the local adviser.

James McBeth's name no longer appears in these advertisements, and there is no further evidence connecting him with the nursery. It seems that Lumsden and McBeth had a partnership arrangement. Both men, together with Stockbridge, were listed as nurserymen in the *Wellington Almanac* of 1853, but McBeth's name did not appear for 1854. In the shipping news for 1853 and 1854, James McBeth appeared twice as a passenger on ships carrying exports of trees and plants to Victoria, but whether he was furthering his or Lumsden's business through exports of plants to Australia is conjecture.[7]

The nursery in Tinakori Road continued. On 24 May 1859, Lumsden and another nurseryman, John Watson, each shipped 7 bundles of trees on the steamer *Queen* to Lyttelton. Watson's trees went to the Canterbury nurseryman W. Hislop, who advertised as follows:

> The *Lyttelton Times* May 28, 1856 ex Steamer *Queen* from Wellington.
> 795 English yews, laurels, and laurestinus etc. just arrived from Wellington.
> **W. Hislop**

Lumsden's trees may also have formed part of the stock advertised by Hislop.[8]

Like Stockbridge, Lumsden too came to an unfortunate end. Intending to visit the Wairarapa to look for plants on the Rimutakas, he apparently got lost and no trace of his body was found. He left a widow and a large family. In 1862, Mr Huntley, a teacher at St Mary's School who was later to become the Overseer of Government Domains in Wellington, wrote, 'Lumsden was an intelligent man and indefatigable in his business ... what I know of gardening I got principally from him.'

F.W. Hurst, Camden Vale, Karori

F.W. Hurst, a foundation member of the Wellington Horticultural Society and an early prize-winner with his seedling geraniums, had a nursery garden in Karori called Camden Vale. The *Wellington Independent* of 29 January 1851 noted that the garden was well worth visiting. Later that year, this advertisement appeared (left).

No further advertisement has been found, perhaps because of other nurserymen going into business about this time.

> 'The undersigned begs to announce that he has for sale at his Nursery Grounds Camden Vale, Karori, a collection of fruit trees of the following sorts, all named and warranted'.
>
> | | |
> |---|---|
> | Apricots | Gooseberries |
> | Apples | Plums |
> | Cherries | Pears |
> | Currants | Vines |
>
> Several hundred rhubarb plants Roses in varieties. Also a few cucumber seeds
> **W. Hurst**
> Apply to F.W. Hurst at the store of Mr Spinks.
> May 7, 1851.

Robert Donald, Eden Vale, Karori

Robert Donald, a gardener from Insch in Aberdeenshire, and his wife Jane arrived in 1850 on the *Tranvancore*. They chose to settle in Karori, where they bought a five-acre block with house (part of the original Yule Section 36) from a Mr Edwards. For around ten years, Edwards had run a boys' school from this place, surrounding the property with a holly hedge,

[7] James McBeth in 1853 is officially listed as a merchant, Lambton Quay. The relationship between James and John McBeth is unknown.

[8] Watson had lent money to Hislop, which may explain Challengers' remark, 'It is interesting to note that Hislop appears to have gone outside the Province for his stock rather than patronising his obvious supplier but competitor – William Wilson'. Challenger, S., 'Pioneer Canterbury Nurserymen', *JRNZIH*, 1979.

some of which remains to this day. Donald settled into his new home and immediately established a vegetable and fruit garden. In an amazingly short time, he invited the public to visit him.

Karori was still a long way from the city, and Donald could see the sense in offering city families a place for picnics when they came for their fresh market produce. He did not advertise from 1854 to 1857. In 1858 and 1859, he increased his holding by purchasing two more five-acre lots from the original Yule block. He exhibited flowers and vegetables in the professional section of the Wellington horticultural shows, and achieved recognition for his trimming and shaping of trees. In 1872, he presented 48 plants to the Botanic Garden, then in 1875 he sold them 100 *Pinus halepensis*, 100 *P. sylvestris*, 12 *P. benthamiana*, 12 *P. laricio*, 50 totara trees, and 4 variegated hollies.

From advertisements in the 1875 *New Zealand Times*, it appears that Eden Vale was both a specialist tree nursery and a tea garden. Conifers were mentioned in the 18 June 1877 *New Zealand Times*. The heyday of pine planting had arrived, but Donald was astute enough to advocate a wider range than just *Pinus insignis* and *Cupressus macrocarpa*. It is not known whether he raised trees from seed, or bought them from a firm such as the Norwich Nurseries, Nelson.

Robert Donald, Gardener, intimates to the inhabitants of Wellington that he has commenced a Pic Nic and general fruit garden at Eden Vale, Karori and will be open daily, the Sabbath excepted.
Only a limited quantity of strawberries and gooseberries can be supplied this season.
P.S. Orders taken for supplying vegetables in large quantities and at very moderate prices if delivered on the ground.

Eden Vale, Karori
November 7, 1853

Wellington Independent, November 12, 1853

TO PARTIES PLANTING

Whilst planting freely of Pinus insignis and Cupressus macrocarpa, the favourite trees, it would be well to try a few of other varieties.

The following sorts, when the locality is suitable, will not disappoint the planters:-

Pinus austriaca	*Abies douglasii*
Pinus ponderosa	*Cupressus lawsoniana*
Pinus excelsa	*Cupressus lambertiana*
Larix europeus	*Cedrus atlantica*

A general list may be seen, and orders taken at Mr Logan's store, Lambton Quay. Growing samples from 2 to 20 feet, at R. Donald's Tree Nursery, Karori.

On Sale

SURPLUS STOCK OF PINE TREES FOR SALE
AT S. BOLTON'S
NORWICH NURSERIES NELSON

10,000	*Pinus insignis*, 1 to 2 feet, 20s. per 100, £7 per 1,000
3,000	*Pinus jeffreyi*, 1 foot, 40s. per 100
10,000	*Pinus austriaca*, 1 foot, 10s. per 100, £4.10s. per 1,000
10,000	*Pinus pinaster*, 1 foot, 10s. per 100, £4 per 1,000
5,000	*Pinus pinaster*, 2 feet, 12s. per 100, £4.10s. per 1,000
2,000	*Abies douglasii*, 1 to 2 feet, (very fine), £3 per 100
5,000	*Cupressus macrocarpa*, 2 feet, £2 per 100

The above were all transplanted last Spring. Large quantity of QUICKS, 2 years old, 6s. per 1,000.

The *Wellington Almanac* for 1877 listed Robert and James Donald as farmers. (The tea garden is not mentioned.) In 1882, the property was extended with the purchase of 11½ acres from John Campbell. From the simple beginning of providing city families with picnicking facilities and this acquisition of more land, the Donald family developed Eden Vale into a very well known nursery and tea garden.

R. DONALD
EDEN VALE
TREE NURSERY AND TEA GARDEN,
KARORI

[Above] Robert Donald, c 1880s.
Karori Historical Society

[Above] Jane Donald, c 1880s
Karori Historical Society

[Above right] Hatton Street, Karori, May 1913.
Alexander Turnbull Library, National Library of New Zealand, Te Puna Mātauranga, F-111583-1/2

Robert Donald died on 4 March 1895, aged 84. The property was leased to Lucy Young, widow, and nurseryman William Henry Young for three years, on the understanding that the gardens and pleasure grounds were to be carefully maintained. At the end of the three years, the Youngs could then purchase the property for £1,650.

Many early photographs of Karori show the extent to which macrocarpa and pines were planted by settlers for shelter after the bush was cut down. The photograph of Hatton Street taken around 1913 shows pines that would have been planted about the time that Donald was advocating their sale in his Tree Nursery advertisements. Besides the macrocarpa stumps still found on some Karori properties today, two fine examples of these trees can be seen at the corner of Hatton Street and Homewood Avenue.

Henry Woouldom and the 'Soot and Manure' Nursery Willis Street

Henry William Woouldom, aged 30, accompanied by his wife and two children, arrived at Port Nicholson on the *Martha Ridgeway* on 8 July 1840.[9] Fourteen months later, he wrote to his father:

> Henry Wouldon to W. Wouldon
> Gardener near the John Bull,
> Old Ford,
> Box,
> Middlesex
>
> Please to send me plenty of garden seeds for we cannot get any seed here. Please to send me some Scarlet Runners for they are £2 a quart and please to send me a 12 Rubbut roots (rhubarb) for they only two on the island and they won't sell them. If you don't come please take those seeds to my master Revent M. Saxon.

New Zealand Journal, September 18, 1841

[9] Sometimes there is a variation in the spelling, with 'Woouldom', the same spelling as a village in Kent, becoming the final form.

By the end of 1841, Woouldom was delighted with Wellington:

> Thanks be to God, I have been harty and weel since I left home . . . . I shall never think of coming to England whiist I can get pleanty of Pork . . . Father, Pray do come in the Next Ship and I will look out for you, and mind and bring the chirldren with you . . . . Please to tell all young men and ther wives to come to New Zealand, For they will soon get fat as hogs.[10]

Henry's father did come to Wellington, and worked at various occupations. 'Henry Woouldom, gardener', was shown living at Dixon Street in 1848 and 1849. William advertised as a rabbit fancier, Henry as nightman and chimney sweep, but the *Wellington Independent* of 14 May 1851 carried the advertisement on the right.

FRUIT TREES

For sale Fruit Trees. Warranted free from blight and named.
Apply to
H. Wouldom

In 1852, William was living at Willis Street and was listed as gardener as well as nightman. In May 1857 he was a 'rabbit fancier' of Willis Street, near the church, while the newspaper of 22 July 1857 referred to Wouldon, 'the original sweep and nightman'. An advertisement on 15 December 1858 indicates Henry Woouldom had become both a florist and seedsman, and this is confirmed in an advertisment in the 1863 *Almanac*.

W. H. WOOULDOM,
RABBIT FANCIER, WILLIS STREET,
NEAR THE CHURCH.
May 20, 1857 .

Wellington Independent, *May 20, 1857.*
Alexander Turnbull Library, National Library of New Zealand, Te Puna Mātauranga

H. WOOULDOM,
SEEDSMAN AND FLORIST,
WILLIS STREET,
WELLINGTON.

Wellington Almanac, *1863.*
Alexander Turnbull Library, National Library of New Zealand, Te Puna Mātauranga, B-K 443-2, P REF 919.31 WEL

There was yet another development – *Wellington Independent*, January 1861:

> H. Wouldom's Menagerie, Willis Street, gigantic Antipodean Diorama.

The story of Henry Woouldom shows how an immigrant from a working class background with certain skills could, with perseverance and hard work, achieve a measure of independence that may not have been possible back in England. Where he obtained his first fruit trees from is not known. But it seems only natural that in those days a trained gardener, with soot and manure at his command, should make use of it in the business of seedsman and florist.

---

[10] *New Zealand Journal*, 1841.

JOHN WATSON
NURSERYMAN,
SEEDSMAN, FLORIST
Willis Street
Wellington

Blue Gum Seeds for the —— 200 BLUE GUM SEEDS will be delivered free, with instructions for sowing, on receipt of £1 cash, giving the unequalled opportunity to possess this magnificent tree, suitable for ornament or shelter. White-thorn, Quicks, England Fruit Trees, and also a collection of garden seeds, warranted.

Willis Street Nursery,
Wellington.
August 26, 1850.

John Watson and William Mansill

John Watson was the only other nurseryman of any consequence in Wellington in the 1850s. The Willis Street Nursery is listed in the 1856 *New Zealand Gazette* as being under the management of John Watson, gardener. However, Watson's first advertisement appeared in the *Wellington Independent* as early as 26 August 1850.

In October and December1854, Watson offered roses of several kinds, possibly being the first nursery in Wellington to list rose varieties. In 1856, it seemed he advertised another first for Wellington: hollies:

JOHN WATSON
NURSERYMAN, SEEDSMAN, FLORIST
Willis Street, Wellington

Begs leave to offer the ladies and gentlemen of Wellington and the neighbouring colonies, a selection of hybrid, perpetual, Bourbon, Noisette and tea-scented roses; 20 varieties of geraniums, 20 varieties of Verbenas, 9 varieties of Calceolaria, etc. Myatt's Surprise Strawberry 12s. per dozen, or #5 per 100; Queen ditto, at 6/- per dozen or #2.10 per 100 Holly at #2.10 per 100, Berberis aquifolia, fine hybrid rhododendron, Whitethorn quick, Plums, Pears, Medlars. Damson's, etc.
The roses, geraniums, verbenas, and strawberries are warranted imported from England and of the finest description.

Gardens attended to by the day or by contract.

P.S. Plants ordered will be delivered the ensuing spring and autumn.

Specimens to be seen at the Nursery during the summer.

October 20th 1854.

Wellington Independent, October 21, 1854

JOHN WATSON
NURSERYMAN
Willis Street, Wellington

Begs leave to offer for Sale, the finest lot of English Holly ever offered for sale in New Zealand: 15,000 fine transplanted Holly from 4 to 9 inches high, at £2.10s per 100, or £15 per 1,000. English Yew, two years, same price. Warranted seedling plants. Fine stock of Cherry, Plum, Pear, etc., of the best varieties in cultivation.

P.S. Early orders are earnestly solicited.

June 3, 1856.

Wellington Independent, August 27, 1856

In 1857, Watson relinquished the Willis Street Nursery in favour of William Mansill.

Watson must have had some means. Challenger records that in 1858 Watson lent William Hislop, gardener to the Deans family, £250 towards establishing a nursery in Christchurch, his two pieces of nursery land being used as security for the loan. Although the loan was due for repayment by 1859, it was not repaid until 1862.[11] According to Challenger, the initial loan may have been used to purchase stock for the nursery, and we have seen that in 1859 both Lumsden and Watson sent plants on the *Queen* to Lyttelton. The shipment included yews, laurels, and laurestinus, and possibly Wellingtonia.

William Mansill was listed in the 1856 and 1857 *New Zealand Gazette* as a Gardener, leasehold, Town Belt. Mansill, then forty years of age, was a gardener from Warwick, with three years' gardening experience in Sydney. The following advertisements notified the Wellington citizens of the nursery's change of ownership:

> J. Watson Begs leave to thank the inhabitants and the neighbouring settlements for the liberal manner in which they have supported him during his stay in Wellington and to inform them he has assigned his business in favour of William Mansill, of Wellington, and hopes they will continue to him their liberal support.
> **J. Watson**
> March 26, 1857.

> William Mansill, in commencing the Business of Nurseryman, begs leave to call the attention of the inhabitants of Wellington and its vicinity to his fine fruit trees in variety, of the best description, whitethorn quicks, blue gums, laurestinus, holly, yew from two to three years old, and other shrubs and trees too numerous for insertion, and hopes by strict attention to business, to merit that liberal support bestowed upon his predecessor.
> N.B. Garden seeds and plants of all descriptions.
> *Willis Street Nursery, Wellington.*
> March 26, 1857.

The next advertisement for Mansill appeared in the *Wellington Independent*, 18 August 1857:

> **William Mansill**
> Nursery and Seedsman
> Willis Street, South
> All orders attended to.

The name 'Willis Street Nursery' was dropped, and from 23 August 1860 until 7 March 1862 the following advertisement appeared in the *Wellington Independent*:

> **PORTOBELLO TEA GARDENS**
> **Willis Street, Te Aro**
> William Mansill, Nurseryman begs very respectfully to inform the inhabitants of Wellington that he has laid out the above gardens regardless of expense and they are now open as a place of recreation and amusement. The grounds command a splendid view of the bay. Visitors may rely upon every attention shown them.
> Tea, Curds, and Whey, etc.

Concurrently with the tea garden advertisement, Mansill sometimes advertised as follows:

---

[11] Challenger, S. 'Pioneer Canterbury Nurserymen', *JRNZIH*, 1979.

WILLIAM MANSILL

Quicks, Quicks, Whitethorn Quicks W.M. has a fine sample of 3 year old quicks and it is absolutely necessary that persons desirous of planting whitethorn hedges this season should be quick in giving their orders as the stock is limited. Price moderate for cash. A general assortment of nursery stock and garden seeds on hand of the best quality. Orders carefully packed for the coast.

Willis Street, South.

Wellington Independent, June 21 to October 8, 1861

Advertisements for Portobello as a tea garden ceased on 7 March 1862. The Mansills' five-year-old daughter died around this time.[12] However, the *Almanac* for 1863 mentioned the Portobello Nursery, with an address in Nairn Street, top of Willis Street. W. Mansill was noted as a resident on the west side of Nairn Street in 1863,[13] occupying three Town Acres, two containing houses and one, the nursery, planted and fenced. Town Acre 51 had a glasshouse and further planting as well as a house.

Mansill's nursery operations continued. At the Agricultural and Pastoral show on March 1864, he won a prize for strawberries and a special prize for a 'very good collection' of yew and holly. Twelve months later at the next March show, he exhibited some very fine 'Hallett's' pedigree wheat and, together with Mason from Taita, carried off a number of prizes for various collections of apples.

For over twenty years, the Willis Street–Portobello Nursery made an important contribution to the stocking of the town's gardens. It in not known whether Mansill was a propagator, or whether he followed his predecessor's example and imported much of his material, for he was familiar with nurseries in Sydney.

Mansill owned the business, not the land. It appears that Watson sold the business to Mansill, but kept the land, offering it as security on the loan to Christchurch's William Hislop. When the debt was repaid in 1862, Watson sold the land to a Mr Daniel. Mansill paid the rates from 1857 until his death in 1867, when the Cemetery's Sexton, David Robertson, took over managing the business until 1870. In 1871 Robertson and market gardener Heinrich Bunckenburg managed the property and paid the rates jointly. From 1872, Bunckenburg operated the business as a market garden. The changes from 1870 to 1890 can be seen in the Bragge and Burton Brothers panoramas in Chapter 5.

WILLIAM MANSILL,

NURSERYMAN & FLORIST,

PORTOBELLO,

Nairne Street, top of Willis Street,

WELLINGTON.

W.M., has the honor to offer for sale this season a very large and choice collection of

FRUIT AND FOREST TREES, EVERGREEN

AND

Desiduous Shrubs.

CHOICE FRUITS,

True to name, and

APPLE TREES,

Warranted free from Blight.

A fine collection of

CALCEOLARIAS,

AND FLOWERS OF EVERY KIND.

Garden Seeds and Plants always to be had.

ORDERS FROM ANY PART OF THE COLONY EXECUTED WITH PROMPTITUDE.

Wellington Almanac, *1863*.

Alexander Turnbull Library, National Library of New Zealand, Te Puna Mātauranga, B-K 443-1, P REF 919.31 WEL

12 *Wellington Independent*, June 1861, *JRNZIH*, 1979.

13 Ward, Louis E., *Early Wellington*, Whitcombe & Tombs, 1928.

The early Wellington nurserymen

By introducing trees, shrubs and plants of all kinds, including those urgently required to give shelter, Wellington nurserymen played a significant role in humanising Wellington after the removal of the bush. Shipping notices show they also sent parcels of fruit trees to Christchurch between 1853 and 1858. Wellington's nurserymen certainly fulfilled the settlers' requirements, but never reached the importance of their counterparts in Canterbury.

No known catalogues of the period 1840–65 exist for Stockbridge, Lumsden, Watson, and Mansill, and reliance has to be placed on advertisements and incomplete information about imports and exports. It certainly seems probable that an introduction of Wellingtonia gigantea (*Sequoia wellingtonia*) to Canterbury came from a nursery in Wellington. (See the tables of imports and exports 1850–60 at the end of this chapter for more information.)

Thomas White, Fruiterer, Seedsman, and General Storekeeper

T. WHITE,

LAMBTON QUAY, NORTH.

RETURNS his sincere thanks to the Nobility, Gentry, and the Public in general for the extensive patronage he has hitherto received, and begs to assure them that nothing shall be wanting on his part to render his Establishment the first of its kind in Wellington.

T. W., has also a large and well assorted stock of Fish Lines and Hooks. Also, Rimmell's Perfumery, in endless variety, together with a regular stock of Groceries, too various to particularize.

Thomas White's advertisement. Wellington Almanac, *1852 and 1863.*
Alexander Turnbull Library, National Library of New Zealand, Te Puna Mātauranga, B-K 443-3, P REF 919.31 WEL

The earliest recorded catalogue from Wellington was Thomas White's vegetable and seed catalogue, issued in 1866, a copy of which was found among the miscellaneous papers of Sir George Grey. White was typical of many settlers in the variety of ways he gained his living. He was a general storekeeper in the 1850s, but in the next decade he specialised in selling garden and farm seeds and implements. White was well patronised. In 1867, James Hector bought from him 10 packets of vegetable seeds, 10 packets of assorted seeds, as well as seed of larkspur and mignonette. As in the 1840s, the catalogue shows numerous varieties of vegetable seeds and provides a useful list of annual and perennial flowers available and obviously popular in the mid-1860s, just after Wellington had become the capital city. However, there is no evidence that White raised his own seed, unlike his contemporary, the Wellington seedsman Frederick Cooper.

F. COOPER

BEGS to inform his friends and the public that he has just commenced in the above business, where he intends to keep constantly a fresh supply of the choicest

FRUITS AND VEGETABLES,

Which he will be enabled to do through arrangements made with several leading Horticulturalists, and trusts by careful attention to public requirement to receive that liberal support which it will ever be his earnest endeavour to merit.

F. C. has landed a choice selection of

FLOWER AND GARDEN SEEDS,

Which he can guarantee good and true to name.

Town and Country Orders punctually attended to.

NOTE THE ADDRESS

F. COOPER,

Greengrocer, Fruiterer, and General Storeman,

MANNERS STREET, WELLINGTON.

Wellington Almanac, *1866.*

Alexander Turnbull Library, National Library of New Zealand, Te Puna Mātauranga

F. Cooper Limited, Seed Merchants

'The firm began with the city.' So begins Cooper's centennial publication. Established by a twenty-year-old on a piece of land in Taranaki Street in 1860, the firm flourished for nearly 130 years. Its centennial publication has furnished much of the information that follows.

In October 1841, among the passengers on the ship *Oriental* that arrived at Wellington were Samuel Cooper, a tailor, his wife Elizabeth, and their six children. The youngest was baby Frederick, aged six months.

As a boy, young Frederick Cooper demonstrated a keen interest in gardening. Most families were dependent on their gardens and young Frederick's interest was valuable in a country in urgent need of primary produce. By careful selection, he gradually improved the varieties of plants that he obtained, until his requests for free plants and seeds from the public became an embarrassment. In order to provide funds for more and better plants he began to sell some of his output.

In 1860, he opened a nursery at the top of Taranaki Street. Land was not cheap, finance limited, and it took time to build up suitable stocks. By 1865 Frederick Cooper and his wife Ellen were able to open a shop on the south side of Manner's Street, to the west of Herbert Street, while retaining the nursery in Taranaki Street (see Panaroma 1, Chapter 4). Known as 'the boy and girl shopkeepers', they worked from 7 a.m. until the last customer left – some time between 8 and 10 p.m.

In 1866, about the same time that Thomas White issued his printed catalogue of seeds, Frederick Cooper advertised in the *Wellington Almanac*. The Coopers operated a general store, and specialised in garden seeds. Wellington had just become the capital and the time was right for such a business to become successful. According to his advertisements, all seeds sold were tested and 'guaranteed to grow and to be true to name'. In 1869, new premises were built adjoining the original shop.

The nursery at Taranaki Street and an additional one in Hopper Street eventually became inadequate. In 1880, Frederick Cooper bought land at Alicetown in the Hutt Valley, and named the property Bijou Nurseries. The firm continued to expand. Ten years later, in 1890, they bought another site in Manners Street, on the opposite side of the road. By now, the Coopers had six daughters and two sons, Frederick junior and George. The girls concentrated on the florist side of the business, while the two boys joined the firm. Frederick senior moved to his nursery at the Hutt, where he employed ten to twelve men.

Both boys received some training with the Dunedin firm Nimmo and Blair. Young George began his career at the age of nineteen, visiting the England in 1898. By the turn of the century, the name of Coopers' Seeds had spread throughout New Zealand. The firm's success continued until late in the twentieth century.

Manners Street, Wellington, in the 1870s. The first shop of Mr Cooper was at the far end on the right-hand side of the road. The second was on the same side, but nearer, and the third nearly opposite the second. The site of his third shop was a few doors past the Duke of Edinburgh Hotel, which is on the left of the illustration.

Alexander Turnbull Library, National Library of New Zealand, Te Puna Mātauranga

The First Generation

[Left] Frederick Cooper as a young man. Founder of F. Cooper Ltd, Seed Merchants, Wellington, New Zealand.

100 Years of Growth, 1860 - 1900

[Right] Frederick Cooper in later life.

Cyclopedia of New Zealand, 1897

The Second Generation

Mr George Cooper.

100 Years of Growth, 1860 - 1900

Mr Frederick Cooper.

100 Years of Growth, 1860 - 1900

Cover of booklet issued to mark the centenary of the firm of Coopers Seeds.

100 Years of Growth, 1860 - 1900

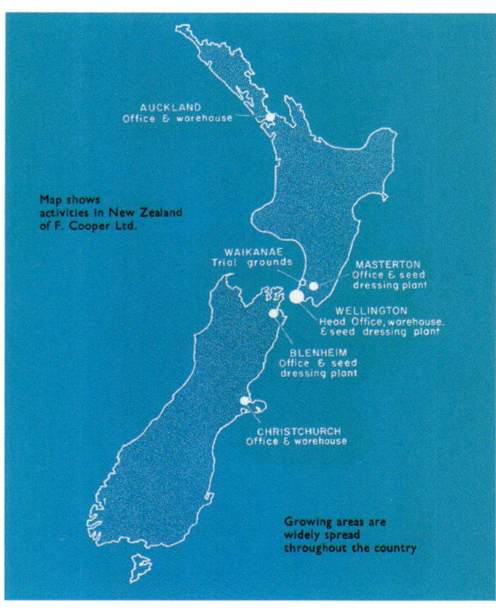

Map showing extent of operations for the firm of F. Cooper Ltd in 1965.

100 Years of Growth, 1860 - 1900

The third shop occupied by F. Cooper Ltd, on the north side of Manners Street, Wellington. The founder, Mr Frederick Cooper, is standing in the doorway of the shop, c 1890s.

Imports of plants and seeds to Wellington
1850-1860

Imports and Agents
Place of Origin

Year	From	Agent or Private*	Nature of Material	Date	Ship	Reference
1850	Nelson	J.E. White	200 fruit trees	June 12		Wellington Independent, Jun. 12, 1850
1850	Nelson	J. McBeth** Lambton Quay	500 lbs grapes	June 12		Wellington Independent, Jun. 12, 1850
1850	Hobart Town	J. McBeth** Lambton Quay	Onion seed	October 29		Wellington Independent, Oct. 29, 1850
1850**	Hobart Town	"	3 crates trees		ex *Munford*	Wellington Independent, Aug. 13, & 28, 1850
"	"	"	1 case garden seeds	"	"	"
"	"	"	2 packages seeds	"	"	"
1850***	Sydney	William Bannister. For sale Crown & Anchor	Selected fruit trees	June 16	*Scotia*	Wellington Independent, Aug. 10, 1850
1851	Hobart Town	"	1 bag seeds	April 12		Wellington Independent, Apr. 12, 1851
1851	Hobart Town	"	6 cases plants & seeds	April 16		Wellington Independent, Apr. 16, 1851
1851	Hobart Town	Bannatyne & Co., Willis Street	4 bags seeds	June 11	John & Charlotte	Wellington Independent, Jun. 16, 1851
1851	"	"	5 cases trees	"	"	"
1851	"		3 bags seeds) meadow & 4 casks seeds) others	"	"	"
1851	"	"	1 box bulbs	"	"	"
1851	"	"	3 casks blackthorns	"	"	"
1851	"	"	1 cask blackthorns	"	"	"
1851	"	"	1 case plants	"	"	"
1851	"	"	1 case seeds	"	"	"
1851	Hobart Town	Levin & Co.	18,000 white thorns	June 21	"	Wellington Independent, Jun. 21, 1851
1852	Nelson	"	3 packages plants			Wellington Independent, Jul. 10, 1852
1852	New South Wales	"	1 case plants (N.S.W.)			Wellington Independent, Sept. 15, 1852
1853	Port Victoria	"	1 case seeds			Wellington Independent, Apr. 30, 1853
1853	Hobart Town	Waitt. For auction. Terms at sale	10 doz. apple trees	June 29	ex *Munford*	Wellington Independent, Jun. 29, 1853
1853	"	"	10 doz. pear trees also cherry, plum, peach & filbert trees	"	"	"
1853	London	John McBeth Lambton Quay	Seeds, Forest Trees, Scotch fir, Silver fir, Larch fir, Beach mast, Ash keys, Alders, Norway spruce, Weeping birch	Sept. 23	*Admiral Grenfell*	Wellington Independent, Oct. 1, 1853
1854	Nelson	Bethune & Co	2 parcels plants		in the *Nelson*	Wellington Independent, July 19, 1854
"	"			1 case trees	"	"
1854	Sydney	W. Spinks*	1 case bulbs & shoots	July 29	*William Alfred*	Wellington Independent, July 29, 1854
"		"	1 package plants	"	"	"
1854	Nelson	Ludlam*	1 case plants			Wellington Independent, Sept. 30, 1854
1857	Hobart Town	R.J. Duncan & Co., Custom House Street	20,000 fine Van Dieman Land Quicks		*Helen*	Wellington Independent, May 20, 1857

****For details refer section on James McBeth Tinakore Nursery**
*****For details refer section on Agents**

Table 3

Exports of plants and seeds fromWellington
1850-1860

Exports

Year	Destination	Nature of Export	Consignee	Ship	Reference
1851	Victoria	6 packages fruit trees	Longden & LeCrew Auctioneers	*Fly*	Wellington Independent, June 11, 1851
1851	Lyttelton	4 bales	"	"	Lyttelton Times, July 19, 1851
1853	Port Victoria	7 bundles	"	"	Lyttelton Times, June 15, 1853
"	"	2baskets plants	Waitt	*Shepherdess*	Lyttelton Times, Aug. 20, 1853
"	"	1 case fruit trees	"	Schooner, *Wellington*	Lyttelton Times, July 23, 1853
"	"	12 packages trees & plants	"	"	"
"	"	2 casks plants	"	*Mary Jane*	"
"	"	1 box	"	"	"
"	"	3 bundles plants	"	"	"
1854	"	1 bundle trees	W.B. Rhodes & Co.	*Eagle**	Lyttelton Times, July 1, 1854
" "		3 bundles trees	Bethune V. Hunter	"	"
"	Port Cooper & Otago	1 bundle fruit trees	"	*Nelson*	
1857	"	6 bags seed	"	*Canterbury*	Wellington Independent, May 23, 1857
1859	Lyttelton	2 cases apples	Stockbridge Smith & Co.	*Queen*	Wellington Independent, May 6, 1859
"	"	1 case plants	"	"	"
"	"	7 bundles trees	J. Watson[x]	*Queen*	Wellington Independent, May 24, 1859
"	"	7 bundles trees	Lumsden	*Queen*	Wellington Independent, 24 May 1859

[x]Lyttelton Times, May 28, 1859 ex steamer 'Queen' from Wellington
795 English Yews, laurels and lauristinus etc. just arrived from Wellington
W. Hislop
***James McBeth again a passenger as he was in 1853**

Table 4

Chapter 8

TEA GARDENS

Gardens that provided entertainment and refreshment for the public had their origins at first as part of a plant nursery business. (A modern form of this idea is still seen in Wellington today, in places such as California Home and Garden, with its attractive café in Miramar.) In nineteenth-century London, gardens such as Ranelagh provided organised entertainment – music, balls, and firework displays. Later, more flamboyant entertainment was provided by the Chelsea Cremorne Garden.

In 1843, a dairy on Wellington's Terrace and another at Evans Bay offered customers new bread with fresh milk, so it is perhaps not surprising to find that fledgling nurseries soon began offering refreshment or entertainment to their visitors.[1] In the 1860s, Henry Woouldom in Willis Street advertised a menagerie, a so-called 'gigantic antipodean diorama', at the same address from which he operated as seedsman and florist.[2]

At the top of Willis Street, nurseryman William Mansill advertised his newly laid out garden-nursery as the Portobello Tea Gardens. There were other small 'pleasure gardens' in the suburbs, for example, Heginbotham's at Kilbirnie and Bishop's at Newtown, all contributing to the social life in the young colony. Some were more elaborate than others, and from the 1850s through to the end of the century they made a major contribution to the social life of Wellington and the Hutt Valley. They included Wilkinson's Tea Garden at Oriental Bay; Edenvale, Donald's Tea Garden and Nursery at Karori; McNab's Pleasure Garden at Woburn (formerly Alfred Ludlam's garden and later known as Bellevue Gardens); and Mason's Tea Garden at Avalon.

Advertisement for Bishop's Tea and Pleasure Gardens.

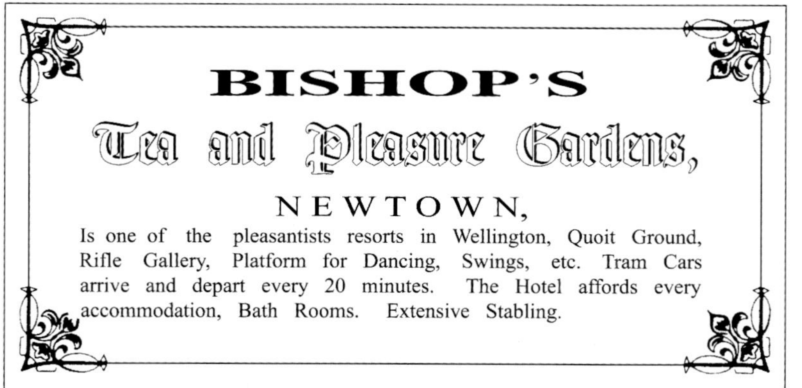

Wilkinson's Tea Garden was possibly the first to open in Wellington. David Wilkinson, aged 28, arrived with his wife and young daughter on the *Olympus* in May 1841. Born in Ayr and described as a 'Gardener', he was

Wilkinson Tea Gardens, Oriental Bay

NOTICE
To the inhabitants of Wellington and vicinity
David Wilkinson
of Roseneath Cottage Oriental Bay
Will open his Botanic Gardens on 6th Inst. Parties will be supplied with tea, curds and cream, ginger-beer, fancy bread, Burns' cakes and fruit in season.
All arrangements will be made for Pic Nic parties as there are a good many arbours with seats, parties will enjoy a treat.
No dogs admitted
Wellington,
November 4, 1850

Wellington Independent, November 9, 1850

1 Mrs Petre's Diary, 1843, Alexander Turnbull Library.
2 *Wellington Independent*, January 1861; *Wellington Almanac*, 1863.

recommended by James Crawford. In 1844, he is shown as a nurseryman living at Wadestown;[3] in 1848 he is shown as a 'Gardener, Thorndon Flat';[4] in 1850 he is shown as a 'Sawyer, Thorndon Flat';[5] in 1852 he is shown as a 'Gardener, Oriental Bay' on freehold land;[6] in 1882, still listed as gardener, he is shown as having Town Acres numbers 424 and 426 Oriental Bay.[7] Such changes of occupation were common. Settlers had to turn their hand to anything as they established themselves in the new colony. Both Wilkinson and James Bryant, the gardener who came out to work for Francis Molesworth, were at times listed as sawyers.

Wilkinson became a Foundation Committee Member of the Wellington Horticultural Society shortly after his arrival in town. At the Society's first show in January 1842, he won first prize for turnips, second prize for cauliflower, second prize for beetroot, and first prize for a bouquet. He was again successful at the December show that year, securing firsts for cauliflower, turnips, twelve strawberries, and a floral device.

A month before this show an interesting advertisement appeared in the newspaper.[8] Was there a particular story behind it?

> David Wilkinson begs to inform the public that he has now ready for sale plants of that beautiful new seedling *Mimulus wilkinsonii*, the varieties *youngii* and *smithis* are not to be compared to it – the blossoms are neat and regular in form and most distinctly marked with crimson or yellow ground. The flowers are produced in abundance and renders the plant very showy and produces a brilliant appearance. The plant is easy to increase.
>
> P.S. Flowering plants 2/- each.

In March 1843, Mrs Petre visited Wilkinson's Nursery Gardens at the top of the hill by Wellington Terrace: 'The view of the Bay and the town is very lovely and the gardens are very nice.' She visited Wilkinson's Gardens again at the end of that month, walking through the bush to get there.[9] Wilkinson was listed as living at Wadestown in 1844, and it is not known how long the garden remained on The Terrace or even exactly where it was situated, but in the 1852 *Wellington Almanac* David Wilkinson is shown as 'Gardener for the Government Domain' at a salary of £70 pa. The Government Domain in 1860 was:

> all that piece of land situated in the City of Wellington containing 5 acres, 2 roods and 16 perches, more or less and known as the Government House Domain; bounded towards the north by Sydney Street, 834 links; towards the north-east by Charlotte Street, 528 links; towards the south-east by Lambton Quay, 283 links, towards the south by Kumutoto Street, 818 links; and towards the west by Town Section No. 505, 556 links.[10]

---

3 *New Zealand Gazette and Wellington Spectator*, Survey List, 1844.
4 *Province of New Munster Gazette*, 1848.
5 Ibid, 1850.
6 Ibid, 1852.
7 Burgess Roll for Cook, 1882.
8 *New Zealand Gazette and Wellington Spectator*, 16 November 1842.
9 Mrs Petre's Diary, 1843, Alexander Turnbull Library.
10 Act to Provide for Management of Government Domains, 1860.

The position of 'Government Grounds Superintendent' was only recently disestablished.

Wilkinson's move to Oriental Bay occurred about the same time as he received his appointment as Government Gardener. The two Town Acres he bought were originally purchased by Mr Duppa from his ballot in 1840. Duppa sold them to the Collector of Customs, Mr Hogg, who in turn sold them to Wilkinson. The two acres were developed into a Tea Garden with glasshouses, from which he sold grapes in the autumn. Citizens young and old promenaded round the bay on a fine Saturday or Sunday afternoon and, after a walk through the gardens enjoying the trees and rose gardens, took a cup of tea in one of the shady arbours. The quality of Wilkinson's grapes was so good that he became known as the 'Father of Wellington Viticulture'.

Wilkinson's imagination and enterprise did not stop with the formation of his Tea Garden.

> **Mr D. Wilkinson is about to enclose a suitable place in the waters of Oriental Bay and make other arrangements suitable for the inhabitants of Wellington and its visitors to indulge with safety in the luxury of sea bathing, and proposes to carry out his plan by collecting sufficient subscribers to meet the amount which will be required for the outlay. Gentlemen wishing to forward the above are respectfully requested to leave their names at the store of Mr William Lyon.**
>
> ***New Zealand Gazette and Cook Strait Guardian*, October 9, 1855**

Sadly, the proposal went no further.

Wilkinson died in 1903, and his son subsequently built a row of houses along the promenade, thereby reducing the area of the garden by one half. The place lost its position as a place of public resort and, save for old families who still bought grapes from Wilkinson's hothouses in the autumn, the

Oriental Bay, Wellington Harbour, 1886 *by David Turner. The view is looking east towards the position of Wilkinson's Tea Garden.*

Wellington Maritime Museum Collection

[Right] *Oriental Bay looking towards the city, watercolour by Christopher Aubrey, 1889. Wilkinson's Tea Gardens are on the left.*

Alexander Turnbull Library, National Library of New Zealand, Te Puna Mātauranga, C-030-023

[Below right] *To the left are houses built along Oriental Bay Promenade, with the remains of Wilkinson's Tea Gardens behind, c 1910. Note the lack of sand.*

Postcard

[Above] *Early residence in what is now known as Grass Street, Oriental Bay, c 1900. The background trees are possibly part of Wilkinson's Tea Garden.*

Museum of New Zealand Te Papa Tongarewa B19454

garden, once the lover's lane and promenade garden of Wellington, became a private domain. In 1923, the gardens disappeared altogether when the beneficiaries of the estate erected two handsome, semi-detached brick buildings of two storeys each, containing 4–5 roomed flats with a frontage to Grass Street.[11]

Wilkinson himself did not contribute greatly to early plant introductions. In 1860, he ordered seeds from Backhouse in London and was disappointed when they sent him vegetable seeds, not ornamental shrubs or trees as he had wished. He exhibited an 'exquisitely beautiful' collection of fuchsias at the 1865 March show.

At the time Wilkinson's Tea Garden folded early in the twentieth century, all the Wellington tea gardens were under pressure and eventually they all disappeared. Wilkinson's Garden commanded an outstanding position, but today there are few reminders of it – Duppa and Wilkinson Streets, a giant mulberry, and little else.

McNab's and Bellevue Gardens, Woburn, Hutt Valley

When Alfred Ludlam died in 1877 there was no one to succeed him, and it was feared for a time that his garden might be sold and subdivided. James McNab, who owned a nursery in Thorndon, later bought Ludlam's property at Woburn, and opened it to the public as McNab's Gardens. He continued to develop the thirty-year-old property for another eighteen years. Many photographs come from both this and the next period, when the garden was immensely popular.

---

[11] *Evening Post*, 7 April 1923.

[Above left] Built by Ludlam in 1848, the grounds around the home are now mature, c 1880s. Climbing 'Cloth of Gold' roses screen the verandah and trees on the lawn soften the garden.

Hutt City Library

[Above right] Summer House, McNab's Gardens, c 1880s. Note the prevalence of nikau palms, cabbage trees and mamaku tree ferns.

Museum of New Zealand Te Papa Tongarewa B.16967

An outstanding Victorian botanical artist, Marianne North, stayed with the Premier in March 1881, four years after Ludlam's death. One of her remarks is illuminating:

> Going by railway three miles along the shore and then to a garden which had once been made by a man of taste, and now a nurseryman. Here I got good studies of the nikau palm, the most southern of all palms.[12]

In August, a few months after Marianne North's visit, Augustus Hamilton, who in 1903 would become Director of the Colonial Museum, visited the garden. On noting the lawn dotted with many large beautiful nikau palms, he said:

> Some Cordylines (Dracaenas, from Australia were doing very well) – and there were a lot of rare conifers that I would like to have examined. The ground was gay with tulips wherever it was not cultivated. One thing I must note. The Erythrina trees – the trunks were enormous and stood in the open without the slightest protection! The base of the stem must have been at least a foot in diameter. I should like to see them when in flower – the garden contains a very large number of bulbs and small flowering shrubs – the greatest show is made by the Azaleas and Ericas – one of the latter, carnea, I think, was particularly striking .... I saw the Chatham Island Lily in full flower.[13]

In 1882, the garden was described as follows:

> On entering the gate, an avenue some 70 yards long, bordered with handsome tree ferns, leads up to the house, a quaint gabled building, smothered in a cloth of gold roses. In front of the house is a smooth cropped lawn dotted over with some of the finest specimen conifers in the Colony. A labyrinth of walks conducts one through the flower garden. In addition to excellent specimens of native trees and shrubs there are fine single specimens of cedar, abies pine, piceas, oranges, lemons, and louquet trees .... erythrina, jacaranda side by side with the old fashioned sweet smelling favourite of British gardens.[14]

After fifteen years McNab put the garden on the market. It was bought by

---

12 North, Marianne, *Recollections of a Happy Life*, Journal pub. 1892.

13 Hamilton, A., Diary, Museum of New Zealand, 1881.

14 Bishop's Guide to Wellington, 1882.

[Above left] Bellevue Gardens, c 1907.
Postcard

[Above right] Lawn, band rotunda, and a range of conifers, c 1900.
Postcard D. Duthie

[Opposite] Bellevue Gardens, carpet bedding, c 1905.
Hutt City Library

Mrs Ross, a widow with a large family, and renamed Bellevue Gardens.[15] The garden reached the peak of its popularity in the 1890s, becoming a favourite venue for tourists and visitors from all walks of life, even royalty. The property consisted of 40–50 acres of farm, kitchen, and show garden. The house had been enlarged, with large stables at the back capable of housing 24horses. Those attending to the horses lived in quarters at the back and helped as waiters during weekends. Besides these men, the staff consisted of two maids, a laundry woman, two to three gardeners, and several Chinese to manage the vegetable garden.

Bellevue Gardens were open to the public every Sunday, and on public holidays, including Christmas. Such was their popularity that two trains ran there on a Sunday, as well as what seemed like every horse-drawn vehicle from Wellington. Hot scones, homemade butter and jam, fruit cake, and seed cake were served with tea. All the food was produced on the farm.

Mrs Ross also catered for special dinners, banquets, and dances. There were two full-sized pianos, and the dining room had large folding doors that could be opened up. Pies of all description, corned beef, roasts, jugged hare, and jellied tongue were provided with vegetables, salads, fruit, and cream – nearly all of it grown on the property. Men who were headed for the Boer War camped there before embarking to go overseas.

At the height of Bellevue Gardens' fame, there were two disastrous floods. Since the property was so close to the river, considerable damage occurred. The flood water swept over the lawn, destroyed the monkey cages, wreaked havoc with the garden, and entered the house. It was all too much for Mrs Ross, and she put the property up for sale.

Bellevue Gardens was bought by A.R.V. Lodder, who ran Orr's City Buffet,

---

[15] *Evening Post*, 8 November 1969.

The Bellevue Gardens
and Hotel
(LATE McNAB'S)
L O W E R H U T T

THE MOST SCIENTIFIC AND
ORNAMENTAL GARDENS
IN THE SOUTHERN HEMISPHERE

Mr A.R.V. LODDER has pleasure in announcing that the BELLEVUE GARDENS are now ready to receive visitors. The residence now having been thoroughly renovated and re-furnished, patrons may rely on finding everything first-class. Private dinner and picnic parties arranged for. Permanent boarders and tourists will find excellent accommodation at the Bellevue Gardens. The Gardens and their Beautiful picturesque surroundings are so well known that the Proprietor finds it needless to describe them in this announcement. Correspondence invited, addressed either to the Manager, Bellevue Gardens, or to the Proprietor Mr A.R.V. Lodder, City Buffet Hotel, Lambton Quay, Wellington.

THE BEST BRANDS OF WINE AND
SPIRITS IMPORTED BY THE
PROPRIETOR
Telephone 702-

The Place to Spend
Your Holidays

****

**BELLEVUE GARDENS,
LOWER HUTT**

****

DINNER ON CHRISTMAS DAY
AT 1 O'CLOCK

DINNER ON BOXING DAY AND FOLLOWING
DAYS at 12 o'clock

Hot Water Provided for Picnic Parties

CORDIALS & LIGHT REFRESHMENTS
AT TOWN PRICES

BAND WILL PLAY ALL DAY

ON BOXING DAY, NEW YEAR'S DAY, AND
ANNIVERSARY DAY

Advertisements Free Lance, 27 December 1902.

later the Gresham Hotel. The house, refurbished, was advertised as a hotel.

Bellevue Gardens and Hotel were still immensely popular, but the garden itself began to decline. The government was asked to help and suggested that the local council form a trust to manage the garden. If it had acted, Lower Hutt might have had its own Botanic Garden today. Instead, sections were sold off, leaving a small garden area of about $1\frac{1}{2}$ acres.

A fire destroyed part of the hotel in 1914. The building was reconstructed on a more modest scale, and run by a Mrs Shine along the lines of an English inn. In 1923, the year that Wilkinson's Gardens finally disappeared, the remaining garden of Bellevue Gardens was also sold. However, Bellevue Gardens Hotel still operates in Woburn Road.

In 1923, a small part of the subdivided Bellevue property was bought by J.W. Cooper of Coopers Seeds. He built a house there, designed by a Wellington architect named Fielding. Many of the original plantings were retained, and the remainder was planted more or less in keeping with the original. J.W. Cooper occupied the house until 1951, when it was bought by a religious order. In 1989, it was bought by the Te Omanga Hospice Trust, to be used as a hospice to care for the terminally ill. The garden continues to receive loving care and many donations of plants have been added to the older conifers, rhododendrons, puriri, nikau, and other trees planted last century by Alfred Ludlam.

Conifers at Te Omanga Hospice, originally planted 1860s – 1870s.
J. Wilson, Historic Places Trust

Grounds of the Te Omanga Hospice.
J. Wilson, Historic Places Trust

The original Ludlam house was occupied by Colonel Wakefield when Ludlam went to Sydney to fetch his bride in 1849. It was home to Ludlam and his wife for 25 years, and for over 40 years it was the most popular tea garden for Wellingtonians and their visitors. Ludlam's historic home and garden continue to play an important role in the lives of many.

Another of those subdivided properties in Woburn Road merits special attention: the home of the American Ambassador. Both this residence and Te Omanga Hospice, and adjacent gardens, are of regional horticultural significance today.

Eden Vale – Donald's Tea Garden and Karori Pleasure Grounds

From 1853, for over 50 years, the public was invited to Eden Vale, which was owned by Robert Donald and his wife (as we saw in Chapter 7). It was visited by Sir George Grey in 1867, who planted a holly tree there. From the 1870s, Eden Vale was an immensely popular tea garden. The *Wellington Independent* of 18 December 1871 carried this article:

> By a back gate we enter Edenvale Gardens, the property of Mr Donald: A patch of quaking grass engages attention, it is the finest we have seen; the stem is 18 inches in height. The most prominent features in the gardens are the grand and sombre holly hedges which are 12 feet high in some instances to 18 feet in others, and are impenetrable; the winds pass over them without withering their youngest leaf, whilst among willows, blue gums, peaches, poplars, and other smaller plants innumerable, a serious damage is still observable from the last south-east storm that swept over a portion of the Wellington province; were these gardens then depending upon any other natural or artificial shelter ruin to their owner might possibly have been the painful result. Native shrubs of surpassing loveliness of foliage and variety of tone, borders of dark green box, evenly sanded walks of bold firm outline and wealthy breadth, compel you to admiration and enjoyment; but the flowers, in single stateliness, in profuse masses, heaps, long compact lines, phalanxes of beauty scattered from the cornucopia of flora, and occupying every point of vantage all displaying variety of tint, magnificence of colour, and breathing a fragrance more tender, awaking

remembrances more sweetly melancholy than perhaps even music itself can exert in her subtlest witcheries over the human heart. We cannot pass a white rose, the 'Lucy Gray', without looking at her sweet face, and inhaling the fragrance of her perfume. Close by stands a totara clipt into form, shewing its fitness for hedges. In the vinery the grapes are in their green infancy, full of promise; in the many conservatories are rare and beautiful plants and flowers. On the summit of a bold hill in the grounds is a summer house, from which an extensive view is obtained; and on the same hill, among a grove of the *Olearia forsteri* stands, in a circular bed, a fine holly tree; eight feet in height, and on it a label, painted and glassed, preserves the following inscription:

ILEX AQUIFOLIUM;
PLANTED BY H.E. SIR G. GREY

15TH OCTOBER, 1867

It is surely a pleasing trait in the character of our late Governor thus to find him taking pleasure in entering with zest into the kindly pursuits of arboriculture, and giving to posterity a remembrance of himself linked with no public act, but merely from his own goodness and largeness of soul he has planted with his own hands, in the soil of the country he loves so well, a beautiful and picturesque tree, whose presence always reminds us of a far off isle ....

Entering by the front entrance; we see two sister ponds of water, with a small fountain playing in each; the sound of falling water adds an indescribable charm to the place; here are avenues of Lombardy poplar, and quaint summer houses; smooth-grassed lawns, so fit for picnic parties and holiday-keeping, folk from the dusty street home of Wellington. We turn homewards as the sun is flooding with soft warm light the gardens and village homes of Karori.

Today, the holly tree planted by Sir George Grey can be seen on a property in Donald Crescent. It is registered by the RNZIH as a notable tree. In 1981, it had a spread of 12 metres, was multi-stemmed, and had reached a height of 9.5 metres. The circumference of one branch 1.4 metres from the ground was 1.01 metres.

The entrance from Donald's Road (known as Donald Street today) gave access to the original house at approximately the site of number 89 today, where the vestiges of holly hedges that may have been planted by Edwards in the 1840s can still be seen. The house was two storeyed, with a steep gabled roof that was later covered with corrugated iron. A wide verandah ran along the north and part of the western side of the house. The gardens were designed to be viewed from the veranda, and from the drawing room, where tea was provided.

The entrance to the stables was approximately where the right-of-way to Numbers 83 and 85 Campbell Street is today.

Robert Donald was 84 years of age when he died in 1895. The tea garden, renamed the Karori Pleasure Grounds, remained open under the management of Lucy Young, a widow, and nurseryman William Henry Young.

In the plan of 1900, the kitchen garden was quite small, probably much smaller than in the

Donald's house with farmland behind, c 1920s. The house was condemned and demolished in the 1930s.

Karori Historical Society

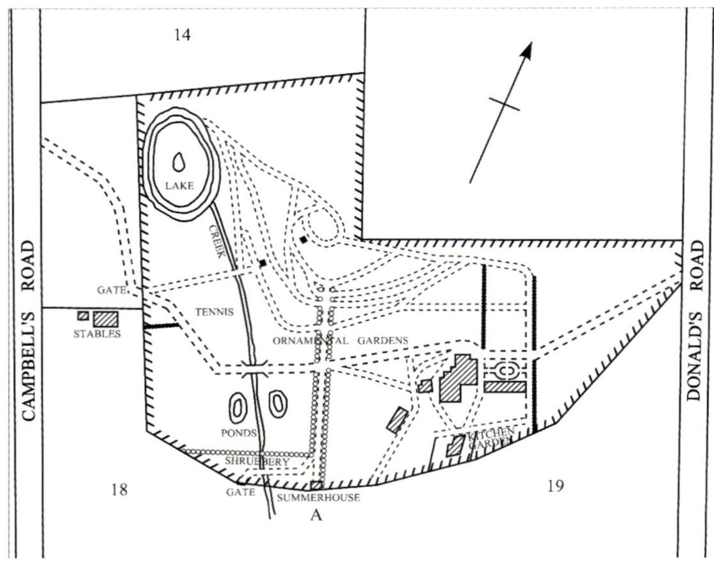

Plan of Edenvale by A.W. Seaton, c 1900.

Alexander Turnbull Library, National Library of New Zealand, Te Puna Mātauranga

1850s.[16] A creek flowed through the property and fed the lake at the low western corner near Campbell Street. How much of the development shown in this plan was due to Young is not known, but he is said to have dug the six-foot-deep lake with its central island.

Karori Pleasure Grounds were said to be much improved under William Young's management. Ornamental gardens lay to the north and east of the property, while native bush was retained on the south side. There were tennis courts and children's play areas. A two-roomed cottage, initially servants' quarters, was made available for a permanent gardener. A conservatory for choice plants lay to the east of the house while on the south boundary was the summer house with its punga roof.[17] Nearly thirty years on from the description of the garden given in the 1871 *Wellington Independent*, the *Cyclopedia of New Zealand* had this to say of the garden:[18]

> **The Karori Pleasure Grounds** are situated about a quarter of a mile to the south of the State School. Nestling among the hills, the gardens are protected alike from the cold of the prevailing winter winds and the heat of the summer sun. Although it is within the last two or three years only that they have been brought prominently before the notice of the public, the gardens are by no means a new institution. Their age may inferred by the fact that a tree is pointed out to the visitor as having been planted by Sir George Grey in 1868. About three years ago the present proprietor, Mr W.H. Young, acquired the property from Mr Donald, who had owned it for many years. Under the new *regime* the gardens have been greatly improved, and now form one of the most pleasant spots near Wellington. The property consists of thirty acres, of which fifteen compose the pleasure grounds, while the remainder are open fields. A pleasant surprise awaits the visitor as he enters at the eastern gate and makes his way towards the house. On one side the path is planted with a holly hedge, and on the other flowers abound in endless profusion. Entering the house to rest after walk or drive from town, the visitor may refresh himself with .... Having satisfied the claims of the inner man, the traveller may now explore the other parts of the garden. From the house, which occupies a central position, the ground towards the western gate suddenly declines for about fifty yards, and thence stretches a flat of some distance. On this flat, fishpond, the lake, and the croquet and tennis courts meet the eye of the visitor. The tennis courts, which are always well-patronised in summer form one of the most pleasing features of the garden. Many residents in town look forward with delight to Saturday afternoon, when they may take a trip to the gardens and enjoy a game of tennis. It is not an

A picnic in the Platts-Mills garden, formerly Donald's Tea Gardens, c 1900. The pines in the background are consistent in size with an 1870s planting.

Karori Historical Society

[16] Seaton, A.W. , Plan of Edenvale, produced for subdivision sale by a consortium of six, Alexander Turnbull Library, c. 1900.

[17] Ingerson, John and Barbara, *The Donald Tea Gardens*, 'The Stockade', Vol. 1, No. 2, 1973.

[18] *Cyclopedia of New Zealand*, Vol. 1, 1897.

uncommon sight to see several parties waiting their turn for the use of the courts. A short distance from these the lake is situated on which a boat is always ready for those who wish to use it. The northern portion of the gardens is intersected with beautifully shaded walks, on the sides of which are seats for the convenience of the public. In these cool places may be obtained such rest from the summer sun as would have satisfied the heart of the poet when he sighed for the valleys of the fabled Haemus. On the south side there are also many pleasant walks and summer houses. Here, too, are the swings and other means of amusement for children. Having seen the many sights of the gardens, the visitor may, before returning home, obtain an excellent tea at the house; and, as flowers are always in abundance, may if he wishes, take a bouquet to town with him. It must not be supposed, however, that the proprietor's functions are exhausted with the entertainment of day visitors. On the contrary, provision is made for honeymoon parties and others who wish to take a longer holiday at the gardens. For anyone in need of a complete rest, no better place could be found. Here the invalid may enjoy the fresh bracing air of the country, and at the same time be within easy access of the town. Coaches run between Wellington and Karori, and the gardens are some three or four hundred yards from the coach line. Mrs Young and her family do all in their power to make the Karori Pleasure Grounds a thoroughly agreeable resort for all classes.

View of Karori Pleasure Grounds, c 1890s. Hollies, pines, and box edging can be seen.

Karori Historical Society

The Karori Pleasure Gardens were popular for staff picnics and church outings, and honeymooners could stay there. The Youngs continued to advertise regularly. *New Zealand Times* of 18 November 1897 ran the advertisement on the right.

SPECIAL SHOW DAY
at the
KARORI PLEASURE GARDENS

Tennis boating etc. refreshments. Young's brakes will run to the Gardens leaving Fitzgerald's Corner 10, 12, and 2. Return fares including admission 1/6 Sundays 2 p.m. 2/-.

Eden Vale's popularity continued after its first owner died, but as with other tea gardens in Wellington, economic pressures began to bite as the nineteenth century came to an end. After nearly fifteen years on the property, the Youngs sold out to a small consortium, which unsuccessfully tried to sell off land near the Campbell Street entrance. They subsequently sold most of the garden to J.F.W. Mills and his wife Dr Platts.

The Platts-Mills, as they were known, kept the grounds open and served teas with the help of various caretakers. By the beginning of World War I, however, the house was empty and the grounds had deteriorated badly. The lake's banks had collapsed and the area was a swamp. By the 1930s, the house was so derelict that the Wellington City Council served a demolition order on the ninety-year-old residence. The property was bought by the well-known City Architect, Mr Hammond, who subdivided and sold the land.

Today, little remains of this once famous nursery and tea garden. Remains of the holly hedges can be seen behind properties in Campbell Street, along Ellerton and Masefield Ways, and around 89 Donald Street. The holly planted by Sir George Grey is still alive.

There is a small plant museum at 10 Masefield Way. In 1976, encouraged by the owner, Mrs Orgias, the Wellington City Council designated the area 'a place of scenic beauty' and placed it on the Regional Plan.

Karori Pleasure Grounds, c 1912. This photo shows two ponds, hedging, a cabbage tree, and a house in the background.

Karori Historical Society

Chapter 9

THE CITY LANDSCAPE

Although most of Wellington's original plant cover has been lost or modified, many botanists believe that before human settlement most of the ridges and hills were clothed with a temperate broadleaf-podocarp forest, except for Eastbourne, where there was and still is a dominance of beech (*Nothofagus*). Nearer to the sea, the forest became semi-coastal, with kohekohe prevailing. Flax, toetoe, fern, and tutu dominated both the windswept plain at Petone and the swamp at Te Aro.

At the time of European settlement, to judge from contemporary illustrations, there was little sign of podocarp or coastal forest on the north-facing slopes from Mt Victoria to Mt Albert at Melrose, and no obvious stumps or other remains of past forest. The land seems to have been covered with scrubby plants such as manuka, kanuka, tauhinu, flax, fern, and native grasses.[1] Matagouri was recorded on the Miramar Peninsula and also on the Mt Victoria ridge.[2] In 1842, Jerningham Wakefield described the plant cover at settlement as 'natural pasturage' with fern:

> The rapid improvement of the condition of the sheep and cattle on the natural pasturage of the hills south and south-east of the town, was no less remarkable. The fern, through which we used to ride up to the knees of our horses, had been trodden down in many places, and grasses, had sprung up in its room.[3]

In 1878, the botanist Kirk found the herb *Oreomyrris colensoi* growing, which confirms that the eastern and south-eastern hills had been unforested for some considerable time.[4]

To the east of the present city, the north-facing slopes are dry ridges, semi-arid for parts of the year. The scrubby plant community found there at the time of European settlement probably developed in response to the exposed conditions, frequent north-west gales and, in summer, little fresh water at the surface. Fire, not necessarily caused by people, may have periodically cleared the vegetation. Manuka-kanuka scrub, not coastal forest, may have always occupied this area. Wardle has suggested that this kind of scrub is not necessarily successional vegetation:

> Kanuka and manuka stands are not always transient but can maintain themselves as more or less stable communities for reasons that include frequent fires; harsh environments ... kanuka may have a permanent place in woody vegetation on dry ridges and in semi arid districts.[5]

---

1 *Leptospermum scoparium/Kunzia ericoides, Cassinia leptophylla, Phormium tenax.*

2 *Discaria toumatau.*

3 Wakefield, E. Jerningham, *Adventures in New Zealand,* 1845.

4 Kirk, T., *Transactions of New Zealand Institute*, Vol 2, 1878, p. 467.

5 Wardle, Peter, *Vegetation of New Zealand*, Cambridge University Press, 1991.

Without the benefit of pollen analysis or archaeological work on these slopes, and with Brees's 1843 panorama of Mt Victoria featuring cattle grazing in low scrub, as far as we know this was the type of vegetation on the eastern side of Wellington at the time it was settled by Europeans.

Things were very different on the western side of the city. In 1839–40 there were extensive stands of tall kanuka-manuka forest estimated to be 75–90 years of age. In his various views of his Hawkestone Street property,

[Above] Panorama taken from the summit of Mt Victoria in the form of a circle, c 1843. Evans Bay is on the left, Wellington Town and Harbour in the centre, Somes Island and the Tararua Ranges in the distance. Scrub vegetation amongst which cows are already grazing.

S.C. Brees

Brees used artistic licence in the placing of a solitary kahikatea tree in different positions. Only one view shows tree stumps. The solitary tree does seem to confirm Kilmister's comment that Tinakori Road, when formed, seemed to be the dividing line between bush and manuka-kanuka country.[6] In 1850, Walter Mantell said of the heavily forested Tinakori Hill:

> there are trees a 100 feet or more high, some most magnificent some covered with the gorgeous flowers of our crimson myrtle .... Some trees six men could not span – they are more than 10ft in diameter.[7]

On the eastern side of what is now Tinakori Road, the manuka-kanuka forest extended over the slopes that have become the Botanic Garden and Bolton Street Cemetery, and along The Terrace to Aro Street.

Some gullies in the Botanic Garden contained patches of bush. Soldiers felled and cut up a large matai in a small bush remnant in the gully that is now Anderson Park.[8] There was, and still is, bush in other valleys of the Botanic Garden. Large pukatea (*Laurelia novae-zealandiae*) grew in the valley at the top of Tinakori Road.[9] Mature pukatea still grow in a Botanic Garden gully near the Pukatea Stream, which enters the garden from The Glen in Kelburn.[10] A sketch in 1852 by Quaker T.

[Below] Bush on Tinakori Hill, Wadestown, c 1890s. Tall podocarps and other emergent trees with a dense understorey can be seen.

Denton Album, Alexander Turnbull Library, ational Library of New Zealand, Te Puna Mātauranga, F-19604-1/2, PA1-o-131-09-4

[Above right] Wellington Botanic Garden, c 1885. A view from today's Herb Garden ridge looking towards Salamanca Road over an extensive area of kanuka forest, a small area of which has been cut.

E.R. Williams Collection, Alexander Turnbull Library, National Library of New Zealand, Te Puna Mātauranga, G-25555-1/1, PAColl-0975

6 Kilmister, Albert, 'Some Early History of the Kilmister family and Early Wellington as they remembered it', MS, Alexander Turnbull Library.

7 Mantell, W., Letter to his mother, Mantell papers, Alexander Turnbull Library.

8 Kilmister, Albert, ibid.

9 Kilmister, Albert, ibid.

10 Shepherd W. & Cook W., *The Botanic Garden, Wellington 1840-1987*, Millwood Press, 1988.

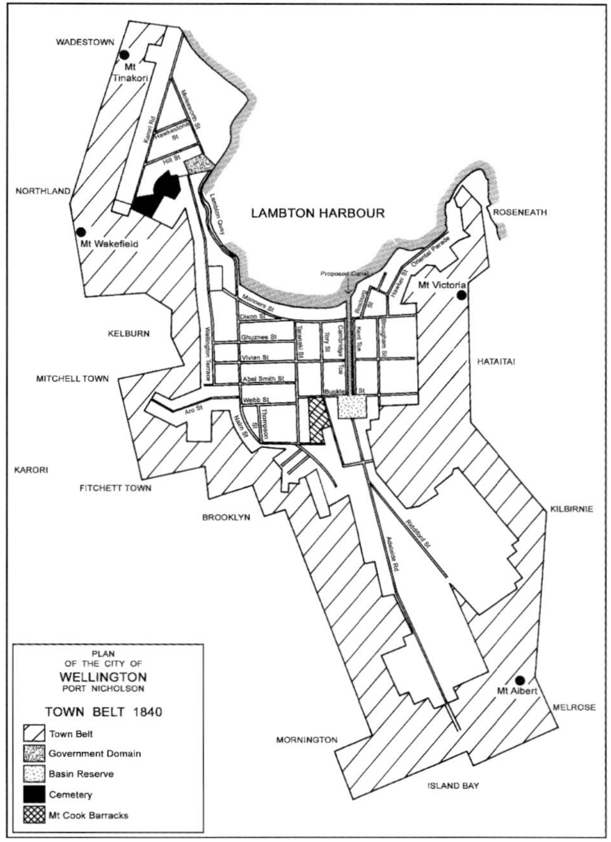

[Left] The Town Belt drawn by K.W. Shepherd, 1840.

Botanic Garden Archives, Museum of New Zealand Te Papa Tongarewa

[Right] Drawn about the time the Kumototo Block was given to the Wesleyan Church Mission, c 1852. The sketch shows fairly dense bush on what is possibly the Glenmore slope above the Pipitea Stream in the Botanic Garden.

T. Mackie, Traveller Under Concern

Mackie shows bush on a 13-acre strip of the Botanic Garden between the Glen and Tinakori Road.

Wellington's Town Belt, 1840–1870

The New Zealand Company's surveyor, as we have seen, was instructed to provide a green belt of open space to separate the town from the country acres. Marked as Public Reserve Land on the map, it was referred to as the Town Belt. It was and remains a conspicuous feature of the city, and one of the oldest surviving historical structures. Estimations vary as to its original size and range from 1519 acres to 1320 acres 2 roods 34 perches.[11] This reserved land ran from Mount Victoria to Mount Albert at Melrose, across to Brooklyn, across Aro Street to where Victoria University is now sited, through what is now the Botanic Garden, and on to Mount Tinakori, ending at Mount Wakefield.

Its appearance was most unlike the Town Belt of today, where the dark, even colour of the pine trees provides a backdrop to the city below. Nor was it evenly covered with native forest, a factor overlooked or not understood by many who advocate returning some parts of the public reserve to that state. The photograph overleaf shows forest on the Brooklyn hills. There were appropriations from the Town Belt shortly after the Survey was completed. In May 1844, land was taken for a cemetery, for the Botanic Garden, and for residences for the Wesleyan and Scotch clergymen and the Catholic

[11] *Wellington Town Belt Management Plan*, Wellington City Council, December 1995; Town Belt Boundaries, Mantell papers, Alexander Turnbull Library.

The Union Bank of Australia and manager's house, built in 1852, on the corner of Willis and Boulcott Streets, the site now occupied by the St George Hotel. The land behind has been cleared and fenced for grazing, while to the right is a large area of uncleared bush. Note the lack of drainage and the poor state of the city's roads.

Alexander Turnbull Library, National Library of New Zealand, Te Puna Mātauranga, G-731-1/1

priest.[12] In 1852, 75 acres were given to the Wesleyan Mission and, in 1872, 143 acres were given for Wellington College, the Wellington Hospital, and an asylum that occupied the site on which Government House now stands. Early in the 1900s, more Town Belt land was taken for Victoria University. Sports club rooms, scout dens, and the Winter Show Buildings were all built on Town Belt land. Some parts have been sold and are now covered with housing. Over 150 years, all these pressures have resulted in approximately one-third of the area of the original Town Belt being lost for public use.

The original limits within which the Town Belt could be used were established in the 1840s. No buildings were ever to be erected on it.[13] For a time, some areas provided grazing land for farmers supplying town milk and animals for transport. Through the 1840s and 1850s, given the Company's difficulties in securing land titles for the settlers from the Crown, title to the Town Belt remained with the Crown. By 1862, however, the Crown handed the Reserve over to the Superintendent of Wellington, to be held in trust for its citizens until such time as they would be able to administer it.

In 1863, the Town Council surveyed the Town Belt into 65 sections for leasing for 14 years, the rents to be used for roading through and planting on the Town Belt.[14] Some trees were planted, but the idea of embellishing the Town Belt in order to enhance the appearance of the city was not generally accepted until the latter part of the century.

The denuded Town Belt

By the late 1860s, nearly all the original vegetation had been cleared from the Town Belt and elsewhere throughout Wellington's environs. A photograph

---

[12] Shepherd, W. & Cook, W., 1988.

[13] Ibid.

[14] Wellington Ordinances 1853-65, Sessions IV, No 14, An Act to provide for the management of certain parcels of land in the town of Wellington, 19 June 1862, National Archives.

taken in 1867 with Wakefield's Government House in the foreground shows only the remains of the heavy podocarp forest, described by Mantell, that once covered the entire Tinakori Hill section of the Town Belt.

By 1871, when the new Government House had replaced Wakefield's house, the removal of the forest from Tinakori Hills was complete. The view from the new Government House across the harbour to Mount Victoria was also bleak, the scrub having been removed from that area too. All land around the town was bare, open, windswept, and ugly. Wellington's settlers had created what has been termed the 'first colonial landscape'.[15]

Forest clearance Tinakori Hill, c 1867. Dense forest is giving way to steep fenced pastureland.

Alexander Turnbull Library, National Library of New Zealand, Te Puna Mātauranga, F.2974½

The landscape shown in these photographs was typical of much of the North Island. The forest was pushed back and, as logs and stumps were removed, a shelterless pastureland developed across the hills and valleys. The towns within it were built of wood, almost treeless, and very exposed. Shelter was needed urgently. Settlers' letters and nursery catalogues reflect

[Left] Government House, built in 1871, with the now completely bare slopes of Mt Victoria in the background.

Museum of New Zealand Te Papa Tongarewa, B.14103

Scrub clearance on the Mt Victoria/Mt Albert ridge, c 1865. Open dry pastureland replaces the natural vegetation.

Alexander Turnbull Library, National Library of New Zealand, Te Puna Mātauranga, G-697-1/1

[15] Shepherd, W. & Cook, W., 'A vanishing Colonial landscape', *Onslow Historian*, Vol. 19 No. 4. 1990.

the demand for shelter plants such as gorse, hawthorn ('quicks'), hollies, and willows, plants with which the settlers were familiar. When deciduous trees such as elms and oaks were planted, their leaves were burnt by the relentless wind. The lessons were not easily learned. Nor have they been remembered, as a new settler in Ohariu Valley found in 1990, when his perimeter plantings of silver birch were burnt off by the wind at about 15 feet.[16]

Francis Molesworth at the Hutt seems to have been the first to establish a thorn hedge, in 1843. Chapman imported bundles of quicks from Hobart Town, while the nurserymen Stockbridge, Watson, and Mansill all advertised quicks and hollies. At Taita, Thomas Mason advertised 'quicks' for sale.[17] Thompson's *Gardeners Assistant* listed holly as 'suitable for coastal conditions'. In Karori, Donald planted holly hedges, and some of them can still be seen in Donald Street today. The holly hedge planted about 1870 around the Botanic Garden's fledgling nursery still flourishes, protecting what is now known as the Sunken Garden.

[Above left] Wellington Botanic Garden. A holly hedge planted c 1870 surrounds the nursery.

Botanic Garden Archives, Museum of New Zealand Te Papa Tongarewa

[Above right] Wellington Botanic Garden. The same holly hedge protects today's Sunken Garden.

W. Shepherd, Aug 1999

Quicks and hollies seen today in Ohariu Valley probably date from the period before the introduction of conifers. A holly hedge still shelters the Anglican Church on its eastern side. The cherry laurel *Prunus lauras ceracus* was also common, one such hedge being planted along Junction Path in the Botanic Garden.

Gorse hedges began to appear in the 1860s, an example being the boundary of Mr Moxham's Upland Farm with the western edge of the Botanic Garden.[18] Early paintings and photographs, especially of the Thorndon area, show that gums and poplars were proving to be quick-growing shelter trees.

The replanting of the Town Belt

By1865, the bare Town Belt was slowly being colonised by the native cottonwood, tauhinu, and successful exotics such as gorse and broom.

[16] Shepherd, W. & Cook, W., ibid.
[17] Shepherd, W. & Cook W., 1988.
[18] Ibid.

From the late 1860s through to the early 1880s, anxious to find industries that would secure the country's economic future, the government introduced seeds and plants with economic potential. They were trialled through the Geological Survey, headed by James Hector, who was also Manager of the New Zealand Institute and, from 1868, Manager of the Wellington Botanic Garden.

The growing realisation that New Zealand trees were unsuitable for tree cropping was causing concern about how the country would meet its future timber requirements. Tree species were introduced, hardwoods as well as the increasingly popular softwoods, the conifers from America and the Himalayas that were as new to Britain as they were to New Zealand. Between 1876 and 1885, large quantities of conifer seed were imported and distributed by the Geological Survey to Provincial Superintendents, botanic gardens, nurserymen, and private individuals.

Through the 1870s to the mid 1880s, the Wellington Botanic Garden raised plants from the seed, planting some in the Garden as well as distributing them free to those who requested them. The distribution of plants and seed for this period and the 48 conifer species introduced are detailed in the book on the history of the Garden.[19] Because of James Hector's position, the Wellington Botanic Garden was central to the generation of this new landscape, not only for Wellington but also for New Zealand. By the 1880s, the Wellington Botanic Garden had itself become an oasis of green in an otherwise stark landscape of bare land.

The success of the conifer seed created what can be termed the 'second colonial landscape'.[20] Some shelter plants planted as hedges in the first period, such as gorse and broom, were too successful and gradually colonised the bare hills to form an integral part of the 'second colonial landscape'. Broom and gorse became conspicuous on Wellington's hills. Kipling, visiting in 1891, wrote of 'Broom behind the windy town, pollen of the pine.'[21]

View from Northland overlooking north-west corner of Botanic Garden towards Kelburn and Mt Victoria Town Belt, c 1910. An oasis of green in an otherwise barren landscape, showing conifers on the western boundary before the formation of the Magpie lawn, the fine landscape planting of the Botanic Garden Board, the housing development, and the hills of Mt Victoria, which are barren except for a plantation at Pirie Street.

S.C. Smith Collection, Alexander Turnbull Library, National Library of New Zealand, Te Puna Mātauranga, G-019651-1/1, PAColl-3082

Radiata pine and macrocarpa, two conifers from the Monterey Peninsula in California, were extremely successful in the plant trials, and the 'second colonial landscape' can still be seen, with conifer plantings around cemeteries, churches, schools and homesteads throughout New Zealand. In Wellington, the conifers proved their worth in the face of north-westerly gales, salt-laden winds, and clay soils. In 1872–73, 642 pines and cypresses were planted around the asylum. In 1874, W.T.L. Travers secured 600 selected conifer plants for planting behind Wellington College. Further plantings of *Pinus insignis*, *P. maritima*, Wellingtonias, and macrocarpa were made on Somes Island and at the Basin Reserve and the asylum. When conifer trees were supplied to the Town Council for the first plantation on the Town Belt in 1880, the *New Zealand Times* said: 'We are pleased to see that a large section of the Town

[19] Shepherd, W. & Cook W., 1988.
[20] Shepherd, W. & Cook, W., 1990.
[21] Kipling, Rudyard, *The Flowers*, 1895.

Belt at the top of Pirie Street is being planted with trees such as macrocarpa, *Pinus insignis* and others known to stand high winds.'

Many of those early plantings, including the Pirie Street stand and those at Wellington College, Government House, and Somes Island, are still extant. Their significance often goes unrecognised.

Basin Reserve, looking south-east, c 1885. Young pines have been planted on the Town Belt (top left corner). Older pines can be seen around the Basin and Wellington College. Gorse and broom are spreading on hills. The second colonial landscape has formed.

Museum of New Zealand Te Papa Tongarewa, B.16966

Mt Victoria slope, looking west across to Brooklyn hills, 1884. The stark first colonial landscape is about to be broken with this 1881 Pirie/Ellice Street planting of pines.

Burton Bros Collection, Alexander Turnbull Library, National Library of New Zealand, Te Puna Mātauranga, G-2237-1/1-BB

Basin Reserve with the barren Town Belt in the background, 1908. A similar view to that shown above. The Pirie/Ellis Street pine plantation is now 20 years old and those around Basin Reserve and Wellington College are 30 years of age. Both the Pirie Street conifers and some around Wellington College and Government House are extant today.

S.C. Smith Collection, Alexander Turnbull Library, National Library of New Zealand, Te Puna Mātauranga, G-19898-1/1, PAColl-3082

Somes Island, c 1878. Planted in 1874 conifers raised in the Botanic Garden are starting to soften the harshness of the Island's landscape. Immigration barracks are on the skyline.

Fitzgerald Album, Alexander Turnbull Library, National Library of New Zealand, Te Puna Mātauranga, F-154610-1/2

By the 1880s, pines planted in private gardens added their contribution to the developing inner-city landscape. Christopher Aubrey's 1889 watercolour shows conifer boundary plantings on a property in Brougham Street. The conifer plantings around John Kirkcaldie's house in Thompson Street were also conspicuous. Conifers were planted in private gardens even in Oriental Bay.

The planting of the Town Belt with conifers continued, with the addition of some eucalyptus species that were also proving useful. The city side of Mount Victoria was completed by 1932. In 1924, the final planting on the belt along Alexandra Road began. The plantings on the southern end of Tinakori Hill date from 1913–15, and those to the north (from the Grant Road Scout Den) from between 1930 and 1940. These trees are therefore 50 years younger than the Pirie Street plantation. Newtown Park was planted in the 1880s, and the Nairn Street Reserve in 1886–8. During the 1925 season, J.G. Mackenzie, Director of Parks and Reserves, reported that the nursery sent out 26,526 trees for planting on the Town Belt.[22]

[Above left] Brougham Street, Mt Victoria, Wellington, watercolour by Christopher Aubrey, 1889.

Alexander Turnbull Library, National Library of New Zealand, Te Puna Mātauranga, C-030-005

[Top right] Cuba Street, looking south, 1880s. Extensive conifer planting has occurred on the property of J. Kirkcaldie at the top of Thompson Street.

Holmes Album, Alexander Turnbull Library, National Library of New Zealand, Te Puna Mātauranga, F-125042-1/2, PA1-q-120-23-2

[Lower right] Conifers in private gardens, Oriental Bay, 1910. Trees from Wilkinson's Tea Garden are on the top left.

S.C. Smith Collection, Alexander Turnbull Library, National Library of New Zealand, Te Puna Mātauranga, G-19756-1/1, PAColl-3082

Planting of Tinakori Hill with pines and eucalypts has begun, c 1913.

Postcard, Godfrey Phillips Ltd

The conifer legacy

Throughout Wellington, and indeed throughout New Zealand, the success of the conifer plantings of the 1870s–80s is still apparent, although it remains to be seen how long these trees will last. To see how conifer shelter belts and plantings were used around houses, look for old plantings in Ohariu Valley

[22] 'Report on tree planting for the 1925 season', Wellington City Council, 1925.

and Makara. The photographs that follow show conifers planted in the 1870s and 1880s in the Ohariu and Makara Valleys, the Town Belt, the Karori Waterworks Reserve, the Botanic Garden, and the old Gaol Reserve.

Ohariu Valley – Makara

Panorama of Ohariu Valley, looking north from top of Rifle Range Road, showing conifer plantings following the base of the valleys, c 1990.

R. W. Shepherd

[Above left] Bonsai-looking radiata pines on the right with further mature radiata in the background, D.J. Weaver's property on Ohariu Valley Road, c 1990. The property was originally owned by George Best, recipient of Botanic Garden seed in 1879.

W. Shepherd

[Above centre] Makara Lawn Cemetery, Returned Services Section, c 1991. Pines and macrocarpas planted last century border the cemetery. The open pastureland behind is becoming gorse covered. An excellent example of the second colonial landscape.

W. Shepherd

[Above right] Makara Lawn Cemetery, looking northeast towards recently planted pines and gorse clad hills, c 1991. A modern landscape repeats the success of conifers introduced to New Zealand between 1870–85.

W. Shepherd

[Left] Radiata pine on the southern church boundary, planted around 1880, Ohariu Valley, photo c 1990.

W. Shepherd

Pinus radiata and *Cupressus macrocarpa*

Planted c 1870-1885

From left to right:
(a) Pinus radiata, Wellington Botanic Garden.
(b) Pinus radiata, Ohariu, original property owner Mr G. Best, who obtained conifer seed from the Botanic Garden in 1879.
(c) Cupressus macrocarpa, upright form well suited for timber production, Makara.
(d) Cupressus macrocarpa, Ohariu, umbrella shape not suited for timber production.

(a) 1987. John Johns, (b) - (d) 1990. W. Shepherd

Te Aro flat from Gaol Hill, 1878. Taken at the bottom of Native Reserve 15 on Gaol Reserve 10 on Wellington Map of 1840. This is above the Terrace between Vivian and Abel Smith Streets. The pines planted on the Government Gaol Reserve were supplied from the Botanic Garden in 1873/74/75. A few are extant today.

Museum of New Zealand Te Papa Tongarewa, Te Papa Tongarewa, James Bragge

Macrocarpa, Homewood Avenue, planted 1870s, photo November 1999.

J. Nauta, Museum of New Zealand Te Papa Tongarewa

Looking south from Te Aro School grounds, originally the Gaol Reserve, c 1997. The few trees shown in are now mature specimens recognised by the school for their shelter, age, and landscape qualities.

W. Shepherd

Waterworks Reserve, Karori, c 1905. This shows the growth of the conifer trees.

Postcard, F.T. Series No. 527

Wellington City conifers

Planted 1870-1885

The illustrations chosen are but a few examples of past and present landscapes. Today many remaining fine specimens of old pines and macrocarpas remind us of their place in Wellington's history, trees that softened the landscape and gave valuable shelter, improving the bare landscape created by the settlers. In the Botanic Garden, remnants of the podocarp-broadleaf rainforest were protected by conifers planted from 1870–85. These are among the oldest pines in New Zealand, providing the Garden with a distinctive skyline, the forerunner of that seen on the Town Belt today.

[Left] Looking west from the Botanic Garden Education Centre towards Magpie Hill and stand of the first pines planted in the Botanic Garden in 1871, c 1997.

W. Shepherd

[Right] Looking east from the Botanic Garden Education Centre towards Druids Hill and an early planting of pines, c 1997.

W. Shepherd

Into the twenty-first century

Today, the Town Belt, clad mainly in conifers with some eucalyptus, is a distinctive feature of Wellington's landscape, and is as important to the physical, emotional, and spiritual health and well-being of the citizens of Wellington as it was at its beginning. In recent years, there has been a growing recognition of this importance and the need to secure the Town Belt's boundaries and provide for its management.

An 'Outer Town Belt' was initiated in the 1960s under the direction of Ian Galloway, with the Wellington City Council Parks and Recreation Department responsible for developing it. It too was designed to separate the now expanding city from the country with a further zone of open space. Only part of the land intended for this Outer Town Belt is currently in Council ownership, but necessary additions are being acquired or protected as land becomes available. For example, in January 1999 a further 265 hectares were added to the Outer Town Belt when the hills above Chartwell and Crofton Downs were bought by the Council from Brian Kilmister.

The Otari Native Botanic Garden, with its remnant of podocarp forest, falls into the Outer Town Belt. It seems more or less likely that New Zealand native plants will eventually dominate the Outer Town Belt, but no decisions have yet been made.

In the early 1990s, after public consultation, the Wellington City Council formulated a Management Plan for the Town Belt proper, and it was approved on 14 December 1995. This detailed and worthwhile document, which outlines complex management policies, should go a long way to ensuring the preservation and management of this valuable bequest to the city by its founders. The Council's foreword to the Management Plan is explicit:

> Since being set aside in 1841 management of the Town Belt has occurred pretty much on an ad hoc basis both under the Crown's and Council's jurisdiction. As the city expanded numerous demands for land occurred and sadly it was the Town Belt land that was often exploited.
>
> Until now a comprehensive plan outlining the future management policies for the Town Belt has not been prepared. It is with considerable pride that the Council has prepared such a plan.[23]

Under this plan there will be no further encroachments on the Town Belt, and in some cases provision has been made to return land to the Reserve. In order to rationalise a few areas, other land will be taken into the Town Belt. Some southern areas, including Mount Albert, are zoned to be returned to coastal forest, but provision has been made to protect meadowlands and areas rich in wildflowers Conifers are to be retained on the inner Mount Victoria slopes, but are to be removed from Tinakori Hill, which is to revert to native forest.

> The present vegetation must be accepted collectively as the starting point for future vegetation and its management. The forest cover we have on the Town Belt today has taken many years, and a great deal of effort from early Wellingtonians, to develop. This forest environment has been hard won and must be protected.
>
> A forest is a living system and as such, is constantly changing through natural processes to achieve not only a more ecologically sustainable result, but also one which will cost us less in the long run ....
>
> The variety of vegetation types on the Town Belt offers a range of recreational and visual experiences much valued by the people of Wellington. There are those who will argue for the creation of pure

---

[23] *Wellington Town Belt Management Plan*, Wellington City Council, December 1995.

[24] Ibid.

> native forest cover, and those who prefer the open understorey of the coniferous forest. There is scope to accommodate a range of preferences. The landscape and micro climates are varied enough to carry a variety in vegetation cover and, as this is a public reserve, the desires of as many of the community as practicable should be accommodated.[24]

The changes will be slow and difficult. In the majority of cases, where seed sources for forest trees are lacking, trees will have to be introduced by hand and carefully nurtured. The satisfactory dark green backdrop to the city provided by the Town Belt at the start of the new millennium will be changed by these major plans for re-vegetation. It is to be hoped the changes will be aesthetically pleasing, and not result in an indeterminate mix of mahoe, kawakawa, and the other undistinguished plants that pass for 'native bush'. Invasives such as *Clematis vitalba* (Old Man's Beard) will always need monitoring. The native vegetation on the Tinakori Hill and elsewhere may cause the hills to blend into the colour of the Outer Town Belt and be less visually satisfying than they are today with their mantle of conifers.

Over the last century Wellington has re-vegetated the public reserve that the city's first generation of settlers had devastated by 1870. The Wellington City Council, with its admirable Town Belt Management Plan, has a

[Right] Mt Victoria/Mt Albert Ridge section of the Town Belt. It is a portion of the continuous open space through the city, separating and defining urban localities and providing a 'natural' backdrop to the densely developed land on each side.

L. Homer, Wellington City Council Town Belt Management Plan

[Below] Golf Links Area. In the south are gentler contours with large areas of open ground for sporting activities. Few conifers are to be retained, large areas are to be native vegetation.

L. Homer, Wellington City Council Town Belt Management Plan, CN.11118

Tinakori Hill is the largest area on the Town Belt where a return to native vegetation is proposed, presenting an opportunity for scientific study and education about the ecological processes involved. Conifers on lower slopes will be gradually thinned.

L. Homer, Wellington City Council Town Belt Management Plan

difficult and onerous job in the years ahead to retain both the satisfactory use of Wellington's most important and historic landscape artifact, and preserve its visual harmony. This work of nature and man forms a cultural landscape worthy of inclusion on the World Heritage List. It is to be hoped that tomorrow's citizens will remember the lessons of the past.

The wildflowers of Wellington

Another distinctive feature of the present Wellington landscape is its wildflowers. These are wayside plants originating from discarded garden refuse, or succeeding by their own devices, seeding on to dry, rocky slopes or, like the foxglove, into damper areas. An endless array of species can be found, but only the commonest are illustrated here. In spring, Wellington's roadside banks are transformed by wildflowers, with purple, cream, and yellow being the predominating colours. Summer flowers are few, mainly roses that still continue after the main spring flush is over, while in late summer and autumn montbretia, purple linaria, and the occasional nasturtium add vivid colour to the banks.

The commonest rose is the rambler *Rosa* 'Alberic Barbier', which was planted in numbers by the Wellington Beautifying Society and the Parks Department in the time of McKenzie. Thus it is not a true garden escape or wildflower.[25] Fortunately for the city and its environs, plants of the sweet briar, *Rosa rubiginosa*, are few in number, even though it was one of the earliest plants to be introduced to Wellington. This stands in stark contrast to its over-success in other parts of New Zealand.

Wildflowers, together with the pines, eucalypts, deciduous trees, gorse, broom, and pasture make up the special visual character of the capital city. It is this landscape, uniquely ours, that we take into the twenty-first century.

South African Daisy, Senecio glastifolius, *Wellington hillsides, Happy Valley Road, November 1999.*

J. Nauta, Museum of New Zealand Te Papa Tongarewa, C.T.15697/3-5

---

[25] Duthie, D., 'The Wild White Rose of Wellington', *Newsletter*, Friends of the Wellington Botanic Garden, No. 3, 1994.

Senecio glastifolius, *Brooklyn Bank, November 1999.*

J. Nauta, Museum of New Zealand Te Papa Tongarewa, C.T.15697/6-8

Red spur valerian, Centranthus ruber, *Wadestown, November 1999.*

J. Nauta, Museum of New Zealand Te Papa Tongarewa, C.T.15704/14-16

Mixed colours spur valerian, Ngaio Gorge, November 1999.

J. Nauta, Museum of New Zealand Te Papa Tongarewa, C.T.15700/19-20 or 28-32

Rhododendron ponticum, *Karori bank, December 1999. The author first observed these self-sown plants on this bank in the 1960s.*

J. Nauta, Museum of New Zealand Te Papa Tongarewa, C.T.15703/23-25

Nasturtium, Tropaeolum majus, *on a Kelburn bank, December 1999. This plant is originally from the Andes in South America.*

J. Nauta, Museum of New Zealand Te Papa Tongarewa, C.T.15698/3-7

Everlasting pea, Lathyrus latifolius, *Greta Point, November 1999.*

J. Nauta, Museum of New Zealand Te Papa Tongarewa, C.T.15705/13-18

Spanish broom, Spartium junceum, *Bowen Street, December 1999.*

J. Nauta, Museum of New Zealand Te Papa Tongarewa, C.T.15704/40-44

Canary Island broom or a hybrid of Teline canariensis, *October 1999. A sweet scented branching shrub flourishing on a Karori road. In the 1920s, B.C. Aston is credited with spreading the seed in this vicinity as he walked to work.*

J. Nauta, Museum of New Zealand Te Papa Tongarewa, C.T.15697/33-35

Bone seed, Chrysanthemoides molifera, *covering a hillside in Happy Valley Road, October 1999.*

J. Nauta, Museum of New Zealand Te Papa Tongarewa, C.T.15696/9-12

Oxeye daisy, Leucanthemum vulgare, *Wilton, December 1999.*

J. Nauta, Museum of New Zealand Te Papa Tongarewa, C.T.15703/2-4

Marguerite daisy, Argyranthemum frutescens, *above the Karori tunnel, December 1999.*

J. Nauta, Museum of New Zealand Te Papa Tongarewa, C.T.15703/10a-12a

Wild freesias, Brooklyn Road, October 1999.

J. Nauta, Museum of New Zealand Te Papa Tongarewa, C.T.15696/17-23

Foxgloves, Digitalis purpurea, *gorse background, Makara, December 1999.*

J. Nauta, Museum of New Zealand Te Papa Tongarewa, C.T.15698/38-41

Honesty, Linaria annua, *Kelburn, October 1999.*

J. Nauta, Museum of New Zealand Te Papa Tongarewa, C.T.15697/41-43

Arum lilies, Zantedeschia aethiopica, *Makara, December 1999.*

[. Nauta, Museum of New Zealand Te Papa Tongarewa, C.T.15698/33-37

Succulent garden escapes, Greta Point, December 1999.

J. Nauta, Museum of New Zealand Te Papa Tongarewa, C.T.15072/17-20

Rose, 'Albéric Barbier', *Khandallah, November 1999.*

J. Nauta, Museum of New Zealand Te Papa Tongarewa, C.T.15700/6-8

Periwinkle, Vinca major, *Holloway Road, Te Aro, November 1999.*

J. Nauta, Museum of New Zealand Te Papa Tongarewa, C.T.15696/30-32

Watsonias, *Karori bank, December 1999.*

J. Nauta, Museum of New Zealand Te Papa Tongarewa, C.T.15703/28-30

Broom, Cytisus scoparius, *Khandallah Road, Ngaio, November 1999.*

J. Nauta, Museum of New Zealand Te Papa Tongarewa, C.T.15700/1-6

Watsonia bulbilfera, *Karori Main Road, December 1999.*

J. Nauta, Museum of New Zealand Te Papa Tongarewa, C.T.15703/41-44

[Right] Linaria purpurea, *Wadestown, November 1999.*

J. Nauta, Museum of New Zealand Te Papa Tongarewa, C.T.15704/8-9

Chapter 10

WELLINGTON'S PARKS

Wellington's landscape at the beginning of the twenty-first century features the Town Belt, clad mainly in conifers and eucalypts, its inner-city parks, and four Botanic Gardens. They all enhance and beautify the capital city, which is now vastly different from the bleak, windswept, ugly town of the 1860s. Three of the Botanic Gardens and the inner-city parks are examined in this chapter; the fourth, the Otari Native Botanic Garden, was discussed in Chapter 5.

The Wellington Botanic Garden and its environs

In London in 1839, the New Zealand Company provided for a botanic garden in the instructions it laid down for the Survey at Port Nicholson. Mein-Smith, the Surveyor General, was unable to fulfil all the Survey's requirements immediately, and it wasn't until 1844 that an appropriation of 12 acres 1 rood 19 perches of Town Belt land was designated as the Botanical Garden Reserve.[1] Known today as the '13-acre strip', it ran alongside 'Karori Road', now Glenmore Street. The formal development of the Garden did not commence until 1868, by which time residents had removed much of the scrub covering the lower part of the Reserve for firewood. The Town Belt on the east side of the 13-acre strip was eroded even further when, in 1847 under the McCleverty Awards, 52 acres 2 roods 37 perches were given to Kumototo Māori in compensation for their pā and cultivations taken by the 1840 survey.

In 1851, the Kumototo Māori sold this block of land back to the Government for £159, together with an exchange of land at the Hutt. In the following year, Sir George Grey gave the same block to the Wesleyan Church Mission for educational purposes, and it became known as the Wesleyan Reserve.

The first and perhaps the only home on the Reserve was that of John Dutton, Henry St Hill's gardener. He was granted a seven-year lease over two acres of the Wesleyan land adjoining and overlooking the Botanic Garden Reserve. His entrance was through the Botanic Garden Reserve. 'On a ridge overlooking a gully of bush dense with tree ferns' he built a lean-to close to where the Tree House is today. However, about 1858, Dutton surrendered his lease and moved to Christchurch. A Mr Grey was offered a seven-year lease over the land, provided that he built a pig-proof fence around the property. He did not take up the lease, but it was taken up by William Randall, brickmaker, in 1860, who seems to have also purchased the cottage from Dutton.

---

[1] See Shepherd, W. & Cook, W., *The Botanic Garden Wellington*, Millwood Press, 1988, for the full story of the Botanic Garden.

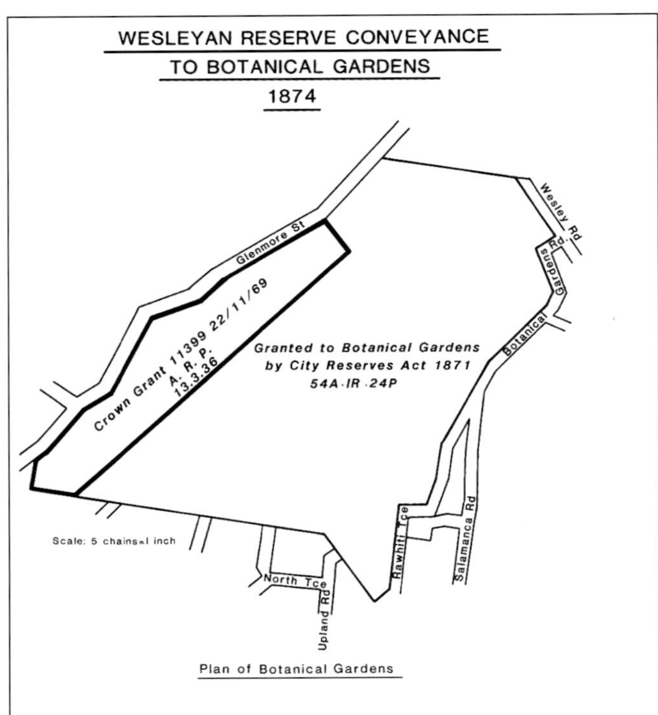

The original 13-acre Botanic Garden Reserve, fronting on to Glenmore Street, and the 54 acres 1 rood 24 perches acquired from the Wesleyan Reserve in March 1874 and granted under the City Reserve Act 1871.

Re-drawn by K.W. Shepherd from original in Deed pkt. 749. Wellington City Council

In 1865, as the Wesleyan Church Mission was making no use of the land, Government authorised the Superintendent to purchase the Wesleyan Reserve to develop as a public park for Wellington.[2] Randall sold the cottage to David Hall in 1868, although both parties were aware of the possible change of ownership. Two years later, and unfortunately for Hall, he was forced to sell this cottage to the Botanic Garden Board and it became the home of the newly appointed keeper of the Garden, William Bramley. Under the 1871 City Reserves Act, most of the Wesleyan Reserve land was transferred to the Botanic Garden.

At the time Hall purchased the cottage, James Hector, Director of the Colonial Museum, had been appointed Manager of the Garden. The next year, in 1869, when the Botanic Garden Act was passed, the Botanical Reserve was entrusted to the care of the New Zealand Institute, the forerunner to the Royal Society of New Zealand. Hector continued as manager from 1869 to 1891. The Botanic Garden was developed by the New Zealand Institute to meet three needs:

a) Trial grounds for examining the economic potential of plants for industries such as sugar, silk, olives for oil, flax and more importantly for forestry.

b) For scientists to study and develop collections of native flora and establish exotic plants.

c) For the public a place of recreation and enjoyment

View looking south over the Botanic Garden, with conifers encroaching on the Entrance Gate, c 1885. There are bush remnants below Magpie Hill ridge, poplars along Glenmore Street, and eucalypts to the left of the entrance.

E.R. Williams Collection, Alexander Turnbull Library, National Library of New Zealand, Te Puna Mātauranga, F-2707-1/1

The Garden was fenced and mapped, and paths were formed and named. The lawn that today is known as Soundshell lawn was levelled by hand and laid out as a labelled teaching garden. Areas of native forest were encircled with trees to provide shelter. The ridges were planted mainly with conifers. The depression of the 1880s caused the Government to withdraw financial support for the Botanic Garden. There was no money for gorse eradication, fence repairs, or general running expenses. This led to a change in the control of the Garden. The Botanic Garden Board was dissolved under the 1891 Vesting Act, which gave the Garden to the Wellington City Council on condition that the original 13-acre strip be maintained as a botanic garden in perpetuity. The original division between Botanic Garden and Park was enshrined in the Vesting Act and still continues today. Also under the Act, six acres, part of the original Wesleyan Block, were set aside as an Observatory Reserve. Contrary to the fears of many, when the Garden did come to the City Council it was well formed and well planted.

From 1870, William Bramley, a professional gardener from Yorkshire, was appointed Gardener/Keeper of the Botanic Garden, a post he held until he retired in 1889 at the age of 70. He and his family lived in the cottage vacated by Hall. The main drive in the Garden, William Bramley Drive, honours this man who for nearly twenty years,

helped build the framework of the present Garden and planted so many of its trees. Bramley described his career on retirement: 'A great portion of my time has been occupied in nursery work for the benefit of the colony as both seeds and plants have been distributed far and wide at the instance of General Government'.[3]

Bramley was succeeded by George Gibb. Besides attending to over 60 acres of the Botanic Garden, in 1891 Gibb was designated 'Chief Horticultural Advisor to the Council'. Gibb bridged the two administrations, and continued in the position until 1901, when, as a result of an unfortunate accident, both of his legs were amputated below the knee. For a time, he continued to live on in the Garden in a four-roomed bungalow built in 1892 to replace the old cottage.

George Glen, professionally trained in Scotland, became the new Head Gardener and was fortunate enough to occupy the new custodian's house, which was finished in 1902. In 1904, Glen was appointed Superintendent of Baths and Reserves, the first horticultural officer to manage the Botanic Garden as well as other city reserves. This was the beginning of nearly a century of service to Wellington from directors of the Garden.[4] With the exception of the last two directors, Richard Nanson and Rosemary Barrington, they all lived in the Botanic Garden in the house built in Gibb's time, which has been modified and extended over the years.[5] From the time of George Glen, the Botanic Garden Directors, or Directors of the Parks Department, as they became known, have left their mark on Wellington.

Three stages in the development of today's Soundshell lawn are shown below.

[Above left] The Director's House in the time of Ian Galloway – the heart of the Garden, c 1970s. It is adjacent to the site of the original cottage.

Karen Angus, Wellington City Council

[Above] George Gibb outside the old cottage, c 1892.

Lent by the Gibb family

[Left] Looking south over the Main Drive and the first bridge from the slope of Druid's Hill showing the original slope of the lawn, c 1880.

Alexander Turnbull Library, National Library of New Zealand, Te Puna Mātauranga, F-29236-1/2

[Right] The Teaching Garden developed after the levelling of the lawn and very much as it had been laid out by the Botanic Garden Board. The beds have not yet been divided up in the process of change that culminated in the area becoming a rose garden. The right background shows Glen's remodelling of the Garden, the cabbage trees along Glenmore Street, and curved paths below. To the left of these is Picea sitchensis, *still a feature along William Bramley Drive, c 1906.*

S.C. Smith Collection, Alexander Turnbull Library, National Library of New Zealand, Te Puna Mātauranga, G-20191-1/1, PAColl-3082

3 Letter from W. Bramley to Botanic Garden Board, 31 July 1889, Museum of New Zealand.

4 Shepherd, W. & Cook, W., 1988.

5 Today the house provides an office for the World Wide Fund for Nature (WWF), the library, and a custodial flat.

Soundshell lawn, c 1990s.
Neil Price, Wellington City Council

Since 1869, major land modifications have altered the two Reserves comprising the Wellington Botanic Garden. Early in the twentieth century, there was a need for a recreation ground in the Thorndon area. As land for a new cemetery had been found at Karori, the little-used gully, part of the original Cemetery Reserve, was filled in with spoil taken from a spur beginning in the Botanic Garden and running parallel with Tinakori Road. Under Glen's direction, and by hand, Anderson Park was formed. Today we can only wonder at the undertaking.

In 1918, the commercially-trained J.G. McKenzie, Curator of Oamaru Public Garden, succeeded Glen. Under him, hand-filling of the gully's head to the south of Anderson Park was finished in 1934.

With the completion of Anderson Park, McKenzie turned his attention to the southern end of the Garden. The top of Magpie Hill was flattened to form a lawn, and the spoil was used to fill in the gully below. The Pipitea Stream, which flowed along this gully, was piped, allowing the formation of Glenmore Lawn and the west entrance to the Garden.

McKenzie, who perhaps more than any other Director understood the significance of the remaining conifers in the Garden, replanted the ravaged spur above Anderson Park with more pines. He worked closely with botanist Dr Cockayne in gaining recognition for the native bush in the Garden as well as supporting the botanist in his bid to establish the Open Air Native Plant Museum at Otari. Pohutukawa, a favourite of the Director, were planted not just in the Garden but plentifully around Wellington, and McKenzie was dubbed 'Pohutukawa Mac'.

In 1947, English-trained Edward Hutt succeeded McKenzie. Under him, the last of the landfills in the Garden was completed with the formation of the Rose Garden. Sir Charles Norwood was a great benefactor of the Garden. The Rose Garden, called The Lady Norwood Rose Garden after his wife, opened in 1953. The Rose Garden was followed by the building of the Norwood Begonia House and the Peace Garden.

[Below left] Anderson Park, newly completed, c 1910. The fill came from the badly scarred spur.
L.I. Parton Collection, Alexander Turnbull Library, National Library of New Zealand, Te Puna Mātauranga, F-111167-1/2

[Above middle] Filling the valley, now the site of the Lady Norwood Rose Garden and Begonia House, 1932. The children's playground was moved to its present position in the Main Garden.
Evening Post Collection, Alexander Turnbull Library, National Library of New Zealand, Te Puna Mātauranga, G-EP-2485-1/2

[Above right] Looking east from the position of today's Herb Garden lookout, c 1885. This spur planting did not survive the filling of Anderson Park but remains were replanted with pines under McKenzie.
Wellington Harbour Board Maritime Museum

The 1.21 hectare area of the Rose Garden includes 102 formal beds growing a large number of traditional and established varieties, as well as recent hybrid teas, floribundas, climbers, heritage, shrub, and miniature roses – flowering right through summer from October to April. November is the peak viewing time, and Rose Sunday is celebrated during that month.

Besides these major developments in the Garden, Hutt followed his predecessors' example by continuing to enrich the City by planting trees and introducing displays of bedding plants. More and more, the Director worked away from the Botanic Garden, in charge of a department that grew as the

[Left] Magpie lawn, looking east past 1870s pines on Magpie Hill, c 1950.

Wellington City Council

[Right] Glenmore lawn, created from spoil removed from Magpie Hill above, 1951.

New Zealand Free Lance Collection, Alexander Turnbull Library, National Library of New Zealand, Te Puna Mātauranga, G-100357-1/2

[Left] The Rose Garden takes form, overlooked by the constabulary cottage built in 1874, c 1950s.

[Right] The Lady Norwood Rose Garden from the Herb Garden, c 1990s. In the background of this photograph is Norwood Path leading down from Salamanca Road.

Neil Price, Wellington City Council

city expanded. The Parks Department became the best funded in the country and was the first employer to take on women as horticultural apprentices. With recreation expanding rapidly, the Department was renamed the Parks and Recreation Department. Staffed by a team of keenly motivated people, the Department trained many, including its next Director, Ian Galloway, who had been one of the Garden's apprentices.

In 1973, Ian Galloway took up his position as Director, living in the Garden. Because he had started as an apprentice in the Garden, he had a greater interest in it than his predecessor. He consulted with his staff, seeking new ideas. He elaborated and enriched the unfinished parts of the Garden so that its presentation was greatly improved, although he was against the labelling of plants. Galloway encouraged foreman Donal Duthie and employees Greg Hooker, Walter Cook, Robin Lucas and later Mick Reece, who formed an excellent team, their enthusiasm benefiting the Botanic Garden. Two results were the development of the Herb Garden and the beginning of the dwarf conifer collection. The Herb Garden, designed by landscape architect Ron Flook of the Parks Department, was sited overlooking both the Rose Garden and Anderson Park on the very spur used to create those areas.

Ian Galloway is to be credited with the inspirational idea of forming the Outer Town Belt. I well remember his pleasure and excitement when he showed me the proposal and plans in the early 1970s. When shown the early history of the Garden, Galloway put in motion the resources necessary to write an account of the Council's management of the Garden since its takeover in 1891. The Garden in which he lived took on a new dimension for him.

Galloway died suddenly in 1987. Richard Nanson, his deputy, succeeded him in February 1988. The story of the Botanic Garden was published that year, and was followed by the production of a Management Plan for the Garden in 1990, a major achievement. Nanson, aware the Garden needed an administrative heart, organised the construction of the Environment

[Above left] Framed by a scarlet gum, a waratah, tree ferns, and other plants, the Tree House overlooks the Sunken Garden.

Neil Price, Wellington City Council

[Above middle] The view north towards the Herb Garden lookout. On the right, golden marguerite; opposite, the camphor daisy and cotton lavender.

Neil Price, Wellington City Council, c 1990s

[Above right] From the Herb Garden Trachelium x halteratum *in flower.*

Neil Price, Wellington City Council, c 1990s

Centre, which was opened by David Attenborough in 1991. It is known more familiarly as the Tree House.

This administrative centre highlighted the need for a curator. Mike Oates, a horticultural tutor, was appointed. It was not long before his responsibilities included the Otari Native Botanic Garden, the Bolton Street Cemetery Memorial Park, and the Truby King Park. All these gardens were run on more professional lines. Plants were named and entered on a database, while plant collections were established, especially of endangered species.

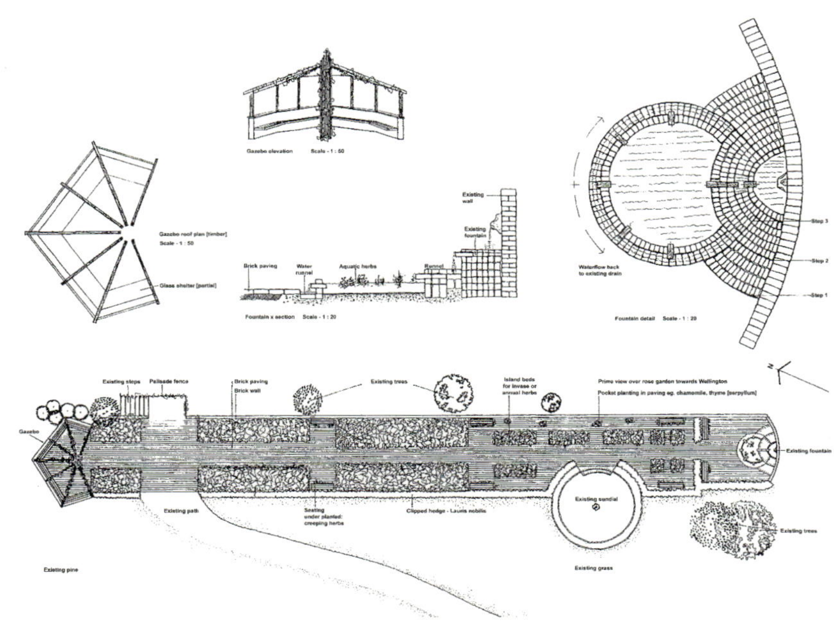

Design for Herb Garden.

R. Flook, Wellington City Council Parks Department

On 21 September 1991, at the end of the year, the Botanic Garden celebrated 100 years of management under the Wellington City Council. The Founders of the Garden, the Early Settlers and Historical Association, and the Royal Society of New Zealand (previously the New Zealand Institute) donated a bronze amillary sphere sundial, which was installed on Soundshell lawn in 1993.

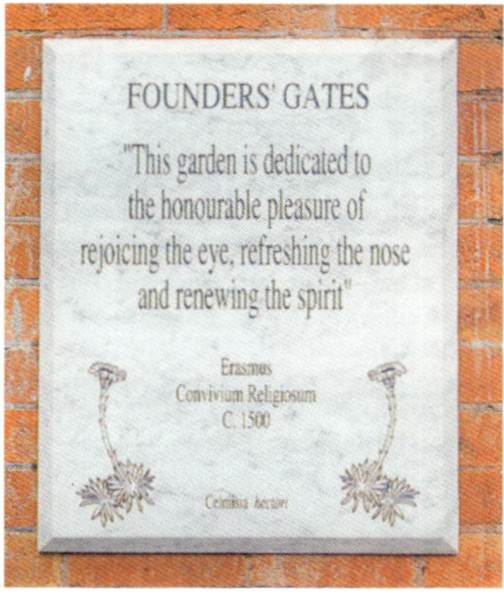

[Left] Amillary sphere sundial on Soundshell lawn with WCC, Royal Society, and Early Settlers Association representatives, 1993. From left, John Gilberthorpe, Reverend Worsfold, Joan Ombler, and Helena Taylor.

Neil Price, Wellington City Council

[Middle and right] 21 September 1991. James Belich, Mayor, together with Peter Hector and Alan Mason.

Neil Price, Wellington City Council

The Memorial Plaques at Founders' Entrance are unveiled.

Neil Price, Wellington City Council

To celebrate the centennial itself, the Mayor, James Belich, was challenged to thank 'The Founders' of the Garden for their part in establishing the well-formed Garden that the Wellington City Council inherited in 1891. Together with Peter Hector, a descendant of James Hector, Manager of the Garden 1868–91, and Alan Mason, a descendant of Thomas Mason, last Chairman of the Botanic Garden Board, the Mayor unveiled the plaques at the entrance to the original 13-acre reserve set aside in 1844. At last, the City had acknowledged the work of the Botanic Garden Board.

For a year, from 21 September 1991, the Garden celebrated this Centenary of Management. In 1992, a pictorial guide entitled *Celebration of a Garden* was published, a practical booklet, and a suitable companion to the larger book on the history of the Garden. During the year, Nanson launched 'The Friends of the Botanic Garden', a group who were to assist the Garden.

Since then, the Tree House has been manned at weekends, paths have been labelled, the Duck Pond remodelled in 1996, guides for the Garden have been trained, and the curator Mike Oates funded for an overseas study of children's garden and play areas. The late Sir Walter and Lady Norwood, wonderful benefactors of the Garden, gave generous donations to The Friends of the Botanic Garden. Appropriately, the City's Arbour Day planting for 1992 was held in the Botanic Garden in the presence of the Governor-General, Dame Catherine Tizard. Together with Peter Hector and two children from nearby Kelburn school, Her Excellency planted the first tree in the recently designated James Hector Pinetum.

In 1993, at the request of Richard Nanson, the author mapped, photographed, and documented all the old plants, trees, features, and entrances in the Garden. This was presented to the Council after the Culture and Recreation Department was restructured.

Time ran out for the Culture and Recreation Department and for Nanson himself. Although voted Council's best-run Department, Nanson was removed from office in 1994, his place filled by a non-horticultural manager, Rosemary Barrington. Barrington was sympathetic to the Gardens and what they stood for and was helped by the progress Mike Oates was making in consolidating technical matters concerning all four Gardens. Under Barrington's management, the Department's greatest achievement, however, was having the Town Belt Management Plan accepted.[6]

[6] John Gilberthorpe, Chairman of the Reserves Committee, together with a few dedicated Councillors and an extensive team of experts from both inside and outside the Department, developed the plan.

Reserves Chairmen have played important roles in the re-greening of Wellington. Logan Houston, whose father Dr Francis Houston forwarded native plant specimens to J.D. Hooker at Kew, was Reserves Chairman in the 1870s and 1880s, when the conifers were planted above Pirie Street, along the median strip between Kent and Cambridge Terrace, and at Newtown Park. More recently Chairmen such as Dame Elizabeth Gilmer, Robert Archibald, Keith Spry, and John Gilberthorpe have all made important contributions.[7]

From the time of Glen's appointment in 1902, and the gradual build-up of the Parks and Recreation Department with its team of designers, horticulturists, and arborculturists, Wellington has been well served. The parks, including the pocket parks, the Outer Town Belt, the planting of a median strip along Lambton Quay, and the planting of trees in the inner city have all come about from the inspiration of those who headed the Department.

Now the skills and experience of a well-run Council Department are no longer available. Councillors lobby among themselves as to the solution, while the public are forced to lobby the councillors. The city is deprived of the vision and professional training of men like Glen, McKenzie, Hutt, Galloway, and Nanson. Councillors come and go, but the continuity of a specialist department dealing with parks and reserves (whatever its name) had much to recommend it. Wellington enters the new millennium feeling the consequences of the fragmentation of what was once a well-run and co-ordinated Parks Department. A few signs are positive. In 1997, a Botanic Garden Advisory Board was set up to assist and advise the Curator. Mike Oates, appointed Asset Manager, Horticulture for a short time, is now back as Curator/Manager of the four Botanic Gardens. A revised Management Plan to cover the Botanic Garden, Anderson Park, and Bolton Street Memorial Park is being prepared. Along the upper part of Glenmore Street, a new fence replaces the old.

Dame Catherine Tizard, together with Peter Hector, descendent of Sir James Hector, and two children from Kelburn school plant the first pine in the James Hector Pinetum, August 1992.

Neil Price, Wellington City Council

Modern sculptures have appeared in the garden. In 1990, Ron Flook, Walter Cook, the author, and Richard Nanson walked the Garden, considering particular places that might be enhanced by a sculpture, such as Druid Hill (named by the Botanic Garden Board in 1875).[8] At the time of the Management Centenary, the Sculpture Trust arranged for a Chris Booth sculpture to be placed on the lawn below Druid Hill. This was the first of several sculptures placed in the Garden by the Trust. 'Peacemaker' suits the site well.

Five other works, the last called 'Rudderstone', have been positioned in the Garden since then, and Henry Moore's 'Bronze Form' has been re-sited to Salamanca Lawn from Midland Park. There has been concern, however, about the appropriateness of the designs for the Garden. The new Management Plan outlines a policy for all future artworks.

1. Donated or commissioned artworks shall be sought for pre-

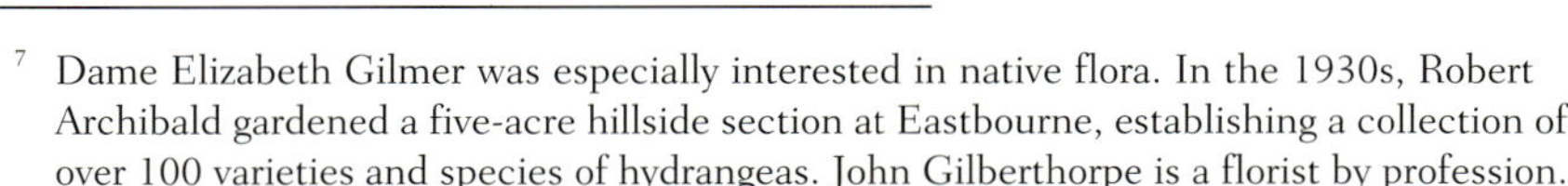

[7] Dame Elizabeth Gilmer was especially interested in native flora. In the 1930s, Robert Archibald gardened a five-acre hillside section at Eastbourne, establishing a collection of over 100 varieties and species of hydrangeas. John Gilberthorpe is a florist by profession.

[8] The photograph of Druid Hill at full moon was taken by Neil Price, with a scuplture project in mind.

Druid Hill is situated on a knoll above the main garden. As its name implies, it's a magical place. "Stand in the centre, twirl on your heels and enjoy the panorama, or walk the circle slowly, breathe in the fresh air of pine and sense the aura." The strong, gnarled trunks of the old pines frame enchanting views.

Neil Price, Wellington City Council

The Chris Booth sculpture 'Peacemaker'. Nearby grows a New Zealand kahikatea and Chamaecyparis lawsoniana, *'Gracilis'.*

Neil Price, Wellington City Council

determined sites according to specific requirements in preference for accepting ad hoc donations.

2. Donated artwork or proposed cultural projects shall be subject to the Wellington Botanic Garden Advisory Board taking into account whether a suitable site can be found where the proposed feature would be appropriate to the immediate context and setting and whether the proposed feature contributes to the overall cultural character and cultural associations in the Garden.

The Sculpture Trust's involvement in the Garden, in particular Andrew Drummond's 'Listening Device' on Druid Hill, ended all thoughts of trying to develop a significant area complementing the name of the hill.

Mature conifers dominate the Botanic Garden's skyline. The oldest are thought to be those on Magpie Slope above the Duck Pond and are probably now one hundred and thirty years of age. The Druid Hill pines are nearly as old.[9]

[9] Shepherd, W. & Cook, W., 1988.

Looking south from the Glenmore hillside to the Botanic Garden, c 1992. Almost the earliest planted in the Garden, they are now 130 years of age.

Neil Price, Wellington City Council

A provisional list of the Garden's old conifers of historic and genetic importance was provided by Ray Mole in 1986. Replacement of these conifers is not assured. Although cloning of these old trees, especially the pines, is desirable, no decision has yet been taken. It is ten years since the history of the Garden focused attention on the genetic importance of these conifers, their landscape quality, and the protection they give from the wind. As it will take twenty years or so for any replacements to give similar protection, the matter needs urgent attention. Indeed, it may be too late if many more of these trees are lost, for example, the *Pinus canariensis* was struck by lightning in 1947 and *Abies nordmanniana* was lost in a gale.

PROVISIONAL LIST OF OLD EXOTIC CONIFERS	
Abies alba	*Picea orientalis*
A. nordmanniana	*P. sitchensis*
A. pinsapo	*P. smithiana*
A. x vilmorinii	
	Pinus halepensis
Araucaria bidwillii	*P. muricata*
A. columnaris (tentative)	*P. nigra* sub sp. *Laricio*
A. cunninghamii	*P. palustris* (tentative)
A. heterophylla	*P. pinaster*
	P. pinea
Cedrus atlantica	*P. radiata*
C. deodara	*P. roxburghii*
C. libani	*P. torreyana*
Chamacyparis lawsoniana	*Pseudotsuga menziesii*
C. pisifera	*Sequoia sempervirens*
C. p. plumosa	
Cryptomeria japonica	*Sequoiadendron giganteum*
Cupressus lusitanica var. benthamii	*Taxodium distichum*
C. macrocarpa	*Thuja plicata*
C. sempervirens	
[10 Feb. 1986 Wellington City Council Parks Department]	

Since the 1992 Arbor Day planting in the James Hector Pinetum, a path has been formed with money from the Denton Trust, and conifers already growing in the area have been identified: three *Pinus halepensis*, one *Araucaria bidwillii*, five *Agathis australis*, and a clump of *Sequoia sempervirens* (redwood). Planting of new conifers, however, has been extremely slow, only the following, chosen for a teaching garden not for landscape value, have been planted.[10]

Pinus aristata	1	Bristle cone pine Rocky mountains
" *canariensis*	3	Canary Is. pine
" *coulteri*	1	Big cone pine. California & west Mexico
" *griffthii*	3	
" *Jefferyii*	1	Jeffrey's Pine. Oregon to Mexico
" *mugo*	2	(1 dead) Alpine pine. Switzerland
" *nigra ssp. Callasiara var. pryamiarta*	5	
" *patula*	3	Jelecote pine. Mexico
" *pinea*	1	Italian stone pine. Italy
" *sabiniara*	1	Digger's pine. California
" *sargentii*	3	
" *tabulaeformis*	3	Chinese pine. Northern & central China
" *torreyanna*	5	Southern California & Santa Rosa Island
" *cambroides 'Monophylla'*	(dead)	
Abies koreana	1	Korean fir. Korea mountains in the south
" *homolepsis*	3	Nikko fir. Japan
Larix decidua	3	European larch
" *kampfera*	3	(all dead) Japanese larch
Callistris oblonga	3	Cypress pine. Tasmania
Cupressus duclouxiana	1	China, west Yunnan. Szechwan to Kansu province
Pygmaea	3	Dwarf form developed from seed. Carshalton Nursery, England 1929
" *sargentii 'California'*	3	Coastal California
" *bakeri ssp. Matthewii*	3	Modoc cypress. Northern California
Tsuga heteropylla	1	West American. Hemlock
Podocarpus flavidus	1	
Prumnopitys ardina	2	
?Taxus ascerdens 'Toilia'	3	
Taxus mucronatus pendulum	3	

The conifers, the bush remnant, and the paths have the most historic value in the Garden. Although possum control has allowed titoki, pukatea, fuchsia, and other seedlings to germinate on the forest floor, no young trees are evident, and further intervention is needed. Except for tōtara, there is a complete absence of podocarps to provide a seed source. Regeneration can only be

[10] Oates, M., Letter to author, 12 March 1998.

expected to come from kohekohe, rewarewa, the ubiquitous kawakawa, and māhoe if the pukatea, rata, hinau, maire, and titoki fail to establish.

Provided the Management Plan is adhered to by trained staff and there are no further funding cuts, the Garden's future seems assured as a garden both for pleasure and for education. The 1891 Botanic Garden Vesting Act provided for 13 acres to be maintained as a true Botanic Garden in perpetuity, but while it is not practical for the original 13-acre strip to be used for botanical purposes only, the 1891 Vesting Act can be fulfilled in principle by maintaining an equivalent area for this purpose. The wide range of plant collections and displays, and the botanical collections of the Garden, are already spread throughout, namely the flax, the old conifers, the dwarf conifers, the camellias, the ericas, and the Australian collection, etc. In the main, they have developed as a pragmatic response to topography and climate. Some do well, others, such as the introduced fern collection and the camellias, are not flourishing. Perhaps the choice of site has been wrong or, in some cases, like the ericas, another position may have attracted more public attention. Land available for establishing new collections or extending old ones is limited. Species of magnolias that do well in the Garden could be extended further to the Glenmore Lawn area by re-siting the erica collection in this area to a slope where it would be more conspicuous.[11] The numbers of maple species here could be increased. Roses, tulips, and begonia displays in season will always attract visitors, while the children's playing area, Joy Fountain, and the Duck Pond attract young folk and their families.

The Wellington Botanic Garden is a major attraction in the capital city and has a history and a fragment of original bush that goes back to the time of settlement. The more one learns about and understands the Garden, the more enjoyment it provides, encapsulating as it does all the difficulties and results experienced in Wellington gardens. At the time of writing, a landscape redevelopment plan is being considered for the Garden. Hopefully, with skilful handling, New Zealand's most historically significant public garden will not lose its importance. As the new century progresses and changes are introduced, the hope is too that the ambience of the Garden evoked by Katherine Mansfield in 1907, and still true in the year 2000, will always remain.

> They are such a subtle combination of the artificial and the natural – that is, partly, the secret of their charm.
>
> From the entrance gate down the broad central walk, with the orthodox banality of carpet bedding on either side, stroll men and women and children – a great many children, who call to each other lustily, and jump up and down on the green wooden seats. They seem as meaningless, as lacking in individuality, as the little figures in an impressionist landscape.
>
> Above the carpet bedding, on one hand, there is a green hedge, and above the hedge a long row of cabbage trees. I stare up at them, and suddenly the green hedge is a stave, and the cabbage trees, now high, now low, have become an arrangement of notes – a curious, pattering, native melody.

---

[11] This suggestion builds on the fact that Robert Stokes, First Treasurer of the Horticultural Society had by 1842 a magnolia growing on his property St Ruadhan in Woolcombe Street (now The Terrace).

[Left] The waterfall and exit of the Pipitea Stream as it leaves the pond, 1992.

Neil Price, Wellington City Council

[Right] Overlooking the newly designed Duck Pond from the Tree House on the slope above, c 1998.

Neil Price, Wellington City Council

In the enclosure the spring flowers are almost too beautiful – a great stretch of foam-like cowslips. As I bend over them, the air is heavy and sweet with their scent, like hay and new milk and the kisses of children, and further on, a sunlit wonder of chiming daffodils.

Before me two great rhododendron bushes. Against the dark, broad leaves the blossoms rise, flame-like, tremulous in the still air, and the pearl rose loving-cup of a magnolia hangs delicately on the grey bough.

Everywhere there are clusters of china blue pansies, a mist of forget-me-nots, a tangle of anemones. Strange that these anemones – scarlet, and amethyst, and purple – vibrant with colour, always appear to me a trifle dangerous, sinister, seductive, but poisonous.

And, leaving the enclosure, I pass a little gully, filled with tree ferns, and lit with pale virgin lamps of arum lilies.

I turn from the smooth swept paths, and climb up a steep track, where the knotted tree roots have seared a rude pattern in the yellow clay. And suddenly, it disappears – all the pretty, carefully-tended surface of gravel and sward and blossom, and there is bush, silent and splendid. On the green moss, on the brown earth, a wide splashing of yellow sunlight. And everywhere that strange indefinable scent. As I breathe it, it seems to absorb, to become part of me – and I am old with the age of centuries, strong with the strength of savagery.

Somewhere I hear the soft rhythmic flowing of water, and I follow the path down and down until I come to a little stream idly, dreamily floating past. I fling myself down, and put my hands in the water. An inexplicable, persistent feeling seizes me that I must become one with it all. Remembrance has gone – this is the Lotus Land – the green trees stir languorously, sleepily – there is the silver sound of a bird's call. Bending down, I drink a little of the water. Oh! is it magic? Shall I, looking intently, see vague forms lurking in the shadow staring at me malevolently, wildly, the thief of their birthright? Shall I, down the hillside, through the bush, ever in the shadow, see a great company moving towards me, their faces averted, wreathed with green garlands, passing, passing, following the little stream in silence until it is sucked into the wide sea ....

There is a sudden, restless movement, a pressure of the trees – they sway against one another – it is like the sound of weeping ....

I pass down the central walk towards the entrance gates. The men and women and children are crowding the pathway, looking reverently, admiringly, at the carpet bedding, spelling aloud the Latin names of the flowers.

Here is laughter and movement and bright sunlight – but behind me – is it near, or miles and miles away? – the bush lies hidden in the shadow.[12]

---

[12] Mansfield published this sketch, 'In the Botanical Gardens', under the name Julian Mark in the *Native Companion*, Melbourne, December 1907.

Bolton Street Memorial Park

The Bolton Street Cemetery is a botanic garden in its own right and, like the main Botanic Garden, has its own history.[13] The relationship of the three areas is clear from the map, but not the steepness of the land from the top cemetery entrance down to just above The Terrace. This map shows how the motorway cut right through the Cemetery in 1968. The scars have healed gradually, and the remaining area is now known as the Bolton Street Memorial Park, although the true park itself is the special area created at the bottom to include the repositioned graves. The entire area is a Historic Reserve under the 1977 Reserves Act and a Heritage area under the District Scheme.

In 1857, at about the time that Dutton left his cottage in the Wesleyan Reserve, a cottage backing onto a portion of the Jewish section of the Cemetery was built for the Public Sexton, David Robertson. Here Robertson, a professional gardener, and his family lived until the cottage was demolished in 1908 after the death of Robertson's widow. A photograph of the cottage taken in the 1880s shows two shrubs in front of the cottage, but by 1900 there was a colourful flower border in front of the house with climbers and roses around the door. Robertson kept a cow, grew fruit in the Cemetery Reserve, and supplemented his income with landscaping work and managing properties such as the Nairn Street Nursery.

As the original kānuka-mānuka scrub was removed, Robertson, together with Sir George Grey, who lived nearby in Government House, studied native plants in the Cemetery and Botanic Garden Reserves, and collected ferns.

In the 1880s, the Botanic Garden supplied a number of trees, mainly conifers, to the Cemetery Reserve. Today these trees are a distinctive and

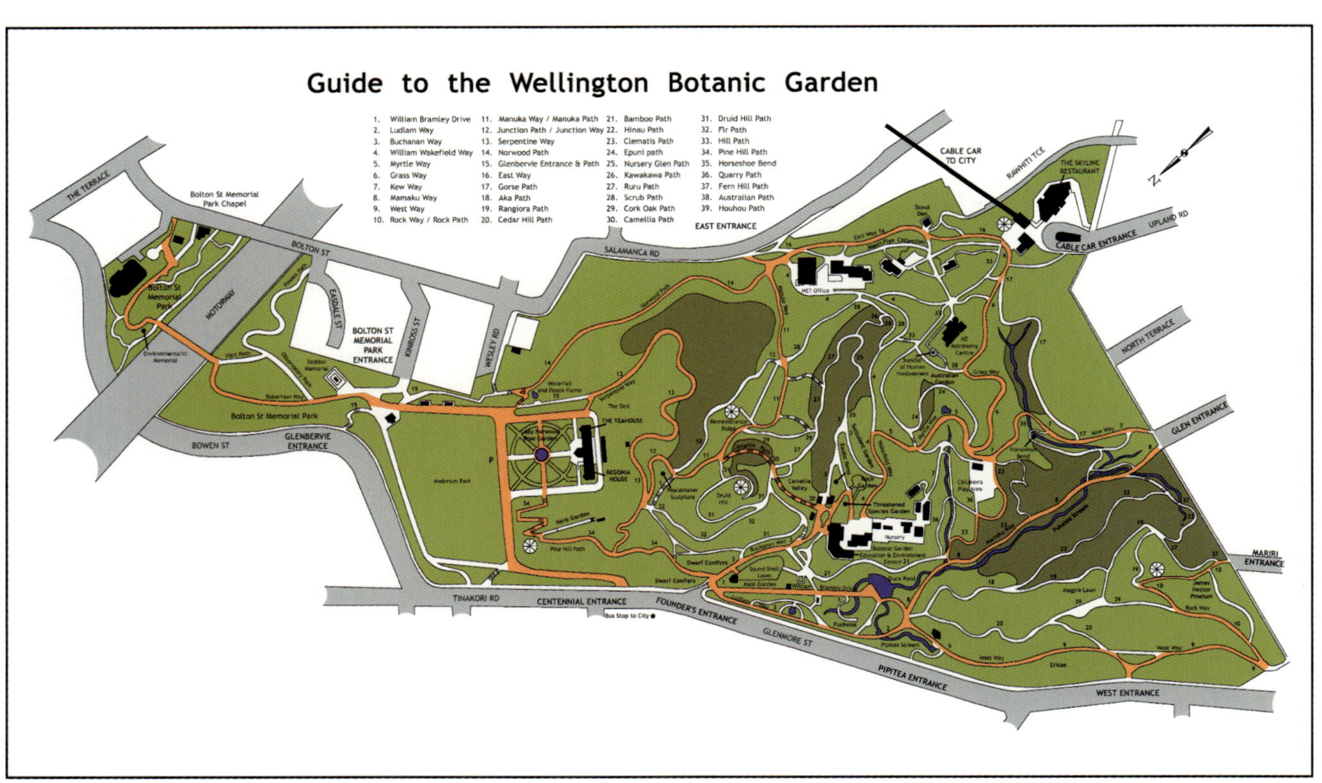

Map of the Botanic Garden and Bolton Street Cemetery Reserve.
Wellington City Council, 1992

[13] Alington, M., Unquiet Earth.

[Left] Design for Bolton Street Memorial Park showing position of existing Sexton's cottage, the new replacement Chapel, and, in the centre, steps surrounding the area for re-positioned graves.
Ron Flook, Boffa Miskell Ltd

[Above] The public Sexton's cottage is a typical early cottage re-roofed with iron, c 1900. Flower borders, climbers, and roses surround the door. The cottage was demolished around 1908.
Alexander Turnbull Library, National Library of New Zealand, Te Puna Mātauranga, F-2851-1/2

dominant feature in the Park, echoing similar trees in the Botanic Garden. Some, like the radiata pines in John Johns' beautiful photograph, used as the frontispiece, soften the skyscrapers of today.

Ron Flook, the landscape architect for Parks and Recreation Department, in consultation with the Friends of the Bolton Street Cemetery, drew up a design to reposition the graves disturbed by the motorway that was duly executed. This repositioning remains controversial in some quarters today.

The proposed Management Plan for the area aims to preserve the semi-wilderness, the mature trees, and to establish 'old fashioned garden plants with historical associations'. Some of the roses mentioned in nursery advertisements of the 1850s and 1860s might have been expected to have survived in the Cemetery Reserve, but there are only four candidates, according to Rodney Reid, horticultural custodian of the Botanic Garden, who lived in the Botanic Garden for many years. Reid was particularly interested in roses and in the Cemetery Reserve. He remembers five roses predating the motorway, all of which were common in early Wellington.[14]

Reid believes there were more, but, following the motorway construction, power scythes and herbicides were used to clear the entire area and plants were lost. From 1978, roses obtained from either Tony Griffiths in Timaru or from Frank Mason in Feilding were planted in the Cemetery, but until 1987 records of these plantings were inadequate. From that date, under Reid's supervision, each planting introduced was given an accession number, whether bought or donated. In 1991, new labelling was introduced that showed the name of the rose, the type, and year of origin.

A number of Council staff have taken a particular interest in the Cemetery roses – Bruce and Christine Harkness, Donal Duthie, Peter Tyson, Rosemary Heather – as well as the Heritage Rose Society and others. The Management Plan proposed for the Cemetery Park states: '"Heritage roses" are appropriate to the Memorial Park both for their historic association and for their informal growth habits which compliment the wild and overgrown planting character.'

Species roses, Gallicas, Damasks, Centifolias, Rugosas, Albas, Bourbons, hybrid perpetual, and hybrid musks are all planted in this Memorial Park.

Wellington Almanac, *1873.*

Alexander Turnbull Library, National Library of New Zealand, Te Puna Mātauranga

No. 122 *Rosa banksiae lutea* – picket fence of the Sexton's cottage

No. 49 *Rosa banksiae alba plena* L10-06 on Map B217

No. 16 *Rosa indica major*[15] M07-03/08 on Map B217

No. 46 *Rosa* 'Félicité et Perpétue' L09-06 on Map B217

Rosa 'Cécile Brunner'

[14] Reid, Rodney, Letter to author, 1998.
[15] In the 1950s, R. indica major was favoured as the root stock for budding on new varieties.

Recently developed David Austin roses are included as well. There is no restriction limiting plants to those in cultivation before the Cemetery's closure in 1910.

In October 1968, Ray Mole identified 180 different plants in the Cemetery Reserve. The list is published in *Unquiet Earth*.[16] Of the conifers noted, eighteen species are also found in the Botanic Garden. Pines include *Pinus coulteri, P. ponderosa*,[17] *P. pinaster*, and *P. radiata*. Many native plants listed in the Cemetery are also to be found in the Botanic Garden.

The list includes many introduced plants favoured by the early settlers: *Camellia japonica, Magnolia grandiflora, Erica arborea, Datura suaveolens, Rhododendron ponticum, Viburnum japonicum, Geranium robertianum*, eucalypts, flowering red currant, lilac, hawthorn, holly, laburnum, sweet bay, arum lily, grape hyacinth, watsonia, and onion weed. How many were lost as a result of the motorway is not known, as no recent survey appears to have been carried out.

The lower section of the Bolton Street Cemetery Park, that is the Memorial Park itself with the repositioned graves, is the first in a series of city parks originated by Ian Galloway and designed to bring plants into the city's open spaces.

The parks of the inner city

The majority of Wellington's inner-city parks were formed at the end of Edward Hutt's directorship and during that of Ian Galloway. Galloway, following the completion of his horticultural apprenticeship with the Parks Department, received further training in England at the Royal Botanic Gardens, Kew and at Brighton. During this time, he developed firm ideas for inner-city street plantings, ideas that were carried out when he became Director, the results of which we all enjoy today.

This inner-city greening started with the development of 'pocket parks' – wherever Galloway saw a small empty space, a tree would be planted, a seat added and a few more shrubs and flowers. The first of these small open spaces, in Victoria Street at the entrance to the Lombard Car Park, was funded by the Denton Trust. The idea grew of a chain of these pocket parks linked together with the larger parks, spaced through the City at 500-metre intervals or so. The area around the War Memorial site at the bottom of Bowen Street is but one example.

When work on Midland Park began in 1982, Galloway convinced the City Engineer and the Council to create a median strip of small trees and flowers along Lambton Quay that would emphasise the position of the original shoreline and link the open spaces. These green oases are one of Galloway's legacies to Wellington.

Starting from the old Government Building, the first of the inner-city Council Parks is Midland Park. (Justice Park, at the northern end of Lambton Quay, is merely a temporary park, with large steel portals into an area bounded by the back wall of the old law court building. Although managed by the Council, it was not of their design.)

---

[16] Alington, M., *Unquiet Earth*, Wellington City Council and Ministry of Works & Development, 1978.

[17] Re-identification of this species is desirable.

Heritage roses used in the Bolton Street Cemetery.

Neil Price, Wellington City Council

Midland Park was to have been followed by a park on the old Bank of New Zealand site, then Pigeon Park and Glover Park. The new Bank of New Zealand building was allowed to go three storeys higher than provided for by the city ordinances on the understanding the old bank building would be demolished and the area would become an inner-city park. The old bank building has now been strengthened and made into a shopping complex.

Frank Kitts Park lies between the old Bank of New Zealand site and Pigeon Park, at the harbour's edge. From Lambton Quay to Courtenay Place, 'pocket parks' have been formed: at the junction of Grey Street and Lambton Quay; Featherston Street and Lambton Quay; Mercer Street and Willis Street; Mercer Street and Victoria Street; and Taranaki Street and Manners Street.

It was also Ian Galloway who tentatively proposed the formation of pedestrian malls, the first to be in Cuba Street. Surprisingly, the citizens approved, and Galloway decided to close off Manners Street and create a mall. Later, when trees were planted at the western end of Manners Street and in Willis Street, the whole inner city was transformed. The trees on the corner of Wakefield Street by the City Council offices are a recent addition in the tradition of Galloway's pocket parks.

According to Ken Clarke, the city's town planner, the change from the old Wellington to the new has not been easy. High-rise buildings create problems with wind. The Bank of New Zealand building, fourteen storeys

Wakefield Street corner looking north-west, January 2000. The traffic intersection is graced by deciduous trees and ornamental plantings.

Neil Price, Wellington City Council

War Memorial Park, a pocket park at the lower end of Bowen Street and its intersection with Lambton Quay, January 2000.

J. Nauta, Museum of New Zealand Te Papa Tongarewa, C.T.15708/9-21

Cuba Street Mall looking south, January 2000.

J. Nauta, Museum of New Zealand Te Papa Tongarewa, C.T.15708/1-8

high, caused considerable down-draught. Special wind-diffusing prisms had to be built and, since that experience, wind reports have been called for on all new buildings.[18]

Midland Park

Midland Park is built on the foundations of the Midland Hotel, which was identified as an earthquake risk and demolished. With an area of 1,654 square metres, the land presented an opportunity for Galloway and his talented team to provide an oasis of green among high-rise buildings in a sophisticated shopping street. Ron Flook, in consultation with Galloway and Nanson, overcame a number of obstacles. Because the site was on reclaimed land, test holes had to be dug to ensure that tidal flow would not flood the site. Then, with the possibility that the adjoining building housing the police station could be demolished some time in the future, the design of the back of the park had to be flexible. A series of block forms set at different levels, ideal for use as seats and also for staging entertainments, formed the structure of the park.

This 'stage 1' was opened to the public while work continued on stage 2, the back wall. Flook, a firm believer in the therapeutic effect of water, designed a water cascade 12 metres long and 4 metres high. It was extremely effective, but it is remarkable how some citizens always find something to complain about. Besides the waterfall, the back wall incorporated hanging gardens and a sheltered seating area.

The Park has been a huge success, with lunchtime crowds flocking to find seats, some even stripping off to sunbathe on fine days in summer. There have been buskers, street theatre, rock bands, choirs, and retail promotions.[19] Midland Park, with its covered footpath and graceful Chinese elm trees *Ulmus parvfolia*, gives shelter and relaxation. It won the Tourist Design Award for the year in 1984. A Henry Moore sculpture donated by the Fletcher Challenge Company under the city's Art Bonus Scheme was placed on the lawn next to Brandon Street.

The structure of Midland Park shortly after its formation in 1984, looking north to Lambton Quay.

R. Flook

Alterations to the park came when the police vacated their premises in 1995. The Henry Moore sculpture, always too large in scale for the park, was moved to a more satisfactory position on Salamanca Lawn, overlooking the Lady Norwood Rose Garden in the Botanic Garden. The cascade waterfall, hanging gardens, and seats were removed from the back wall as they had been designed to be. A café, as envisaged by Flook, opens out to the park, looking on to a new fountain in the forecourt. The mature park, besides being popular, is a visual focus for this part of Lambton Quay.

[18] Regrettably, the precedent set by the height of the new Bank of New Zealand building also allowed the new Majestic Centre in Willis Street to exceed the previous height allowed by the city ordinances.

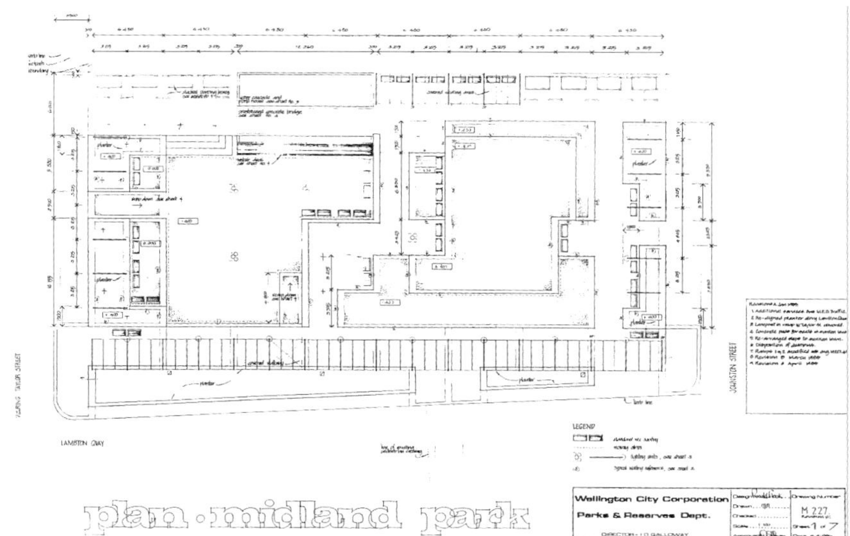

[Left] Plan for Midland Park.

Wellington City Council Parks and Reserves Department, Director Ian Galloway, Landscape Architect R. Flook

[Right] Midland Park, c 1999.

J. Nauta, Museum of New Zealand Te Papa Tongarewa C.T.15699/13-15

Frank Kitts Park

'A VIBRANT CITY PARK, THE JEWEL OF LAMBTON HARBOUR'. That was how the *Dominion* of 28 August 1990 described Frank Kitts Park, Wellington's newest park and a Lambton Harbour development. It doubled the size of an area formed in 1974, providing a 600-seat amphitheatre and a tree-lined boulevard. The 106-year-old Boating Club building was moved to a new position and the mast of the ill-fated *Wahine* re-erected. In 1985–86, Tanya Ashken's striking white water sculpture 'Albatross' highlighted the park.

The awkward land contours are the result of accommodating an underground car park, a modification that has irked users of the park since it was built. The small children's play area, with its lighthouse slide and other activity equipment, is well used, but there is public criticism that spaces and seating facing the sea are inadequate.[20] At present, the park features a number of native trees such as ngaio, the large leafed puka, *Meryta sinclairii*, cabbage trees, and flax, with Australian shrubs and trees as well as rosemary, aralia, and agapanthus.

Tanya Asken sculpture 'Albatross' with boating shed in new position, c 1998.

W. Shepherd

Frank Kitts Park from the air, looking north. To the left, the rear mast of ill-fated Wahine, which sank on 10 April 1968 with the loss of 51 lives, is now erected in Frank Kitt's Park as a poignant reminder of the power of the sea, c 1999.

Neil Price, Wellington City Council

[19] *Midland Park – The Landscape*, April 1983.

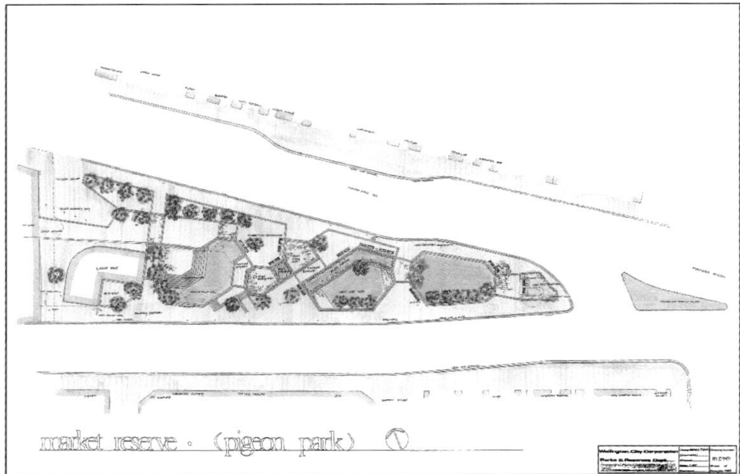

[Left] Te Aro Park, as designed by Shona Rapira Davies, viewed from the air, June 1994.

Neil Price, Wellington City Council

[Right] Design for Pigeon Park, 1984.

Ron Flook, Wellington City Council Parks Department

Te Aro Park

Two busy thoroughfares, Dixon and Manners Streets, edge what is now known as Te Aro Park. The park marks the site of what was Te Aro Pā, where on 9 June 1839 the first Christian service was held with local Māori. One hundred years later, a Memorial Stone commemorating this event was erected. The stone reads: 'Close to this spot at Te Aro Pa on Sunday 9th June 1839 a Christian service with the Maoris was conducted by Reverend S. Bumby and Reverend J. Hobbs, Missionaries of the Methodist Church DEDICATED 11th JUNE 1939'.

There have been many changes to this particular piece of land since the pā was vacated. It has been used for police, fire, and electrical stations and for a Turkish Baths. In 1928, the site was designated as Market Reserve. Two Norfolk Island pines, pohutukawa, and pigeons dominated 'Pigeon Park', as it was popularly known for many years. The park attracted lunchtime crowds brave enough to risk the pigeon droppings. During World War II, girls from the Hannah Shoe factory took their lunch break in this square, which was near the main entrance to the factory.

Memorial Stone commemorating a Christian Service at Te Aro Pa, June 1939.

J. Nauta, Museum of New Zealand Te Papa Tongarewa, C.T.15706/43-44 or 1-5

In 1984, a new women's toilet was decorated with Bill Mackay's vibrant murals depicting women of all races and their fashions. About this time, upgrading of the site was considered necessary and, after discussion and some preliminary sketches, a design by Ron Flook was accepted and approved by the Council. The design included a small amphitheatre for regular Salvation Army meetings and for the many buskers in that area of town. Deciduous trees that would allow the winter sun to penetrate the site were chosen, and positioned to give protection from the wind as well as shade from the summer sun.

Work was delayed, and the nearby Wesley Church in Taranaki Street, remembering their first contact with Māori on this site, pressed the Council for Māori involvement in the design for the Park. The Council invited

[20] Boffa, Frank, Ian Galloway memorial lecture, *NZ Garden Journal*, Vol 2, No 2, June 1997. The 1997/98 Lambton Harbour Design Team's proposed changes, which included a hard edge, several storeys high, along Jervois Quay, with the loss of both the harbour view and the Norfolk Island pines, were rejected in the year 2000 by the citizens of Wellington.

[21] Ibid.

further designs from Māori only. Of the six submitted, that of Shona Rapira Davies was chosen.

Te Aro Park opened in May 1992. One pohutukawa remains, so the pigeons continue to enjoy the area but now have limited perching space. Kōwhai trees placed to represent the canoe's oarsmen have since been replaced by cabbage trees. The design described on the plaque needs to be seen from a high vantage point in order to be fully appreciated.

> This was the site of the Te Aro Pa, settled by Te Atiawa people up to the 1890s. By 1845 the Wesleyan Church had erected several buildings including a Mission House and Maori Chapel. The Park has also been the site of police, fire electrical stations and Turkish Baths. In 1928 the site became Market Reserve and in 1839 the stone memorial was erected to commemorate the 1939 Christian Service at Te Aro Pa between Maori and Methodist Church Missionaries. In 1989 planning of the site as a sculptural park was begun by the Wellington City Council. New Zealand sculptural artist Shona Rapira Davies was commissioned to design the Park in conjunction with the W.C.C. landscape architect and then to prepare the artwork and manufacture of the tiles. The Park was completed and opened in May 1992. Symbolic features of the Park include water representing the life principle, cleansing, blessing and renewing. It flows diagonally across the site and reflects the stream and the original Te Aro shoreline. The pools with female figures represent three generations of women. Old women, young women, and young girls. The strong horizontal elements of the walls from weaving patterns and symbolise the female principle. The prow and other vertical elements symbolise male principles. Only men were allowed to paddle war canoes. The nine kowhai trees are symbolically placed to represent the oarsmen of the canoes.

Mural by Bob Mackay on the women's toilet in Te Aro Park just prior to removal in 1998.

W. Shepherd

The Park is still controversial and considered by some authorities to be not 'user friendly' and lacking a focal point.[21] There is no doubt, however, that the design acknowledges the importance of the site and provides a special open space to reflect on the history of the capital city.

Glover Park

Glover Park, lying between Ghuznee and Garrett Streets, was largely funded from Lewis Glover's bequest to the city. The park was constructed in 1971, at about the time extensive planting along the chasm of the motorway was finished. It was the first of the inner city-parks and the first of the inner-city plantings with trees.

Although it is a very pleasant sheltered park, and the autumn colours of

[Left] Glover Park, Ghuznee Street under construction, 1971.

Evening Post Collection, Alexander Turnbull Library, National Library of New Zealand, Te Puna Mātauranga, F-18511-1/4

[Right] Looking south down on Glover Park, c 1996.

Neil Price, Wellington City Council or J. Nauta C.T.15699/30-31

deciduous trees contrast well with the evergreen *Pinus radiata*, this open space has not been as successful as it might have been if it had been connected to or linked with Cuba Mall in some way. Hopefully, in time, a way will be found to improve the use, popularity, and safety of this attractive inner-city park.

The parks on the Town Belt

There are many parks and playing fields on the Town Belt. As in the Botanic Garden, a number of these flat areas have been formed by extensive land filling, for example Kelburn Park.

When Brooklyn road was formed, it skirted a section of the Town Belt now known as Central Park. A certain amount of fill spilled over on to the reserve land. Later, more fill was added over the city refuse tip when it was closed in 1940. The design for Central Park, a very hilly park, is shown below. Pines and eucalyptus planted around the western and southern borders give considerable protection from the wind, and, because of this shelter, fine specimens of lime trees and evergreen oaks (*Quercus ilex*) have matured here without wind distortion. The park is notable too in that it contains a huge rata tree, a remnant of the original forest.

[Top] Kelburn Park under construction, c 1896.

Pollock Bros. B.11948, Alexander Turnbull Library

[Lower top] Upper end of Central Park, c 1907, showing spoil from Brooklyn Road. Note pines in Nairn Street Park.

Wellington Public Library Collection, Alexander Turnbull Library, National Library of New Zealand, Te Puna Mātauranga, G-25451-1/1, PAColl-5448

[Above left] Central Park entrance, November 1999. Iron gates donated, c 1916.

J. Nauta, Museum of New Zealand Te Papa Tongarewa, C.T.15699/30-31

[Above right] Central Park Gardens.

Wellington City Council Collection, Alexander Turnbull Library, National Library of New Zealand, Te Puna Mātauranga, G-24202-1/1, PAColl-5448

Truby King Park, Melrose

It is appropriate to end this chapter with Truby King Park. The park is noteworthy not only because it was established by Sir Truby King, but also because of its structure. Today it is one of Wellington's four Botanic Gardens. Richard Nanson was Director of Parks in 1990 when the City Council purchased 1.9 hectares of land adjoining the inner Town Belt on a Melrose ridge overlooking Evans Bay, Lyall Bay, and Newtown. There were three parcels of land: the late Sir Truby King's house and garden, which had been in the Plunket Society's ownership, and two adjoining properties. The amalgamation of these has formed Truby King Park, and, because it adjoined the inner Town Belt, the land has been re-zoned from Residential A1 to 'Inner Town Belt'.[22]

In purchasing Sir Truby King's property, the City Council gave an undertaking to the Plunket Society and to his daughter, Mary White, that the following would be maintained:

1. The homestead and grounds of the property would remain intact.

2. The brickwork, associated landscape areas, the grave and the house would be retained in their more or less original condition.

3. The site would be known as Sir Truby King Park.

4. The library, if the Plunket Society so wished should remain and that the Society, should they wish, have occasional use of the house and garden.

Sir Truby King's house and garden, Mt Melrose, 1934.

S.P. Andrew Collection, Alexander Turnbull Library, National Library of New Zealand, Te Puna Mātauranga, F-18464-1/1, PAColl-3739

Mary White was delighted, but asked that the area be known simply as Truby King Park.

Truby King's devotion to the care of mother and child is well known. The garden he created was unique, an exceptional example in its use of extensive brick walls to develop an exposed and hilly Wellington section. Most of the brick walls were built by King himself. Although they are not so elaborate, the brick walls built by Dr Cohen on his property Merivale in Homewood Avenue suggest that King's prowess in the use of bricks could have influenced others in the medical profession. The construction work carried out by both King and Cohen took place around the time the landscaper, Buxton, was laying out Homewood.

Sir Truby King's house and garden, Mt Melrose, c 1943.

Pascoe Collection, Alexander Turnbull Library, National Library of New Zealand, Te Puna Mātauranga, F-437-1/4, PAColl-0783

Photographs show King's house protected from the wind by radiata pines, and a luxuriant garden within an extensive framework of brick walls, arches, and pergolas.

After acquiring the property, Council commissioned a management plan for the park, which was in a decrepit state – far from its former glory when rhododendrons, azaleas, roses, flowering cherry walks, hedges, yew trees, and the walls were such a feature. The Management Plan provided for:

- Reconstruction, repairs and maintenance of garden walls, pergolas and other structures in a sensitive manner.
- Reconstruction where possible of the nature and form of the original garden landscape.

As far as practicable the rhododendron dell, azalea and rose plantings and other horticultural features to be reinstated.

Truby King Garden was extensively modified in the early 1950s. The head gardener, Yoop Tetteroo, having initially removed the 'overgrowth', appears to have modified the garden developed by Truby King, c 1950.

Bill Scott, retired manager, Karitane Products Society

Truby King's garden was known especially for its rhododendrons, obtained from many overseas sources. Losses from such consignments were high – many rhododendrons or various other types of grafted or layered cuttings or seedlings were dead on arrival. But rhododendrons and roses were King's favourites and he told Victor Davies that from the curved, semi-circular band rotunda he could look down on 300–400 rhododendrons.

A list of rhododendrons available in New Zealand prior to 1933 is given in the Truby King Park Conservation and Management Plan, and in the mid-1990s a list of some species of hybrid rhododendrons suitable for Wellington was compiled from Truby King's invoices.

[22] The New Zealand Historic Places Trust noted that the house was relatively unassuming in contrast with its extensively landscaped gardens.

[Left] Garden walls throughout the Park requiring restoration.
Truby King Management Plan

[Right] Looking south down the drive to the main entrance of Truby King's place and the Karitane Hospital, c 1960s.
Bill Scott

[Above] The rebuilt steps and walls leading up to the mausoleum, July 1999.
W. Shepherd

[Below] The Moongate before renovation, c 1990.
Truby King Management Plan

Suitable for Wellington – species and hybrid rhododendrons prepared from Truby King invoices:

Species

R. arboreum	*R. bullatum*
R. catawbiense	*R. smirowii*
(? Baron de Bruin)	*R. maddenii, var. virginalis*

Hybrids

Princess Alice	Pink Pearl
Chevalier Felixide Sauvage	Prince Camille de Rohan
Betty Wormald	Unknown Warrior
C.B. van Ness	Beauty of Littleworth
Baron de Bruin	Cornubia
Dr Stocker	Helen Schiffner
Ivory's Scarlet	J.G. Millais (= Mrs John)
Loder's White	Loderi
Earl of Athlone	Boule de Neige
Christmas Cheer	Cunningham's White
Countess of Haddington	*R. fastuosum plenum*
	R. boddartianum

An example of an invoice sent to King is shown opposite. With this list, together with funding from the Denton Trust, rhododendron replanting at Truby King Park was completed in 1998. Colours have been grouped and include the heritage rhododendrons, as it was decided not to plant a separate historical section.

A bed of *Azalea mollis* has been re-established. There are no yellows and it is unclear whether Goldsworth yellow and *Azalea Broughton aurea* were planted or established. To date, rose replanting has not yet commenced. The cherry walk has been replanted and two areas of native flora are being enhanced. Redevelopment of Truby King Park is slow, but continues as funds become available. When the newly planted rhododendrons and other plants mature, visitors will appreciate the foresight shown in 1991 by

Truby King house today, looking out over Evans Bay, January 2000.
Boffa Miskell

Wellington City Council and its Parks Department in securing this property for public enjoyment.

Planning the city's parks

There are other important spaces within the city besides the main parks, gardens, and open areas that have been described. Public input into planning without a functioning Parks Department has become difficult. Commenting on this difficulty, Frank Boffa, an outstanding landscape architect says:

> In the days when there was a City Planner and a Parks Director it was relatively straightforward and easy to make approaches and gain some measure of confidence that consideration and/or action would result. Today it is considerably more difficult to identify who is responsible for what and how best one should direct one's enquiries.[23]

Continuity is needed, and someone who can appreciate the wider picture, as did those Parks Directors who served the city for nearly 100 years and directed the formation of the Wellington Botanic Garden. They served Wellington City well in the twentieth century. The appointment of three Curators in 1998/99 for the Town Belt, the four Botanic Gardens, and, more recently, the city's parks does not answer Boffa's concerns, but augurs well for the continuity of these important features.

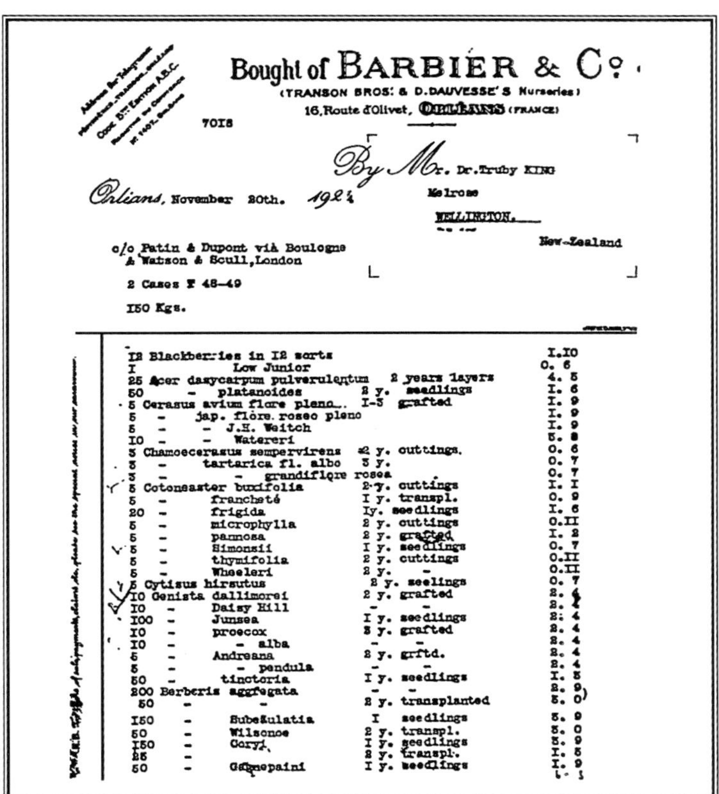

Bought of BARBIER & Co.
(TRANSON BROS: & D.DAUVESSE'S Nurseries)
16, Route d'Olivet, ORLÉANS (FRANCE)

7018

Orléans, November 20th. 1924

By Mr. Dr.Truby KING
Melrose
WELLINGTON.
New-Zealand

c/o Patin & Dupont via Boulogne
à Watson & Scull, London

2 Cases F 48–49

150 Kgs.

Qty	Item		Price
I2	Blackberries in I2 sorts		I.IO
I	Low Junior		O. 6
25	Acer dasycarpum pulverulentum	2 years layers	4. 5
50	- platanoides	2 y. seedlings	I. 6
5	Cerasus avium flore pleno..	I-3 grafted	I. 9
5	- jap. flore. roseo pleno		I. 9
5	- - J.H. Veitch		I. 9
IO	- - Watereri		5. 8
3	Chamoecerasus sempervirens	2 y. cuttings.	O. 6
3	- tartarica fl. albo	3 y.	O. 7
3	- - grandiflore rosea		O. 7
5	Cotoneaster buxifolia	2 y. cuttings	I. I
5	- franchetê	I y. transpl.	O. 9
20	- frigida	Iy. seedlings	I. 6
5	- microphylla	2 y. cuttings	O.II
5	- pannosa	2 y. grafted	I. 2
5	- Simonsii	I y. seedlings	O. 7
5	- thymifolia	2 y. cuttings	O.II
5	- Wheeleri	2 y. -	O.II
5	Cytisus hirsutus	2 y. seelings	O. 7
IO	Genista dallimorei	2 y. grafted	2. 4
IO	- Daisy Hill	- -	2. 4
IOO	- Junsea	I y. seedlings	2. 4
IO	- proecox	3 y. grafted	2. 4
IO	- - alba	- -	2. 4
5	- Andreana	2 y. grftd.	2. 4
5	- - pendula	- -	2. 4
50	- tinctoria	I y. seedlings	I. 5
200	Berberis aggregata	- -	2. 9
50	- -	2 y. transplanted	5. 0
I50	- Subulatia	I seedlings	5. 9
50	- Wilsonoe	2 y. transpl.	5. 0
I50	- Coryl.	I y. seedlings	5. 9
25	-	2 y. transpl.	I. 5
50	- Gagnepaini	I y. seedlings	I. 9

Invoice to Truby King from Barbier & Co. France, 1924.

23 Boffa, Frank, Ian Galloway memorial lecture, *NZ Garden Journal*, Vol 2, No 2, June 1997.

Chapter 11

NURSERY CATALOGUES AND EARLY PLANT INTRODUCTIONS

What were the expectations of the first intending immigrants to New Zealand about what they could grow in the new country? One source of information was the reports of the Australian experience.

> Potatoes, cabbages, carrots, parsnips, turnips, peas, beans, cauliflowers, broccoli, asparagus, lettuces, onions, and in fact all the species of vegetables known in England are produced in this colony; many of them attain a much superior degree of perfection but a few also degenerate .... The colony is justly famed for the goodness and variety of its fruits, peaches, apricots, nectarines, oranges, lemons, citrons, loquets, guavas, cherries, almonds, medlars, quinces, grapes, pears, plums, figs, pomegranates, raspberries, strawberries, and melons of all sorts attain the highest degree of maturity in the open air .... The climate however of Port Jackson is not altogether congenial to the growth of the apple, currant, and gooseberry .... These fruits however arrive at the greatest perfection in every part of Van Dieman's Land.[1]

Fifteen years later, in 1835, Charles Darwin observed the missionary settlement at the Bay of Islands:

> Fine crops of barley and wheat were standing in full ear and in another part fields of potatoes and clover. These were large gardens with every fruit and vegetable which England produces and many belonging to a warmer climate. I may instance asparagus, kidney beans, cucumbers, rhubarb, apples, pears, figs, peaches, apricots, grapes, olives, gooseberries, currants, hops, gorse for fences, and English oaks; also many kinds of flowers. Around the farmyard were stables, a thrashing machine and a blacksmith's forge, and on the ground was that happy mixture of pigs and poultry lying comfortably together as in every English farmyard.[2]

From about 1820, various Europeans, many from Australia, had been coming to New Zealand in search of whales, seals, flax, and timber. By the time the first settlers arrived at Petone, introduced plants were already established at points on the Kapiti coast, thanks to the whalers, including fruit trees, melons, vegetable varieties such as pumpkins, potatoes, and turnips, and some crops, particularly wheat and Indian corn.

The wealthier colonist could purchase packets of seeds from commercial sources, either prior to sailing, or on arrival in New Zealand, by requesting seed to be sent out. Settlers also brought with them seeds from the gardens they left behind, or from those of their friends and relatives, which resulted

---

[1] Wentworth, W.C., 'A Statistical, Historical and Political Description of the Colony of New South Wales and its Dependent Settlements in Van Dieman's Land.' Advice to Emigrants, London, 1820.

[2] Darwin, Charles, *A Naturalist's Voyage around the World*, 1848.

in many varieties being grown here that were not common in the trade. In addition, there were seeds and plants obtained from ports of call such as Madeira, Tenerife, South Africa, or Australia.

Contact with Australia increased after 1840. Henry Petre visited Australia four months after his arrival, bringing back plants. Robert Stokes familiarised himself with Sydney's plant nurseries and had established a remarkable number of plants in his garden in Woolcombe Street by 1842.

The nursery catalogues published in the early years are invaluable in dating plant introductions, because they list the plants that were available at the date they were published. John Harvey's book on early English catalogues, published in 1972, allows the reader to make a comparison of plants available in earlier centuries with those of the nineteenth century, just prior to the New Zealand Company's colonisation of Port Nicholson.

It has been assumed that the plants listed in Flanagan and Nutting's 1837 catalogue represented the plant material commercially available to English settlers about to voyage across the world. But for a marked increase in the number of varieties listed, the Flanagan and Nutting catalogue list of seeds for vegetables and flowers does not differ greatly from those given in the William Lucas catalogue issued 160 years earlier. Favourites from the past were included together with the latest varieties or species.

The 1837 catalogue lists 26 varieties of peas, 16 of broccoli, 20 of cabbage, 24 of lettuce, and the New Zealand spinach (*Tetragonia expansa*). The range of vegetable seeds can be compared with those available in early Wellington (see Appendix). Fashionable flowers in 1837 included hyacinths, narcissus, tulips, gladiolus, ixia, anemone, ranunculus, dahlia, geranium, pansies, and calceolaria.[3] For arbours were the sweet briar, honeysuckles, clematis, jessamines, tamarisk, roses, and whitethorn. The jessamine probably included the common white *Jasminium officinale*, and the yellow winter flowering *J. fruticans*. Naturally, New Zealand immigrants wanted these familiar plants around them, and nurserymen endeavoured to supply them.

American research has identified the source of horticultural plants grown in that country before 1900. Monticello in Virginia, the home of Thomas Jefferson, maintains a world-renowned collection of historic American plants. In Australia, the Ornamental Plant Collections Association, based at the Royal Melbourne Botanic Garden, has recognised the value of nursery catalogues in documenting the range of nineteenth-century plants brought in to that country.

The earliest known Australasian catalogue is that of James Dickinson of Hobart, dated 1845. Early Wellington contact with Hobart is well documented. In February 1841, agents John and George Wade advertised fruit trees for sale from Van Dieman's Land.[4] Any of the plant material

---

[3] The range of different species grown in southern England several hundred years earlier can be deduced from the varieties mentioned by the poet Geoffrey Chaucer: alder, apple, ash, aspen, poplar, beech, birch, box, cherry, chestnut, elm, fir, hazel, holly, laurel (bay), lime, maple, medlar, oak, peach, pear, pine, plane, plum, poplar, quince, thorn (hawthorn) willow, and yew. Chaucer had served a term as Forester of Petherton Park, and was obviously familiar with many of the plants he mentioned in works such as 'The Parlement of Foules' and the Knight's Tale.

[4] *New Zealand and Wellington Spectator*, 13 Feb 1841.

Fourcroya gigantica, *listed as* Furcrea gigantic *in Dickinson's 1845 Tasmanian Catalogue, flowers in the main drive of Wellington's Botanic Garden in the 1880s.*

Museum of New Zealand Te Papa Tongarewa, B.17357

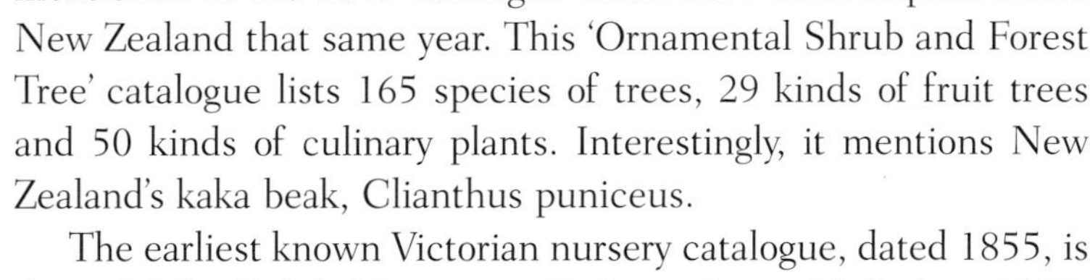

mentioned in the 1845 catalogue could have been imported into New Zealand that same year. This 'Ornamental Shrub and Forest Tree' catalogue lists 165 species of trees, 29 kinds of fruit trees and 50 kinds of culinary plants. Interestingly, it mentions New Zealand's kaka beak, Clianthus puniceus.

The earliest known Victorian nursery catalogue, dated 1855, is that of John Rule's Nursery at Richmond, established in 1850. Ten years after the Hobart catalogue, it lists 870 species and cultivars including 44 roses and 20 orchids. Two years later in 1857, Rule's stock had expanded to 1,455 items, including 64 under the heading 'Conifers and Taxads', 74 camellias, 48 fuchsias, and 21 gladioli.

In New Zealand, Charles Challenger of Lincoln University has researched the Canterbury nurserymen, and the Mount Albert Research Centre in Auckland has built up a collection of New Zealand nursery catalogues.[5] The study of nineteenth-century exotic plants in New Zealand is still in its infancy. Even when it is known that a plant was here at a certain date, old varieties of fruit trees, carnations, dahlias, and others may no longer be available.

At first, Wellington settlers' needs were supplied by the Nelson and Australian nurseries. The popularity of certain nineteenth-century plants in Australia and New Zealand and elsewhere can be gauged from the nursery catalogues. For example, conifers increased rapidly from the late 1850s to the 1870s as newly discovered species were introduced to cultivation. Camellia cultivars increased as hybridisation accelerated. Like the conifers, the number of rhododendron species increased as new discoveries were introduced, and hybrids also extended the numbers as they were developed.

New Zealand catalogues began to appear in the 1860s: David Hay in Auckland, William Hale in Nelson, William Wilson and others in Christchurch, Reids and the Australian-linked Thomas Lang and Co. in Dunedin, with its excellent plant engravings. The earliest known Wellington catalogue is the small 1865 seed catalogue of Thomas White of Willis Street. Many of the plants we still grow and enjoy were available in Wellington by 1870. From Dickinson's Tasmanian catalogue of 1845 and Hale of Nelson's catalogue of 1861, and White's of Wellington seed catalogue of 1865 it is possible to gauge what was available here in those first years. The catalogues are reproduced in the Appendix. Further information may yet emerge as more early diaries and letters are found.

The Appendix also provides examples of bedding plant designs common at the end of the nineteenth and beginning of the twentieth century.

Glenbervie Terrace, January 2000. The gardens in front of these replicated old houses have been sensitively planted. The bouganvillea is a wonderful plant, but is not shown in any of the catalogues reproduced in this book.

J. Nauta, Museum of New Zealand Te Papa Tongarewa, C.T.15707/12-14

[5] Challenger, C., 'Studies of Pioneer Canterbury Nurserymen', *RNZIH Annual Journal*, No 7, 1979.

APPENDIX

James Dickinson Catalogue, Hobart, 1845

CATALOGUE
OF
ANNUAL AND HERBACEOUS PLANTS,
FLOWERING BULBS AND TUBERS,
ORNAMENTAL SHRUBS,
FOREST TREES, FRUIT TREES,
AND
CULINARY PLANTS AND SEED,
On Sale
BY JAMES DICKINSON
39, MURRAY STREET.

Hobart Town, Van Diemen's Land:
PRINTED AND PUBLISHED BY
WM. GORE ELLISTON, COURIER OFFICE, COLLINS STREET.
1845.

PREFACE

The following Catalogue will, of course, be looked upon as an advertisement of goods on sale. But the writer has also another object in view. Professing to exchange plants as well as to sell them, the publication of a Catalogue of those already in his possession will enable individuals, inclined to treat with him, to ascertain what additions they can make to their stock, at the expense of any plants not found in the Catalogue, which will be gladly received in exchange.

The paucity of the Catalogue is accounted for by the statement that it is only the second season, with very limited capital, since the Collection was attempted. As soon as sufficient encouragement is obtained to warrant it, a second edition will be published, in which the Plants will appear in systematical arrangement.

Tasmanian Plants are, except in very few instances, omitted; yet Seed is always on hand and Plants supplied when required.

39, *Murray Street*
November 1st 1845

Botanical Name	English Name
Azalea Indica,	Azalea, Indian.
" " phoenicea	" "
" viscosa,	" viscid.
" " odora,	" " scented.
Asclepias salicifolia,	Swallow-wort, willow-leaved.
" Curassavica,	" Curassoa.
Arbutus Unedo,	Strawberry tree.
Amygdalus communis,	Almond, sweet.
" persica pendula,	Peach, weeping.
" " sempervirens,	" evergreen.
" " " pleno,	" double-flowered.
Aloysia citriodora,	Aloysia, lemon-scented.
Alonsoa linearis,	Alonsoa, linear-leaved.
Artemesia abrotanum,	Southernwood.
" absinthium,	Wormwood.
" vulgaris,	Mugwort.
Aster sinensis sp.,	Aster, China, many sp. and var.
Aucuba japonica,	Aucuba, blotched-leaved.
Araucaria excelsa,	Norfolk Island pine.
Acacia, varius,	Acacia, many.
Acer pseudo-platanus,	Sycamore.
" saccharum,	Maple, sugar.
" platanoides,	" Norway.
Abrus precatorius,	Bead tree.
Bouvardia triphylla,	Bouvardia, three-leaved.
Brugmansia suaveolens,	Brugmansia, scented.
Bignonia radicans,	Trumpet-flower, scarlet.
" suaveolens,	" scented.
" jasminoides,	" jessamine-like.

Botanical Name	English Name
" stans,	" branching.
" excelsifolia,	" ash-leaved.
Buxus sempervirens,	Box tree.
" " suffruticosa,	" dwarf.
Caprifolium periclymenum,	Honeysuckle or woodbine,
" japonicum,	" japanese.
" flexuosa,	" slender.
" dioicum,	" small-flowered.
Coffea arabica,	Coffee tree.
Cassia Capensis,	Cassia, Cape.
Cotyledon ovata,	Naval-wort, ovate-leaved.
Cydonia japonica,	Quince, flowering.
" " alba,	" white.
Cactus, speciosimus,	Cactus, most beautiful.
" speciosus,	" beautiful.
" mammilarius,	" mammillary.
" triqueter,	" least triangular.
" triangularis,	" triangular.
" truncatus,	" truncate.
" Jenkinsonia,	" Jenkinson's.
" opuntia,	" Indian-fig.
" horrida,	" Horrid.
" cochinelifera,	" cochineal-fig.
" flagelliformis,	" creeping cereus.
" Mallinsonia,	" Mallinson's.
" tomentosus,	" woolly.
" Ackermannia,	" Ackerman's.
Cactus phyllanthus,	Cactus, spleenwort-leaved.
" pendula,	" naked.

Botanical Name	English Name
" pereskia,	" Barbadoes gooseberry.
Cratoegus crus-galli,	Hawthorn, cockspur.
" pyracantha,	" evergreen.
" oxyacantha,	" common.
" " pleno,	" double-blossom.
" " rosea,	" red-flowered.
Cottoneaster microphylla,	Cottoneaster, small-leaved.
Chimonanthus fragrans,	Chimonanthus, scented.
Cistus ledon,	Rock rose, many flowered.
Clerodendrum fragrans,	Clerodendrum, scented.
" tomentosus,	" tomentous.
Celsia linearis,	Celsia, linear-leaved.
" Cretica,	" Cretan.
Cheiranthus cheiri,	Wall-flower.
" " pleno,	" double.
" " " rubra,	" " bloody
" mutabilis,	" changeable.
Camellia bohea,	Bohea tea.
" japonica,	Camellia.
" " pleno rubra,	" double red.
" " " carnea,	" kew blush.
Cytissus laburnum,	Laburnum.
" capitatus,	" Portugal.
Colutea arborescens,	Bladder-senna, common.
" cruenta,	" oriental.
Citrus limonum,	Lemon.
" aurantium,	Orange.
Cineraria arborea,	Cineraria, tree.
Castanea vesca,	Chesnut, edible.
Carpinus betulus,	Hornbeam, common.
Corylus avellana,	Hazel-nut.
" " rubra,	Filbert.
" " grandis,	Cob-nut.
Cupressus sempervirens,	Cypress.
" " stricta,	" upright.
" " patens,	" spreading.
Clianthus puniceus,	Glory-pea.
Calampelis scabra,	Calampelis, rough.
Coronilla picta,	Coronilla, painted.
Daphne ponticum,	Daphne, Pontic.
" odora,	" scented.
Dracocephalum canariense,	Balm of Gilead.
" altiense,	" Altaic.
Duranta Ellesii,	Duranta, Ellis's.
Daulbergia scandens,	Daulbergia, climbing.
Euonymus japonica,	Spindle-tree, Japan.
" variegata,	" " striped.
" europea,	" common.
" sp.,	" sp.
Esculus hippocastanum,	Horse-chesnut.
Erythrina corallodendron,	Coral-tree, smooth-leaved.
" caffra,	" Cape.
" crista-galli,	" cockscomb.
Epiphyllum Hookeri,	Epiphyllum, Hooker's
Eccramocarpus scabra,	Eccramocarpus, rough
Edwardsia microphylla,	Edwardsia, small-leaved.
Fuchsia coccinea,	Fuchsia, scarlet.
" gracilis,	" slender.
" conica	" conical.
" microphylla,	" small-leaved.
Fuchsia globosa,	Fuchsia, globe-flowered.
" " erecta,	" " erect.
" " rosea,	" " rosy.
" floribunda,	" many flowered.
" Chandlerii,	" Chandler's.
" fulgens,	" crimson.
" Rickertonii,	" Rickerton's.
" pulcherima,	" very beautiful.

Botanical Name	English Name
" Yuellii,	" Yuell's.
" carnea,	" flesh-coloured.
" tricolorum,	" three-coloured.
" corymbiflora,	" cluster-flowered.
" corymbosa,	" clustered.
" defiance,	" defiance.
" Dulstonii,	" Dulston's.
" Devonsiana,	" Duchess of Devenshire's.
" conspicua arborea,	" tree.
" Dicksonii,	" Dickson's.
" Venus' Victrix,	" Venus' Victrix.
" delicata,	" delicate.
" Prince Albert,	" Prince Albert's.
" Brennus,	" Brennus.
" transparens,	" transparent.
" grandiflora,	" many flowered.
Fraxinus excelsior,	Ash, common,
Ficus carica,	Fig, "
" Bengalense,	" Bengal.
Friesia peduncularis,	Friesia, peduncled.
Furcrea gigantea,	Furcrea, gigantic.
Gardenia florida,	Gardenia, Cape jessamine.
" thunbergia,	" starry.
Gossypium arboreum,	Cotton-tree.
Glycine sinensis,	Glycine, Chinese.
Gloxinia superba,	Gloxinia, superb.
Heliotropium Peruvianum,	Turnsole, Peruvian.
Hedera helix,	Ivy.
" " vegeta,	" Irish.
" Africana,	" Cape.
Hoya carnosa,	Honey-dropper, fleshy-leaved.
Hydrangea hortensis,	Hydrangea, changeable.
Hyssopus officinalis,	Hyssop.
Hibiscus Patersonii,	Hibiscus, Norfolk Island.
" cannabina,	" hemp-leaved.
" rosa sinense,	" Chinese.
" " pleno,	" " double.
" heterophyllus,	" various-leaved.
" rotundifolia,	" round-leaved.
" trionum,	Bladder ketmia.
" vesicarius,	Hibiscus, African.
Jasminum officinale,	Jessamine, scented white.
" fruticans,	" yellow.
" gracilis,	" slender.
Justicia adhatoda,	Malabar nut.
Ilex aquifolium,	Holly, common.
Indigofera tinctoria,	Indigo, East Indian.
" cytissoides,	" cytissus-like.
" Australis,	" Australian.
Juglans regia,	Walnut, common.
" alba,	Hickory-nut.
Juniperus Suecica,	Juniper, Swedish.
Inga xylocarpa,	Inga, apple.
Kerria, Japonica,	Kerria, Japan.
Botanical Name	English Name
Ligustrum vulgare,	Privet, common.
" " sempervirens,	" evergreen.
Laurus nobilis,	Sweet-bay.
Lavendula spica,	Lavender.
Lavatera arborea,	Tree-mallow.
Lophospermum scandens,	Lophospermum - Tree-foxglove.
" erubescens, blushing.	"
Lycium Europeum,	Box-thorn, European.
Lonicera xylosteum,	Lonicera, fly.
Lagerstraemia regina,	
Melia Azederach,	Bead-tree, common.

Botanical Name	English Name
Myrtus communis,	Myrtle common small-leaved.
" " romana,	" " broad-leaved.
" " tarentina,	" " box-leaved.
Magnolia grandiflora,	Magnolia, large-flowered.
" purpurea,	" purple-flowered.
" annonefolia,	" annona-leaved.
Melianthus major,	Honey-flower, great.
Maurandya Barclayana,	Maurandya, Barclay's.
" semperflorens,	" red-flowered.
" antirrhiniflora,	" blue-flowered.
Melaleuca fulgens,	Melaleuca, splendid.
Morus nigra,	Mulberry, black
" alba,	" white.
" Italicum,	" Italian.
Maclura aurantica,	Osage orange.
Mimosa sensitiva,	Mimosa, sensitive.
Mammillaria stellata,	Mammillaria, star.
Matica cerulea,	Marica, blue.
Metrosideros speciosa,	Bottle-brush, splendid.
" lanceolata,	" willow-leaved.
Metrosideros Patersonia,	Bottle-brush, Patterson's purple.
" squamea,	" small.
Nerium oleander,	Oleander.
" " pleno,	" double.
" grandiflora,	" great-flowred.
" " pleno,	" "
double.	
Nauclea orientalis,	Nauclea, oriental.
Olea Americana,	Olive, American.
" europea,	" common.
" " longifloria,	" " Italian fruiting.
" " " var.,	" " " 4 variet.
Ornus europeus,	Ash, flowering.
Othonna abrotanifolia,	Ragwort, southernwood-leaved.
" pectinata,	" wormwood-leaved.
Opuntia vulgaris,	Opuntia - Indian-fig, common.
" horrida,	" " horrid.
" cochinelifera,	" " cochine.
Protea?	Protea?
Physalis edulus,	Cape gooseberry.
Pittosporum spectabile,	Pittosporum, showy.
" bicolor,	" two-coloured.
Podalyria sericea,	Podalyria, silky.
Punica granatum,	Pomegranate.
" " pleno,	" double.
" " albiflora,	" white.
Prunus lusitanica,	Portugal laurel.
" laureo-cerasus,	Common "
Pyrus aucuparia,	Mountain ash.
" japonica,	Japan pear.
Pentstemon gentianoides,	Pentstemon, gentian-like.
" grandis,	" great-flowred.
Pentstemon levigata,	Pentstemon, smooth.
" Bradburii,	" Bradbury's.
Passiflora cerulea,	Passion-flower, blue.
" edulus,	" fruit-bearing.
" racemosa cerulea,	" racemous blue.
" " rubra,	" " red.
" Buonapartea,	" Buonaparte's.
" linearis,	" narrow-leaved.
" Colvillii,	" Colville's.
" cuprea,	" copper-coloured.
" pinnatistipula,	" pinnated-leaved.
Pelargonium,	Geranium.
"	" 42 splendid
varieties.	
Polygala speciosa,	Milkwort, showy.
" virgata,	" twiggy.

Botanical Name	English Name
" myrtifolia,	" myrtle-leaved.
Psoralea aphylla,	Psoralea, leafless.
" sp.,	
Platanus occidentalis,	Plane-tree, American.
Pinus sylvestris,	Scotch fir.
" pinea,	Pine, stone.
" halipensis,	" Aleppo.
Phoenix dactylifera,	Date-palm.
Populus nigra,	Poplar, black Italian.
" dilatata,	" Lombardy.
Petunia nyctaginiflora,	Petunia, white.
" phenicea,	" purple.
Pereskia aculeata,	Barbadoes gooseberry.
Parkinsonia aculeata,	Parkinsonia, prickly.
Quercus robur,	Oak, common.
Quamoclit vulgaris,	Quamoclit, common.
Rosemarinus officinalis,	Rosemary.
Rhamnus theezans,	Buckthorn, tea.
Ribes aureum,	Currant, yellow-flowering.
" sanguineum,	" purple-flowering.
" oxyacanthoides,	" hawthorn-like.
" speciosa,	" beautiful.
Rhus typhina,	Shumach, Venetian.
Rhododendron ponticum,	Rose-bay, pink.
" " alba,	" white.
Rhipsalis cassutha,	Rhipsalis, naked.
Rubus apiifolium,	Bramble, parsley-leaved.
Ricinius communis,	Castor-oil.
Ruscus aculeatus,	Butcher's broom.
Rosa spinosissima,	Rose, Scotch.
" damascena,	" damask.
" "	" " York and
	" Lancaster.
" centifolia,	" cabbage.
	" " Provins'
" " mucosa,	" " moss.
	" " "
	blush.
	" " "
	white-cluster.
" gallica,	" medicinal.
" " & var.,	" " many varieties.
" alba var.,	" maiden's-blush.
" rubiginosa,	" sweet-briar.
" Indica,	" China blush.
" " luteo,	" " yellow.
" " centifolia,	" " cabbage.
" sempervirens,	" evergreen.
" multiflora,	" bramble-flowered.
Robinia pseud-acacia,	Acacia, common thorn.
Robinia viscosa,	Acacia, clammy.
" hispida,	" rose.
" " rosea,	" " upright.
Russelia juncea	Russelia, rush-like.
Syringa vulgaris,	Lilac, common.
" " violacca,	" purple.
" " alba,	" white.
" Persica,	" Persian.
Salvia officinalis,	Sage, common.
" coccinea,	" scarlet.
" splendens,	" splendid.
" violacea,	" violet.
" sp.,	
" "	
Solanum giganteum,	Nightshade, gigantic.
" dulcamara,	Bitter-sweet.
" incertum,	
" lanciniatum,	Nightshade, cut-leaved.

Botanical Name	**English Name**
” pseudo-capsicum,	Winter cherry.
” aculeatissimum,	Prickly nightshade.
Stapelia bufonia,	Stapelia, toad-flower.
” asterias,	” star-flower.
Sempervivum arboreum,	Houseleek, tree.
” tectorum,	” common.
Spirea hypericifolia,	Spirea, hypericum-leaved.
” corymbosa,	” corymb-flowered.
” sp. novum,	” new species.
Spartium junceum,	Broom, Spanish.
” multiflorum,	” white Portugal.
” scoparium	” common.
Salix babylonica,	Willow, weeping.
Botanical Name	English Name
Salix sp.,	Willow, several.
Symphora racemosa,	Snowberry, clustered.
Spondias mucronata,	Spondias - Hog-plum.
Stachytarpheta mutabilis,	Stachytarpheta, changeable.
Tilia rubra,	Lime-tree.
Thymus vulgaris,	Thyme, garden.
” ” variegata,	” silver.
Tephrosia grandiflora,	Tephrosia, great-flowered.
” suberosa,	”
Thuya occidentalis,	Arbor-vitie, American.
Taxus baccata,	Yew-tree.
Tacsonia pinnatistipula,	Tacsonia, pinnated-leaved.
Veronica formosa,	Speedwell.
” labiata,	
” sp.,	
” ”	
Vinca major,	Periwinkle, greater.
” minor,	” lesser.
” rosea,	” Madagascar.
Vitis vinifera,	Vine, common grape.
Ulmus campestris,	Elm, English.
” suberosa,	” cork-barked.
Viburnum, tinus,	Laurestine.
” opulus,	Guelder-rose.
Ulex europeus	Furze, common.
Wistaria consequana,	China glycine.
Yucca gloriosa,	Adam's-needle, superb.
” filamentosa,	” thready.

FRUIT TREES

Botanical Name	**English Name**
Amygdalus communis,	Almond sweet.
” ” amara,	” bitter.
” persica,	Peach.
” ” nectarina,	Nectarine.
Bromelia ananas,	Pine-apple.
Berberis vulgaris,	Berberry, common.
Coffea arabica,	Coffee-tree.
Cydonia vulgaris,	Quince, common.
Botanical Name	**English Name**
Castanea vesca,	Chestnut, edible.
Corylus avellana,	Hazel-nut.
” ” rubra,	Filbert.
” ” grandis,	Cob-nut.
Citrus limonum,	Lemon.
” aurantium,	Orange.
Eriobotria japonica,	Loquat.
Fragaria eliator,	Strawberry, hautboy.
” vesca,	” Alpine.
Ficus carica,	Fig, common.
Juglans regia,	Walnut, common.
” alba,	Hickory-nut.
Juniperus suecica,	Juniper, Swedish.
Mespilus germanica,	Medlar.
Morus nigra,	Mulberry, black.
” alba,	” white.
” Italicum,	” Italian.
Olea Americana,	Olive American.
” europea,	” common.
Olea europea longifolia,	Olive, common, Italian fruiting.
” ” ” var.,	” ” ” 4 varieties.
Physalis edulus,	Cape gooseberry.
Punica granatum,	Pomegranate.
Prunus domestica,	Common plum.
” cerasus,	Cherry.
” insititia,	Bullace.
” spinosa,	Sloe.
” armeniaca,	Apricot.
Pyrus communis,	Pear.
” malus,	Apple.
” prunifolia,	Siberian-crab.
Passiflora edulus,	Passion-flower, fruit-bearing.
Phoenix dactylifera,	Date-palm.
Pereskia aculeata,	Barbadoes gooseberry.
Ribes rubrum,	Currant, red.
” ” album,	” white.
” nigrum,	” black.
” grossularia,	” gooseberry, rough.
” uva-crispa,	” ” smooth.
Rubus idaeus,	Raspberry.
” ” alba,	” white.
” fruticosus,	Bramble.
Solanum lycopersicum,	Love-apple.
” melongena,	Egg-plant.
Sambucus nigra,	Elder.
Vitis vinifera,	Vine, common grape.

William Hale Catalogue, Nelson, 1861

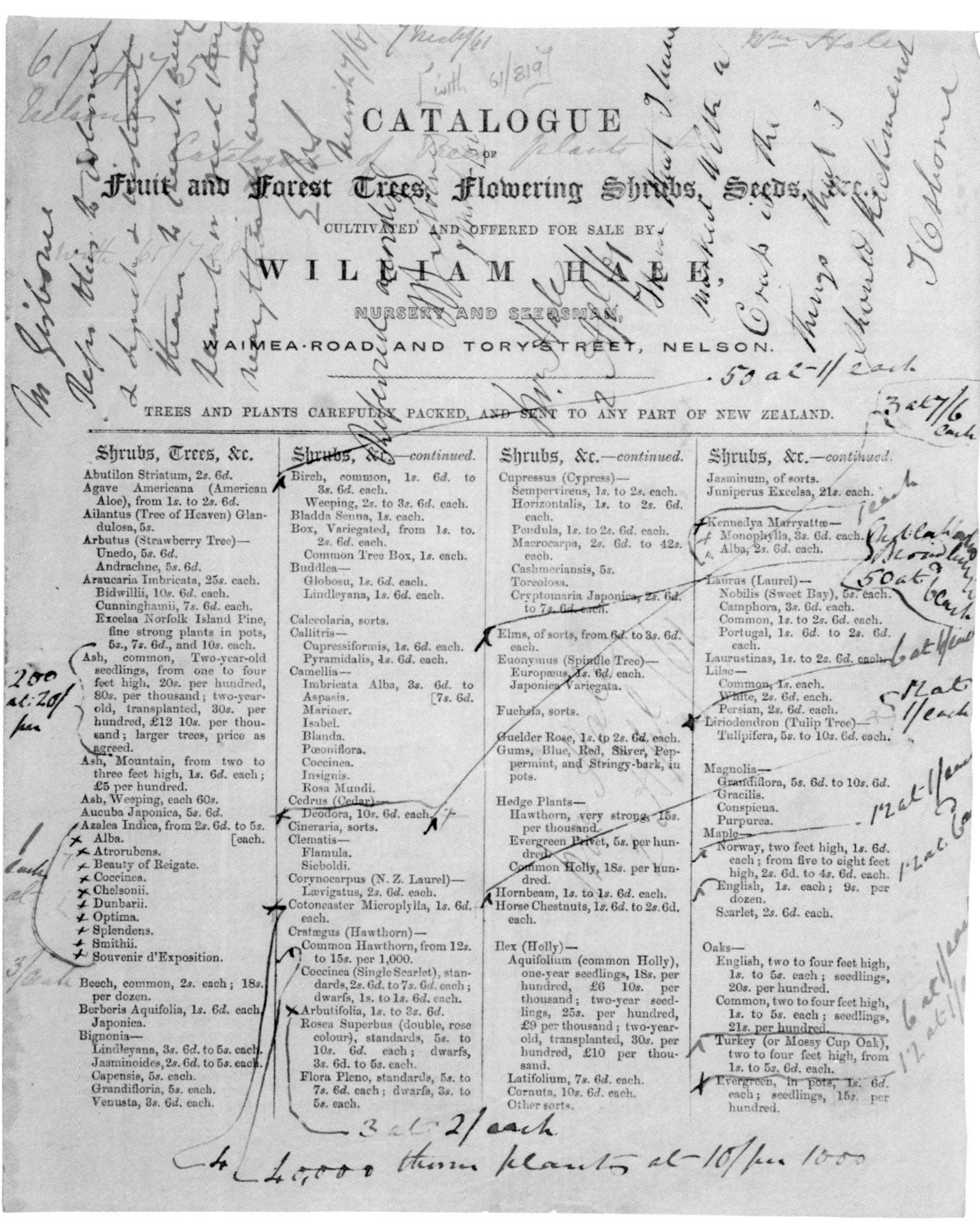

CATALOGUE

OF

Fruit and Forest Trees, Flowering Shrubs, Seeds, &c.

CULTIVATED AND OFFERED FOR SALE BY

WILLIAM HALE,

NURSERY AND SEEDSMAN,

WAIMEA-ROAD AND TORY-STREET, NELSON.

TREES AND PLANTS CAREFULLY PACKED, AND SENT TO ANY PART OF NEW ZEALAND.

Shrubs, Trees, &c.

Abutilon Striatum, 2*s.* 6*d.*
Agave Americana (American Aloe), from 1*s.* to 2*s.* 6*d.*
Ailantus (Tree of Heaven) Glandulosa, 5*s.*
Arbutus (Strawberry Tree)—
Unedo, 5*s.* 6*d.*
Andrachne, 5*s.* 6*d.*
Araucaria Imbricata, 25*s.* each.
Bidwillii, 10*s.* 6*d.* each.
Cunninghamii, 7*s.* 6*d.* each.
Excelsa Norfolk Island Pine, fine strong plants in pots, 5*s.*, 7*s.* 6*d.*, and 10*s.* each.
Ash, common, Two-year-old seedlings, from one to four feet high, 20*s.* per hundred, 80*s.* per thousand; two-year-old, transplanted, 30*s.* per hundred, £12 10*s.* per thousand; larger trees, price as agreed.
Ash, Mountain, from two to three feet high, 1*s.* 6*d.* each; £5 per hundred.
Ash, Weeping, each 60*s.*
Aucuba Japonica, 5*s.* 6*d.*
Azalea Indica, from 2*s.* 6*d.* to 5*s.* each.
Alba.
Atrorubens.
Beauty of Reigate.
Coccinea.
Chelsonii.
Dunbarii.
Optima.
Splendens.
Smithii.
Souvenir d'Exposition.

Beech, common, 2*s.* each; 18*s.* per dozen.
Berberis Aquifolia, 1*s.* 6*d.* each.
Japonica.
Bignonia—
Lindleyana, 3*s.* 6*d.* to 5*s.* each.
Jasminoides, 2*s.* 6*d.* to 5*s.* each.
Capensis, 5*s.* each.
Grandifloria, 5*s.* each.
Venusta, 3*s.* 6*d.* each.

Shrubs, &c.—*continued.*

Birch, common, 1*s.* 6*d.* to 3*s.* 6*d.* each.
Weeping, 2*s.* to 3*s.* 6*d.* each.
Bladda Senna, 1*s.* each.
Box, Variegated, from 1*s.* to 2*s.* 6*d.* each.
Common Tree Box, 1*s.* each.
Buddlea—
Globosu, 1*s.* 6*d.* each.
Lindleyana, 1*s.* 6*d.* each.

Calceolaria, sorts.
Callitris—
Cupressiformis, 1*s.* 6*d.* each.
Pyramidalis, 1*s.* 6*d.* each.
Camellia—
Imbricata Alba, 3*s.* 6*d.* to 7*s.* 6*d.*
Aspasia.
Mariner.
Isabel.
Blanda.
Pœoniflora.
Coccinea.
Insignis.
Rosa Mundi.
Cedrus (Cedar)—
Deodora, 10*s.* 6*d.* each.
Cineraria, sorts.
Clematis—
Flamula.
Sieboldi.
Corynocarpus (N. Z. Laurel)—
Lævigatus, 2*s.* 6*d.* each.
Cotoneaster Microplylla, 1*s.* 6*d.* each.
Cratægus (Hawthorn)—
Common Hawthorn, from 12*s.* to 15*s.* per 1,000.
Coccinea (Single Scarlet), standards, 2*s.* 6*d.* to 7*s.* 6*d.* each; dwarfs, 1*s.* to 1*s.* 6*d.* each.
Arbutifolia, 1*s.* to 3*s.* 6*d.*
Rosea Superbus (double, rose colour), standards, 5*s.* to 10*s.* 6*d.* each; dwarfs, 3*s.* 6*d.* to 5*s.* each.
Flora Pleno, standards, 5*s.* to 7*s.* 6*d.* each; dwarfs, 3*s.* to 5*s.* each.

Shrubs, &c.—*continued.*

Cupressus (Cypress)—
Sempervirens, 1*s.* to 2*s.* each.
Horizontalis, 1*s.* to 2*s.* 6*d.* each.
Pendula, 1*s.* to 2*s.* 6*d.* each.
Macrocarpa, 2*s.* 6*d.* to 42*s.* each.
Cashmeriansis, 5*s.*
Toreolosa.
Cryptomaria Japonica, 2*s.* 6*d.* to 7*s.* 6*d.* each.
Elms, of sorts, from 6*d.* to 3*s.* 6*d.* each.
Euonymus (Spindle Tree)—
Europæus, 1*s.* 6*d.* each.
Japonica Variegata.

Fuchsia, sorts.

Guelder Rose, 1*s.* to 2*s.* 6*d.* each.
Gums, Blue, Red, Silver, Peppermint, and Stringy-bark, in pots.

Hedge Plants—
Hawthorn, very strong, 15*s.* per thousand.
Evergreen Privet, 5*s.* per hundred.
Common Holly, 18*s.* per hundred.
Hornbeam, 1*s.* to 1*s.* 6*d.* each.
Horse Chestnuts, 1*s.* 6*d.* to 2*s.* 6*d.* each.

Ilex (Holly)—
Aquifolium (common Holly), one-year seedlings, 18*s.* per hundred, £6 10*s.* per thousand; two-year seedlings, 25*s.* per hundred, £9 per thousand; two-year-old, transplanted, 30*s.* per hundred, £10 per thousand.
Latifolium, 7*s.* 6*d.* each.
Cornuta, 10*s.* 6*d.* each.
Other sorts.

Shrubs, &c.—*continued.*

Jasminum, of sorts.
Juniperus Excelsa, 21*s.* each.

Kennedya Marryattæ—
Monophylla, 3*s.* 6*d.* each.
Alba, 2*s.* 6*d.* each.

Laurus (Laurel)—
Nobilis (Sweet Bay), 5*s.* each.
Camphora, 3*s.* 6*d.* each.
Common, 1*s.* to 2*s.* 6*d.* each.
Portugal, 1*s.* 6*d.* to 2*s.* 6*d.* each.
Laurustinas, 1*s.* to 2*s.* 6*d.* each.
Lilac—
Common, 1*s.* each.
White, 2*s.* 6*d.* each.
Persian, 2*s.* 6*d.* each.
Liriodendron (Tulip Tree)—
Tulipifera, 5*s.* to 10*s.* 6*d.* each.

Magnolia—
Grandiflora, 5*s.* 6*d.* to 10*s.* 6*d.*
Gracilis.
Conspicua.
Purpurea.
Maple—
Norway, two feet high, 1*s.* 6*d.* each; from five to eight feet high, 2*s.* 6d. to 4*s.* 6*d.* each.
English, 1*s.* each; 9*s.* per dozen.
Scarlet, 2*s.* 6*d.* each.

Oaks—
English, two to four feet high, 1*s.* to 5*s.* each; seedlings, 20*s.* per hundred.
Common, two to four feet high, 1*s.* to 5*s.* each; seedlings, 21*s.* per hundred.
Turkey (or Mossy Cup Oak), two to four feet high, from 1*s.* to 5*s.* 6*d.* each.
Evergreen, in pots, 1*s.* 6*d.* each; seedlings, 15*s.* per hundred.

William Hale Catalogue, Nelson, 1861

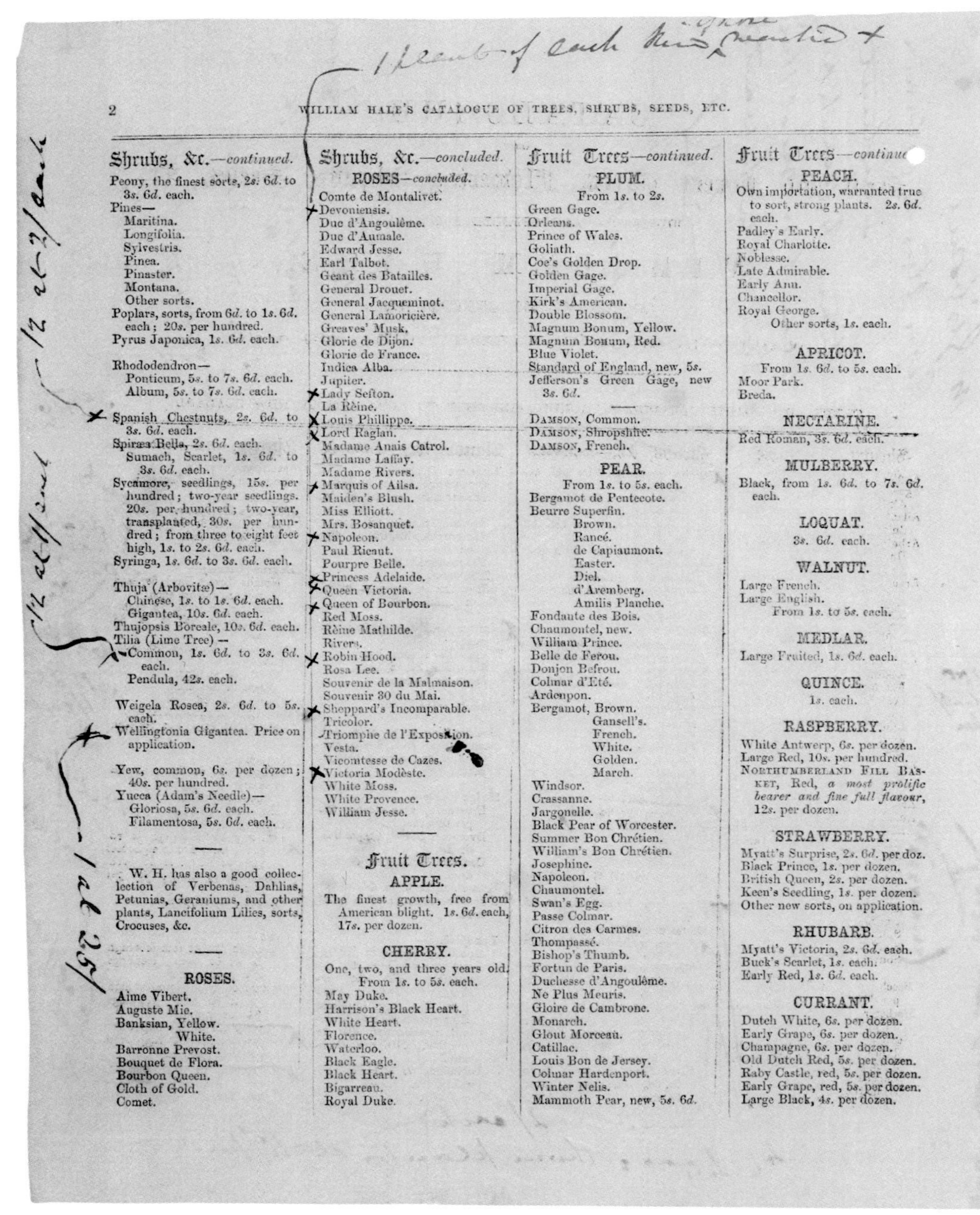

2 WILLIAM HALE'S CATALOGUE OF TREES, SHRUBS, SEEDS, ETC.

Shrubs, &c.—*continued.*

Peony, the finest sorts, 2*s*. 6*d*. to 3*s*. 6*d*. each.
Pines—
Maritina.
Longifolia.
Sylvestris.
Pinea.
Pinaster.
Montana.
Other sorts.
Poplars, sorts, from 6*d*. to 1*s*. 6*d*. each; 20*s*. per hundred.
Pyrus Japonica, 1*s*. 6*d*. each.

Rhododendron—
Ponticum, 5*s*. to 7*s*. 6*d*. each.
Album, 5*s*. to 7*s*. 6*d*. each.

Spanish Chestnuts, 2*s*. 6*d*. to 3*s*. 6*d*. each.
Spiræa Bella, 2*s*. 6*d*. each.
Sumach, Scarlet, 1*s*. 6*d*. to 3*s*. 6*d*. each.
Sycamore, seedlings, 15*s*. per hundred; two-year seedlings. 20*s*. per hundred; two-year, transplanted, 30*s*. per hundred; from three to eight feet high, 1*s*. to 2*s*. 6*d*. each.
Syringa, 1*s*. 6*d*. to 3*s*. 6*d*. each.

Thuja (Arbovitæ)—
Chinese, 1*s*. to 1*s*. 6*d*. each.
Gigantea, 10*s*. 6*d*. each.
Thujopsis Boreale, 10*s*. 6*d*. each.
Tilia (Lime Tree)—
Common, 1*s*. 6*d*. to 3*s*. 6*d*. each.
Pendula, 42*s*. each.

Weigela Rosea, 2*s*. 6*d*. to 5*s*. each.
Wellingtonia Gigantea. Price on application.

Yew, common, 6*s*. per dozen; 40*s*. per hundred.
Yucca (Adam's Needle)—
Gloriosa, 5*s*. 6*d*. each.
Filamentosa, 5*s*. 6*d*. each.

W. H. has also a good collection of Verbenas, Dahlias, Petunias, Geraniums, and other plants, Lancifolium Lilies, sorts, Crocuses, &c.

ROSES.

Aime Vibert.
Auguste Mie.
Banksian, Yellow.
White.
Barronne Prevost.
Bouquet de Flora.
Bourbon Queen.
Cloth of Gold.
Comet.

Shrubs, &c.—*concluded.*

ROSES—*concluded.*

Comte de Montalivet.
Devoniensis.
Duc d'Angoulême.
Duc d'Aumale.
Edward Jesse.
Earl Talbot.
Geant des Batailles.
General Drouet.
General Jacqueminot.
General Lamoricière.
Greaves' Musk.
Glorie de Dijon.
Glorie de France.
Indica Alba.
Jupiter.
Lady Sefton.
La Rèine.
Louis Phillippe.
Lord Raglan.
Madame Anais Catrol.
Madame Laffay.
Madame Rivers.
Marquis of Ailsa.
Maiden's Blush.
Miss Elliott.
Mrs. Bosanquet.
Napoleon.
Paul Ricaut.
Pourpre Belle.
Princess Adelaide.
Queen Victoria.
Queen of Bourbon.
Red Moss.
Rèine Mathilde.
Rivers.
Robin Hood.
Rosa Lee.
Souvenir de la Malmaison.
Souvenir 30 du Mai.
Sheppard's Incomparable.
Tricolor.
Triomphe de l'Exposition.
Vesta.
Vicomtesse de Cazes.
Victoria Modèste.
White Moss.
White Provence.
William Jesse.

Fruit Trees.

APPLE.

The finest growth, free from American blight. 1*s*. 6*d*. each, 17*s*. per dozen.

CHERRY.

One, two, and three years old. From 1*s*. to 5*s*. each.
May Duke.
Harrison's Black Heart.
White Heart.
Florence.
Waterloo.
Black Eagle.
Black Heart.
Bigarreau.
Royal Duke.

Fruit Trees—*continued.*

PLUM.

From 1*s*. to 2*s*.
Green Gage.
Orleans.
Prince of Wales.
Goliath.
Coe's Golden Drop.
Golden Gage.
Imperial Gage.
Kirk's American.
Double Blossom.
Magnum Bonum, Yellow.
Magnum Bonum, Red.
Blue Violet.
Standard of England, new, 5*s*.
Jefferson's Green Gage, new 3*s*. 6*d*.

DAMSON, Common.
DAMSON, Shropshire.
DAMSON, French.

PEAR.

From 1*s*. to 5*s*. each.
Bergamot de Pentecote.
Beurre Superfin.
Brown.
Rancé.
de Capiaumont.
Easter.
Diel.
d'Aremberg.
Amilis Planche.
Fondaute des Bois.
Chaumontel, new.
William Prince.
Belle de Ferou.
Donjon Befrou.
Colmar d'Eté.
Ardenpon.
Bergamot, Brown.
Gansell's.
French.
White.
Golden.
March.
Windsor.
Crassanne.
Jargonelle.
Black Pear of Worcester.
Summer Bon Chrétien.
William's Bon Chrétien.
Josephine.
Napoleon.
Chaumontel.
Swan's Egg.
Passe Colmar.
Citron des Carmes.
Thompassé.
Bishop's Thumb.
Fortun de Paris.
Duchesse d'Angoulême.
Ne Plus Meuris.
Gloire de Cambrone.
Monarch.
Glout Morceau.
Catillac.
Louis Bon de Jersey.
Colmar Hardenport.
Winter Nelis.
Mammoth Pear, new, 5*s*. 6*d*.

Fruit Trees—*continued.*

PEACH.

Own importation, warranted true to sort, strong plants. 2*s*. 6*d*. each.
Padley's Early.
Royal Charlotte.
Noblesse.
Late Admirable.
Early Ann.
Chancellor.
Royal George.
Other sorts, 1*s*. each.

APRICOT.

From 1*s*. 6*d*. to 5*s*. each.
Moor Park.
Breda.

NECTARINE.

Red Roman, 3*s*. 6*d*. each.

MULBERRY.

Black, from 1*s*. 6*d*. to 7*s*. 6*d*. each.

LOQUAT.

3*s*. 6*d*. each.

WALNUT.

Large French.
Large English.
From 1*s*. to 5*s*. each.

MEDLAR.

Large Fruited, 1*s*. 6*d*. each.

QUINCE.

1*s*. each.

RASPBERRY.

White Antwerp, 6*s*. per dozen.
Large Red, 10*s*. per hundred.
NORTHUMBERLAND FILL BASKET, Red, *a most prolific bearer and fine full flavour*, 12*s*. per dozen.

STRAWBERRY.

Myatt's Surprise, 2*s*. 6*d*. per doz.
Black Prince, 1*s*. per dozen.
British Queen, 2*s*. per dozen.
Keen's Seedling, 1*s*. per dozen.
Other new sorts, on application.

RHUBARB.

Myatt's Victoria, 2*s*. 6*d*. each.
Buck's Scarlet, 1*s*. each.
Early Red, 1*s*. 6*d*. each.

CURRANT.

Dutch White, 6*s*. per dozen.
Early Grape, 6*s*. per dozen.
Champagne, 6*s*. per dozen.
Old Dutch Red, 5*s*. per dozen.
Raby Castle, red, 5*s*. per dozen.
Early Grape, red, 5*s*. per dozen.
Large Black, 4*s*. per dozen.

Thomas White Catalogue, Wellington, 1865

CATALOGUE

or

VEGETABLE,

FLOWER, AND AGRICULTURAL

SEEDS,

SOLD BY

THOMAS WHITE,

SEEDSMAN AND GENERAL STOREKEEPER,

LAMBTON QUAY,

WELLINGTON.

1866.

Thomas White Catalogue, Wellington, 1865

6

FLOWER SEEDS.

BIENNIALS AND PERENNIALS.

Antirrhinum Majus (Snapdragon) ......
Anemone Coronaria ....
Aquilogia Formosa ....
„ Glandulosa ....
„ Skinneri ....
Calceolaria Hybrida ....
Campanula Carpatica ....
„ Medium (Canterbury Bell) ......
„ „ Alba (White) ....
Chrysanthemum Indicum ....
„ Nanum Pompou ......
Cineraria Hybrida ....
„ Maritima ....
Dahlia ....
Delphinium Chinensis ....
„ Formosum ....
„ Magnificum ....
Dianthus Caryophyllus (Carnation) ......
Dianthus Cary. Punctatus (Picotee) ......
„ Plumarius (Pink) ....
Digitalis (Foxglove) various ....
Fuchsia Hybrida ....
Gentiana Acaulis ....
Gladiolus ....
Hedysarum Coronarium (French Honeysuckle) ....
Heliotropium Peruvianum ....
Hollyhock ....
Humea Elegans ....
Hesperis Matronalis (Purple Rocket) ....
Ipomopsis Elegans ....
Ipomea Horsfalliæ ....
„ Rubro Cœrnlea ....
Lathyrus Latifolius (Everlasting Pea) ...
Lobelia Cardinalis ....
„ Erinus ....
Lobelia Paxtoniana ....
„ Ramosoides ....
„ Speciosa ....
Lychnis Chalcedonica ....
„ Fulgens ....
Mathiola Incana (Brompton Stock) ......
„ „ Alba (White) ....
„ „ Coccinea (Scarlet) .....
„ „ Purpurea (Purple) .....
„ Imperialis (Emperor Stock) ......
Mimulus Cardinalis (Monkey Flower) ....
Mirabilis Jalapa (Marvel of Peru) ......
Myosotis Palustris (Forget-me-not) .....
Nierembergia Gracilis ....
Œnothera (Evening Primrose) ....
„ Drummondii ....
„ Macrocarpa ....
Passiflora (Passion Flower) ....
„ Cœrulea ....
Pelargonium (Geranium) ....
„ Zonale (Scarlet Geranium)
Pentstemon Gentianoides Coccineum ....
„ Murrayanum ....
Petunia Hybrida ....
Phlox Perennis Hybrida ....
Primula Auricula ....
„ Polyantha (Polyanthus) ....
„ Sinensis (Chinese Primrose) ......
„ Veris (Cowslip) ....
Ranunculus Asiaticus ....
Salvia Patens ....
„ Splendens ....
Verbena Hybrida ....
Viola Tricolor (Pansy) ....
„ Hybrida ....

Bedding plant designs from Thompson's *Gardener's Assistant*

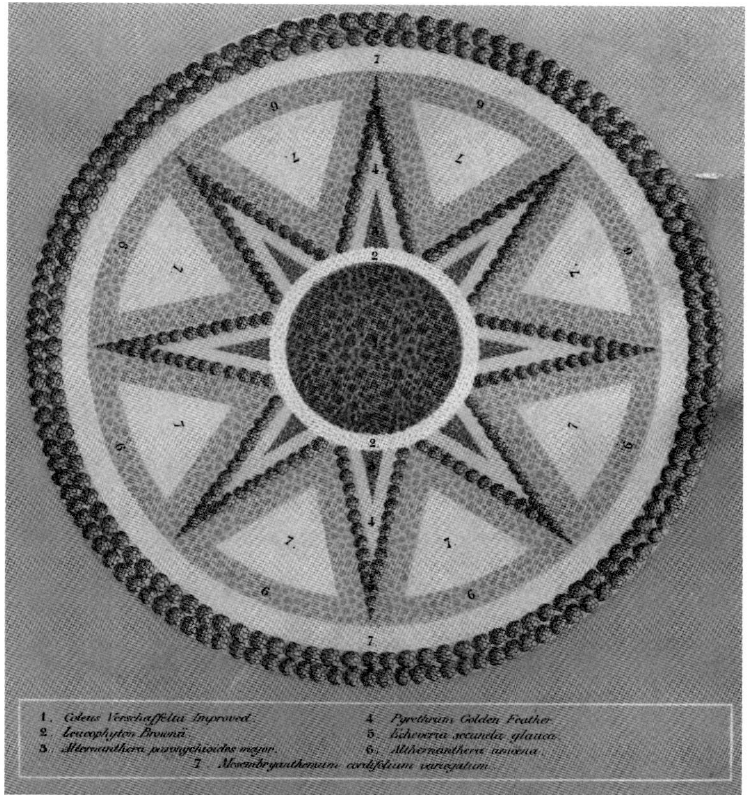

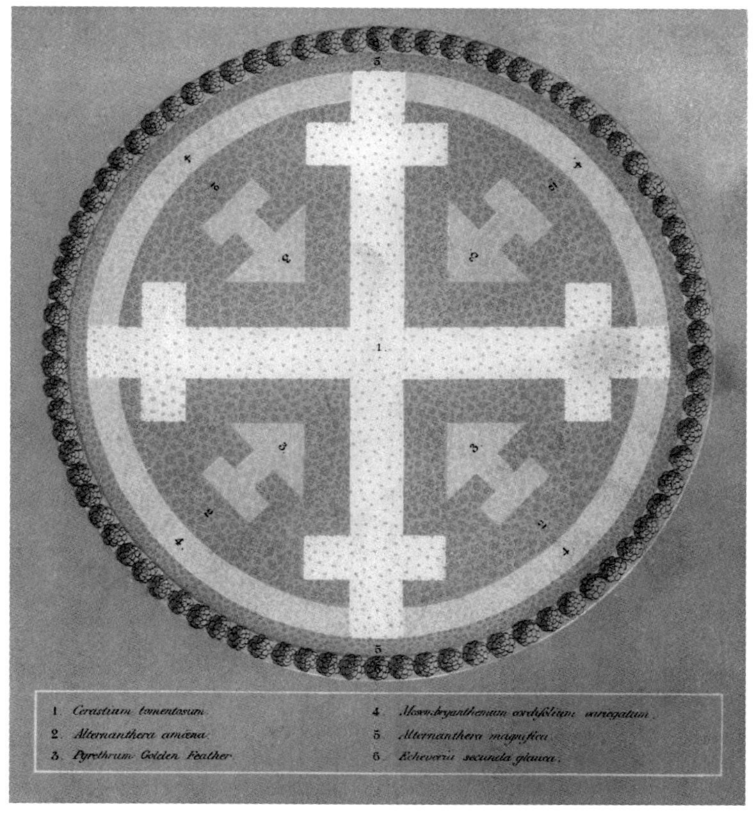

INDEX

A

Abraham, Charles John, **113**
Allom, Thomas, 6, **6**
Alston, Pat, 142
Alston, Robert, 142
Alzdorf, Baron Charles Von, 12, 18, **25**, 25–6, 26, 51, **126**, 152, **153**
Archibald, Robert, 224
Asken, Tanya, **235**, 235
Attenborough, David, 221–2
Aubrey, Christopher, **50**, **188**, 204, **205**
Aubrey, Harcourt Richard, 23

B

Baines, Mr, **153**
Baker, Major, 152, **153**
Bamford, Mr, **122**
Bannatyne, W.M., **112**, **145**, **182**
Bannister, William, **153**, **182**
Barraud, C.D., 162
Barrington, Rosemary, 219, 223
Barton, R., 152, 162
Battersbee, Captain, 161
Bayly, William, 23
Beattie, Sir David, 133
Beauchamps (Katherine Mansfield's family), 67, 74, **113**, 113, **116**, **120**, 143, 146
Belich, James (historian), 4
Belich, James (mayor), **223**, 223
Bell, F.D., 29, **29**
Benthell, J.P., **77**
Berry family, 79
Berry, William, 60
Best, Alfred, **90**
Best, Elsdon, 75–6, **116**
Best, George, **206**
Best, Lieutenant, 99
Best, Margaret, **90**
Betts-Hopper, Edward, 44
Bledisloe, Lord, 131
Boardman, Alfred, 116
Boffa, Frank, 241
Bolton, S., **173**
Booth, Chris, 224, **225**
Boulcott, Mr, 158
Bould, Robert, 76
Bowen, Sir George, 129
Bowler, Mr, 157
Bradey, Alfred, 87–8
Bradey, Francis, 13–14, 64, **86**, **87**, 87–8, **88**, **89**, 96, 98, 155
Bradey, Frederick, 87–8
Bragge, James, **52**, 123, 148, **149**, 178
Bramley, Annie, **103**
Bramley, William, 218–19
Brandon, A.d'B., **98**, 151
Brees, S.C., **19**, **24**, 24–5, **25**, 71, **98**, **99**, 99–100, **135**, 198, **198**
Broderick, Anne, 85
Broderick, Creasy, 85
Brook, J.T., 35
Brown, Capability, 95
Bryant, James, 22, 28, 88–90, **89**, 186
Bryant, Josephine, **90**
Bryant, William, **90**
Buchanan, John, 55
Buck, Captain, 160
Bumby, Reverend S., 236
Bunckenburg, Heinrich, 148, 178
Burcham, Mr, 19, 152, **153**, **154**
Burnet, Mr, 157
Burstall, B., 34
Burton Brothers, 148, **149**, 178
Buxton, Alfred, **131**, 131–2, **132**, 135, 140–1, **141**, 142, 239

C

Campbell, John, 173
Campbell, Thomas, 4
Carnegie, D.F., **165**, 165
Carter, C.R., 160
Catchpool, E., 12, **153**
Challenger, Charles, 165, 168, 176–7, 244
Chapman, Harry, 61, 64
Chapman, H.S., 20, 26, 60, **61**, 61–6, **65**, 66, 68, 70, 87, 92, 98, 138, 139, 202
Chapman, Kate, 46, 61, 65
Chapman, Martin, 70
Chew, John, **79**, 80, 92
Christenson, Louis, **103**
Clark, George, 80, **81**
Clarke, Ken, 233
Clayton, William, 129
Clere, Frederick de Jersey, **109**, **113**
Coates, Gordon, 136
Cobham, Samuel, 7–8, **8**
Cockayne, Dr Leonard, 70, 220
Coglund, G.H., 11–12
Cohen, Dr, 239
Collins, Richard, **136**, 136, **137**, 161, 162
Collinson, Bernard, 125
Cook, John George, 23
Cook, Walter, 14–15, 53, 221
Cooley, Isaac, **52**
Cooper, F., **166**
Cooper, Frederick, 51, 179, 180, **180**, **181**
Cooper, Frederick jr, **181**
Cooper, George, **181**
Cooper, J.W., 191
Copeland, Mr, 162
Cotter, Thomas, **50**
Crawford, James Coutts, 55–7, **57**, 185–6

D

Daniel, Mr, 178
Daniell, Captain, 75, 76, 95
Daniell, Juliette, 76
Daniels, Edwin, 29
Darvill, Captain, 152
Darwin, Charles, 242
Davies, John, 72
Davies, Shona Rapira, **236**, 237
Davies, Victor, 239
Davis, H.W., **114**
Denton, George, 107
Denton, William, 107
Derby, Lord, 57
Dickinson, James, 243
Dieffenbach, Dr, 167
Dixon, Edward, **102**
Domett, A., 125
Donald, James, 173
Donald, Jane, 172, **174**, 192
Donald, Robert, 44, 60, 161, 162, 163, **166**, 172–4, **173**, **174**, 192–3, **193**, 194, 202
Drake, Selina, 84–5
Drake, Thomas, **84**, 84–6, 104
Drake, T.J., 22
Drake, Walter, 86
Drummond, Andrew, 225
Duncan, R.J., **182**
Duppa, George, 14, 44, 187
Duthie, Donal, 221, 231
Duthie, John, 52
Dutton, John, 217, 230

E

Eagles family, **92**
Earp, William, 86, **86**
Eaton, the late Mr, 12, **23**
Ebden, Mr, 162
Edwards, Mr, 172–3, 193
Edwards (seed distributors), 40
Evans, Dr, 44, 152
Eyre, Mrs, 100

F

Featherston, Dr I.E., **145**, 151, 152, **153**, **154**, 157, 158
Fell, Dr Walter, **109**, **119**
Ferguson, F., 126–8
Fielding, Mr, 191
Fitzherbert, Sir William, **52**, 52
Flook, Ron, 144, 146, 221, **222**, 224, 231, 234, **235**, **236**, 236
Fox, William, 76–9, **78**, 92, **97**, 97
Fuller, Mr, 157

G

Galloway, Ian, 209, **219**, 221, 224, 232–3, 234
Galway, Lord, 131
Garrett, Mr, 29
Gibb, George, 219, **219**
Gibbs, Lieutenant Colonel, 29
Gibbs, Mr, 157
Gilberthorpe, John, **223**, 224
Gillies, Mr, 162
Gilmer, Dame Elizabeth, 224
Glen, George, 219, 220, 224
Glover, Lewis, 237
Godley, Charlotte, 100–1, **101**
Gold, Charles Emilius, **96**
Golder family, **118**, 118
Graham, Mr, 68

Greenwood, Anne, 114
Greenwood, Sarah, **114**
Grey, Mr, 217
Grey, Sir George, 34–5, 179, 192, 193, 194, 217, 230
Griffiths, Tony, 231

H

Hale, Alan, 36, 165
Hale, William, 128, 244
Hall, David, 218
Hamilton, Augustus, 189
Hannah, Robert, 143
Hanson, R.D., 25, 152
Hardie-Boys, Sir Michael, 133, 135
Harkness, Bruce, 231
Harkness, Christine, 231
Harrison, George Henry, **44**
Hart, Mr, 87
Harvey, John, 243
Hay, David, 244
Heaphy, Charles, **5**, 5–6, **9**, **12**, 45, 59, 71, 74–5
Heather, Rosemary, 231
Heberley, James 'Worser', 57
Hector, James, **111**, **112**, 129, 179, 203, 218, 223
Hector, Peter, **223**, 223, **224**
Henry, Mr, 152
Hill, Martin, **120**, **148**, 149
Hine, Reverend Vesey, 55, 56
Hislop, William, 172, 176–7, 178, **183**
Hobbs, Reverend J., 236
Hochberg, Count Fritz, 120
Hodder, Edwin, 101
Hodges, Carter, 81, **82**
Hogg, Mr, 187
Holm, Captain F., 116
Holmes, John, **79**, 79
Holmes, Lancelot, 79
Holmes, Mary, **79**, 79
Hooker, Greg, 221
Hooker, J.D., 224
Hooker, William, 45, 49
Hooper, John, 72
Horsfall, John Atherton, **39**
Houston, Dr Francis, 224
Houston, Logan, 224
Howe, Sir Edward, 159
Hunt, Mr, **153**
Hunter, Bethune V., **183**
Hunter, G., 161
Hunter, George, 109, 135–6
Huntley, Mr, 172
Hurst, F.W., 12, 66, 152, **153**, 157, **166**, 168–9, 172, **172**
Hutson, Peter, **117**, **119**
Hutt, Edward, 220, 224

I

Iggleston, Charles, **108**

J

Jackson, Henry, 28
Jackson, Mr, 126, **127**, 162
Jacob, Angela, **15**
James, Mr, **153**, 157
Johnson, Frank, 82–3
Johnston, Charles, 138–9
Johnston, D., **153**
Johnston, E., 152, **153**
Johnston, Henrietta Charlotte, 138
Johnston, John, **113**, 138, 142–3
Johnston, Judge, 115
Johnston, Mr, 157
Johnstone, E., **153**
Johnstone, J., 161
Joseph, Joseph, **112**, **115**

K

Keti, E., **153**, 154
Kilmister, Alfred, 60, 68, 198
Kilmister, Brian, 209
Kilmister, Frances, 68
Kilmister, John, 11, 13, 68, **101**, 104
Kilmister, John jr, 68
Kilsby, Jim, **90**
King, Sir Truby, 238–40, **239**, **240**, **241**
Kipling, Rudyard, 203
Kirk, H.B., 197
Kirkcaldie, John, 204, **205**
Knowles, H., **153**

L

La Trobe, Mr, 49
Laing, P., 162
Lancaster, Stephen, **66**, 67
Lawson, Mr, 157
Levin, Nathaniel William, **135**, **136**, 136, **182**
Levin, W.H., **112**
Lewis, D., **153**
Liardet, W.F.E., **73**
Lindsey, Robert, 39
Lindsey, Sarah, 39
Littlejohn, Wilson, 79
Lochart, T. and C., 10
Lodder, A.R.V., 190–1, 191
Logan, Mr, **173**
Loudon, Jane, 15
Loudon, John Claudius, 7, 15, 35, 165
Lowe, E.W., 73
Lucas, Robin, 221
Ludlam, Alfred, 18, 24–5, 27, **27**, 27–35, 28, **29**, 30, **30**, 31, 31–3, **32**, **33**, 34, 36–7, 38, 44, 50–1, 52, 53, 62, 88, 92, **115**, 126–7, 152, **153**, 161, 163, 165, 188, 189, 191–2
Lumsden, William, 12, 157, **166**, **170–1**, 170–2, 177, 179, 183
Lyon, William, 11–12, 14, 187

M

McBeth, James, 12, 159, 160, 163, **166**, **170–1**, 170–2, **182**, **183**
McBeth, John, 12, 167, **168**, **182**
McCleverty, Mrs, 100
MacDonald, Thomas Kennedy, **109**, 109–10, **110**
McFarlane, Reverend J., 152
MacGregor, Rob Roy, **116**
McHardie, Mr, 157
Mackay, Bill, 236, **237**
McKenzie, J.G., 205, 220, 224
Mackie, Frederick, 39–40
Mackie, T., 198–9
MacLagan, Mr, **153**
Maclean, Sir Donald, 105
Maclean, Sir Douglas, 105, **106**
McLeod, Mr, 161
McNab, James, 33, 185, 188–90
Mallaby, Lady, 142
Mansfield, Katherine, 67, 74, 113, 116, 143, 145–7, **146**, **147**, 228–9
Mansill, William, 148, 162, 163, **166**, **176–8**, 177–8, 179, 185, 202
Mantell, Walter, 28–9, 68, **101**, 101, **101**, **111**, 160, 198, 200–1
Manthell, Vivian, **138**, 138
Marshall, Major, **47**, 75
Marshall, Mary. *see* Swainson, Mary (WS' daughter)
Martin, Alexander, **118**
Martin, John, **122**
Martin, Mary, **118**, 118
Martin, Robert, **118**, 118
Mason, Alan, **223**, 223
Mason, Frank, 231
Mason, Jane, 37, 39, 41
Mason, John, 37
Mason, Thomas, 8, 18, 29, 31 fn 40, **37**, 37–44, **38**, **39**, **40**, **41**, 41–2, **42**, **43**, 43, 47, 50–1, 52, 53, 161, 162, 163, 170, 185, 202, 223
Maxton, Samuel, 69–70
Mein-Smith, William, 7–8, **22**, 24, **94**, 95, **115**, **153**, 217
Melville, H., **135**
Mills, Charles, 121
Mills, E.W., 160
Mills, J.F.W., **194**, 195
Minifie, Mr, 161
Minto, Fanny, 29
Mole, Ray, 226, 232
Molesworth, F.A., **153**, 157
Molesworth, F.D., 152
Molesworth, Francis, 18, **19**, 21–5, **23**, **24**, 27, 28, 30, 35–7, 44, 51, 55, 56, 88, 165, 186, 202
Molesworth, Sir William, 21–2
Moore, George, **108**, 161
Moore, Henry, 224, 234
Moore, Johnson, 12
Moore, R.P., 139, **139**
Moreing, Henry, 18, **20**, 27
Moxham, Mr, 59, 202
Murphy, M., 152, 157

N

Nairn, Robert, 165
Nanson, Richard, 219, 221–2, 223, 224, 234, 238
Nattrass, Luke, 11–12, 57
Nightingale, Florence, 147
Nisbet, Bruce, 133
North, Marianne, 189
Norwood, Lady, 220, 223
Norwood, Sir Charles, 220, 223

O

Oates, Mike, 222, 223, 224
Ombler, Joan, **223**
Orgias, Mrs, 195

P

Palmer, Sir Geoffrey, 137
Park, Geoff, 17
Parker, Thora, 84
Parnell, S.D., 66–7, 68, 98
Paton, Claude, 130
Patrick, M., 60
Paxton, Sir Joseph, 147
Pearce, John, **104**, **127**
Percy, Earl, 157
Percy, J.H., 21, **29**
Petre, Eleanor, 20–1, 24, 100, 186
Petre, Francis, **112**
Petre, Henry, 10, 18, 19–21, **20**, 29, 36, 44, 50, 61, 87, 100, 243
Pharazyn, E., **153**
Pharazyn, Robert, **113**
Phillips, G., 96, 157
Platt, William, **140**, 140
Platts, Dr, **194**, 195
Plimmer, Isaac Harold, 145, 160, 162
Pope, Mr, 30, 36, 165
Pulley, Charles, 139

R

Randall, William, 217, 218
Read, C.R., **125**, 125, 162
Reece, Mick, 221
Reeves, Lady, 133
Reeves, Sir Paul, 137
Reid, Rodney, 231
Repton, Humphrey, 95
Retter, Samuel, 72
Revans, 58
Rhodes, Barney, 115
Rhodes, Captain, 161
Rhodes, W.B., 73, 92, 161, **183**
Riddiford, Daniel, 19, **19**, 21, 29, 66–7, 157
Robertson, David, 161, 178, 230, **231**
Robertson, Mr, 162, **166**
Robertson, Nasmith, 158
Robinson, Abraham, 136
Robinson, Lesley, 136–7
Roskell, T., 11–12
Ross, Mrs, 189–90
Rule, John, 244
Russell, Lord John, 57

S

Savage, Michael Joseph, 137
Saxton, J.W., 13
Scott, Sam, 143
Scutchings, Mr, 157
Seaton, A.W., **194**
Sellars, James, 161
Seymour, Michael, 135–6
Sharp, Captain, **108**
Shaw, John, 101
Shepherd, K.W., **199**
Shine, Mrs, 191
Smith, Captain, 152, **153**, 157
Smith, Mr, 10, 58, 157
Spinks, W., 12, 161, **166**, **182**
Spry, Keith, 224
St Hill, Henry, 152, 157, 160, 217
St Hill, James, 87, **98**, 100, **136**
Stanley, Owen, 75, **75**
Stebbings, Benjamin, 90, 92
Stebbings, Eileen, 90
Stebbings, Eva, 90–1
Stebbings, Henry, 90
Stebbings, Mr, 29
Stirling, James, 133, 137
Stock, A.H., 100, **101**, 160, 161, 163
Stockbridge, Mary, 167, 169
Stockbridge, Stephen, 12, 157, 159, 163, **166**, 167–9, **168**, **169**, 171, 179, **183**, 202
Stokes, Robert, 13, 26, **99**, 99, 104–5, **105**, **106**, 107, 152, **153**, 154–5, 157, 158, 159, 160, 161, 163, 243
Stowe, Jane, 114
Stowe, Leonard, 114, **115**, 145
Strang, Robert, **99**, 104–5, **107**, 107
Strutt, William, 84
Sutherland, Benjamin, 131, 139–40, 142
Sutherland, Jean, 142
Swainson, Ann, 44
Swainson, Geoffrey, **20**, 29, 38
Swainson, Lucille Frances, **49**
Swainson, Mary (WS' daughter), 20, 44, 45, 46–7, **47**, 75, **76**
Swainson, Mary (WS' first wife), 44
Swainson, William, **9**, 13, **17**, 18, 19, **19**, 27, 29, 38, **44**, 44–50, **45**, **47**, 48, 50–1, 64, **75**, 75, **76**, 145, 152, 157

T

Taringakuri, 47
Tate, Thomas, 135–6
Taylor, Helena, **223**
Taylor, James, 86–7
Taylor, J.M., 161
Te Puni, 34
Thompson, 127
Tilbury, Nancy, 73
Tizard, Dame Catherine, 133, 223, **224**
Tolley, Wendy, 146
Toomath, Bill, 97
Travers, W.T.L., 60, 77, **78**, **79**, 203
Trotter, William, 21, 27, 28, 35–7, 51, 98, 161, 165
Tschopp, Frederick, 136, **137**, 138
Turnbull, Thomas, **113**
Turnbull Thomson, John, 76–7, **78**, **113**
Turnbull, Walter, **108**
Turnbull, William, 143
Turner, David, **187**
Tyser, Mr, 61
Tyson, Peter, 231

V

Veitch, J.H., 42
'Veronica', 162
Vogel, Julius, 136

W

Wade, George, 12, **167**, 243
Wade, John, 12, 72, 152, **167**, 243
Waitt, **182**, **183**
Wakefield, Edward Gibbon, 3–4, 7–8, 10, 13, 24, 47, 50, **136**, 159
Wakefield, Edward Jerningham, 55, 56, 197
Wakefield, Joah, **98**
Wakefield, William, 99, 125, **125**, 125–6, **126**, 129, 151, 152, **153**, 157, 192, 200–1
Walker, Hilda, **116**
Wall, Anthony, 83–4
Wall, Susan, 83–4
Wallace, J.H., 161
Wallis, William, 147, **147**
Ward, John, 44
Wardle, Peter, 197
Waterhouse, G.M., **113**
Waterhouse, Professor E.G., 32
Watson, John, 148, **166**, **168**, 172, **176**, 176–8, **177**, 179, **183**, 202
Watt, James, 72, 152, 160
Watts, Mr, 44, 151
Weaver, D.J., **206**
Weld, Frederick, 126–8
Wentworth, W.C., 242
Westbury, Frederick, 86
White, George, 26
White, J.E., 182
White, Joseph, 72, 157
White, Mary, 239
White, Thomas, 163, **179**, 179, 244
Wickstead, J.T., 152, **153**
Wickstead, Mr, **98**
Wilford, Sir Thomas, 42–3
Wilkinson, David, 87, 152, **153**, 157, 159, 160, 161, 162, 163, **185**, 185–8, **186**, **187**, **188**
Williams, Ann, **142**
Williams, T.C., **121**
Wilmhurst, Irene, 118
Wilson, Professor, 42
Wilson, William, 244
Wilton, Job, 70
Wilton, N., 161
Woodward, Jonas, 159, 160, 161, 162, 163
Woouldom, Henry, 98–9, **166**, 174–5, **175**, 185
Woouldom, William, 174–5, **175**
Worsfold, Reverend, **223**
Wright, Henry, **98**, 98, 111
Wright, Mr, 95, 96
Wright, Reginald, **98**

Y

Young, Lucy, 174, 193–5
Young, William Henry, 174, 193–5
Yule, John, 61, 68